LCD

WAR ON FILM

WAR ON FILM

The American Cinema and World War I, 1914-1941

Michael T. Isenberg

> The history of democracy should be read, not in the lengthened shadows of the lives of the great, but in the shorter shadows cast by average men.
> —Donald Richberg (1930)

Rutherford - Madison - Teaneck
Fairleigh Dickinson University Press

London and Toronto: Associated University Presses

© 1981 by Associated University Presses, Inc.

Associated University Presses, Inc.
4 Cornwall Drive
East Brunswick, N.J. 08816

Associated University Presses
69 Fleet Street
London EC4Y 1EU, England

Associated University Presses
Toronto M5E 1A7, Canada

Library of Congress Cataloging in Publication Data

Isenberg, Michael T
  War on film.

  Bibliography: p.
  Includes index.
  1. European War, 1914-1918, in motion pictures.
2. Moving-pictures and history. 3. Moving-pictures, Documentary--History and criticism. 4. Historical films--History and criticism. I. Title.
D522.23.18   791.43'0909'3   76-19835
ISBN 0-8386-2004-3

PRINTED IN THE UNITED STATES OF AMERICA

For My Mother
and
In Memory of My Father

Contents

Preface	9
Acknowledgments	13
Introduction	15

PART I Charting *Terra Incognita:* Remarks on Film and History

1	Film: The Unused Evidence	25
2	Historians, Aesthetics, and Film	34
3	Toward a Historical Methodology for Film Scholarship	44

PART II Realism and the War Film

4	The Myth of the "Objective Camera": A Critique of Film Reality	57
5	From Idealism to Nihilism: The Plastic Uses of the Realistic Film	68

PART III The Camera Eye: Focus on War

6	The Mirror of Democracy	85
7	The Trumpet Calls: Commitment and Sacrifice	97
8	What Price Adventure?	114
9	Film against War	128

PART IV The Camera Eye: Images in a Mirror

10	The Threat: The Image of the Enemy	145
11	The Friend: The Image of the Ally	161
12	We Ourselves: The Image of the Home Front	175

PART V The Camera Eye: Variations on a Theme

13	War and Women	189
14	War and Humor	204

Conclusion	215
Notes	220
Bibliography of Primary Sources	249
Index	265

Preface

History in recent years has cast a wide net in its search for relevant historical evidence. As if in response to Harold Cruse's dictum that "the cultural arts are the mirror of the spiritual condition of the nation,"[1] historians have been assiduous in elevating new materials to scholarly respectability. Most important in this broadening of our historical horizons has been the extensive use of literary evidence. Every aspect of literature has been examined, from great books to graffiti. Historians now regard the philosophical memoir of a Henry Adams and the dime novel of a Ned Buntline, if not of equal weight, then at least equally worthy of attention.

The readiness to appreciate new forms of evidence, however, has not generally extended to nonliterary forms. The aural and visual mass communications media spawned by the technological revolution in which we still are living constitute persistent examples of the reluctance of the historical craft to deal with these forms. Myriad aspects of radio, television, and the motion picture remain unexamined by serious historians.

This study is an exercise in the use of motion pictures as historical evidence. It is not a history of the motion picture industry, nor is it a series of biographical sketches of screen personalities, nor is it an aesthetic analysis of the author's favorite motion pictures. The purpose of the exercise and its thesis are one and the same: to show that motion pictures provide a completely reasonable and effective source of evidence for historians of twentieth-century America.

The subject of World War I presents itself first because it already has generated a large body of historical literature, which in turn has been based almost exclusively on traditional evidence; second, because it initiated some intellectual themes in American life and reshaped others, themes which may be studied on film as well as on paper; and third because it produced hundreds of movies which revealed significant ideas, attitudes, and values regarding the war. Just as easily, the "Roaring Twenties" or the Depression could have been chosen. Film evidence abounds for examining both these periods, just as it does for studying questions which are unfettered by chronology.

Mark Twain once remarked that "there are no common people, except in the highest spheres of society."[2] Much ink has been spilled lately, both by historians and by other members of the scholarly community, in trying to establish guidelines between "private" and "popular" spheres of culture. While such efforts may be useful in examining pre-1900 America, any distinction drawn between the "mass" on one hand and some "elite" on the other loses most of its meaning in the complexities of the modern era. Movies have been a truly universal form of communication since the very earliest years of their history. They have reached kings and coachmen, and everyone in between. The study thus contains no attempt to analyze movie audiences in any way. Although this runs against the grain of our current stress on providing statistics for everything, any attempt to create a typical American movie audience would be the sheerest fabrication.

The study likewise may be called "extensive" rather than "intensive." Instead of concentrating on a limited number of "representative" films of the war, the study has tried to gather in as many as possible. Statistically this is good form, but it obviously precludes in-depth treatment of any particular film. No apologies are made for this decision, because the most hackneyed screen melodrama may tell the historian as much, perhaps more, than that rare instance when the screen glows with originality and insight. No claim is made that every film concerning World War I has been included; such a task would swamp a team of researchers. But the study tries to be reasonably inclusive in the hope that what emerges shall have a more solid foundation.

Yet the area of research must be narrowed down at some points. This is, above all, a study in the use of evidence. This premise links the otherwise somewhat disconnected essays. The concentration is on American films with what one hopes is an historical perspective. Videotapes, microfilms, and other substances for registering visual imprints are not included here, nor would they be if they had existed during the period of the study. Finally, the study stops at 1941, although several films are mentioned which were produced after that date. This is not because Hollywood completely forgot the first war in the aftermath of the second. Several films made since 1945 have used World War I for various purposes. Among these have been Stanley Kubrick's introspective *Paths of Glory* and David Lean's adventure spectacular *Lawrence of Arabia*.[3] But the examination of pictures like these would add little but bulk to an already weighty manuscript. The year 1941 provides a convenient end point because it stands on the eve of another and greater war. Viewing one war through the prism of another invites distortion.

It must be emphasized that in no sense may the films in this study be taken as registering anything more than commonly held American ideas, attitudes, and values connected with various facets of World War I. Compared with the total output of the motion picture industry, these films form a humble and almost insignificant group. Most of them are forgotten today, and the prints of many have long since vanished. These pictures are resurrected here neither to reshape the historical scholarship of the war (although they present information which may make a minor contribution in this direction), nor to advocate film as the final step in the evolution of evidential material. That they remain useful historical matter is the central contention; let the reader judge.

Acknowledgments

Academic thank-yous usually tag the long-suffering wife on at the end, almost as an afterthought. I wish to thank Susan at the beginning–for her energy, dedication, and good common sense.

Robert Athearn, Matthew Downey, Charles Middleton, George Pilcher, and Robert Skotheim all helped this manuscript in earlier drafts with their comments. Special thanks go to Ray Cuzzort, who also read the manuscript, and to Phil Mitterling–two gentlemen who helped out during tough times.

Several individuals were kind enough to swap chatter on film teaching and research. I received useful hints and ideas from Les Adler, John Diggins, Louis Giannetti, Gene Gressley, Pat Griffin, Garth Jowett, Henry C. Meyer, and Jack Spears. Some of these gentlemen I have never met; their kindness is the more appreciated for that.

I am grateful to those institutions which allowed me to utilize their film and manuscript collections. A professional historian was an odd commodity in several of these places, but the welcome was no less warm. My deepest appreciation to: Mildred Simpson and the staff of the Academy of Motion Pictures Arts and Sciences Library, Hollywood; Anne Schlosser, James Silke, and the staff of the American Film Institute Center for Advanced Film Studies, Beverly Hills; Patrick J. Sheehan and the staff of the Prints and Photographs Division, Library of Congress; Charles Silver and the staff of the Film Study Center, Museum of Modern Art; William Murphy and the staff of the Film Division of the National Archives; Morrie Roizman and the staff at Time-Life Films, New York City; Susan Davis, who at the time of my visit was the entire staff of the Wisconsin Center for Theater Research, Madison; and the staff of the Division of Rare Books and Special Collections, University of Wyoming Library.

A small grant from the Graduate School of the University of Colorado facilitated the research. Ronald Roth and David Redstone provided that rigorous editing which embarrasses an author but can only improve a manuscript.

Finally my belated thanks to Gerta–constant seminar companion and good friend.

I wish also to thank the following:

The *Journal of Popular Culture*, for permission to use material from my "The Mirror of Democracy: Reflectrions of the War Films of World War I, 1917-1919," reprinted from Volume IX, No.4 (Spring 1976), 878-85 of the *Journal of Popular Culture* with the permission of the editor.

The *Journal of Popular Film*, for permission to use material from my "An Ambiguous Pacifism: A Retrospective on World War I Films, 1930-1938," reprinted by Permission of the Editors of the *Journal of Popular Film* from IV, No.2 (1975), 98-115.

The Museum of Modern Art/Film Stills Archive, 21 W. 53rd Street, New York City, for permission to use all the photographs herein.

Introduction

i

In 1957, two Columbia University professors published a guidebook for scholars and prospective scholars. Barzun and Graff's *The Modern Researcher* attempted to analyze and link research and writing in a meaningful and cohesive fashion.[1] Symptomatic of the attitudes of historians of twentieth-century America, the work contained only one reference pertinent to cinematic resarch. The authors stated that "works of art" such as "certain kinds of films, kinescope, etc." could be considered as "records,"[2] but no methodological assessment of film as historical evidence was present, nor did the reader find our what the certain kinds of film were.

The Modern Researcher exposed, although only to a greater degree than works less bold in scope, the tendency of historians to ignore, for the most part, one of the most constant and pervasive aspects of modern life–the motion picture. Historians have done so at the risk of severely restricting their profession to an almost complete reliance upon more traditional forms of evidence. Broad histories of the modern United States, when mentioning the cinema at all, mention it as a factor in American life with "an influence difficult to overestimate,"[3] and pass on. Such great influence should rate more than a few short sentences, but it seldom does. In like manner, no film evidence has found a place in such works. Yet it is these general studies which voice all that the profession has to say, in a systematic but nonextensive fashion, since virtually no specialized monographs exist.

This material which remains nonevidence comprises possibly the most significant aspect of the mass-cultural phenomenon. Rising rapidly from its humble storefront beginnings, the nascent motion picture industry first had gained a grudging and then an enthusiastic acceptance among the middle classes by the end of the second decade of the twentieth century; the lower classes had always supplied ardent devotees. By 1929, Joseph Wood Krutch dourly estimated that the film was already thoroughly interwoven into the country's social fabric.[4] Within twenty years of Krutch's assessment, mass communication as a powerful social influence had spawned a respectable body of scholarly literature.[5] Sociologists were intrigued by the deep effect film, as part of this phenomenon, seemed to have upon society as a whole; anthropologists dissected Hollywood moguls as one would examine a primitive tribe; psychologists and educators showed great concern over the direction in which the perceived educational potential of the cinema seemed to be moving; and everyone debated whether the motion picture actually delineated the "national psyche" in bold if brutal form. The literature of film aesthetics grew to enormous proportions, in volume if not in sapience.

The attention many of the social sciences have given film certainly seems merited, if only from statistical evidence. As early as 1910, the influence of American-made films spanned the globe. "The newspaper with the largest circulation on earth is a mere mouse in the presence of this mammoth," wrote one concerned observer, "and the 'best seller' in the book world is, by comparison, something still smaller."[6] During the fiscal year 1918, for example, the United States exported 160 million feet (over 30,000 miles) of film valued at $7 million; this was a war-necessitated drop from the 230 million feet which had been shipped two fiscal years previously.[7] By 1921, the number of movie theaters throughout the world was estimated somewhat haphazardly at 87,000; the United States was credited with 16,900 of these.[8] During the 1920s the American film industry solidified its dominance over world markets.[9] Foreign audiences, whether or not they believed what they saw on the screen, thus were exposed vicariously to American life. If cultural emulation of America is any indicator, this dominance indicated not only economic imperialism, but cultural imperialism as well.[10]

Domestically, the film industry displayed a similarly robust health. Attendance by 1914 was generously estimated at 15 million daily, which meant a gross of about $1 million dollars a day. The total investment capital of the industry was already $500 million; 100,000 people were endlessly and profitably engaged in producing and marketing the shimmering strips of celluloid. By 1922, a more conservative assessment had forty million tickets sold weekly; eight years later, this figure had risen to 100 million.[11] A leading film historian, pondering all this, remarked that Thomas Edison had invested $24,000 in his work on the motion picture. By 1926 the infant had become a young giant, ranked variously as the fifth to eighth largest industry in the country; by this time it boasted a total investment of $1.5 billion.[12]

Impressive numbers, yes; but so huge as to be almost meaningless except in a statistical sense. Boiled down to the size of a community such as Muncie, Indiana, these numbers meant that Muncie theaters enjoyed 31,000 admissions a week out of a population of 38,000.[13] Movies rapidly took on a rural as well as an urban base. The new mobility provided by the automobile made trips to the nearest town to see Wallace Reid's latest exploits a real, but casual, treat. In short, a great and heterogeneous section of the American populace had developed a movie going habit, a habit conditioned by a well-organized complex of production, distribution, exhibition, promotion, and exploitation–the "studio system." Here, at least, is proper material for the social historian, since it provides a foundation for the examination of social thought and social custom.

Not even the Depression could curb greatly the industry's success. Its total investment had risen to $2 billion as of January, 1931. The total weekly attendance in 1930 topped 100 million, and might have reached 115 million. The advent of sound played a great part in sustaining interest. Although critics bemoaned the passing of a mimetic art which was only beginning to attain maturity, almost 75 percent of the nation's theaters had been wired for the new marvel by 1931.[14] Clearly, the commercial motion picture was itself a mass phenomenon which by its very nature had metamorphosed into a major leisure aspect in the lives of many Americans. A member of the President's Research Committee on Social Trends estimated in 1933 that with the possible exception of the radio concert, the motion picture reached more individuals than any other avenue of communication, and "in any future survey of this character it is sure to occupy a commanding position."[15]

ii

Behind these impressive figures lay a theory unique to America. A country that continuously preached the virtues of the democratic faith, both to itself and to the rest of the world, had little difficulty in justifying the popularity of motion pictures within its borders. The justification lay in assuming that since film was so obviously a mass form of communication, it was *de facto* democratic in nature. Had not movie theaters, at first confined to the more squalid urban areas, soon proliferated into the expanding suburbs and beyond, to rural America? No person, it seemed, was beyond their reach. Largely because of this conception, it was argued that film was a major avenue for the dissemination of the national culture.[16]

Not only were Americans in city, town, and countryside perceived by both friends and enemies of the film as subject to the "shadow stage." The same argument which praised the democratic aspects of the motion picture also lauded the global nature of American film domination. This stance, an intellectual inheritance from turn-of-the-century imperialist thought, made it possible to endow the movies with humanitarian as well as democratic virtues. World War I, seen through this prism, was a vast misunderstanding caused primarily by the vicious nature of national stereotypes. Film, as an international language needing no translator, served to erase frontiers, remove misconceptions, and kill prejudice. The international role of the motion picture, couched in these terms, was to banish hatred and promote peace.[17]

This humanitarian argument gained its ultimate appeal from reasoning implicit in earlier imperialist thought. The promotion of American democracy overseas was inseparable from other aspects of film exportation. Like imperialism, such promotion had an ethical and religious base. If some saw the quality of American movies as low, others reveled in the idea that the world could be Americanized in such a smooth and profitable fashion. Vachel Lindsay, one of the few intellectuals to grasp the great potential of the new medium, lost no time in securing a position as movie critic for the *New Republic*. From this post, the poet beat the drums for a one-world ideal, to be cemented in part by the film. "We Americans should look for the great photoplay of tomorrow that will mark a decade or a century, that prophesies of the flags made one, the crowds in brotherhood." In this crusade, the movies would be the "new weapon of men"; under the onslaught, "the face of the whole earth changes." The moviemakers, who would lead the crusade, were styled "God's thoroughbreds."[18]

Such bombast should not obscure the basic democratic, humanitarian, and even Messianic nature of film's appeal. Lindsay himself viewed film as a kind of mirror for democracy:

> The possibility of showing the entire American population its own face in the Mirror Screen has at last come. Whitman brought the idea of democracy to our sophisticated literati, but did not persuade the democracy itself to read his democratic poems. Sooner or later the kinetoscope will do what he could not, bring the nobler side of the equality idea to the people who are so crossly equal.[19]

Here is the imperialistic ideal of "uplift" in all its splendor, reflected back into American society itself. What was good for the aborigine, Lindsay argued, would do for a country where egalitarianism was more preached than practiced. Such a concept merged nicely with the ideals behind the war itself; what could be more natural than to see the motion picture as a double-edged celluloid sword, at once promoting democratic ideals and at the same time providing a loyal population with well-earned entertainment? A leading film magazine put it thus:

> As our world-war goes on, the light behind the flying celluloid must grow brighter and brighter. The time is promoting democracy in things other than government. For one thing it is making a democracy of amusement, and the photoplay is the most democractic of diversions, not only in its price, which is more alluring in adversity than in prosperity, but in its all-encompassing appeal.[20]

The moviegoing public had been concerned that motion pictures would not be declared an essential industry; with this unease put to rest, the war was made more bearable, at least for the fans at home. By the Armistice, even a conservative organ such as *Harper's Magazine* could print an article praising the motion picture as a "great American institution."[21] All other forms of amusement, such as the theater, baseball, and the Sunday comics, were completely dwarfed by the new Goliath.

The film industry in the immediate postwar years proved to be a prime force in the formation of what George Mowry has called the "mass-production-consumption culture."[22] The smoothly running studio system turned out a consistent, consumer-responsive product, which was buoyed up even more in the public mind by an aura of glamour. This was carefully cultivated through the gross publicity generated by the "star system" and the astronomic salary scales offered by the industry. Film executives tolerated the former but despaired of the latter, except when applied to themselves. Such devices led automatically to increased film budgets, which in turn demanded a search for the widest possible audiences.

Nor was the avenue of the commercial cinema the only route by which film assisted in standardizing American culture. The new advertising industry, for example, turned readily to the equally new avenue of communication. A spokesman argued that motion pictures could and should be used as a means of promotion; they were the "logical medium of thought and idea conveyance."[23] Newsreels presented public figures and instant celebrities visually to all corners of the country. Educators and bureaucrats were quick to see the possibilities of the film for instruction, and governmental propaganda experts proved equally adept at exploiting the new medium.

Whether used for promotion, propaganda, or just plain entertainment, the motion picture was construed by friend and foe alike as a democratic institution. The movie industry itself was far from democratic; methods of production and distribution continued to carry that taint of economic jungle warfare which had been both the thrill and the bane of motion picture companies from the cinema's earliest years. But the chief effect of the commercial film clearly lay in the direction of a leveling of American culture and a standardization of values. Aesthetic considerations aside, as Mortimer Adler put it in 1937, "the motion picture theatre is the theater of democracy, and the motion picture is its most popular poetry."[24]

It is this theater of democracy which largely remains unexamined by historical scholarship. Until historians take a different view of the possibilities of using film and film evidence, they cannot be "modern researchers" in any total sense–for to research the complexities of the twentieth century, one must use not only traditional forms of evidence but also those newer forms which permeate so much of modern life.

WAR ON FILM

Part 1

Charting *Terra Incognita:* Remarks on Film and History

> We believe that we have as much right to present the facts of history as we see them . . . as a Guizot, a Bancroft, a Ferrari, or a Woodrow Wilson has to write these facts in his history.
> —D.W. Griffith (1916)

> They have built their business upon a foundation of morons . . .
> —H.L. Mencken (1927)

1

Film: The Unused Evidence

i

The starting place for any student of film is of course film itself. Yet this simple statement marks a rather radical departure for historians, particularly historians of ideas. John Greene once commented that "although the intellectual historian works with the same materials that are used by the political historian, the student of literature, and the historian of science, he handles them in a different way with a different object in view."[1] This observation has not been extended to include film. In the case of film, historians in part must forsake print to work in a new medium of communication, one which calls for an assessment of the value of the evidence it has to offer.

The film industry has a call on the historian's attention in a variety of ways. The industry itself was and is huge, and its vagaries have had a telling effect on the local and even the national economy. But it has had few capable historians. The industry is composed of individuals, some powerful, some bizarre, even some with talent, but many of greater interest than their effusive press clippings might warrant. Few scholars trouble to write their biographies. Of more pertinent interest to this discussion is the fact that a medium of mass expression, in all three modes–production, diffusion, and reception–is inevitably a carrier of ideas. It is true that cinema rarely has staked a claim to originality; its ideas are most commonly conveyed in the form of attitudes, preconceptions, or stereotypes. Yet such material would, it seems, comprise proper evidence for historians, particularly those interested in the intellectual history of the modern United States. However, no serious work on the film has been done by the profession from this angle, and few pertinent methodological questions have been posed.

Literature on the film, on the other hand, is awesome in its bulk. Primarily this is because a consumer-oriented culture is responsive to the latest Hollywood tidbits, but also because a ticket to the cinema, unlike seats to a debating match, seems automatically to confer critical acumen upon its holder, and critical acumen breeds the written word. Little if any of this commentary has been produced by professional historians; minuscule scholarly spadework has been done. Daniel Boorstin has lumped the study of film into a group of "academic outcasts" which includes radio, television, and travel.[2] Despite this situation, doctoral candidates in many instances are discouraged from research in these areas, or more commonly, they probably never realize that this option is even available. Although this study does not concern itself with film history per se, the relatively narrow area of research encompassed herein admits the force of Boorstin's complaint.

Historians of the First World War have paid little or no attention to the role played by film in presenting (advocating, explaining, exculpating, dramatizing, castigating) the conflict to the American mass public. The war has been seen on film as commercial entertainment, news, or "analysis"; in some cases these different aspects are difficult to distinguish. Yet no assessment of the American involvement in the war has treated this dimension in any adequate manner. Charles Callan Tansill's ponderous *America Goes to War*[3] contained no reference to film. His opening chapter, entitled "American Public Opinion at the Outbreak of the World War," relied on traditional sources such as newspapers, memoirs, diaries, biographies, and manuscripts. Another historian of the neutrality period, Charles Seymour, ignored films in his treatment of the causes of American intervention.[4] In fact, propaganda as a causative factor received only brief mention, and that in the form of newsprint. In like vein, another scholar argued that newspapers provided the "bases of contemporary American opinion."[5] The author of an article called "The World War and the Arts" ignored films completely, concentrating instead on literary evidence, such as novels, poetry, and drama.[6]

Historians of war propaganda have been equally loathe to use film evidence. Harold D. Lasswell, the dean of this school, paid no attention to motion pictures in his chief work, with two exceptions: he gave one line to the formation of a British film committee, and he recounted very sparingly the *Patria* episode (*Patria* was the fruit of William Randolph Hearst's production company, a serial which included racial defamations of the Japanese to such a degree that the hideous Orientals were more acceptably styled "Mexicans" after public protest–to capitalize on the then current border difficulties). Lasswell drew his evidence almost directly from an account in *The New York Times*.[7] James Duane Squires, a student of British propaganda efforts in the United States, ignored film completely. Squires used as evidence material sent to this country by Sir Gilbert Parker and Professor W. MacNeile Dixon, the propaganda overlords of Wellington House. Under a "Checklist of British propaganda sent to the United States Between 1914 and 1917," which he felt was "fairly complete," Squires included printed sources only, overlooking the considerable amount of film which the British shipped to the United States both before and after this country's entry into the conflict.[8] These examples form virtually the complete pattern. When film propaganda has been mentioned, it has been largely in connection with notorious "faked photographs," the motion picture receiving slight, if any, attention.[9]

If general histories of the war and interwar periods discuss film at all, they usually are confined by the exigencies of space and scope to saying something to the effect that motion pictures have "nationalized American popular culture."[10]

When more substantive comments are made, they invariably are distorted or mistaken. Thomas Pressly, in a general comment on the "climate of opinion" in the Thirties, observed that hostility to war was preached in novels, plays, and poems, but he did not mention the several pertinent motion pictures of the period.[11] When the film is mentioned in this regard it is usually in the vein exemplified by George Mowry: "Novels, poetry, and most movies and plays of the twenties and thirties were almost unanimous in condemning America's entry into World War I and in questioning whether any modern war was worth fighting."[12] Such a statement betrays, not poor historical work, but the abysmal nature of the historian's relationship to film. Historians of broadly conceived chronological periods, while forced to make some comment on film because of its perceived influence on American society, simply do not have at hand that standard evidence which is available to them in other areas—dissertations, articles, monographs, and readily accessible primary source material. Film evidence in either the primary or secondary sense does not exist in many cases in cohesive, reliable form.

ii

What of the film evidence we can isolate, track down and study? Those who seek to study films as historical documents begin at a disadvantage. There is no place in the United States which serves as a central repository for positive screening prints. As early as 1921 critics were calling for government to take a hand in preserving film records.[13] The National Archives and the Library of Congress have responded nobly with what personnel and money they could muster, but their work has just begun. Archivists were slow to recognize the chemical instability of nitrate-based film, and many negatives have been lost or irreparably damaged through decomposition. Work in film archives must take place in widely scattered areas; the cost of film-lending programs is individually prohibitive. In addition to those in Washington, D.C., leading film repositories in this country include the Museum of Modern Art in New York City, Eastman House in Rochester, New York, and the Wisconsin Center for Theater Research in Madison. The scholar utilizing films made in the early twentieth century must be content with viewing them in these locales, unless he knows private collectors or has the backing to examine the leading overseas collections such as those in Paris and Leningrad. Until recently there existed no dependable bibliographic work on American films. The American Film Institute's giant Film Catalog project[14] will, it is hoped, rectify this situation.

Some films that do exist and are available to the student are accompanied by little or no background information. This information would include who shot the film, when and where the shooting took place, under what conditions, and for what purpose. Many film clips are available to the historian only in second-hand form; they have been taken from long-vanished newsreels or feature presentations and used for a different purpose from that originally intended. Film editors at times have few scruples about assembling useful film footage to make a point without unduly concerning themselves about the real origin of that footage.[15] For these reasons films must have the most complete categorization possible insofar as the situation surrounding their creation is concerned.[16] Once the background of a film has been thoroughly examined, it can be treated as primary source material.

Beyond film itself as a primary document stands the Everest of written material on the cinema. The researcher has available several avenues of approach to the study of film through the written and printed media. Film reviews, specialized monographs, periodical articles, biographies and autobiographies, film scripts, and various manuscript collections can prove helpful just as they do in other areas of research. But all these sources of evidence need strong qualification before they can be used; *Moving Picture World* is not the *Congressional Record*.

In 1964 Richard D. MacCann published an introductory primer for film research.[17] Obviously aimed at the beginning student, MacCann's book included a section entitled "Suggested Topics for Library Research." This section listed a number of periodicals and books for further study. Since his approach was limited to secondary evidence, MacCann included films and reviews in his list but omitted scripts, manuscripts, and studies of the filmmakers themselves. Unfortunately, the omission of this evidence, intentional or not, underscores the shallow methodology of most film historians. Film scholarship with rare exceptions never has been distinguished by the caliber of its research and analysis. At mid-century it was characterized as carefree and slipshod, a condition which has changed little in the years since. The field remains in James Card's words a "quagmire of gossip and guess," dominated not by the researcher but by the raconteur.[18] Books on film history tend to be confined to films and to anecdotal accounts of and by the filmmakers. The scholarly apparatus of footnotes and bibliography usually is either badly attenuated or completely lacking.[19] Attention to such mundane matters might seem to be overly compulsive unless one realizes that many of the works on film history were written by individuals close to the industry, either as film critics, editors of film magazines, businessmen, producers, or filmmakers.[20] Thus much of their material comes from memory and experience. What seems to the historian to be a crying need for documentation apparently is for many of these individuals only ponderous pedagogy which would inhibit, not enhance, their work.

Film reviews provide a partial check on the casual memoir and are a key source of evidence for those films the researcher has never seen. Reviews in trade journals are particularly good in this regard, since they are concerned more with informing the exhibitor of the plot than in making critical comment. Reviews in the mass media, such as magazines and newspapers, tend to submerge the plot outline in a flood of aesthetic criticism. This is especially true of the reviews of the interwar period, when serious reviewers were beginning to analyze the motion picture as an acceptable art form. Reading the review is no substitute for viewing the film, but where no print of a specific picture is available for viewing a comparison of the reviews can in many cases provide an adequate idea of the film's plot.

Film magazines of today have degenerated greatly from the position they once held. Where now they are simply pulps aimed at a puerile and sensation-seeking audience, in the early years of the industry they served in part as vehicles for reasoned commentary on all aspects of the film. Magazines such as *Photoplay* would present stories written directly from screen scenarios. These stories, though useful for grasping a given plot, cannot be used as evidence because of the difference between the literary and motion picture media.[21] Of course *Photoplay*, *Motion Picture Magazine*, and their ilk do not offer the types of evidence usually thought of as reliable, unless one is dealing with attitudes. Most of their space was taken up by standard gossip items, trivial information on stars, fan correspondence, and still pictures. Not even national crises could make inroads on this fare. While World War I was being fought it received relatively little attention in the pages of these magazines, either philosophically or in relation to the industry's output. Trade journals such as *Moving Picture World* and *Motion Picture News* offer much more reliable evidence in assessing the attitudes of the industry, since they were aimed at the exhibitor and not the audience. In recent years a glut of periodicals devoted exclusively to film have been established. Most of these are unbearably "precious" in the aesthetic sense and wander aimlessly through the constantly shifting sands of taste. The best of these newer journals, and those which have some historical perspective, are *Sight and Sound* and *Films in Review*.

When scholarship focuses on the individuals in the film industry, as it must (since even under the studio system, films were made by people), research problems are compounded. Filmmakers, whether they participate in the creative process from behind or in front of the camera, usually have been ill-served by their biographers. Those in front of the camera–the "stars"–traditionally have been assessed at one of two wildly oscillating biographical poles. These works usually can be categorized either as hagiography or as scandal-mongering. They range from Mrs. Bertha Westbrook Reid's nauseating memoir of her son Wallace to Ezra Goodman's muckraking exposé of Hollywood.[22] The star phenomenon is mythic in its proportions.[23] The concern to either retain the myth or destroy it dominates most biographies of these luminaries. The same can be said for autobiographies. The record presented in these literary exercises is more often clouded than clear, largely because zealous press agents and production assistants excel in manufacturing the past. The historian finds such functionaries to be formidable impediments to scholarship.

When attention is focused behind the camera the same situation pertains to a somewhat lesser degree. That is, biographies and autobiographies of film executives, producers, and directors are heavily larded with anecdotes and related in a glib and sometimes slapdash style. Nowhere in any of these works, save for the rare exception,[24] will one find the slightest pretense to scholarship. These men and women bring the style and adroitness of their craft to their writing. It is no consolation that many such books are ghosted by persons whose concern for accuracy is equally nonexistent.

Are any of these individuals of more importance than others in the study of film? Certainly, but the situation varies with the picture. If one ascribes to the "auteur theory,"[25] which dictates that the director is the true creator of any film and that the film serves to communicate the director's attitudes to his audience, then knowledge of the director becomes mandatory in the course of studying the film. The present work views the aspect of film creation in somewhat broader scope. It assumes that the primary act of creation in motion pictures varies with the individual film. In general, creativity is seen as occurring mainly behind the camera, as a coalition between director, producer, and scriptwriter(s). On different occasions actors, editors, cameramen, and light and sound specialists may be involved actively in the creative process. The period of this study encompasses the rise of the studio system, which tended (though by no means always) to submerge creative individuality and emphasize "product."

The effectiveness of this creativity is shaped by our sense of shared experience with the filmmakers. Just as the novelist brings a mixture of experience and theory to his work and expects us to judge him if possible from our own experience in the same context,[26] so too does the filmmaker seek to tell his story through a shared sense of experience. The problem, of course, is that there *is* such a thing as the artistic imagination, and it *can* convince us at times, even against our will. Many of our best war films, for example, were made by people who never experienced the Western Front or even wore a uniform. To be sure, a few did have such a background. William Wellman, the director of the aviation epic *Wings*, flew with the Lafayette Flying Corps, and James Whale, director of *Journey's End* and *The Road Back*, spent time in a German POW camp. But Wellman and Whale were the exceptions. Lewis Milestone, the architect of the finest and most sensitive pacifist film made about the war *(All Quiet on the Western Front)* spent the war as a noncombatant in the Signal Corps. Charles Chaplin had never seen Flanders when he created *Shoulder Arms*. There was always advice available from veterans, of course–King Vidor faithfully reflected the memories of many vets in *The Big Parade*, yet he himself spent the war struggling to make his name as a director in California. The fact that a successful artist need not have undergone the actual experiences he helps translate to the screen is of course an argument in favor of the aesthetic imagination, not an unlimited approach to historical methodology.

The experience, whether actually reflected or imaginatively concocted, was felt immediately on the visual and (later in our period) the aural levels by the audience. The scholar can go further and use the written word to help evaluate this experience. Since a majority (57 percent) of the plots of our World War I films originated in the medium of the printed page, we might assume that these "originals" would comprise part of our evidence. But such is not the case. The process of "adapting" literature into film is one which, even though it may keep the thrust and scope of the literary work intact, invariably presents a different viewpoint to the audience. As one critic remarked, "the best written word has in itself very little film magic."[27] This situation is the result of the different communicative aspects involved in reading and viewing. But there is an area of evidence which offers a compromise between literature and the final motion picture product. This is the movie script.

Scriptwriters lured to Hollywood by the high salaries or the artistic potential of the film soon became sobered by the complexities of the medium. Seemingly everyone had a hand in the writing of a script[28] and literary integrity was more often than not sacrificed in the process. Once the script was completed there was no guarantee that it would be reflected completely in the finished film, and in fact it seldom was. The vagaries of film shooting conditioned that portion of the script which reached the screen. Nevertheless, the ideas, attitudes, and values expressed in film scripts are of interest, because they form part of the creative process which is linked to the production of the film itself. This is not the case with an original literary work upon which a film is based. Script evidence must be supplemental, although it may be considered to be primary. If one has read the script but not viewed the film, one never can be sure that the film completely reflects the script. Assumptions from script evidence alone are invalid; this evidence must be buttressed by the other types already noted. However, reading the complete written version of a completed film, sometimes called the "Dialog Cutting Continuity," is the next best thing to viewing the film itself.

Finally, the historian can rely on written evidence in the form of manuscript collections. The traditional source materials in this regard, namely, letters, memoranda, diaries, and memoirs, are noticeably lacking in the case of filmmakers. Existing collections center around scrapbooks, publicity releases, and various newspaper clippings. This material is useful in itself, but it never can replace those written sources which tend to detail the more intimate side of the persons concerned.

Written materials in various forms provide what knowledge we have of the filmmaking process. Taken as a whole, and particularly for the early years of the industry, these materials in a meaningful sense are irritatingly sparse. Yet they do offer bits and pieces of evidence concerning the attitudes, prejudices, and behavior patterns involved in the manufacture of motion pictures. Together they help to form an intriguing mosaic, a glimpse into the world behind the world depicted on the screen.

iii

Both visual and written evidence concerning the film prove to be of little avail unless one recognizes the difference between the study of the history *of* film and history *in* film. The myths and falsehoods initiated and perpetuated by the motion picture industry on a nation-wide scale deserve to be damned by historians, but condemnation should not obscure the necessity of examining both variants of movie history. Since this study is concerned with the communication of ideas, attitudes, and values, it focuses primarily on history *in* film–with what the industry communicates as history to its mass audience.

During the nascent period of the movies, their most avid supporters claimed that visual history eventually would replace the written and printed word. Sidney R. Kent, the general manager of the Famous Players-Lasky Corporation, predicted in 1925 that

> History will be screened for us, and not written. Even today elaborate plans are being formulated for the preservation of all films of an historical nature. One hundred, two hundred years from now our ancestors *(sic)* will see thrown upon the screen animated pictures of men who have guided the destinies of our nation. Historical events will be pictured in all their vividness.[29]

David W. Griffith once remarked that motion pictures could carry the burden of the "truths of history." We believe that we have as much right to present the facts of history as we see them," he declared, "as a Guizot, a Bancroft, a Ferrari, or a Woodrow Wilson has to write these facts in his history."[30] Thomas H. Ince went so far as to boast that silent movie titles would someday "rank with the masterpieces of history."[31]

Using the motion picture, it still would be possible "to dramatize history to a certain extent, while at the same time keeping within the bounds of historical truth."[32] Many critics deplored the poor history in films, yet insisted film held far greater potential in this regard than the written and printed word. Motion pictures had an almost "magic quality of diffusing knowledge," according to W. Stephen Bush. "One of the great missions of the motion picture," he argued, was "to substitute the picture for the book, in order that all may profit where before only a few were benefited."[33] George Parmly Day, treasurer of Yale University, hailed the appearance of the Yale Historical Series as the application of the "galvanic power of the screen" to the depiction of American history.[34]

The relationship here made was between the visual record of reality and reality itself. On this simplistic level, the champions of film confused visual details with the stuff of history. One of these even claimed that a moving picture of King John signing Magna Carta could have portrayed that event completely.[35] The gross overextension of claims for the film as a communicator of history tended to overshadow the fact that film provided valuable visual records for posterity. Movie people were engaged in compiling a "kind of secret *dossier* of the nation . . . an amusing and valuable body of evidence for future historians . . . ."[36]

Sociologist Ian Jarvie has noted the lack of "historical sense" in Hollywood productions.[37] This lack connotes a tendency to subordinate the natural drama inherent in history to situations defined by those artificial dramatic modes that have been found to be so congenial to mass audiences. David W. Griffith, probably the best of the early filmmakers, was extremely conscious of this type of criticism. Stung by the attacks on his *Birth of a Nation*, some of which claimed he had falsified history, he inserted footnotes to several of the titles in his next film, the classic *Intolerance*. The most sympathetic critics viewed Griffith not as a filmmaker, but as an historian who happened to work in another medium. Thus Arthur Gleason, in a plea for Griffith to make more historical films, argued that Griffith's "fertile talent" could extend to the screen the powerful prose of masters like Gibbon.[38] Such proposals died aborning; rich historical writing did not (or could not) leap the gap between page and screen.

Other filmmakers readily conceded the necessity of giving the primary role in historical vehicles to drama. Producer Irving Thalberg once was asked how much weight he would give to historical accuracy in a film, where historicism might clash with dramatic content. He replied, with revealing ambiguity:

> There, of course, it depends on the importance of the historical fact. There is a problem that we in pictures are faced with in working on an historical subject. It is sometimes very hard to stage things with historical accuracy when you have to do so with a certain amount of dramatic emphasis . . . . If, in telling a story, we find it impossible to adhere to historical accuracy in order to get the necessary dramatic effect, we do change it and we feel that it is the right thing to do. Where it is changing the basic ideal of the man, where it is actually changing history in its effect, why, of course, in my opinion, it is a great mistake . . . .[39]

William Dieterle, a successful director of historical films, also stressed the difference between the visual and written media. "History no doubt figures that it will get its message across sooner or later," he surmised.

> But a director has a different problem. He is trying to convey to it some definite idea, something that must be developed emotionally. In order not to distract attention, the events of the story being told must come in an orderly, consequent procession, the one following the other in logical sequence.
> That, I think, justifies some slight rearrangement of history .... I suppose it is impossible to make a historical picture without some compromise.[40]

The attitudes expressed by Thalberg and Dieterle obviously would be completely unacceptable to the academic historian. The necessary oversimplicity of the cinematic approach to history, coupled with the desire for dramatic effect, has led to a gross overemphasis on Great Men and Great Events. While this tendency in theory might have gladdened the heart of a Carlyle, in actuality it has created incredible distortions of fact along with burlesques and caricatures of historical figures. The historian must accept the idea that no commercial feature motion picture will give him "real" history which satisfies his methodological considerations and his objectivity.

The subtle nuances of history simply are not within the scope of film. But it is the mental constructs concerning historical personages and events which interest us in this context. History *in* film affords historians an opportunity to examine these patterns in a substantive and coherent manner. Close attention to film should be substituted for the raised eyebrow and the sardonic comment; only then may film in its entirety be accepted as useful evidence upon which to base studies of modern America.

2

Historians, Aesthetics, and Film

i

It is extremely difficult to separate the logic-centered idea of film as evidence from the aesthetic-centered idea of film as art. If it be true that the most precious values of a culture are displayed in its arts, then the study of these arts becomes proper for the historian. But, as Barry Ulanov has noted,[1] a twentieth-century democracy produces two kinds of culture. The first, or "private" culture, contains those arts in which the artist speaks only to himself and to the individual who sympathizes or understands. It is this culture that includes the "high thought" that intellectual historians have regarded as their special scholarly preserve. The second, or "popular" culture, is geared to profit, and hence to the perceived values of the widest possible audience. Without doubt the commercial film lies within this area. While serious students of the film do not deny that art–in the traditional sense of something connoting beauty and taste–can exist in popular culture, nor that the popular nature of the film in any way inhibits film art, professional historians have not subscribed to this view. Clio's aesthetic impulse has tended to ignore the screen.

Historians form but a subgroup in American intellectual life. Intellectuals as a class began both to appreciate and to denigrate the commercial film in the second decade of the century; by the Twenties, these diverse critiques had been developed fully.[2] Either reaction tended to embrace aesthetic considerations, which followed naturally as one either accepted or rejected the claims of the motion picture to any artistic standards. The major concern seemed to be that the popularity of the movies might in some way inhibit their art.[3] Although this argument never was made with any clarity, the comparison with the virtuous and independent private artist was implicit and highly unfavorable to the film.

In recent years, this rather haughty view has moderated among intellectuals sympathetic to both the aims and the handicaps of the film. Lyman Bryson argued in 1948 that "we cannot judge popular art as if it were trying to be something else."[4] Scholars such as Russel B.Nye have displayed enthusiasm and understanding, not condescension, in studying film as part of popular culture.[5] In spite of this moderation, however, the basic premise regarding the study of film remains a tendency to judge cinematic products on aesthetic grounds alone—on whether or not the products meet predefined standards of beauty and taste established for the arts of private culture.

Americans long have been proud of their indigenous arts. Largely due to the nature of the wilderness experience and to their great distance from the cultural centers of Europe, these men and women created their own "vernacular tradition" in the arts, first and foremost in the area of technology.[6] This tradition, interacting with the "high culture" imported from Europe, has shaped the history of American art. The motion picture industry is very much a part of this technologically inspired vernacular tradition; without the machine, the industry ceases to exist. But it is precisely the machine that has given many intellectuals pause. One does not have to belabor the deep soul-searchings of a Henry Adams to realize that intellectuals considered as a class of aesthetic critics always have been highly suspicious if not intolerant of machine-inspired culture, for it is a culture beyond their ability to define or control. The movie machine thus becomes tolerable only if it produces art.

Some aesthetes go to great lengths in arguing that art does exist in popular culture, and that this art is "an unusually sensitive and accurate reflector of the attitudes and concerns of the society for which it is produced."[7] But this high ground, if indeed it has been conquered, seems to have been won at great cost. For if film is approachable in a scholarly way only through its arts, or lack thereof, then the ideas, attitudes, and values the film conveys become at best interesting to the aesthetician and the philosopher and at worst the reflectors of the artistic biases of everyone. While the historian may be sensitive to these perspectives as an intellectual, the study of beauty and taste should not perform a major function in his professional methodological formulations.[8]

To date, the historian of ideas has been concerned primarily with the thought of social and intellectual elites.[9] In part, this is a congenial notion: the historian as intellectual consorts with other intellectuals through the continuum of time. But the problem of causation continues to vex even our best scholars. The connection between idea and act can be a very intangible one indeed. Traditionally the tendency has been to recognize this problem of causation in theory and ignore it in practice. The upper classes or elites were assumed to set the intellectual tone for the nation to a great degree. It was these groups that left written records without which traditional history could not function. Such assumptions may carry a great deal of weight when applied to the early and middle years of the Republic, but the rise of the mass media in the twentieth century has introduced several new factors. First, it is no longer clear, if indeed it ever was, that American intellectual life is conditioned by any aristocratic or scholarly elite. This notion is obviously a bitter pill to swallow for the historian with any sense of his class status as an intellectual. Second, the ready accessibility of mass media information implies that members of any social stratum may possess and act upon ideas and attitudes at variance with those of social and intellectual elites and thus not generated by these elites. The fact that such information may be distorted or even false should not belie its power to influence social action. Finally, and most abhorrent to intellectuals, they themselves may be victims of mass media influence. Susceptible to ideas and attitudes which previously were the exclusive property of non-elites and hence deemed noncausative by their very nature, intellectuals now must coexist uneasily with other classes in a world dominated by mass culture.

Historians have tended to react to this situation in one of three ways. First, they have simply ignored it, continuing to regard intellectual elites as comprising the sum total of the nation's intellectual life. Second, they have recognized the existence of what one scholar has called the "plebian school" of study, but have argued that members of this school "are required to show, as they clearly imply, that there is a discernible and historically significant reciprocal flow of intellectual influence from the popular culture to the intellectual elite of school and academy."[10] Such an approach has the virtue of implying that the ultimate patterns of American intellectual life still are established by elites. It ignores, however, the possibility that there are now several varieties of intellectual life, some of which may bypass totally Beacon Hill and Harvard Square.

The third view holds the most promise. As early as 1951, John Higham claimed that before any synthesis could be achieved in the broad and diverse field of American intellectual history, historians "must explore more thoroughly the incidence and intensity of widespread, popular attitudes, each followed in its extensive ramifications through a span of time long enough to show significant transitions."[11] Certainly the film is a conveyor of such attitudes. But these attitudes, if they have not been foreign to social and intellectual elites, nevertheless appear to have been given little attention by intellectual historians. Felix Gilbert was correct when he noted that until recently work in intellectual history tended to confine itself to elites, whom he called "prominent individuals," and to ignore the rest of society.[12] Historians of that body of knowledge labeled loosely as "popular thought" have been accorded an inferior position within the field to those scholars who work with more traditional and philosophical modes of evidence.[13] While never denying the usefulness of their own work, students in the newer areas of study have not challenged the dominant conceptions of the "aristocratic school."

There is no major roadblock to the study of mass media material, if the same methodology is used that has been applied to more traditional forms of evidence. It is difficult to disagree with Rush Welter's argument that it is imperative that popular ideas and the forms in which they are communicated be studied in this fashion.[14] However, major questions in the area of popular thought remain, including those of establishing source, assessing influence, tracing causation, and defining the relationship of popular with elitist thought.[15] It may even be the case that modes of thought in both private and popular culture originate in similar premises. The study of the ideas, attitudes, and values conveyed by the motion picture, once freed from the prejudices of scholars, can help answer these questions.

ii

The motion picture industry from its earliest years has been a favored whipping boy of American intellectuals. In part, this attitude is due to the feeling that the movies are masquerading as an art and have no business doing so, either because their aesthetic potential is ruthlessly suppressed by commercialism or because they pander so shamelessly to emotion and crude taste that aesthetic discussion is rendered useless. It is also due to a European-derived instinct that art is the inevitable concomitance of social and intellectual elites, and of no other classes.

This aesthetic approach has dominated the study of film from the beginning. by the second decade of the century, the poet-critic Vachel Lindsay and Hugo Münsterberg, the chairman of Harvard's Philosophy Department, were almost alone in their support of the photoplay.[16] Most intellectual critics judged the film in terms of its perceived impact upon American life. Randolph Bourne, Alfred Kuttner, and Francis Hackett were among those who saw little social idealism and less art in the new medium.[17] Although there was some intramural debate,[18] most intellectuals tended to ignore the film; when they did take note, they commented on it in derogatory terms.

Without defining the "American character," intellectuals interested in the film had little doubt that the movies influenced this character, mostly for the worse. By the twenties such early praise as had existed had almost vanished; small cries of adulation were reserved for the occasional production that was either foreign, and hence implicitly cultured, or the obvious result of some rare genius, such as Charles Chaplin. Liberal and radical critics continued savagely to criticize the motion picture as industry, popular art, and social history.[19]

While movie critics remained apprehensive, they at times showed some sympathy for the film. Cultural critics, on the other hand, cared little for the entire industry. Harold Stearns's great catalog of the woes of American civilization,[20] published in 1922, contained no specific essay on the cinema. In fact, the only mention of the film was by music critic Deems Taylor. He rated the large motion picture house as the "greatest present-day force for good, musically,"[21] since great compositions were being orchestrated as accompaniment for silent photoplays. The virtue appeared to be that the masses cleverly were being exposed to culture, even if the exposure was subliminal in nature. By 1937 Stearns himself was discussing movies, but only in the aesthetic terminology of censorship and morals.[22] When Babylon was revisited in 1938[23] Stearns included a fairly sympathetic article on radio and film by Louis R. Reid, the advertising and publicity manager of William Randolph Hearst's Cosmopolitan Productions and of the *News of the Day. America Now* also contained references to the film in its chapters on industry and public opinion, but nowhere was the film assessed as historical evidence.

The intelligentsia tended to regard film fare as beneath history, as being so mundane and so trivial as not to warrant discussion on an intellectual level. Many regarded with approbation H.L. Mencken's observation that the ideas in movies "were simply the common and familiar ideas of the inferior nine-tenths of mankind." The Sage of Baltimore wrote further of the movie moguls:

> They have built their business upon a foundation of morons, and now they are paying for it. They seem to be unable to make a presentable picture without pouring out tons of money, and when they have made it they must either sell it to immense audiences of half-wits, or go broke–soon or late the movies will

have to split into two halves. There will be movies for the present mob, and there will be movies for the relatively enlightened minority. The former will continue idiotic, and latter, if competent men to make them are unearthed, will show sense and beauty.[24]

"Sense and beauty"–these ideals, locked together with another aesthetic consideration, that of morality, were the linch-pins of the cultural critique of film. George Bernard Shaw, who saw the film at its highest level when it presented Shaw himself speaking to the camera, regarded the commercial cinema as "reeking with morality" but decidedly without virtue.[25] If Hollywood must point a moral to adorn a tale, let it be in conformity with the highest intellectual aesthetic standards. Mencken's plea for movies of this nature for the "relatively enlightened minority" was echoed by writer I.A.R. Wylie, who emerged somewhat shaken from her Hollywood scriptwriting adventures to advocate better films for the better sort of people.[26]

Religious organizations also played a powerful role in attacking what they perceived as a clear lack of moral values in the commercial film. Their attack centered largely around the complaint that the traditional moralistic institutions of American society, such as the home, the school, and the church, were being replaced as educators by the film. The motion picture misrepresented and distorted American life, and exported these distortions to foreign audiences all too ready to believe the worst concerning this country's social habits. Many religious organizations either supported calls for censorship or established censorship committees of their own. Implicit in this movement was the old fear of the power of the film to shape the character of the individual and hence that of the mass.

It is difficult to establish where the well-meaning impulse of religious groups left off and bigotry began. Racists also attacked on moral grounds the themes of alcoholism, sadism, and violence common to screen drama. For example, a writer in Henry Ford's notorious Dearborn *Independent* argued that films that exploited such material only tended to "lower the prestige of the white woman and the white race in general."[27]

Such moralistic criticisms were inevitable in a democratic society undergoing the almost constant flux of the twentieth century. Various segments of a polymorphous society change less rapidly than others; the motion picture industry, playing to all parts of the population, could not miss offending many. As the anthropologist Hortense Powdermaker pointed out, the movies emphasize some selected values over others, and these emphases seem to change with the historical situation.[28] Further, these values tend to lag behind behavior, but apparently not far enough behind for some people. This situation helps to create the tension which in large part impels the critique of the moralist from one side and that of the cultural advocate from the other. The ultimate result of such lines of reasoning is achieved when the film becomes a pawn in the war of conflicting national ideologies. The inductive premise implicit here, that national morality is only individual morality writ large, has been one of the strongest intellectual arguments against the commercial cinema.

The irony in all this is that Hollywood historically has cultivated intellectuals whenever and wherever it could. The film colony, particularly in the years encompassed by this study, had great ambitions and greater pretensions. As one industry employee bluntly put it, "the literati may sneer at the movies; the movies don't sneer at the literati."[29] Lillian Hellman, William Faulkner, and F. Scott Fitzgerald were among the better known of many who graced the commercialism of the industry with their literary gifts. In most cases profit apparently triumphed over art, leaving a bitter taste in the mouths of the vanquished and adding more fuel to an already fiery intellectual critique of the motion picture.

It has been argued that the movies should not be criticized on a different level from the criticism afforded other media, such as newspapers and magazines.[30] Such a defense, which points up the problems that make the film unique among mass media channels of communication, has won over few intellectuals. As a class intellectual film critics remain extraordinarily pretentious. Their own aesthetic outlook shapes their moral universe; their critiques of film are thus unhistorical, given the tradition of historical objectivism. It is no credit to the historical profession that its study of film, such as it is, has been confined within the narrow corridors of aesthetics, rather than being broadened by those methodological precepts it tries to apply so rigorously to other evidence.

iii

What compelled intellectuals generally, and for our purposes historians in particular, toward an excoriation of the commercial film? During the heyday of the studio system, roughly 1920-1950, there seem to have been three areas in which the industry was seen as highly vulnerable. First, it was a business, and thus it barbarously commercialized potential art in the name of profit. Second, it addressed itself primarily to puerile audiences. Finally, it was seen as an intrinsic leveler, even degrader, of the national culture.

"It's not our business to promote the culture of the country, or to make art films," said Metro-Goldwyn-Mayer production chief Herbert Solow in 1969. "It's to make money for the studio."[31] American moviemen are businessmen and operate under the ethos of business. The interwar decades were a period when the gears of the industry generally meshed smoothly and profitably. Apropos of this phenomenon, Terry Ramsaye remarked in 1926 that pictures for intellectuals were not profitable commercially. He predicted optimistically that pictures for the intelligentsia might be produced by Americans within a generation.[32] Certainly by the end of the First World War concerned intellectuals had become discomfited both with the business and popular aspects of the industry.

The garish qualities of Hollywood engendered much criticism. Filmmakers did not cultivate the staid, conservative life style of the older, more established Eastern money. Many lived beyond ostentation and, in the eyes of their critics, beyond redemption. The movie city became a symptom of cultural malaise. It stood for "mental ease" and "self-praise," qualities which appeared to be all too readily apparent in the rest of the culture.[33] Intellectuals would argue, with Parker Tyler, that Hollywood's "pleas for social tolerance can only be a side dish simply because it is never serious about anybody's business but its own."[34] The profit motive which, stripped of social concern, long had been for intellectuals a primary target in its connection with other forms of big business, was highly evident in the Hollywood operation. The grosser aspects of movie promotion were viewed as ploys which unintentionally yet substantially defiled the "American character"[35] even as they helped to shape that character.

The intellectual critique of business aspects of the film industry willfully emphasized, even exaggerated, the distance between commercialism and art. To keep this distance supplied two apparent needs of the intellectual elite: it rendered them pure, and still in possession of "private" culture, and it made the industry appear philistine. As Hortense Powdermaker noted, the belief in this dichotomy was important, even crucial, to the intellectual;[36] he even was made more virtuous by the greater power of his antagonist. "Art and aesthetic goals have always been less important in our society than either business or humanitarian ones."[37] The unimportance of the artist was magnified by Hollywood, and the intellectual's conception of his own importance was thus hardened and sustained by adversity. The critique could be weighted with intellectual reformist impulses as well, since the maintenance of the status quo, meaning the contemporary sociocultural structure, was prerequisite to a smoothly running film organization.

Thus repelled by the crass commercialism of the industry, intellectuals obviously remained unimpressed by the product itself, a product seen as puerile in the extreme. To become a thinking adult was apparently to put childhood behind; this Victorian inheritance cropped up with great frequency whenever the film was discussed. As early as 1916, an editorial in the *Nation* lamented:

> Once the importance of the juvenile audience in the movie business is recognized, it becomes plain that the art of the movies must in large measure be shaped by that factor. The public, to which must be given what it wants, is now drawn from the primary school ages with a fair sprinkling of kindergarten upper-classmen. Obviously, the scenario-writers are now busy upon an art that is democratic with a vengeance. They must cater to an appeal infinitely broader than the playwright must keep in mind when he sets out to please at the same time Broadway and Kankakee. He solves the problem by going in for the elemental emotions which are the same on both sides of the Hudson, by appealing, as the phrase goes, to the child that is in all of us. The movie writer must go further. He must appeal to the infant that is in all of us. That the trick can be done is attested by the present state of the new art. It is all very simple. The infant cannot always understand and like what his parents do. It remains, therefore, to make the parents like what their youngest likes. The thing has been done before in the case of the newspaper "comic". Starting out as a Sunday device for keeping the children quiet while father was asleep, it has become the everyday necessity for father's sporting page and mother's home page.[38]

If adults were degraded by film fare, children themselves, as miniature adults, clearly were unsafe. By 1926 about one quarter of the total cinema audience was comprised of children who were seen as helpless, even willing, recipients of the screen's alluring magic. These children, complained one critic,

> are fed, day in and out, with the stuff of the screen, a diet never prescribed,

certainly, by any Doctor Holt of literature. They are fed with cowboy horses, cattle-rustling villains, marcelled heroines of the lone prairie, society "wolves," glittering debutantes, "romantic," stylized myth-figures conjured up for minds that will be impressed by them.[39]

"The mental standard for the moving-picture producer," acidly remarked two advertising authorities in 1927, "is the intelligence of the fourteen-year-old child."[40]

Movies were seen not only as a common denominator for children of all ages, but also as progenitors of stereotypes which, carried over into adulthood, helped perpetrate wars, social unrest, and political dishonesty. The moral categories of childhood were perpetuated in both international and domestic relations, and in sexual warfare as well. This diagnosis had grim implications for the liberal intelligentsia: "Ku Kluxers, fundamentalists, and super-patriots are products of arrested moral reflection."[41] Nevertheless, at the end of the thirties the dominant appeal of the film still seemed to lie in the direction of America's youth.

Equally pernicious was the notion that the motion picture helped keep the national culture at a depressingly low level. By shamelessly playing upon the emotions, it was argued, moviemakers appealed to the worst in human nature. Subject matter seemed mundane, if not inane. J. Stuart Blackton, one of the founders of Vitagraph and a leading producer of World War I films, remembered that sometime between 1898 and 1902, during the industry's embryonic years, he and his partners had analyzed the day's take of four films, and found:

United States Battleship at Sea	$0.25
Joseph Jefferson as Rip Van Winkle	0.43
Ballet Dancer	1.05
Girl Climbing a Tree	3.65

It seemed obvious that visual reportage and culture ran a poor second to novelty and amusement; the path of the industry was set.[42] Although filmmakers could claim that amusement was their *raison d'être*–that due to the movie palace children were off the streets and saloons were less populated–educated men were at first appalled by, then resigned to, and finally almost perversely proud of the gap generated by the conflicting ideals of entertainment held by different sections of society.

In reflection it was conceded that the sentiments of the masses, and particularly those of the proletariat, found "some harmonious note" on the screen. Clearly, status considerations were involved. The tendency of the American working class to eschew revolution in favor of reform doubtless was strengthened by the bourgeois value structure of the film, even if the film industry could and did support and transmit oligarchic, military and antiproletarian ideals. The movie theater as dream world was thus a "confessional of the masses,"most of whom, it was held, aspired to bourgeois status.[43] Such a situation was a difficult one to live with for those intellectuals weaned on the European tradition of radicalism, which prescribed the implicit virtue of the proletariat–the very proletariat that appeared to be highly susceptible to the seductive wiles of the motion picture. But there it was: movies were popular, successful, infantile, crassly commercial, and possessed of impossibly low cultural standards. Could a transfusion of artistry in the form of literary quality redeem the medium?

iv

Mass communication is no longer dominated by the vehicle of the printed page. The impact of film has been visual and immediate, and hence more "real." While Daniel Boorstin may have been too facile in judging that the new dramatic form of film has encouraged the pen to explore the "boundless non-visual world,"[44] it is difficult to argue against the primacy in our culture of the motion picture in presenting dramatic narrative action. Movies, in most cases, leave little to the imagination. A book offers time for reflection and meditation; the screen presents fast-moving images fused into a transitory but compellingly vivid experience.

The ratio of the movie public to the reading public in the interwar period was estimated to be about six to one.[45] Intellectuals feared that potentially the visual might overwhelm written and verbal modes of communication. The Lynds speculated that the residents of Muncie might be conditioned more by their movie palace than by their preacher,[46] while in 1935 a survey indicated that although the masses were not reading the works of the new proletarian writers, motion picture propaganda in the same vein could prove to be effective.[47] "The scribes who jeer at the screen number their audience by thousands," bragged J. Stuart Blackton. "We of the screen number our audience by countless millions of people in all parts of the globe."[48]

Early critics compared the film to the cheap sensational novel and called for censorship. Just as libraries banned improper books, poems, and plays, so too should the motion picture theaters be regulated. Because of the intrinsic nature of the new medium, the profundity of a book never could be translated to the screen; literature must not be defiled by a "screen version."[49] But in fact Hollywood relied heavily on material that previously had been presented to the public in written form, on the assumption that a known commercial success in one medium would be a success in another. For example, of the 356 films in this study the primary plot authorship of which can be determined, 202, or 57 percent , first appeared in the form of novels, short stories, or plays. Moviemakers never were loath to either borrow plots from other media or attempt to lure writing talent to Hollywood. However, this talent proved to be highly malleable in the commercial world of the motion picture.

The presentation of history in film has provided trained historians, habituated to communicating via the written word, with yet another easy target. Regardless of the origin of a dramatic narrative couched in historical perspective, it is pertinent to ask: What kind of history did these plots produce? In a word–bad. History on film, even in documentary form, almost invariably has been "whiggish," in Herbert Butterfield's sense of the term.[50] That is, it tends to put the perspective of the present on the presentation of the past to a far greater degree than does most conventional history. In addition, the handicap of operating in a dramatic mode conditioned more by commercial exigencies than by historical accuracy has led to distortion and outright falsification. In this respect, a modern critic's contention that "buying a cinema ticket is exactly like buying a book"[51] simply will not suffice.

Originally, ardent proponents of the film, while conceding the poor quality of history in the movies, argued that one of the new industry's great missions was to "substitute the picture for the book"[52] in order to spread the story of the nation's past to a wider mass audience. Educators soon realized that while the film never could supplant the book, it could offer a new perspective in the teaching of history. The ambitious *Chronicles of America* film series produced by Yale University in the postwar years was directed toward examining "those things that the literary tradition has neglected because the literary medium is inadequate to their expression."[53] *The Chronicles of America*, used as a supplementary teaching aid in senior high schools, appears to have been capable of stimulating students to a greater interest in reading history.[54] But such efforts earned little notice from professional historians at the college and university level. The impossibility of imparting depth and dimension to history on film overshadowed the possibility that film might prove to be a useful and suggestive teaching aid.

Such a reception of the idea of history in films, like that accorded the ideas of historical evidence in film and the history of film itself, did little to establish a pattern of methodological flexibility in the profession. Historians who have become comfortable with the concepts of "symbol" and "myth" within the last quarter century have balked at extending these concepts from the literary to the visual media. History has been slower than most of the other social sciences in realizing the social dynamism hidden in such concepts. The movies operate on both symbolic and mythic levels. One ardent proponent of the film even claimed that this situation was ideal for the historian. "It is not the man who describes what actually happens who best tells history," wrote Harry C. Carr in 1918. "It is the genius who symbolizes it for us; who puts it into doses we can take without mentally choking."[55] But even granted that the study of symbols and myths is a powerful, if certainly not a complete, methodological tool, the rare historian who has examined the motion picture in its symbolic and mythic forms has been inclined to make judgments based primarily on aesthetic criteria.[56] Just as literary scholars have been overbalanced methodologically in the direction of aesthetic considerations, so have students of the film downgraded historical methodology in favor of aesthetic criticism.

Historians as intellectuals have every right to be concerned with the quality of American culture, and in their roles as cultural critics the use of aesthetic standards becomes valuable, if not necessary. But the application of such standards does little if anything to put the special skills of the historian to work in examining the problems of modern culture. To study the influence of motion pictures in American cultural life using aesthetic judgment *only* is to denigrate those qualities which make history a viable profession. These qualities include the quest for objectivity, conceptions of value of evidence, and the examination of problems of causation. For the historian properly to examine film evidence, aesthetic criteria must be relegated to a position of secondary importance. The profession's strong suit lies in rigorously applying its concepts of analytical research to that vast body of visual and written evidence which comprises the area of film.

3

Toward a Historical Methodology for Film Scholarship

i

Film is a communicator of great force. The medium is capable of producing reactions in literates and illiterates, children and adults, prince and peasant alike. Theories abound as to the causes, transmission, and effects of these reactions, but few argue the power of film to evoke them. We are concerned with what is actually being communicated, the symbolic context of the medium.

However, most of the research done on the film by the social sciences, when not descriptive, has concentrated mainly on studying the effect of motion pictures on the audience. This perspective arose primarily from a deep concern over the apparent power of film to influence behavior, particularly the behavior of children. Motion pictures were regarded from their earliest years as a potent medium of education, the influence of which was almost universal. By the early 1930s this concern had reached its peak. Under the auspices of the Payne Fund, a privately endowed fund dedicated to social research scholars attempted to study and analyze the effects of movies upon children. The Payne Fund studies ranged far afield; when finished, they offered in twelve small volumes the best that contemporary social science could present on the subject.

Payne Fund scholars found by 1934 that American children "imitate movies, their mental imagery is shaped by movies, their very conduct is affected by them."[1] The motion picture was, in fact, an educational institution. It influenced children's play, provided stereotypes, implanted attitudes, and served as a source of imitation. The movie machine was thus a behavioral machine. It could and did influence behavior for better or worse, although in practice its value in inculcating reform seemed almost nil. Using some rather dubious measuring techniques, the Payne Fund studies found that the retention level of film information, even information which was false or distorted, was high in the case of children.[2] All of this merely reflected what concerned adults long had suspected–that the twenty-eight million minors who attended movies every week, and particularly the eleven million under fourteen years of age, were being exposed constantly to a powerful formative influence.

Not only young children, but adolescents and young adults as well, were seen as susceptible to film communication. In 1938 a highly quantified study dealing mainly with Ohio high schools gathered useful test data from 1,886 individuals, ranging from seventh-graders to adults. The study indicated that all parts of the test population, when exposed to certain documentary films, experienced attitude changes in the direction the makers of the films desired, although individuals reacted differently. No relationship was found between intelligence-test scores and attitude changes. The study concluded that the documentary film was a powerful instrument for propaganda.[3] Another study conducted four years earlier had indicated even college students were susceptible to specific types of film propaganda.[4] Films, it was argued, must be handled like educational dynamite. Used correctly, they could be excellent educational tools.[5] But, especially when presented in a commercial context, they offered little but bias, misinformation, and illusion.

The efforts of the Payne Fund studies and of several of the social sciences to establish empirically the effects of film were accepted without too much argument. Mortimer Adler was nearly the only scholar who challenged the Payne Fund studies, but he did so in such recondite terms that the movie industry engaged Raymond Moley, fresh from his sojourn with the New Deal, to interpret Adler to the public.[6] The Adler-Moley critique claimed that the Payne Fund scholars, with the exception of Ruth C. Peterson and L.L. Thurstone,[7] had not confined themselves to their data and conclusions drawn from that data, but instead had indulged in opinion, speculation, and guesswork. Their work, in short, was unscientific and did not warrant the moral judgments made.

Moley argued that the motion picture industry was its own best regulator. Adler took another tack, still clinging to the dichotomy between the ability of adult and child to appreciate movies. His point was that despite all the attacks upon the motion picture, both scientific and pseudo-scientific, the industry still had some positive value to the culture. Movies were effective in providing entertainment, social education, and emotional relief for their audiences. But these benefits went primarily to adults. "Our common sense and common knowledge," Adler reasoned, "raise the presumption that the balance of positive and negative values weights more heavily on the positive side in the case of adults, and more heavily on the negative side in the case of the immature."[8]

It seems clear that the commercial film was a pace-setter in fashions and manners. But historians should be concerned with whether attitudes of less transient concern were conveyed as well. Part of the problem is that little information is available as to what type of picture played best to what type of audience. In 1923, Clarence Aitken Perry of the National Association for Better Films found that high school boys liked western stories best, followed by comedies, detective stories, and love stories. Girls of the same age voted *The Sheik* as their favorite picture; the boys preferred *The Four Horsemen of the Apocalypse*.[9] Adult tastes appeared to differ little from those of the adolescent. Robert S. Lynd and Helen Merrill Lynd discovered that the citizens of Muncie preferred films with much the same themes. Any effort to break down the

American movie audience of the twenties and thirties by age, class, sex, family, or type of film preference inevitably suffers from lack of data. The only constant factor seems to have been that entertainment films were more popular than "factual" or "realistic" presentations. For example, Yale's *Chronicles of America* series played poorly in commercial theaters. In Muncie, "the children say they get enough history in school, the adults say they are too grown up for such things, and the attendance is so poor that the exhibitor says, 'Never again!'"[10]

In addition to the popular genres of the western, the love story, and standard tales of adventure, moviegoers have tended to favor war films. To present a narrative against the background of a familiar war (the Great War, for example) was to give the audience familiar history, familiar characterizations, familiar adventures–in other words, to endow the film with the gloss of reality. Ideas, attitudes, and values concerning the war itself thus were presented by the moviemakers in a stereotypical, almost unconscious fashion. Action, romance, danger–all the standard ingredients of melodrama could be and were grafted onto war plots. But in the process, the formulation of conceptions about the nature of the war itself became inevitable. Such conceptions, whether presented in documentary or fictional form, guaranteed at least some audience response. As examples, a reviewer of a documentary made in 1918, *Washington Sky Patrol*, reported viewers holding onto their chairs as an air-borne camera performed aerobatics over the Washington Monument.[11] A seventeen-year-old youth said that pictures such as *Wings* and *Lilac Time* had given him the ambition to be an aviator. A girl of the same age stated that *Barbed Wire*, *Legion of the Condemned*, and *The Big Parade* had convinced her that war was a menace, but that disarmament was an ineffectual idea.[12]

There exists some evidence that war films as a genre were popular precisely because of their high entertainment value. The problem of peace groups, argued one disgruntled critic, was to dramatize peace.[13] Only in this way could advocates of the virtues of peace compete with the natural drama of war situations. However, war films with a "message" apart from their entertainment function apparently had some power to change opinion. Two of the Payne Fund researchers found that certain motion pictures with war themes had definite and lasting effects on the social attitudes of children. Using *All Quiet on the Western Front* and *Journey's End*, two 1930 films thought to be anti-war, they found that a group of high-schoolers was less favorable toward war after viewing the former. Of two groups viewing the latter, one showed no change in attitude toward war, while the second showed a small change in the direction of pacifism.[14]

Such bits and pieces of evidence concerning audience response to film, however, offer little hope. We cannot speak in terms such as "motion picture X *caused* this or *caused* that," simply because no data exist upon which to base a causation argument. Further, we cannot assume that since either side of the equation is present, the causative relationship is complete. That is, presuppose a motion picture that presented a certain situation and that directly or indirectly advocated a response to that situation. Further, presuppose an audience to that motion picture which responded in just that way. The assumption is that we then know the motion picture *caused* the response. One counter-example should suffice. During World War II, the United States Army commissioned Frank Capra, one of

Hollywood's most successful directors, to produce a film series presenting the reasons for America's involvement, with the purpose of better motivating military personnel. Capra responded with the critically acclaimed *Why We Fight* series; the soldiers responded by fighting. But there was no causational link. The films themselves had no measurable effect on the men's motivation to serve as soldiers.[15]

Social scientists may continue to devise tests and measurements aimed at delineating audience reaction to films, but the exacting demands of professional standards have not yet been able to cope with an annual film product numbering in the thousands, which plays to an audience in the millions. The historian who relies only on the small amount of data available leaves himself open to all the perils which are entailed by the use of inductive logic in a social context. Clearly, the ideal situation would be to possess complete audience data on every film one wished to study. But such a situation is inconceivable, even given our technology of memory banks and computer sense cards. Film audiences may go to the commercial cinema to be entertained or enlightened, but they do not go to be measured. This is not to discount the evidence so painstakingly accumulated thus far by the social sciences. Within their sphere many such studies are evocative and persuasive. But they are guidelines, not answers. Historians seeking to trace ideas in film must look beyond the reactions of the film audience, to the act of film communication and to the reasons people view films.

ii

"The study of man is the study of talk," Kenneth Boulding has written. "Human society is an edifice spun out of the tenuous webs of conversation."[16] If "communication" is substituted for "conversation," one has a more generalized idea of where to start analyzing the role of the mass communications media in modern society. Communication, in fact, is the key to social events, and mass social events are, more often that not, conditioned at least in part by the mass media.[17] Film, in particular, communicates through the use of imagery. The bright flickerings on the screen are merely shadows–imitations of a perceived reality. The images thus communicated, argued Boulding, influence behavior.[18]

If one divides the act of communication into three parts–the communicator, the medium, and the audience–the medium is that part which has generated the most theoretical discussion in recent years. Marshall McLuhan is only the most famous, or in some circles the most notorious, of the theoreticians mining this lode. To McLuhan, the media themselves, whether moving pictures, television, radio, or whatever, provide the experience of illusion and involvement, and thus by themselves condition behavior. Movies are a "hot" medium, since they offer an "inward world of fantasy and dreams" where the moviegoer "sits in psychological solitude like the silent book reader."[19] But the medium is only one aspect of the total act of communication. The film is a symbolic as well as a physical medium, and as the sociologist Hugh Dalziel Duncan has stated, "The physical alone cannot generate the psychic content of symbolic experience." Thus

> The medium is *not* the message, any more than is sexual cathexsis, or class "rights", or tribal taboos, or human "nature", the sole explanation of human motivation. At best these are but partial explanations of conduct which must be synthesized into a universal proposition which transcends, as it includes, such monistic views. For if social action takes place in space, it also occurs in entities called acts which are formed in social roles, which in turn, are expressed in certain ways to attain certain goals.[20]

Any "message" which may be imparted by the motion picture may have the power to influence behavior, but its "meaning," according to Boulding, is the change it produces in the images. These images depend in the first place on the culture or subculture in which they were developed.[21] If behavioral patterns thus can be changed, social values may be changed as well. In some instances, these values even may be manufactured by the communicative act. It has been proposed that the study of works of art, when such works are viewed as communicative devices, offers the best clues to studying society and the "social order." Art "is the realm where the expression of doubt, ambiguity, and difference is normal." Films especially, in Duncan's words, interpret "experience to the individual as the shared sense of the community of which he feels himself a part."[22]

Historians have here at least a theoretical entry into the study of film. By studying communication in a mass culture, they can learn more about the values and behavior patterns of that culture. The imagery contained in the film, *especially when it is repeated over and over in different contexts,* offers important insights into American society. It is irrelevant if such imagery is "untrue"; "truth" is a rather vacuous term in any historian's vocabulary, and is here better left unused. What is relevant is that the imagery exists, and in its existence via the act of communication it *may* generate certain effects. Such effects are intangible, to be sure, and do not respond to any quantitative research methods. The proof of their existence is simply the continued popularity of the motion picture in our culture.

The medium of film, however, only closes the communicative circuit between originator and audience. It is pertinent to examine this communicator-audience relationship and attempt to establish a pattern of influence. Do movies merely reflect cultural values, do they originate these values, or is there some middle ground?

One begins by agreeing with I.C. Jarvie that the role of movie audiences is at once obscure and complex.[23] Traditional arguments have viewed the audience role in one of two ways. The first view is that audiences sit passively and attentively during a cinema performance, and are "injected" with the message of the film (the "hypodermic" theory). The audience is thus anaesthetized, and the film functions as the "opiate of the masses." Joseph Wood Krutch once voiced the fears of many intellectuals who believed this was very much the case, that the movies were part of a trend toward the "creation of a Robot Utopia whose well-adjusted citizens will have comfortably forgotten that their forefathers believed themselves to be men."[24] Hortense Powdermaker concluded the essential presupposition of filmmakers was that man is a passive creature who awaits, indeed invites, manipulation. In this sense, since it preyed upon this situation, both Hollywood and its methods of operation were totalitarian.[25] The other and less gloomy theory of audience involvement argues that viewers selectively relate to those parts of a movie that most appeal to their own preconceptions and prejudices (the "selective perception" theory). The movies thus serve as agents of reinforcement, not of education. Either view is highly unfavorable to the role of film in social communication.

In practice, film communication cannot be categorized so neatly. It is in line with intellectual fears of the power of the motion picture to distort to impute Machiavellian tendencies to the film industry. It is equally in line with intellectual estimates of the quality of American culture to envision filmgoers either as a passive herd of blank minds or as a collection of bigots awaiting selective proof of their prejudices. Either way, the motion picture appears as an agent of tremendous potent force. "Movies can be used either as an ether cone to wipe out our consciousness and drug us into stupid oblivion," wrote Budd Schulberg in 1947, "or as adrenalin, shot into our failing hearts to stimulate us to new vitality, broaden our knowledge, deepen our understanding."[26]

Why do audiences go to the movies anyway? To a sociological theorist like George H. Mead audiences clearly went to escape the pressures of modern life, the sad activities of "unaesthetic toil." As audiences, they were passive, not creative, components of the communicative act.[27] The star sydrome, it was argued, might impel audiences to identify with their favorite hero or heroine, becoming themselves imbued with the daring of a Douglas Fairbanks or the winsomeness of a Mary Pickford. This was total escape, the submerging of one's own character, even if only for a few minutes, in that of a screen image. Yet the alternative suspicion lingered: Did people go to the movies merely to be distracted, to spend a few hours being entertained, while still in possession of themselves?

The actual relationship between communicator and audience seems somewhat more complex than any of these rather simplistic approaches. There is no one audience, but many. Certainly some individuals ignore movies altogether; others attend simply as a diversion, while even more may escape reality for a few precious minutes in the darkened fantasy world of the theater. But most people actively seek certain ingredients in films–they look for the known quantity and the familiar–the stars, the studio (in our period), the director, perhaps even the scriptwriter. And they seek the familiar plot; they expect it, are gratified by it, and reward it at the box office. John Wayne was not a phenomenon; he was familiar to us and enriched by that familiarity.

Overlying this is the movie industry itself, in part composed of creators who try to put themselves into their creations–to stamp their product with their individuality. The most notable among these are the Griffiths, Fords, and Hitchcocks of the screen world. But the industry is composed of businessmen as well, businessmen concerned with the audience response to their films. Thus both creator and audience, in most cases, affect the composition of the final product. The perceived desires of the movie audience, measured by those film ingredients which seem to moviemakers best to insure box office success, play a significant role in determining film content. The studio system of the interwar years fed the fantasies of a public inured to habitual moviegoing and eager for sensation and diversion. Yet the symbolic universe surrounding common movie themes persisted with remarkable resilience.

Historians, operating on this premise, may isolate by content analysis certain movie themes pertaining to a specific historical situation, say World War I, and by examining these themes may make certain observations concerning the values that most appealed to certain movie audiences. What they cannot do is ascertain the composition of the audience, nor can they be sure what ideas, attitudes, and values made the leap from the screen to the human mind. Nevertheless, such observations become significant in the context of popular culture, although in itself content analysis does not supply a complete methodology for the film.

Popular values may be conditioned as much or more by myths than by perceived "truths." In Parker Tyler's words, "*desires* may have the same power over the mind and behavior, indeed a much greater power, than *facts*."[28] Popular myths, appearing in symbolic form on the movie screen, may be translated into apperceptions of the value structure and behavioral patterns of a considerable part of our society. We gain from our films a strengthened knowledge of the overwhelming patriotic zeal which flooded America during 1917 and 1918. But we also gain a new appreciation of the so-called period of "isolation" and neutrality which followed, an appreciation which sees many Americans continuing to elevate the patriotic, glorious and militaristic aspects of the war over its despair and disillusion.

In this sense, it matters not what reasons brought the audience to the movie theater. What matters is that the audience is there, it is there in great numbers, and by being there it is playing an integral role in the communicative process.[29] This is not to deny that moviegoing is a social and psychological act. But the act itself, that of attending alone or in company, sitting in darkness, and responding emotionally to what occurs on the screen, is subordinate for the historian to what is actually being communicated.

iii

Moviemakers catering to a population of millions constantly must seek common elements of appeal with which to augment their pictures. Psychologists have speculated that when people share a common culture, as is the case with the bulk of the United States populace, they are likely to have certain day dreams in common. Commercial motion pictures, playing to these day dreams, tend when created over a period of time to exhibit certain distinctive plot configurations.[30]

With this psychological perspective, any mode of mass communication may prove a fruitful source of evidence. A scholar of the World War I novel has noted that the novel may be a "very effective method of reflecting and promoting particular ideas in any society."[31] In another vein, William O. Aydelotte has argued that even the commonplace detective story has historical value because it describes day dreams, and that these day dreams "may reveal popular attitudes which shed a flood of light on the motivation behind political, social and economic history."[32] The motion picture compares closely with Aydelotte's observations on the detective-story genre. Like the detective-story reader, movie audiences find repeated formulas of plot to be pleasing and comforting. The scholarly examination of these formulas may provide information on the commonly held ideas, value structures, and attitudes of movie audiences.

Aydelotte described the detective story as simplistic and as endowing its events with significance and glamour. Its popularity could be ascribed at least partly to the notion that it introduced the reader to a "secure universe." Few would debate the contention that the motion picture as a medium relies on simplicity and glamour to help tell its story. But it is the aspect of "security" Aydelotte raised that is of the most interest. If one speculates–and speculation is the most one can do in this case–that the primary ideas, attitudes, and values the viewer takes away from a film are those most comforting to him, one is back with the "selective perception" theory. But if the converse is the case, that is, that the moviemakers through trial and error are gambling that they can tap familiar ideas, attitudes, and values in their audiences, then the historian has a methodological leg upon which to stand. That this argument holds up may be proven to a great degree by the continued popularity of formulaic genres, such as the western film.

This means that the strength of our analysis rests both on the isolation of significant war themes and on the reiteration of the familiar. Aesthetic analysis rests primarily on the "key picture," the *Citizen Kane* or *Birth of a Nation*, which seems to mark significant advances in movie technology or the art of storytelling by visual symbols. Some of these key pictures are successes and trend-setters in the industry, while some are noteworthy because of the obvious skills of their creators, not their box-office appeal.

Key pictures of World War I, in terms of box-office success, are films the caliber of *The Big Parade, Wings,* and *All Quiet on the Western Front.* They deserve emphasis in any study. But the strength of their themes rests not only in their own financial success but also in the symbolic content they spawned or reflected most conspicuously. These themes, traced in some instances to the level of potboiler quickies, are roughly measured here in depth of impact as well.

Novels and detective stories provide useful analogies, but popularity alone cannot condone some of the scholarly speculation concerning the insight such works give into the "mass mind." In motion picture scholarship, such speculation is connected with the work of Parker Tyler and Siegfried Kracauer, dating from the immediate post-World War II period. Tyler began by assuming that the unconscious was a dynamic factor in human action. Film plots tended unintentionally (unconsciously?) to emphasize "neuroses and psychopathic traits discovered and formulated by psychoanalysis." In this view moviemakers were not Machiavellian, but they did put themselves into their product. "Unaware of the precise function of the unconscious mind," declared Tyler, "Hollywood moviemakers are used to combining their own automatism of mental and physical behavior with that of the character in their products."[33] He called his method "psychoanalytic-mythological" and apparently hoped that studying the film with his contentions in mind would provide insight into the "mass unconscious" portion of the "mass mind" of the American people.

Siegfried Kracauer, whose chief work was the brilliant (but erratic and exasperating) *From Caligari to Hitler,* can be credited with popularizing the idea that film not only tells its story, but on a different level reflects the unconscious of the mass audience to which it is directed. Kracauer studied carefully selected German films of both the pre-Hitler and Hitlerian periods, and found that his choices showed that the "inner dispositions" of the German people lay in the direction of the establishment and maintenance of the Nazi state.[34]

To transpose the German experience to American films of the same period would make a shaky analogy indeed, but this is unnecessary, since the hypotheses of both Tyler and Kracauer rest on untenable methodological grounds. Even psychologists might resist the idea of a "collective unconscious." But to link this unconscious, even if it should exist, with the movie screen through the character of the moviemaker, who is seen apparently as a "representative mind," strains scholarship out of all proportion. To say that the screen reflects such a "collective unconscious," without providing the wherewithal to study *how* ideas move from the unconscious to become manifest in their symbolic representation on the screen, is to indulge in mysticism and nothing more.

This is not to say that the assumptions of Tyler and Kracauer, stripped of their psychoanalytic implications, are unimportant. The study of dominant movie themes does not have to be linked tenuously with a "mass mind" to be productive, nor need one indulge in the relatively profitless speculation of whether the neuroses of film directors and producers are representative of those of the rest of the populace.

iv

Historians influenced or even obsessed by the relatively new art of quantification in history may well ponder the possible role of counting in the study of ideas. "While the number and importance of the individuals who hold an idea may be irrelevant to its philosophical stand," calimed Rush Welter, "they are directly relevant to the significance it may have had in a given historic situation."[35] Presumably in the case of the motion picture this remark means that this relevance holds up if one can show causation; but to show causation, as noted above, is difficult if not impossible–given the existing evidence. In the present state of media research, the emphasis on studying the audience constitutes a blind alley. Over twenty years ago Franklin Fearing noted the ambiguity of box-office figures as an index to the relationship between movie themes and audience needs.[36] The audience, except in the extremely rare instances when a minuscule portion of it renders public judgment on a particular film, is inchoate, inarticulate, and invisible. To assume that the predominant themes of a box-office draw were communicated to a mass audience *in toto* is completely unrealistic.

John Hicks in his examination of the twenties, *Republican Ascendancy*, admitted that there was no way of measuring the effects of movies on Americans, but he believed that "viewers took what they saw with deadly seriousness."[37] This view must be contrasted with the Lynds' finding that Muncie residents apparently saw movies as a "darned good show" and largely ignored thematic content.[38] In short, the historian cannot be sure of what *any* audience thought about *any* picture–there simply are no hard data available. A picture's "popularity," measured in box-office returns, is not as important in this analysis as the imitation, both *a priori* and *a posteriori*, of its thematic content. It is in this way that this study attempts to assess "impact," not in the ambiguities of box-office dollar signs.

Of course "How many?" may mean not only audience size but the number of pictures released dealing with significant themes. This question would have a simple answer if films were unified under one theme. We could then make such statements as "This film is about women in war," or "This film is about airplanes in World War I." But themes rarely shake out so simply as this: *The Big Parade*, in addition to its predominant adventure mode, also contains the minor but important themes of class leveling, ethnic humor, and the national stereotype of the French peasant girl. Complicating the census problem is the fact that the statistics on film releases during 1917-1919, the peak years of production on World War I films, are grossly inadequate alongside those produced by the streamlined studio system of World War II.[39]

Even during these peak years, when one- and two-reelers were ground out by the week, the movie industry probably devoted less than 20 percent of its entire output to war films. After 1919, the percentage of films concerning World War I directly was minute compared to the total output. This impressionistic observation does not negate the value of the thematic evidence presented–taken together, this evidence gathered from 1914 to 1941 shows both consistency (the continued appreciation of America's heroic and valued role in the war) and evolution (the development of the pacifist film in the thirties, for example). And for all these productions, there existed an audience.

Since Hollywood appears to be dependent to a considerable extent on its estimates of audience response, there does exist a need to study the audience. But today's graduate student may evolve into tomorrow's professor emeritus and still lack the quantifiable data necessary to assess properly the ideas, attitudes, and values audiences take from a motion picture. The call for an economic data study of the movies by the Director of Research for the Motion Picture Association of America a quarter century ago has gone largely unheeded. This is particularly the case with pre-World War II films, because the data required are difficult to reconstruct from the transient process of motion picture release and distribution. The basic problem in measuring audience response to those and later films still remains: how to devise a scale for measuring that response. The same problem, it may be added, still confronts literary historians. One of these scholars has confessed that, as far as novels of World War I are concerned, "It seems likely that no scientific method could be worked out to evaluate their importance." He concluded that perhaps the historian of ideas should speculate rather than methodologize.[40]

Some historians continue to press for a count on the audience without apparently realizing the difficulties and implications of such measurement. Felix Gilbert has argued that in popular literature the ideas conveyed are of "secondary interest," because they are "simple and repetitive." He called for statistical investigations on size and number of editions, regional distributions, and the like.[41] But it is the very repetitiveness of ideas in mass communications media which makes the media so fruitful a field for historical analysis. The cavil about "simplicity," while fairly made, seems to reflect more scholarly bias than a concern for pointing out new directions of research. Even if all these numbers can be accumulated, then what? Is the historian any closer to tracing the flow of ideas than he was before? From Gilbert's own area of interest, take the case of James Joyce's *Ulysses* or Philip Roth's *Portnoy's Complaint*. It would be difficult to find a critic who would argue that these books sold all their copies on literary merit, as defined by scholars, and not on their prurient reputations.

Closer to this study, movie actress Pola Negri has recalled that of her two movies with World War I themes produced in the mid-twenties, the receipts from *Barbed Wire* dropped after her marriage, but *Hotel Imperial* was a big success.

Miss Negri ascribed the latter's drawing power to the fact that it was released shortly after the death of Rudolph Valentino, with whom she had been linked romantically.[42] Setting the problem of causation aside, should the historian attribute the success of these movies to the ideas of World War I which they conveyed, or to Miss Negri's private life made public, or to what? Historians who rest easier when their contentions are supported by numbers can gain little comfort from this murky situation. All these intangibles in the study of film indicate again that the student of the history of ideas in motion pictures cannot wholly rely on quantification, even in the unlikely circumstance that figures were available.

The commercial film world survives largely on commercial instinct, on the ability of the communicator to guess correctly what the audience prefers to be communicated. Thomas Ince, an early and successful producer, put it succinctly: "The producer with insight and a real desire to perfect his art can and must feel the pulse of the vast American audience, and anticipate its desires and demands."[43] Irving Thalberg, the highly successful MGM production executive who still is regarded in movie circles as the "boy wonder," reckoned that the job of a picture producer was twofold. "He must not only make the customers like the picture they see but he must make them want to see more pictures produced under the same name and the same trade-mark."[44] The movie producer, in short, must create demand, and in this creation he must play to what he feels are the predominant interests of his audience.

Admittedly, the profit motive is a weak hook upon which to hang a methodology for film study. But it is certainly stronger than the idea of a "national unconscious" or the notion that if we merely count the audience we shall arrive at an assessment of the impact of a specific motion picture. Beyond content analysis, so far as evidence is available, the process which went into the manufacturing of the film itself should be studied. The process and the product, not the media or the audience, offer the most concrete evidence at present on the representation of ideas in motion pictures. Such an approach leaves the problem of causation in abeyance, but so have the researches of literary historians and historians of "high thought." In the present embryonic state of motion picture scholarship, the most one can hope for is to establish the existence of certain ideas, attitudes, and values and ascribe their importance to the theoretical structure thus far presented. The problem of tracing the transmission of these symbolic patterns of thought and of assessing their effect must await more sophisticated analytic tools. Yet even then, historians may find the mind tantalizingly difficult to assess; therein lies both the problem and the challenge.

Part II

Realism and the War Film

> Nothing affects us more powerfully than
> the truth when it is preached in pictures.
> —W. Stephen Bush (1912)
>
> The camera is a natural liar.
> —Newton E. Meltzer (1947)

4

The Myth of the "Objective Camera": A Critique of Film Reality

i

The history profession seeks to be meticulous in its search for hard evidence, and rightly so. Unfortunately, graduate students are sifted through a sieve from which their prejudices systematically are cooked into an insipid casserole of levelheaded judgment, only to find that many of the best historians have defiantly asserted their individuality and retained their professionalism as well. The search for hard evidence in the area of film has suffered from blandness and lack of imagination. It has centered on noncommercial, "objective" films such as newsreels and documentaries.

Slowly and with understandable caution historians are beginning to enter the area of film study. Progress thus far remains limited largely to calling for more use of films in both research and teaching,[1] although in the seventies a few historians actually have created their own films. This limitation is an overly narrow constriction. Broadly speaking, the French film historian Phillippe Esnault was correct when he noted that "every film is a document concerning the people who have made it and the people who have seen it."[2] The evidence value of these "documents" must be examined both on individual merit and on their totality, or one is left with the complete methodological formlessness of the present scholarship.

The notion of films as "documents" has led to a serious scholarly bias in favor of "factual" films as the only valid historical evidence, a bias this study will call "documentary prejudice."[3] At the most basic level the camera is a recording instrument, and is thus highly functional in telling us about appearances, mannerisms, structures–in short, how things *looked*. Even commercial films emerge as period pieces in depicting matters such as clothing, furniture, and architecture. Documentary prejudice leads the historian toward the belief that documentaries and newsreels contemporaneous with the events they describe are inevitably the most valuable visual evidence concerning those events.

The major reason behind this prejudice is the artificial differentiation between film history in its dramatic mode and film history in its recording mode—the difference, in other words, between the commercial feature film and the documentary or newsreel. Critic Iris Barry gave an example of this way of thinking when she stated that the commercial feature seemed boring and false, while the documentary-newsreel type had a "very convincing air."[4] This manufactured dichotomy between reconstructions of reality and recordings of reality is at the root of documentary prejudice. Scholars who argue that the feature film is mere drama and that "actuality" is what must be studied are simply ignoring an enormous body of visiual evidence.

It is quite true that no historian of twentieth-century life, in America and elsewhere, should be unaware of the great research and instructional potential of the newsreel and documentary film. This type of film, in its pre-edited form, generally was created "on the spot" and in a sense provides a vividness and immediacy to a given topic that no lecturer can hope to match. Leni Riefenstahl does this for us with her scenes of the Nuremberg hordes at Hiltler's feet; so does Pare Lorentz with his visual poems of dustbowl America. It is certainly the case that in this type of film the ideas, attitudes, and values of a society "come into the foreground and stand naked for analysis."[5] Documentaries and newsreels are important communicative devices for studying such evidence, but they are not the whole story.

The British seem more advanced than the Americans in studying film, but they too have shown signs of documentary prejudice. British scholars are prepared fully to bring to the study of film the same critical apparatus with which historians deal with written evidence,[6] but they have not been willing to extend this apparatus from the newsreel and documentary to the commercial cinema. They agree, and we must as well, that film is in no way the complete research answer for the historian. "Its importance as a source can only seldom rival or surpass that of the written and printed record."[7] they recognize the perils of aestheticism previously discussed[8] and have an excellent grasp of the pitfall of documentary evidence. But further than this British and American historians will not go. Most of those interested in film appear to share the view of Fritz Terveen:

> The term "historical film" can be used only of those films which record a period or a person from a time after the invention of cinematography and without dramaturgical or "artistic" purposes: those films which present a visual record of a definite event, person, or locality, and which presuppose a clearly recognizable historical interest inherent in the subject matter.
> The whole area of the feature film, the film reconstructions, and to a great extent also of the so-called "documentary" can therefore be on principle excluded from the discussion of historical films.[9]

This narrow view is completely unsatisfactory. The tradition of historical objectivism is a powerful barrier standing against the utilization of the commercial film as historical evidence. Even the "factual" film, as Penelope Houston has noted, "carries its own built-in comment with it."[10] Comment is a variable function depending on the nature of the film audience and the circumstances surrounding the viewing. The cheering sea of faces at the Nuremberg rallies appear in a different light to us than it might have to a Sudeten German viewing the film in 1936.[11] Film is never neutral; the historian deludes himself if he believes his professional standards can be upheld only by studying documentaries and newsreels. While objectivity is an admirable goal, it must remain the ideal, never the excuse. Films as historical documents are not only highly subjective; they may lead the historian into subjective patterns of analysis, one of which is the total reliance on aesthetic criticism. Once this situation is recognized the student will be prepared to include all types of films within this purview and not be content to limit himself solely to nonfictional motion pictures.

ii

A curious misapprehension has long existed concerning films that claim to depict reality. The idea that reality is capable of film representation is almost as old as the genre. So is the notion that these films may be neatly divided into categories such as "propaganda" and "nonpropaganda," "fiction" and "nonfiction," or "factual" and "nonfactual." This is due largely to a confusion which too readily relates films of reality to reality itself. Hitler's Stukas dive-bombing Warsaw are seen on screen as the "real" Stukas, not their film images. Film content in this facile sense constitutes truth–a tragic and misleading truth since, as Virginia Woolf observed, a movie "can say everything before it has anything to say."[12]

An early film writer's wistful thought that propaganda films should be confined to national emergencies[13] has never been realized. Much time has been wasted trying to define a boundary between the "propaganda" film, the "educational" film, the "scientific" film, and other equally vague areas of cinema. If one regards propaganda as the "organized dissemination of interested information" which shows the "good side of one side of the question and the bad side of the other sides,"[14] one is forced to regard every motion picture, no matter what its degree of objectivity, as propaganda. There has been no feature film or documentary produced, to this writer's knowledge, that deals with a controversial situation in an "educational" as opposed to a "propagandistic" fashion.

The motion picture camera is a mechanistic tool which, no matter what the intentions of its operator, restricts and distorts reality as defined by the human eye and mind. There are certainly films of greater and lesser degrees of subjectivity, a subjectivity produced by the camera mechanism and by the people involved in the filmmaking process. But for the historian the debate over the propagandistic nature of a specific film is largely irrelevant.

The main barrier in establishing this irrelevance lies in the fact that film traditionally has been regarded by many as a moral weapon; that is, there are "good" films and "bad" films, according to the moralistic impulses of the viewer. The moralist thus welcomes what he regards as "good" propaganda and castigates the "bad" propaganda. For the early critic W. Stephen Bush, any motion picture which portrayed "deplorable social conditions" was an agent for good.[15] War situations were perfect for this moralistic approach. American audiences responded much more readily from 1914 to 1916 to the French and British films of World War I than to German productions; by 1916 the German films had been driven almost completely from American theaters. On screen Germans were the bad guys well before Wilson severed diplomatic relations. This satisfactory establishment of the enemy reflected orthodox patriotism and good business practice as well. In the commercial sense, films constantly faced the dilemma of keeping a mass audience while remaining controversial enough to avoid triteness and yet not alienate those who took comfort in familiar themes with moral lessons to teach.

There was no real debate concerning the factual nature of the World War I films presented to the American public during and shortly after the conflict. There was no need to change attitudes and beliefs, only to reinforce them. The task of the film producer was made easier because there was no substantial argument over the "goodness" and "badness" of the war with the Central Powers. These films mark an instance where propaganda, in our terms, so completely dominated the field that no other definitions present themselves; hence "propaganda" as a connotational term becomes meaningless.

Leo Rosten has argued that not until the international crises of 1936-37 did the United States show any substantial concern about the propaganda potentialities of the screen.[16] Certainly there was no such concern during and shortly after the war. But readers conditioned during the twenties by authors such as Hemingway, Dos Passos, and Cummings were prepared in the early thirties to recognize, say, the film techniques of the Nazis as the skillful propaganda they were. The sensational disclosures of rigged newsreels during Upton Sinclair's EPIC campaign for the California governorship in 1934 did much to enlighten the public concerning the capabilities of the motion picture camera to distort and lie.[17]

Not only films but filmmakers could be perceived as propaganda agents. One of the more notorious instances in American motion picture history concerned the callous treatment meted by Paramount Studios to the Russian director Sergei Eisenstein. After the completion of two draft screenplays, *Sutter's Gold* and *An American Tragedy*, Eisenstein was allowed to film neither because of Hollywood's continued nervousness over anyone with a reddish tinge (Eisenstein was relatively apolitical). The brilliant director moved on to Mexico and his famous imbroglio with Sinclair.[18]

The Eisenstein affair legitimately may be seen as a case of art stifled by irrationality and the dollar sign. When the question of aesthetics intrudes into the definition of film realism, the waters are muddied further. One is then faced with the problem of defining "propaganda art" and "escapist art." The deeper questions of reality and meaning cannot be answered by these semantic techniques, as the philosopher Abraham Kaplan glumly concluded. "In short," he summarized, "if we pose the question whether art is realistic or not, we can answer as we choose, yes or no."[19] This ambiguity is merely a reaffirmation of the intense subjectivity of the filmmaking process and its product.

The "realistic" government-sponsored films of World War I were highly propagandistic by today's standards. The government effectively monopolized the commercial film medium through coercion, persuasion, or in most cases cooperation by the private producers themselves. Basic national values were reinforced by the film presentations of the war, since most Americans agreed that these values did not stand in need of change in the first place. It is quite true that the motion picture industry "was one of the greatest instruments for propaganda in the war," and that "it must be given some responsibility for the hysteria and repressive activities of 1917 and 1918."[20] But in the absence of other alternatives, what is "propaganda" to the viewer with the luxury of a half century of hindsight was "truth" to the relatively unsophisticated filmgoer of the war years.

Films have the uncommon quality of not only reshaping reality but of becoming reality themselves. They can become, in Daniel Boorstin's terminology, a "pseudo-event."[21] In the insular darkness of the theater, they may comprise all the reality available, and they present this reality on the terms of their makers. The audience is forced to take the camera eye as its eye, and the will of the filmmakers constantly impinges on its will. In a situation where there exists no perceptible opposition to film content in the first place (i.e., war audiences were appreciative and enthusiastic in their reactions to films from the "front"), the current of "reality" from communicator to audience flows smoothly and unimpeded. This lack of perceived alternatives, to those who have experienced a second world war and an unsettling cold war, appears infantile and inexcusable. But the historian does a disservice to *his* audience if he accepts this criticism. Where some philosophic traditionalists would presuppose a structured picture of "reality" outside the range of a camera lens, scholars must cope with the fact that on film the image of this reality can never comprise the reality itself.

Thus in the broadest sense all film conspires, whether intentionally or not, to reduce the audience to ready acceptance of its message. The message may consist of entertainment or reportage; bias is nevertheless continually present, in greater or lesser degree. In assuming that all films concerning a specific subject present biases that may not even be central to the intended themes, the historian merely is admitting the subjectivity of the entire filmmaking process and that of its products. Pictures of "reality" are not the only proper subjects of study. There are no such pictures—only images and illusions.

iii

Aldous Huxley once remarked that the cinema could do one thing better than literature or the spoken drama: it could be fantastic. He hoped that this "super-realism" would coexist with the realistic quality of film to provide variety and widen the film's potential.[22] Virginia Woolf was moved by the nostalgic qualities she found in old newsreels, yet she felt that abstractions and "some residue of visual emotion" might be the key to the future of cinema.[23] Gilbert Seldes, an early prophet of the value of film to our culture, wrote approvingly of Woolf's opinions.[24] In the minds of all three—all come to the study of movies from some aspect of literary art—film stayed solidly anchored in "reality" while reaching out to grasp illusion, an effort that was aesthetically stimulating and completely necessary if it was to remain viable as an art form. In the work of recent critics like Parker Tyler and Marshall McLuhan, film has raised anchor and now floats serenely in a dream world where illusion is total and "reality" a myth.[25]

Filmgoers of the World War I era had no such analyses available. Largely unaware of the distortion inherent in the movie camera, they were also susceptible to the confusion arising between the photography and the written or spoken commentary that accompanied it. When Kenneth Boulding observed years later that "the image is universally affected with reality,"[26] he was defining a problem that confronts all historians researching early films and film audiences. We know that these old films are not "real" in any concrete sense, yet we also have a strong inclination toward believing early audiences regarded them as such. Further, each member of the audience looked at the screen through his own preconstructed prism of reality, which told him what was "true-to-life" and what was not. One's experiences outside the theater, which were generally saturated with pro-Ally and anti-German sentiment, became the intellectual and emotional filters of the movie experience. To speak of "fiction" and "fact" in this situation is somewhat irrelevant, since these and like terms necessarily contain a high degree of subjectivity. On top of this the historian places his constant opponent—his own subjectivity. Given these overlying and complex patterns which impede analytical research, historians only create more myths by emphasizing dichotomies where at best the dividing lines are obscure and at worst no such situation exists.

Early critics often confused reality with the photography of reality. Many believed the chief value of the camera lay in the fact that it was a recording instrument. For example, war on film was real because the war itself was real. With motion pictures "we accompany the soldier out upon the field of battle until the 'rocket's red glare' and 'the bombs bursting in air' are translated from poetic metaphor to grim reality."[27] "Truth" was regarded as a readily perceptible commodity available to any film viewer with the sense enough to see it. It was deemed incontrovertible because it was visual, immediate, and afforded no alternatives. "The value of the moving picture as a means of agitating for the betterment of social conditions is self-evident," Bush claimed. "Nothing affects us more powerfully than the truth when it is preached in pictures."[28] Technical improvements in the industry only enhanced film's ability to depict reality, and hence to tell the "truth." As late as 1941, it was argued that improvements in audio, such as volume, range, and direction, and even in smell, were an "advancement in realism" which carried the cinema to the "very door of reality."[29]

Because unexposed film was literally *tabula rasa,* it was conceived to be the perfect recorder, an honest and incorruptible spool of celluloid which somehow operated independently of human beings. Bush put this notion into words, *apropos* of the war:

> The only real and incorruptible neutral in this war is not the type but the film. The moving picture camera is convincing beyond the peradventure of a doubt. As a means of enlightening the public as to the honest truth of the situation it is an invaluable instrument in the hands of any and all of the warring nations. It is utterly without bias and records and reports but does not color and distort.
>
> The prohibition of the motion picture camera at the front is nothing less than a loss to civilization and an additional hindrance to peace.[30]

The motion picture along with the press led the way in bringing home the "full facts" to the American people. These media strengthened endurance and "have given us a valuable foretaste of the perils that were upon us."

It has been much better to witness German atrocities upon the screen than it would have been to sit back quiescently until such atrocities were committed upon the streets of our towns and cities. The screen must be given credit for doing its part in arousing the nation to its present state of preparation.

The condition of the public mind has demanded this. It would be interested or attracted by nothing less than the truth. To bring this truth before the people it has been necessary to picture much of the violence of war . . . .[31]

Once the novelty of the film wore off–and to the sophisticated viewer it had worn off by the early twenties–even the gross assumption that pictures of actuality were the primary function of the filmmaker (because they were capable of moving "reality" through space and time) was not enough. "Every effort to make the film merely realistic," complained Seldes, "has made the film dreary and dull."[32]

Although newsreels and documentaries of World War I provided a nice change of pace, most people preferred distraction to information on their movie screens. Those who had experienced the grim reality of war firsthand had little toleration for its dramatic depiction. Yet they were willing to be distracted and amused–in other words, to submerge reality for a brief moment in imagery and illusion. The majority of Americans, who never saw the Argonne or heard the screech of incoming artillery or smelled the stench of death, took their movie war as actuality. Emotional detachment and emotional involvement were thus both possible.

The illusion involved in presenting the war to the public was helped along by a thriving business in faking war films: Viewers were able to accept dramatic presentations as the artificial creations they were and still were able to become engrossed in the plot, which after all hinged on "reality." But most were unaware that some film reportage, particularly in the early years of the war, consisted of carefully engineered fakes. Producers used electrical charges, gunpowder, spring bayonets, and underground explosives to simulate combat on the Western Front. These fictions were pawned off as "combat footage."[33]

In spite (or perhaps because) of such subterfuge, the motion picture was a potent force during the war. Films were popular among fighting men, even those at the front. Some soldiers gave their dugouts the names of their favorite production companies–"Keystone Kottage," "Vitagraph Village," and so on. Others reversed the cinematic process of creating illusion out of reality by defining reality through illusion. A visitor to the front reported a common saying: that a big battle was a "picture show." A survivor of one of the monstrous, formless battles that continually disfigured Northern France might say something like "I was in the picture show at Ypres."[34] When impresario D.W. Griffith visited the front he remained unimpressed. To him the war was *déjà vu*; it took the shape of a spectacle on the level of *Birth of a Nation* or *Intolerance*, with one exception: it was not being directed by D.W. Griffith. Upon his return he unburdened himself to reporters:

All these things were so exactly as we had been putting them on in pictures for years and years that I found myself sometimes absently wondering who was staging the scene. Everything happened just as I would have put it on myself–in fact I have put on such scenes time and time again.[35]

Griffith's comment carried the confusion between reality and illusion to its extreme but logical denouement. If images of the war could appear real to many at home, the war itself could appear as a bad dream to some participants and observers. Combatants often used this notion as a psychic crutch; when reality proved unbearable, it could be made bearable by converting it to illusion. This confusion demonstrates the myth of the objective camera; it destroys artificial barriers between film "fact" and film "fiction"; and it affords scholars the full play of their skills in analyzing the transmission of ideas, attitudes, and values via the cinematic experience. Skepticism in this area contains more than its usual virtue because, as a later critic bluntly put it, "the camera is a natural liar."[36]

iv

Early newsreels continued the novelty of the very first films by showing events "as they happened" or staging the events after the fact and passing the staged version off as the real thing. They were oriented toward novelty and the bizarre, following the path indicated by Blackton's previously mentioned *Girl Climbing a Tree*. The newsreel pioneers believed themselves to be creating a new journalistic technique, as in part they were, although the subject matter admittedly comprised a less than thorough coverage of the news.[37] Newsreels of war events tended to be shots of Great Men doing Great Things (Wilson signing the declaration of war), actual Signal Corps combat footage (relatively rare due to the cumbersome photographic equipment and the nature of trench warfare), scenes of soldier life behind the lines, or staged fakes of battles.[38]

A modern scholar has defined a newsreel as a straightforward record of an event;[39] while this may be theoretically useful, one would be hard pressed to find a newsreel that would fit such a description. But illusion for a considerable time was not part of the newsreel's vocabulary. For over a decade following the war, there was little debate concerning the nature of the new pictorial journalism. It was the "weekly newspaper of the screen," and the events it depicted were assumed to be "actual" and "important."[40] A sophisticated reviewer admired the newsreels for their power to provide a "more complete catharsis than anything devised for the mind or imagination of Hollywood" through their ability to present the dramatic actualities of everyday life.[41]

In 1926 the newsreel was at the peak of its reputation, a peak not matched until the rise of the "news feature" in the late thirties. Its combined circulation was estimated to reach almost 90 percent of all American theaters. "In this film," enthused one admirer, "the universe was turned back and yesterday seen." The war had been preserved forever on celluloid; its horror would persist undiluted for centuries. "The news film has come to be the greatest historian of all."[42] Newsreel theater chains were functioning by 1931. The vision of the pioneers had been realized; the newsreels were accepted by press and public alike as a form of journalism. The advent of sound quickly made the voices of enforced gaiety, enveloping gloom, and staccato analysis familiar counterparts to screen "reality." One newsreel man remarked in 1938 that the newsreels were enjoying a prestige as extensive as it was deserved, "for in them is seen not only swift and accurate representation of news but the closest approach to the ideal of genuine freedom of the press."[43]

But doubt was growing. Perceptive critics were beginning carefully to scrutinize content. Alexander Bakshy quietly suggested that newsreels could stand more imagination and intelligent selectivity of topics and less sensationalism.[44] Gilbert Seldes noted that about 10 percent of the newsreels he saw were really news; the rest were devoted to "features." Further, post-commentary (a necessary addition, given the existing state of film technology) seemed to destroy the spontaneity of the event. To Seldes newsreels were pictorially accurate, "but the tone becomes entirely false."[45] What news there was often appeared to be trivial in the extreme. "The peacetime newsreel," documentary pioneer John Grierson acidly remarked, "is just a speedy snip-snap of some utterly unimportant ceremony."[46] By the end of World War II, newsreels had been clearly and correctly identified as being largely composed of superficial and escapist material.[47]

Chief among the successes in the film journalism field was the much-praised *March of Time*. In 1938 it went to 11,000 theaters in thirty-five countries. It was lively, entertaining, and due to the devotion and skill of its camera crews covered far more "news" than did its competitors. But even the *March of Time* catered to overdramatization; its format necessarily led to oversimplified presentations and shallow analyses. By the time of its demise in the fall of 1951, after over 160 issues, it nevertheless was widely regarded as the quintessence of film journalism.[48] Even documentarists such as Grierson and Paul Rotha had given it high praise during its lifetime.[49]

Newsreels and "news features" for their entire life span, which may be dated very roughly from about 1910 to the decade of the sixties, were ideal vehicles for the dissemination of biased information. The same totality of approach that governed any feature presentation, shutting out the viewer's options, worked just as effectively in the newsreel. One does not have to be paranoid nor brand newsreel producers as Machiavellian (they were not) to realize the highly selective nature of the "news" that appeared on the nation's screens. A study done in 1935 by college sociology students indicated that newsreels were in large part not news at all. The following is their classification of the contents of 307 items in forty-five newsreels:

Classification	Percent
Sports	24.8
Human Interest	23.1
Militarism	10.4
Disasters	8.2
Imperialism, Fascism	5.9
The New Deal	5.9
Other Politics	5.5
Aviation	3.9
Educational	3.6
Anti-Militarism	3.3
Charity	3.0
Crime	1.6
Religion	1.0

The study determined a "trend toward militarism and reaction."[50] It is significant that at a time when America was semi-officially isolationist and professing itself thoroughly disgusted with the results of the Great War, "militarist" items in its newsreels outnumbered "anti-militarist" items three to one.

Newsreels, in spite of their disinterested and objective pose, were in many cases highly effective "propaganda" devices in the sense that audiences may have known of other alternatives to the film message received. Their mode of presentation was particularly dangerous in a democratic society, not because of the triviality of the information conveyed, but because this information came to the viewer in the guise, whether intended or not, of comprising every aspect of the situation. Some newsreels were more blatant with this technique than others, with Hearst Metrotone News and Pathé News leading the list. The public could not know the machinations which determined what was photographed, much less how much of the photographed footage reached the screen and in what form.

The newsreel was in its day an admirable method for disseminating information in a mass society. But there was nothing admirable in its pose of disseminating *disinterested* information. The newsreel, like the feature film, was not reality. Its limited scope and method of approach were downplayed, while the trite aphorism that "photographs don't lie" remained the underlying justification for its popularity. Historians, who may grant the newsreel a lesser measure of subjectivity than many other types of films, should nevertheless be prepared to accept newsreel situations as the contrivances they generally were. This caution is particularly pertinent for the newsreels of World War I, both commercial and government-sponsored. Several of these can be identified even today as outright fictions, others by their willingness to stretch realism into impossibly elastic shapes.

v

If the newsreel was bound by its format to stress spectacle and simplify complex themes, there remained a significant public for "longer films of reality." This public was the target of the documentary movement. The basic suppositions of leading documentarists may be summarized as follows. The movie camera is mobile and capable of reproductive art. The modern world in all its complexity can best be presented, via this art, in its natural setting. This means no actors, no staged scenes; everything must be "real." The force of this reality must be presented to the viewer by skillful editing. In editing lies the key to the documentary art. It is that part of the process which most determines the shape of the final product.

The finished documentary film seeks to be both a "dramatic picture of reality" and a "social commentator."[51] Documentarists desire a fusion of informative material with dramatic technique. The constant aim is to make the documentary more "real" and "true to life." Richard MacCann has noted what differentiates documentary from the feature film; in general, the documentary "parallels the area of social studies."

> It is subject matter, not method, that counts most in a documentary. It is integrity of purpose, bent upon authenticity of comment, which brings with it

the desire to seek out real places and real people as means. It is characteristic of the documentary writer and producer that they seek subjects for films which will cast light on important public problems. This is the kind of civic responsibility which adds new dimensions to the artist's responsibility and makes documentary different.[52]

Documentaries do not attempt that pose of complete impartiality which cloaks the newsreel but, in Lloyd Ramseyer's words, they successfully create the "illusion of being an authentic representation of fact."[53] In spirit they are halfway houses between the quasi-objective forms of film and the familiar dramatized feature. Since most documentaries have a generous input of social commentary, they are almost axiomatically biased. The successful documentary thus achieves its difficult aim of being informative and theatrical at the same time.

Since most American documentaries concerning World War I were made from a decidedly liberal point of view, the historian may find himself a member of the audience rather than a detached observer. This seductive notion is one measure of the power of "documentary realism." Film presented in this fashion has an enormous capacity for creating sympathetic involvement. "History by hearsay is yielding place to history by eyewitness, and our roles are already being thrust upon us," observed one perceptive critic. "It remains for the actors to be united with their drama, for the involvement as a whole to be envisioned in terms of its portent."[54]

Documentary films usually are subordinate to feature films in terms of audience appeal. Only during wartime do documentaries compete successfully for audience attention. The natural drama of war is an irresistible topic for documentarists, perhaps too much so. The documentary film continually labors under the strain caused by dramatic needs on the one hand and the necessity for achieving realism on the other.

Early documentaries of World War I were of course silents, slapped together out of snippets of archival film compiled during 1917 and 1918. The documentary movement began to take hold in America during the thirties, when the Great War became a favorite whipping boy of documentarists. With these films the narration heightened the carefully chosen images of slaughter and downplayed or eliminated the heroism and sacrifice characteristic of the silent documentaries. Audiences thus were afforded a newer "reality," which actually consisted of films of calculated distortion and emotionalism.

No film can masquerade as reality. Every nonfeature film should be regarded as "interested propaganda" until circumstances prove otherwise. The camera eye is not the human eye, nor are the sensibilities of the lens human. But the camera product unavoidably appears in these "humanistic" guises after it passes through the heads and hearts of cameramen, editors, commentators, and so on. The newsreel, news feature, and documentary comprise some of the most enticing evidence which can confront the historian. Everything is weighted toward the suspension of nonaesthetic criticism; in the absence of balancing evidence, the plea of the "neutral camera" to be believed is powerful and compelling. While no film is without a message, the message received by historians will not necessarily be that intended by the filmmakers. Bias and imaginative content thus can be made to serve the cause of historical knowledge, rather than confound it.

5

From Idealism to Nihilism:
The Plastic Uses of the Realistic Film

i

The documentaries of the World War I period offer a prime example of the plastic qualities of the film medium. From the earliest cinematic compilations of the original combatants through the involvement of the American government in motion picture production and distribution, the record was one of ambiguity and distortion. Yet the ideas conveyed by these films provide concrete evidence of shifting national attitudes regarding the war and America's relationship to it. The plasticity of film is especially evident in postwar documentaries compiled from original war footage but for completely different purposes than those of the wartime era.

The motion picture grew to maturity in the crucible of war. One index of this maturity was the growing involvement of film with the battlefield. Movie cameramen had had limited experience in covering combat situations,[1] so the war served as a school as well as an opportunity. Civilians such as Edwin F. Weigle of the *Chicago Tribune* and J.C. Bee Mason of the Hearst-Selig Company were not content with the European footage reaching neutral America and ventured overseas themselves.[2] Their work provided some American film of the pre-1917 fighting.

The government placed no restrictions on film imports at the beginning of the war. Audiences cautioned to be neutral in both thought and deed had their pick of war films from both the Entente and the Central Powers. This situation continued right up to the eve of American entry; a German war film called *Germany and Its Armies of Today* was introduced in January, 1917, at the Strand in New York City. But the French and the British in particular had long since won the battle of the screen for the support of most Americans. European-made war films, of course, arrived pre-edited by the respective governments. The viewer who desired the perspective of the Allied position could avail himself of compendia such as

Behind the Battle Line in Russia, At the Front With the Allies, Somewhere in France, The Great War in Europe, and *The Italian Battle Front.* Others could get the views of the Central Powers from *Austria at War, On the Firing Line With the Germans, The Log of the U-35,* and *The German Side of the War.*³

Both the Germans and the French were most careful about allowing foreign cameramen near newsworthy events, but coups by Americans occasionally were scored. Weigle and Mason proved adept at circumventing regulations, while W. H. Dunborough surreptitiously filmed the Kaiser at a review in Poland. John Allen Everets was allowed to travel with German troops and filmed their shelling of the town of Przemysl on the Eastern Front. Cameras even tracked the Hohenzollerns into abdication. A hidden photographer took scenes of the Crown Prince at Wieringen which were released to much audience merriment under the title *Hiding in Holland.*⁴ Naturally enough, no pro-German "factual" film was shown in this country after *Germany and Its Armies of Today.* A small attempt was made to resuscitate Germany's war reputation in 1928 with *Germany's Side of the War,* but it was quickly removed from circulation.⁵

Almost none of the documentaries made in Europe made a profit in this country. But American producers were quick to sense the value of films about American preparedness. One of the first in the field was *Guarding Old Glory,* released in 1915, which featured pictures of alleged German atrocities. But the primary purpose of this film was to present the entire spectrum of American fighting men in action. Soldiers, sailors, and aviators went through their paces for the cameras and were supported by footage taken on the Vera Cruz expedition of the year before. The ripeness of the whole effort can be gauged by a few of the titles: "Eternal Vigilance is the Price of Liberty"; "To Be Prepared For War is One of the Most Effectual Means of Preserving Peace"; "God Grants Liberty Only to Those Who Love It and Are Always Ready to Guard and Defend It"; "Our Country. In Her Intercourse with other nations may she always be right, but our Country, right or wrong"; and "Ship for Ship our Navy is Equal, if not Superior, to That of Any other Nation."⁶ This combination of historical Messianism and chauvinistic jingoism was effective and was a portent of things to come. One viewer wrote that "we cannot help feeling that man for man in the army and ship for ship on the sea the United States can hold its own with any power; but we are also convinced that Uncle Sam must give us many more of them in order to do so."⁷

In like vein was *America Unprepared,* unveiled for an elite audience in early 1916. It included the ominous but unverified statements that between Portland, Maine, and the Virginia Capes there were no less than 116 places where an enemy might land, and that our coastal defense guns had only a thirty-minutes supply of ammunition. *Uncle Sam's Defenders* apparently fed a desire to see Americans in combat by following shots of the Plattsburg training camp with the departure of New York troops for the Mexican border. When Villa proved elusive not only to the cameraman but to the military as well, the film recorded our soldiers staging mock battles among themselves. *America Preparing* presented a phalanx of Army and Navy might; one title exhorted, "quality we possess–we must have quantity." "This motion picture," stated *The New York Times* man on the scene, "makes the army and navy inviting."⁸

War made the cinema respectable as well as valuable. Film crossed the line from defense to passive involvement with *The American Ambulance Boys at the Front* (1916), composed of shots of the American Ambulance corps in action in France. It was received enthusiastically, and no wonder; its sponsors included the best names in Eastern society, and it was shown initially at Mrs. Vincent Astor's summer home in Newport. Theodore Roosevelt, the constant Cassandra of preparedness, received a private showing and was greatly impressed. Its producers presented *The Ambulance Boys* in humanitarian, not martial, terms:

> Our American boys–fine, clean, upstanding young fellows from all over the country–have been going over to Europe, not to kill other people's boys, just as fine and upstanding, but to risk their lives in bringing those others out of the devil's pit of war where they have been lying wounded, often unto death. They drag the soldiers out of the trenches; they load them in their own ambulances; they drive swiftly through shell-torn towns and villages, and they work like demons to save lives.[9]

American audiences during the neutrality period saw no domestically produced realistic films that stressed the bitter consequences of conflict, other than the romantic-heroic aspects of patriotic and sacrificial death. These documentaries neither debated the war aims of the European contestants nor questioned the wisdom of America's impending involvement. The compilers of war footage realized the futility of presenting American pacifism in documentary terms.

These documentaries did not chart a safe, nonbelligerent course between the contending European powers. Instead, they gravitated from advocating domestic preparedness to displaying Americans serving on the Allied side. Although *America Unprepared* and *The American Ambulance Boys at the Front* were practically contemporaneous, they marked an acute shift in visual perspective. From a relatively phlegmatic assessment of the nation's defense needs to shots of Americans taking part, albeit passively, in European combat, these two films taken together plotted an emotional path away from detachment and toward involvement. Their overriding themes included a strong, historically conscious patriotism which emphasized military deeds and might; a firm appeal to democratic spirit, in that the films sought to make every citizen conscious of the looming crisis and of his responsibility to help meet that crisis; and the delineation of what might be called the "Cincinnatus syndrome," like Triangle's "upstanding young fellows from all over the country." The nation's private producers, motivated in part by sincere patriotism and in part by the commercial appeal of realism in warlike garb, did their share to deny a neutral stance to Americans.

ii

The central effort in putting actual war on film did not, however, come from private enterprise. The federal government had begun making films in 1911, when the Bureau of Reclamation photographed large-scale agricultural systems to show the East the problems of the Western prairies. The Civil Service Commission followed the next year with a self-explanatory title, *Won Through Merit*. Governmental agencies eventually sponsored hundreds of films promoting their particular interest.

Among these were the training films of World War I. They were not distributed commercially and were shown to limited (captive) audiences, but they did play a distinct part in the war effort. As early as 1915 recruits were being trained by shooting at figures on the screen; when the film was stopped, their marksmanship could be analyzed. A year later, at the request of West Point, a film was made for purposes of drill instruction. This spawned a government-sponsored series of sixty-two training films made by private producers under Signal Corps supervision. These remained in circulation until 1928, when they were declared obsolete by a special War Department Board. America's civilian-soldiers in part were introduced through films to such military exoticisms as tactics, drill, bombs, machine weapons and combat mapping.[10]

Usage of film during the period of American belligerency anticipated that of later conflicts. Aerial photography made its debut. War or military scenes appeared in newsreels, features, and short subjects, and were intended for commercial presentation. There were numerous nontheatrical showings as well– many, like the Astor exhibition, to elite audiences. The job of providing the raw material for these films ultimately fell to approximately 600 men, many of whom had been newsreel employees before the war. The Signal Corps provided exposed film until June, 1918, when it reverted to its original military functions and sloughed off photography to the former newsreelers turned combat photographers. Original negatives remained in France for the duration, while duplicates were sent to Washington to be processed by the Signal Corps, thence to await the will of the Committee on Public Information.[11]

It was the Committee[12] that shaped America's movie effort in the war. Chaired by an energetic and aggressive newspaperman, George Creel, it rapidly intruded into virtually every aspect of domestic film production and proceeded to regulate international film trade as well. After a false start in which he selected three Hearst men to coordinate film activities, Creel settled down with an advisory committee which included the biggest names in the industry. This committee functioned in uneasy harness with an exhibitor's committee and a committee of actors and actresses until war's end. But Creel and his Division of Films had the final say, and under him the CPI operated with a maximum of efficiency, given the disparate forces working with it and within it. An early movie historian, writing from the industry's side, conceded that the Committee was more efficient in its task than were the shipbuilding, aircraft, or railroad industries in theirs.[13]

Creel supervised a steady output of films, ranging from one-reelers to seven-reel features, distributed both domestically and abroad. The products shipped overseas contained appropriate foreign-language captions. The Committee initially did not want to compete with commercial producers, and so it distributed its material at a small price to the newsfilm weeklies. The features were compiled from newsfilm and other stock sources. They at first were shipped to State Councils of Defense and sundry patriotic societies for screening. These early efforts ran the gamut of war activities, short of actual fighting. They presented training sequences, sports shorts, ambulance work, labor union activities, shipbuilding, and so on.[14] Those that survive are standard scenes of what would later be called the "arsenal of democracy," coupled with displays of American military power. Other than their intense promotion of support for the war, they contained little battle footage. The viewer's universe was one of patriotic self-sacrifice; it did not include the revenge motif. Some of these films included fake action; presumably this was to enlist the sympathies of the viewer. Death was almost continuously absent, while instruments of death were omnipresent. But the instruments were displayed as scientifically marvelous and technologically efficient. Audiences thus could enjoy American ingenuity without seeing its results.

The CPI soon found that these small films were overly expensive and were not reaching a wide enough audience.[15] It thus began to produce and exhibit its own feature films, using existing footage. At six-week intervals in 1918 appeared the choicest examples of CPI work: *Pershing's Crusaders, America's Answer,* and *Under Four Flags. Pershing's Crusaders* opened to a full house at the Lyric in New York. As the curtains parted, spectators saw Germany and France modeled in clay bas-relief. Out of the center of Germany rose a volcano, and the "mailed fist of the world" proceeded to scatter lava over the face of France. Then followed a summary of how German agents were behind such domestic events as fires, strikes, and other sabotage. The bulk of the film followed the line laid down by the earlier smaller productions of emphasizing domestic war output, civilian solidarity, and military training. Some of the scenes purporting to be battle shots were faked, but others were not. The chauvinism underlying the entire effort showed most clearly in scenes of American military men. As American soldiers sharpened their bayonets, the insert read "The Boche is afraid of cold steel." Scenes of

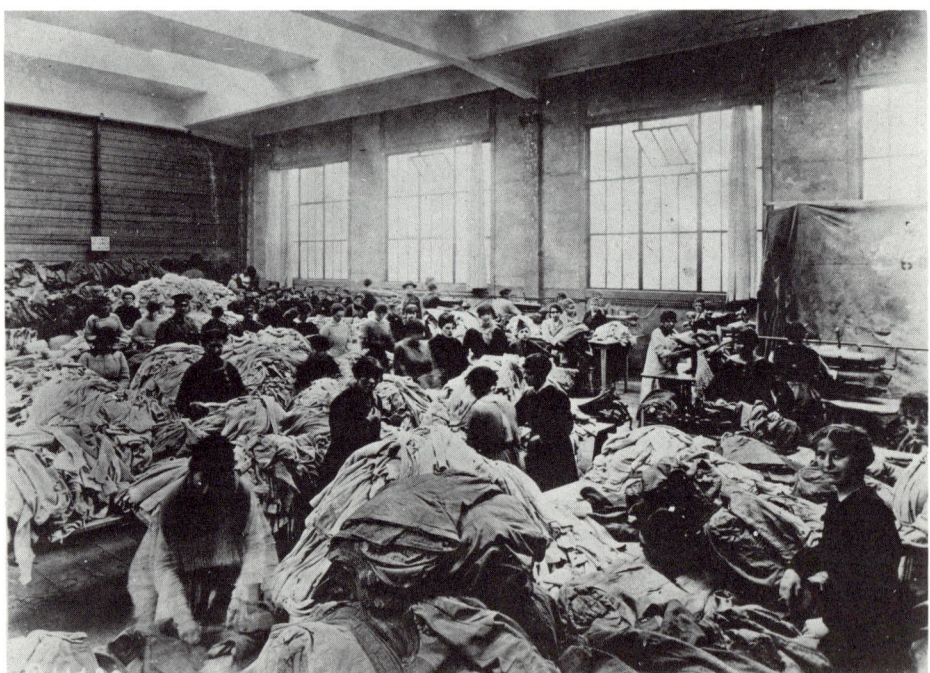

The encyclopedic governmental view of the war effort. Women in the salvage department sorting and repairing doughboy underwear in the documentary *America's Answer* (1918).

Pershing, whose stolid physiognomy graced almost everything the CPI distributed, were intercut with the phrase "Victorious Pershing"–this before American troops had fought as a national unit instead of in isolated groups. No Allied contributions were mentioned. This sublime self-confidence then registered a grimly ironic finale when the American flag was superimposed on a map of Europe.[16]

America's Answer also enjoyed a successful New York opening at the George M. Cohan Theater. Here the emphasis shifted more toward overseas activities, with the usual scenes of marching, reviews, and drills. The entire film was an assemblage of vignettes on soldiering; it said little about the nature, aims, or causes of the war. Labor again was courted. Lumberjacks in service were shown hewing French timber for cantonments. Explaining this toil was the caption: "To the everlasting glory of American labor let it be told that these men have cheerfully accepted a soldier's pay and a soldier's life as their contribution to the cause of Democracy." (It must be remembered that while most of American labor supported the war effort, the IWW troubles were current.) The great cause again was ironically footnoted by two scenes of casual American racism. In the first, four black soldiers were shown dancing in their fatigues after the phrase "Music moves the feet in France as in Our Sunny South." The second showed an American soldier drilling an idiotically grinning Oriental in civilian garb: "The Occident ships a little drill dope to the Orient."[17] *America's Answer* played successfully at home and abroad; for example, it aroused intense Dutch enthusiasm at The Hague. Aided by a lurid advertising campaign ("filmed at the gates of hell and brought back through submarine-infested waters"), it was a box-office success beyond the shadow of a doubt.

A print of *Under Four Flags* has not survived. Like the others, it was received with great enthusiasm, but it arrived at war's end and did not reach as many people. Here the Allied role came to the fore, indicating a more mature vision of the war's cooperative effort. Prominent were shots of French refugees, the Anglo-French war effort, and foreign leaders such as Marshal Foch. The entire thing ended with a *tableau vivant* of the Allies triumphant.[18]

These three features were given the best publicity buildup possible. They played for a week or more in theaters, municipal halls, and ballrooms throughout the country, with high government officials continually providing their imprimatur. The gist of their message was that winning the war required civic solidarity on the economic, social and political fronts. This solidarity could be learned from the military example, and the military would benefit by knowing the citizens back home were behind them. The message was simple and often reiterated. Actual combat stayed in the background and was used only for dramatic effect. Martial maneuvers, candid shots of "average American boys," and standard military ceremonies were juxtaposed with the civilian war effort. Without really showing where it all led, the CPI successfully stressed the familiar format of strength through unity.

The features did not exhaust all the available footage. The government, in cooperation with England, France, and Italy, formed a pool for the provision of war film. In America, the CPI edited the mass and periodically sent out the finished product as the *Allied (Official) War Review*.[19] It purported to be topical and in fact did show scenes of battles only weeks after the fact. These newsreels, appearing eventually at almost weekly intervals, apparently attracted their greatest audiences when the war news was good; obviously, they themselves displayed no "bad" news. Much was made in these films of the Allied "will to win," an understandable attempt to transcend cross-purpose and to make international barriers vanish. The Old Contemptibles, poilus, Polish units, and the like were lauded for their fighting qualities and "unconquerable spirit." By contrast, the enemy was shown in several guises. They might appear as vanquished, like the captured Austrians on the Italian front, or as barbarians deserving democratic retribution, like the Turkish oppressors of Palestine. But rarely was the foe shown in death; the film usually stopped short of this ultimate display of victory. Never was the enemy allowed to indicate his own qualities of patriotism and heroism.

The *Review* promoted the same spirit as the longer films, often placing national qualities in stark contrast. Shots of the ordered confusion of behind-the-lines life were interspersed with commentary such as: "Along the roads the heroes wounded in the fight move back–their only sorrow that they can fight no longer–and with their prisoners, who are glad because they cannot." The *Review* maintained the gentility of the features by promoting pride and courage rather than the more tangible trappings of war. The emphasis was on inter-Allied cooperation, due more probably to the pooling arrangement than to any spontaneity on the part of the United States government.[20]

Creel estimated that over one-half of the 12,000 motion picture theaters in the country exhibited the *Official War Review*. Because of the saturation aspects of regional booking, the actual coverage probably was much higher. The *Review* grossed $334,622.35 during its lifetime, making it the CPI's biggest moneymaker. *America's Answer* took in $185,144.30, *Pershing's Crusaders* $181,741.69, and *Under Four Flags* $63,946.48.[21]

On June 1, 1918, the CPI's Division of Films established a scenario department to provide scripts for independent producers. This project resulted in several one-reel ventures. Paramount-Bray Pictograph released the *Uncle Sam* series,[22] which included such disparate items as training military choirs, operating the War Risk Insurance Bureau and working women's role in the war. Pathé emphasized agricultural problems while Universal did the only known exposition on the war involvement of the American Indians. The C.L. Chester Company produced ten of these films, covering Negroes, engineers, the merchant marine, rehabilitation of the wounded, and other diverse topics.[23] Besides showing a fondness for colorful and alliterative titles these short movies, ten to fifteen minutes in length, helped to provide a comprehensive picture of the CPI ideal. The wide-ranging topics, and particularly the inclusion of oppressed minorities such as blacks and Indians in the war consensus, identified this ideal as one of national solidarity in the fact of threatening adversity. Films such as *Pershing's Crusaders* outlined the threat in bold strokes and dozens of smaller works measured the response at both the military and civilian levels.

This central theme was amplified under the same scenario system for two longer pictures. Chester did one of these, *The Miracle of the Ships* (six reels),[24] that dealt with shipyard construction and was meant to alleviate public concern over sabotage. The W.W.Hodkinson Corporation did the other, *Made in America* (eight reels). It depicted every stage of the soldier's life, from draft to combat. This film used professional actors and actresses and stressed the fighting capabilities of the American civilian–the recurring Cincinnatus syndrome.

Finally, late in the summer of 1918, the Committee produced six films of its own, all two-reelers, and had a second series of six ready to go when the Armistice called a halt. *When Your Soldier Is Hit* was made at Fort Riley, Kansas, and was supplemented by scenes of combat casualties. It sought to reassure the home folks by showing first-aid procedures but was withdrawn because it was too "real." *Our Wings of Victory* dealt with airplane construction, while *Horses of War* was a paean to a military accouterment which technology already had rendered obsolete.

Making the Nation Fit showed mass physical exercises by recruits. The final two films, whose titles—*The Storm of Steel* and *The Bath of Bullets*— displayed a fine alliterative viciousness, were completed but never shown. The first depicted steps in munitions manufacture; the second traced the machine gun through stages of development and use.[25]

Creel had faith in his task. The film work of his committee was aimed not only at presenting "war pictures," but also was intended to present a picture of the nation to foreigners. "The majority of 'war stuff' had to be accompanied by contrasting material," he later reflected. "We wanted the world to see America 'at home.'" Thus the good democratic life went forth in the form of "patriotic celebrations, women voting, Labor Day parades, seashore scenes, baby contests, stock shows, athletic games, and everything else that threw any light on us as a people."[26] What is important here is not so much what was sent as what was left out. The omitted aspects of American life, by being obvious in their absence, indicate why war violence was downplayed in the CPI domestic releases. An America at war was not a violent country, only a righteous and powerful one.

The integration of the war effort. Producer-Director Thomas H. Ince and President Wilson on the steps of the White House.

The Committee rigorously controlled film exports on the following terms: every shipment of entertainment film included at least 20 percent "educational matter";[27] overseas exhibitors who refused to show the Committee's war films were denied the more profitable entertainment films; and no American pictures were permitted to be shown in any theater that presented German-made films. Creel's hammerlock on film exports ensured the promotion of the paradox of a non-violent people engaged in a violent war. The chairman had his own concept of what constituted American life:

It was not only that the Committee put motion pictures into foreign countries. Just as important was the work of keeping certain motion pictures out of these countries. As a matter of bitter fact, much of the misconception about America before the war was due to American motion pictures portraying the lives and exploits of New York's gunmen, western bandits, and wild days of the old frontier, all of which were accepted in many parts of the world as representative of American life.

What we wanted to get into foreign countries were pictures that presented the wholesome life of America, giving fair ideas of our people and our institutions. What we wanted to keep out of world circulation were the "thrillers" that gave entirely false impressions of American life and morals. Film dramas portraying the exploits of "Gyp the Blood" or "Jesse James" were bound to prejudice our fight for the good opinion of neutral nations.[28]

With the government completely dominating all aspects of documentary production, private producers were forced to conform or lose their markets. Several companies sought to combine drama with actuality in a "semi-documentary" mode. The results were films like *Women Who Win*, another look at the female role in war work, and *The Boys From Your State,* which depicted the progress of local units from training to combat. For realism these films depended on CPI leftovers, but so did the Signal Corps itself. At the end of the war the Corps put out its own collection of greatly suspect "war scenes," *The U.S. Army in Action During World War I.* This film achieved a synthesis of modes of American violence by showing American infantrymen as bloodletters of the Wild West variant–they not only shot Germans, they "popped them off." Pathé was more passive. It assembled *Whispering Wires of War,* about the impact of telephonic communications on modern war, and *War Bibles,* which showed the entire bookmaking process on Bibles destined for American soldiers. The studio also distributed a Red Cross film on American combat troops. It certainly is one measure of the complexities of the American character that *War Bibles* and *The U.S. Army in Action* both could advance on the public with the purpose of visualizing part of the war effort.

Novelty sustained other productions. The Prizma color process was responsible for the popularity of *Our Invincible Navy*, which featured naval training, construction, and maneuvers. *Flying With the Marines* was filmed by Marine Corps cameramen and released by the CPI; its aerial photography was a sensation, but most of the footage was of maneuvers near Miami, Florida. Universal was into the field late but effectively with *Crashing Through to Berlin*, a series of war scenes that were familiar but popular, possibly because of the hyperpatriotism of the entire production.

All these films merely rode the tail of the CPI's kite. Without the Committee's approval their ingredients would not have been available, and the Division of Films already had helped to create a receptive atmosphere. The one instance of public disagreement in this area concerned *The Yanks Are Coming*, a Hearst-sponsored Universal film the government claimed showed production secrets of the Liberty engine and of pursuit aircraft. It was made for the Dayton-Wright Company and apparently was innocuous enough, although it caused a Congressional committee investigation concerning charges of corruption.[29]

iii

The war on the screen was by and large a war of civilian effort–in two guises. It was first of all a war involving nearly every imaginable segment of the domestic population, but it was also a war involving citizen soldiers. World War I, in the camera eye, was fought not by military professionals but by Americans in uniform. The government films presented a deep-seated conviction that what was best in our society was nonmilitary and democratic. The problem of advancing this ideal in a military context never was satisfactorily solved. It was approached in part by eschewing the results for the panoply of battle, and in part by stressing humanitarian values in the midst of brutality. The martial spirit, which has been periodically revivified but never sustained in American history, was served by maneuvers, parades, and ceremonies before it was seen in actual combat.

Official films thus registered an interesting composite of America at war. They actively promoted the democratic faith in word and deed. They stressed involvement and commitment, but did not elevate the hero at the expense of the mass. The government never sought to establish a cult of individual heroism. Medal recipients were valued for their representative qualities, not their individual merit. Pershing, the prime candidate for the mantle of valor, could not be depicted doing heroic things from the rear-echelon position modern war demanded of its generals. Instead the hero became Everyman; not the anonymous and helpless Everyman of existentialist thought, but an instinctive egalitarian who displayed the innate virtues of a democratic nation.

The film recorded it all–not merely the story of war, nor any "history" of the war, but an officially sanctioned view of what the war meant to Americans. They believed they were recording the war for posterity, of course; but they were actually recording themselves. Many doubtless thought of the war as the *Official War Review* and *America's Answer*, never dreaming of the reflective qualities which mass society film was beginning to achieve. That war on film *was* important perhaps may best be shown by this classic contretemps of one movie zealot: "Would you care to have this war end without letting the future generations see it for themselves?"[30]

iv

At war's end the Committee on Public Information went out of business, quickly and chaotically dissolving itself by June 30, 1919. But the raw film material that had been part of its arsenal remained, a celluloid legacy which was to demonstrate the complete plasticity of film "reality."

Shortly after the Armistice producer Edward E. MacManus rushed a film called *The Lost Battalion* through to completion. It was based on the exploits of a unit of the Seventy-seventh Division in the Argonne and continued a concept originated in wartime feature films. In casting about for realism, filmmakers had taken to using "real" soldiers, such as Arthur Guy Empey and Bert Hall, to enhance profits and to lend credibility to otherwise empty plots. *The Lost Battalion* mixed professional actors with survivors of the actual conflict. The picture can be called a semi-documentary because it contained some Signal Corps war footage as well as stills of some of the original maps and documents used by the Seventy-seventh. The overriding theme remained that of democratic diversity molding into a powerful unity in the face of war. Bankers' sons, second-story men, Orientals– almost the entire grab bag of American society was put on parade. The "real" war footage was made subordinate to their heroic transmogrifications. In spite of the letdown in national martial spirit, the picture seemed to be well received at its opening, possibly because of the much-publicized deeds of the original lost battalion.

But the MacManus venture proved to be no trend-setter. Filmgoers had had a surfeit of war, especially in reportorial films. War footage languished through most of the twenties; war had become too common, and the seeds of disillusion were beginning to sprout. There were few new releases. A four-reel compilation of shots from the *Official War Review* was released in 1924 under the title *Flashes of Action*, destined for schoolchildren. The American Legion sponsored a film edited by Army officials called *The World War*, using much the same material. Yet a third compilation was made by Sidney B. Lust in 1928 and released as *Over There*.[31] This film was feature length; apparently it stressed the grimness of war without commenting on its futility.

During the twenties, no new themes were introduced in movies using war footage. In fighting the war, Americans were seen as simply doing a necessary job. The Messianism of the pre-Versailles world had vanished, but no counterforce had yet taken its place. The grand totality of civilian effort depicted in the CPI's wartime features disappeared, and scenes of combat dominated what little the decade produced. Also gone was the rather frenetic air of inculcated patriotism and self-sacrifice, which gave way to a passive pride and reflection on a necessary task accomplished. Documentary compilers ignored less noble themes being introduced in literature; war film in the twenties rested content.

The onslaught of the Depression and international militarism in the following decade helped to create an entirely different situation, and producers were quick to both sense the change and to help it along. One of the first fruits of the new intellectual climate was *This is America* (1933), scripted and edited by none other than Gilbert Seldes. Seldes used familiar war film source material as part of an informal look at American society from 1917 to 1932. Drawing almost entirely on newsreel footage, the film's war scenes were tinctured with a certain pathetic air, as in the examination of a lost ideal. This quality was wistful rather than vicious, but it did mark a shift. *Time* offered the following description:

> Front pages screaming WAR. Women knitting, soldiers tramping, Charlie Chaplin selling Liberty Bonds. Swat the Kaiser. Kill the Hun. Ships, ships, ships. "Oh, You Beautiful Doll." The Armistice. The boys come marching home, and the men go marching out of mines and factories suddenly idle....[32]

The same year came *The Big Drive,* which used footage from American, British, French, Italian, German, and Austrian archives, and swiped the opening volcano scene from *Pershing's Crusaders*. Because of this catholicity, Albert L. Rule, its producer, can be credited with some attempt at balance, but the film tended morbidly to sensationalize the bestiality of war rather than measure the meaning of it all. The gross promotion of this aspect of the film was indicated by the following instructions to exhibitors:

> On opening night, have supposedly shell-shocked veteran simulate a seizure. Use this as a basis of letters to editors of all newspapers, arraigning the idea of bringing back the horrors of war. Follow up with a dozen letters from legionnaires, etc., defending the picture as an argument for peace.[33]

Laurence Stallings's *The First World War* (1934), like all preceding efforts, also used Signal Corps combat footage. The film began with truly historic material, a shot of Bismarck taken in 1895, and it built up to a martial crescendo in depicting the early years of the war. Stallings then stressed the growing brutality and irrationality of the entire business. The film was well received critically but it was not regarded universally as a horror story. One reviewer called it a "chant of glory, rather than a cry of bitterness";[34] another commented that "the eagles and trumpets do actually drown out every other note."[35]

Technically *The First World War* was superior in its genre, but Stallings's love for dramatic impact made his message ambiguous. When horror and glory coexist, which is to take the editorial palm? The movie's bias was clearly on the Allied side, and audiences probably reacted to doughboy heroism before they saw the tragedy.

No such ambiguity was present in *Dealers in Death*, a semi-documentary released in 1934. Its thesis was that made current by the Nye Committee, describing an unsuspecting public decoyed into war by profit-seeking businessmen. Pictures of European munitions factories, battle scenes, atrocity shots, and photos of leading munitioneers were mingled with an insipid plot. Even so, it was praised for its "grim power" and called as "effective a document as you could ask for."[36] As its title indicated, the film was sensational and pandered to topical interest. There is some evidence that leaders in the steel and munitions industries may have tried to interfere with its release, but this story may have been merely a publicity gimmick.[37] *Dealers in Death* pushed the conspiracy angle of war causation to its crudest extreme and gained enough notoriety to be shown before the Nye Committee, a remarkable example of reciprocal influence in the causative sense. Yet it indicated a demarcation from the line approached by Seldes and straddled by Stallings.

The year 1937 brought the full force of war weariness in the form of *The Dead March*, a compilation of newsreel shots from 1914 to the then current Chinese struggle. Radio announcer Boake Carter sonorously narrated in voice-of-doom fashion. This film used actors as symbolic figures representing Germany, France, Italy, England, and America. It consciously indulged the macabre by showing the soldiers leaving their graves to tell about their war experiences. The unsettled world conditions of the thirties, more than any other factor, apparently had prepared audiences for this total excoriation of war. It was "worth being kept permanently available" and recommended for school, library, and church use by a film periodical.[38] *The Dead March* reached the ultimate limits, not especially of interwar pacifism, but of the "realistic" depiction of war's brutality and degradation. It was the culmination of the pattern which began with *This is America* and *The Big Drive*. In one decade, the documentary cinema had reshaped war–from a crucial national experience to a nihilistic exercise.

One further film remained, a radical departure from its immediate predecessors both in tone and format. This was *The Ramparts We Watch,* made after the German invasion of Poland by a *March of Time* team led by Louis de Rochemont. Semi-documentary in that it evolved a plot outline out of the same types of scenes used by other producers, *Ramparts* constituted a call for increased attention to national defense. In this it echoed in a more sophisticated fashion the warnings of *America Unprepared* and *Guarding Old Glory. Ramparts* drew upon the fictional experiences of a small American town during the Great War. De Rochemont sought further "realism" by peopling his town with little-known professional actors and some nonprofessionals.

Time's film critic, decidedly unneutralized by circumstances, claimed the film "offered no special pleading,"[39] while *Life* stood in awe of history assuming "human values and truer proportions."[40] This was the cant of professional interest; the film was undeniably anti-isolationist. It demonstrated clearly the "whiggish" impulses inherent in film treatment of history by attempting to tie the experience of the war to America *circa* 1940. The whole thing, naturally enough, was scored by the isolationist press; one writer derided it as a "rhapsodic call to arms" which was "full of hate and hell-fire."[41] *That* prejudiced *Ramparts* was not, but it did effectively reverse the trend and began a new trail which culminated in the documentaries of World War II.

v

The few documentaries produced during the interwar period make generalized analysis hazardous at best. A broad overview nevertheless indicates that World War I scenes were used for different purposes at different times. With the end of the war, the need to emphasize total national effort vanished, and battle footage drifted for some years toward the limbo of memorabilia. The twenties offered no new film interpretation of the war experience, in stark contrast to the genres of literature, poetry, drama and historical writing. The reasons for this can only be speculative. Several feature films with World War backgrounds played to big audiences, some examples being *The Four Horsemen of the Apocalypse, The Big Parade,* and *Wings.* But these fictions, of which more later, tended to glorify the war experience and attempted no reassessment of the stance which had remained popular from the 1917-18 period. So war itself was not passé. But producers and those who compiled war footage may have felt audiences would not accept the stark depiction of combat, preferring instead to sublimate battle to well-known performers and familiar plot lines. Romanticism lingered and made death and disfigurement genteel.

With the thirties a new tone emerged. Economic depression and the foreboding state of world affairs influenced the public receptivity of this reordering of film material, but to what degree is difficult to assess. We can say that the advent of sound–in scoring, narration, and dubbing–greatly assisted the documentarist in putting across his message. Aided by the more immediate qualities of the new technology, documentaries and semi-documentaries moved away from the ritual of recapitulating American involvement toward evaluating the war's role in the American experience, finally arriving at an examination of war itself. This process obviously was tempered by the intellectual climate of the decade, but it influenced that climate as well as partook of it. Evidence to support this contention is sparse, but the involvement of governmental bodies like the Nye Committee and the use of several of these films as educational devices points toward a pattern of social influence.

It should be remembered that these compilations of war film footage were on the fringes of the film world. Although given stature because they contained "reality," they in fact never could compete with the commercial feature film at the box office. Their educational market may have been wide, however. They were important because they mark major shifts in attitudes toward the war experience which did not especially parallel those in other mass media. Even more importantly, they achieved these shifts *using essentially the same film footage*, with the proviso that the later period emphasized horror before glory, rather than vice versa. No more telling argument can be advanced to prove the plastic qualities of the film medium.

Part III

The Camera Eye: Focus on War

> The war we're fighting is different—entirely different . . . . A war impossible to describe to you!
> —young German officer to his father in *Surrender* (1931)

6

The Mirror of Democracy

i

Historians customarily speak of a "democratic faith" in connection with American life.[1] This faith includes a deep conviction that egalitarianism is the primary force underlying the nation's political and social organization. The faith in equality has been shaken, most severely in the slavery crisis of the nineteenth century, but also in the segregation practices and nativism of the past one hundred years. As America passed into the twentieth century, this conviction continued to be based more on faith than on fact. Yet our modern mass society, as it developed, appeared to need the periodic renewal of this faith.

The practices of aristocratic and monarchical governments of Europe always have provided convenient historical contrasts to American egalitarianism. Those idealistic aspects of democracy that form the core of the faith appear most strongly when American democratic ideals seem juxtaposed to the more sordid authoritarian methods of, say, Germans and Austrians. Certainly the motion picture, with its arsenal of symbols and its simplistic approach in depicting both historical events and social interaction, has been an appropriate channel through which the icons of democracy have been kept polished in the eye of the public.

Of all the themes consistently relied upon by the motion picture throughout its history, the most continuous has been that which in some way limns part of the democratic faith. The film critic who said that "In America, we have so many traditions that it sometimes seems as if we have none at all" was only partly correct. The democratic tradition, which is useful precisely because of its ambiguities, is always with us. But the same man's claim that Americans had a strong "nostalgia for the future" was well made.[2] The impulse to give shape to an as-yet-unrealized future is the essence of faith. In a social sense, the motion picture gives reassuring shape to the future by presenting past and present through symbols and myths congenial to mass audiences. It is thus only slightly pressing a point to say that the movie screen has been for this country the mirror of democracy.

This mirror reflects democratic ideals most clearly in times of national crisis, a process that indicates the depth as well as the strength of the democratic faith. World War I was the first such crisis of the twentieth century, and the first one that happened to be contemporary with the motion picture camera. The war, according to one scholar, "integrated" the national spirit.[3] If this view means that the organs of mass communication–such as newspapers, popular magazines, and films–largely were given over to the cause of promoting American involvement in the conflict, then it is substantially correct. Vital to the national spirit was its democratic faith, and it was in presenting this faith that the films of World War I excelled.

Shortly after America entered the war, that National Association of Moving Picture Producers began to work with the government in a plan to make films to be shown on the Allied fronts in France, Russia, and Italy. These films showed a certain brash *hauteur:* to "teach the lessons of democracy to Europe." Apparently this task was to be accomplished mainly by showing "high officials mingling with their fellow men."[4] The Committee on Public Information was even less reticent about advertising the virtues of America. The friends of chairman George Creel were convinced that the Committee had disseminated "the truth about America's participation in the war," while Creel himself introduced a résumé of his activities by claiming that his organisation "carried the gospel of Americanism to every corner of the globe."[5] With fervid impulses like these passing for official policy, it was little wonder that motion pictures were considered to be and indeed became international theological weapons.

Like most societies that see themselves involved in a crisis with the most grave implications, the American public tended to respond to their country's war participation by upholding their most cherished ideals as indivisible from moral and literal "truth." The motion picture supported and promoted this tendency; the capabilities of the cinema, the desires of the state, and the idealism of the people were in almost perfect concord.

ii

In dramatic terms, the logical place for film to commence its depiction of democracy was in the field of individual biography. The representative individual who in himself embodied all that was best in democratic man would seem ideal for cinematic presentation. In fact, historical dramas centering on representative individuals such as Abraham Lincoln and Betsy Ross continued to be popular, and fictional characters constantly were used to depict the complete democratic man. But the representative historical figure for the war, the man who, in John William Ward's apt description of Andrew Jackson, could be used as a "symbol for an age," did not appear on film.[6]

The most legitimate candidates for such a role were President Wilson and General Pershing. Wilsonian quotations appeared in a variety of films, and newsreel shots of the President were included in fiction films from time to time. But Wilson was always more the high priest of democracy than a man of the people. His scholarly and patrician background further mitigated his usefulness as a democratic symbol.

Pershing was something else again. He boasted an extremely varied military career, from the last Indian campaigns to the Filipino wars. He had been in the public eye for years, both as an overappreciated chastiser of Mexican bandits and as a staunch battlefield warrior. But although his looks reflected a bulldog tenacity, Pershing's was a stolid, almost phlegmatic character which was trapped by the command necessities of modern war. He was less the man on horseback than he was the paper strategist. Nevertheless, the movie industry gave him a try. *The Land of the Free* polished Pershing's life to a noble gloss and ended by asserting that specific Germans were guilty of war crimes. The general was also depicted in a particularly vitriolic film called *Why America Will Win,* which again showed his ascent from American boy to international leader. The picture indicated Pershing (William S. Hart patrolling the Marne rather than the Pecos) had "his own personal account to settle with the ruthless Hun."[7]

But Pershing as a representative American did not bear the weight of democratic idealism alone. In fact, his depiction on screen was almost indistinguishable from that of fictionalized soldiers in scores of films. In fiction as in fact, the conviction that a good democrat was also a good patriot amounted to a tautology. *The Man Without a Country,* inspired by the literary classic, featured a man named "Philip Nolan." After hearing him curse the United States, a friend handed Nolan a copy of Edward Everett Hale's novel. Properly enthused, Nolan hustled to the recruiting office. "The average spectator will pass over its slowness of movement, and the lack of engaging qualities in its hero," one industry publication remarked approvingly of the film, "and feel only the fire of its patriotism and the good Americanism it aims to each."[8] Nolan appeared again in *My Own United States,* where he was so persuaded by flashbacks depicting the deeds of Alexander Hamilton, Andrew Jackson, and Abraham Lincoln that he immediately enlisted. In these stories, as in many others, examples from history had medicinal qualities, marvelously curing any antipatriotic disease.

The war itself could become the catalyst for the cure. The hero of *The Thing We Love* was unjustly imprisoned for seven years. Upon his release, as an "advertising aid" put it, "war revives the *inherent patriotism* his ancestors have given him, and when it comes to a choice between self and the country that has wronged him, he places country before self and wins his manhood and happiness."[9] J. Stuart Blackton's *Safe For Democracy* (retitled *Life's Greatest Problem*) took a seriocomic look at the regeneration of two hoboes through military service. A wealthy mama's boy, branded a slacker by his comrades in the National Guard, was *The Man Who Was Afraid*. He became a hero on the Mexican border. Hodkinson's *Made in America,* the semi-documentary picture about the draft process, included a slacker's metamorphosis into a soldier.

Without exception, war films explicitly equated manhood with patriotism and a willingness to fight. A manly love of country was the result of most plots. Ideals concerning pacifism were seen not as ideals at all, but simply excuses to avoid democratic service. Motion pictures went out of their way to indict citizens who did not take part in the great crusade or who were morally unfit for such high purpose. In *Bud's Recruit*, an early effort by King Vidor, young Bud was disgusted by his older draft-age brother, who attended pacifist meetings with their mother.

Bud finally shamed his brother into enlisting, and the film made clear that the younger boy wished he could go as well. *The Common Cause*, an insipid story of a romantic triangle directed by Blackton, had a wife following both her husband and her lover to France. There "the great fire of patriotism . . . burned the dross from their lives."[10]

The purgative powers of war were matched only by the ability of military service to democratize America's warriors. The usual theme was to take a man of Eastern wealth and through a series of training camp and battlefield events transform him into a humble yet courageous democrat. Typical of this approach was *The Brand of Cowardice*, featuring the youthful Lionel Barrymore as "Cyril Van Cortlandt Hamilton." At first declining to join his regiment as it moved to the Mexican border, young Hamilton eventually joined up as a private and distinguished himself in action. The central dramatic device in *The Pride of New York* was a contrast between a working man and a rich man. Since the plot of this film contained most of the common ingredients of the genre, it deserves quotation at length from a sympathetic trade journal. The hero is

> the son of a building contractor . . . hard working and happy. In New York there is another type, one often found—a rich man's son who is an idler who loves the night life and the spending of his father's money. He's a typical snob. To this son is attracted, probably because of their stations in life, the daughter of a millionaire. But one day when she watches George standing smiling on the end of an iron beam, being drawn up twenty stories, with nothing below him but the hard street pavement, she takes an interest in him.
>
> Soon George and the rich man's son are called in the draft. She judges the worth of the two in their soldier's uniforms, and despite George's comparative poverty she comes to believe he is the better man.
>
> Then the soldiers go to Europe, and she follows as a Red Cross nurse. George, genial, smiling, continues to improve in her estimation, while the rich man's son, still a snob and disliked by his fellow soldiers, fades from her esteem. When George, battling for all he is worth, fearing nothing in his fight to uphold the honor of his country, saves this girl from death at the hands of the Germans, she places her hand and her heart in George's keeping.
>
> When the rich man's son sees that his idleness and his snobbish ways have caused him to lose this girl, whose real worth he had never appreciated, his whole disposition changes. He patterns his acts and his conduct after George's and becomes a credit to himself, to his family, and to his country.[11]

Many films joined *The Pride of New York* in the task of leveling. The democratic eraser which smoothly eliminated social barriers usually was accompanied by an amalgam of patriotic purpose and moral regeneration. *For the Freedom of the World* took a spoiled son of wealthy parents and put him in uniform, with the inevitable results. Another individual in the film was used to contrast the noble purpose of the hero. An admiring critic wrote that "The character of the slacker is well portrayed by Romaine Fielding in a manner to inspire disgust for this type of man."[12] A spoiled rich boy, "the decadent son of a society leader," finally was drafted in *Doing Their Bit*, after his mother had tried to protect him by falsifying his birth certificate. *Alias Mike Moran* turned the tables on the idea of class leveling by having a department store clerk who had been "ennobled by bitter experience" in war winning the girl at the fadeout.[13]

The motion picture industry, although lavish in its use of the derogatory term "slacker," reserved it mostly for the wealthy and the cowardly. However, films that took a sympathetic viewpoint toward those who really were unable to serve were relatively rare. *An Honest Man* had a tramp rejected even though he wanted to enlist. *Too Fat to Fight* was a comedy which put an obese fellow through the most excruciating torment. After he was rejected by even the YMCA, he mourned his plight: "I'm too fat to fight and too immoral for the YMCA, but I'd give a leg to be with the boys over there." Sure enough, he went to France, was wounded, and won the girl.[14]

But this type of picture was no counterweight to the continual and savage attack on the more obvious inequities of the American social structure. The war gave moviemakers a chance to exercise a traditional theatrical personage–the spoiled rich boy–in lethal situations where teamwork and trust were of the essence. For those not convinced that wealthy and pampered idlers were being drafted by the thousands, the industry introduced the idea of the "melting pot." This idea would eventually come to dominate the war pictures of a later era, the rich boy vanishing in the mists of the past. In 1917, though, the notion was relatively new.

Take members of various minority groups, mix generously with people representing various classes, put them all in uniform, and let their racial and social differences be resolved in battle. That was the formula. It operated on a fairly superficial level, since both racial and social stereotypes remained cinema standbys past mid-century. The formula was used in *The Lost Battalion,* the semi-documentary by Edward A. MacManus. The members of the Seventy-seventh Division were depicted as just plain Americans, "out of the heart of Manhattan." The group included the dregs of society, but "out of this mixed, and they said, 'despicable mass,' was to be forged a thunderbolt to be hurled against the proudest army in Europe."[15] The soldiers were clearly meant to be representative Americans whose conduct under fire exemplified the best in American life.

Equally blatant was *The Unbeliever,* the last film made by the Edison Company. Much of the picture was filmed, with the cooperation of the Marine Corps, in Quantico, Virginia. The story was the usual one, with a young American aristocrat losing his sense of class under fire. *The Unbeliever* was more than usually top-heavy with egalitarianism. As his buddy died in his arms, the hero sent him on his way with this benediction: "You've taught me to judge people as people, Lefty, old pal, and class pride is junk!" In addition, the film was one of the last "God on our side" epics. After its presentation the happy circumstance of Christ directly aiding democracy was seldom seen on American screens. The religious angle was introduced when Jesus appeared in a vision on the battlefield, and faith and democracy were united as a rabbi succored a dying Catholic. But the ultimate message of the picture was the promotion of democracy as a universal political and social system. When an outraged German enlisted man killed his Prussian officer (played by Erich von Stroheim, the movie war's villain for all seasons), he screamed "Down with militarism! Long live Democracy!"[16]

Since the themes of democracy as class leveler and democracy as melting pot were repeated so often in 1917 and 1918, it is safe to assume that film's depiction of the powers of democracy as both faith and as a mode of political and social organization echoed deeply felt sentiments in the mass audience. The connection between democratization and the American fighting man is in fact one of the more enduring themes in motion picture history.

iii

The fever pitch of the war years could not be maintained without the heat of war itself. In the twenties, few war films presented democratic ideals as openly and crudely as films made during the war, but most of them contained familiar assumptions about democracy. An otherwise bland romance entitled *Puppets* had a puppeteer from New York's Little Italy integrate into a wartime fighting unit. The fact that the melting-pot idea was incidental to this film was probably an indication of the idea's ready acceptance by moviemakers and audiences alike. Minorities were not courted as they had been during the war, however, *The Vanishing American* being an exception. While primarily concerned with the domestic plight of the Indian, it ennobled him as a war hero.

The heroic American democrat in action. Karl Dane simultaneously dispatches two Germans in *The Big Parade* (1925).

There was still room for society dudes, though. *Corporal Kate* was a Red Cross worker who was "half Irish and All American."[17] She was in love with a private in the AEF, a gay blade who in civilian life just happened to have been a champion polo player. The picture explicitly applauded democratization. The polo player's ex-valet was now his sergeant, while the heroine selflessly came to the aid of the hero's wounded socialite girl friend, who also had found her way to France as a Red Cross worker (such being the nature of movie plots).

It is significant that almost without deviation the heroes in films of trench warfare, regardless of their civilian situations, were privates. Since aerial warfare usually required officers, the democratization theme was more commonly found on the ground. The soldiers in *Marianne*, an early sound musical designed to showcase the talents of Marion Davies, were typical. Bright, sassy, and afraid of nothing, these young men contrasted sharply with their leaders. In this film, as in so many others, the enlisted man was the wit and the successful lover, while officers and older noncoms played the buffoon.[18] The unspoken conviction was that democracy was antithetical to authority. This tension provided fuel for many comic and dramatic plots.

The most famous film of the twenties to show the leveling process in action was *The Big Parade*. The picture made a strong contrast between the labor of a steelworker and a bartender and the inherited ease of a rich youth. Yet the three men became close friends in uniform. In the famous shell-hole scene the democratization process was completed when the aristocrat yelled to his steelworker friend: "Why should you take the chance to be picked off? You're no better than we are!"[19] Other big money-earners of the period were not so explicit, relying more on adventure and romance to thrill the audience. Most heroes, however, still donned democratic virtue with their uniforms.

So catholic was the motion picture's interest in democracy that practically anyone or anything was used to wage war. *Into No Man's Land* set some kind of record for a preposterous plot. It had a gangster so upset over a romance between his daughter and a young district attorney that the hood joined the army. *Find Your Man* and *Dog of the Regiment* enlisted Rin-Tin-Tin in the cause. In the former, the canine star appeared as "Buddy," a noble Red Cross auxiliary. The latter featured him assisting his female owner in front-line medical work. In *The War Horse*, cowboy actor Buck Jones was forced to go to France to search for his steed, which had been appropriated by the cavalry.

The plots of such pictures were usually silly in the extreme, and they tended to revolve around novelty rather than common sense. But while a gangster, a dog, or a horse was stretching things a bit, audiences could accept actors like the lean and taciturn Gary Cooper as representative Americans. Here was the more noble and dedicated aspect of the American soldier–a paragon of resolute manhood who complemented the flip brashness of the men of *Marianne*. Cooper made a mini-career out of playing war roles. In *A Man From Wyoming*, for example, he portrayed two American myth-figures in one film: a cowboy who became a warrior-democrat.[20]

The spineless cowards still were needed to make a war plot go. In *Comrades* a manly hero went to war in place of a milquetoast. *Dugan of the Dugouts* was a ridiculous quickie which had a wastrel enlist and follow his Red Cross girlfriend to France, where he inevitably achieved manhood under fire. *Dangerous Business*, a Constance Talmadge vehicle, was in the same vein, showing the maturation process of a male secretary in the front lines. Finally, Hoot Gibson appeared as *Blinky*, a mild-mannered society boy who used his Boy Scout experience to become a hero during the troubles on the Mexican border.

Probably the most dramatic instance of war-inspired regeneration during the decade was displayed in *The Patent Leather Kid*. The story was trite enough, showing the growing cowardice in a soldier who had been a tough prize fighter. Wounded in a charge against an enemy machine gun, he was taken to a field hospital where, naturally, his sweetheart was on hand as a Red Cross nurse to ease him back to health. The film, a silent, was scored in such a way that when the hero's arm moved in salute to the flag in the crucial postoperative scene, the audience was treated to the Star Spangled Banner. "One of war's miracles," wrote a sympathetic reviewer.[21] But Pare Lorentz, later to make his name as a documentarist, had different ideas. He criticized the film aesthetically as an unbearably crude manipulation of patriotic symbols. The operating scene in the hospital, in which the hero was ministered to by his girl while taking the knife *sans* ether, Lorentz called "the most sickening exhibition of bad taste I have ever witnessed."[22]

The reception of such films as *The Patent Leather Kid* indicated that democracy's war, fueled by patriotic impulse and sustained by memories of victory, was becoming passé. The reason for this change undoubtedly was the seemingly prosperous state of the nation, which optimistically looked ahead to a future of plenty, not back to the self-denying emergency of the war years. The atmosphere of national crisis had long since passed. Audiences found films that remorselessly crammed symbols of a cause which had been fought for and won into already tortured plots to be ludicrous rather than inspiring.

iv

Since the Depression was treated primarily as a national internal crisis by motion pictures, there were no martial causes to be won and no downtrodden foreigners to be saved. War themes were either too bitter or too reliant on pure adventure to use democratic symbols to the extent of previous years. The thin thread of war adventure films running through the thirties was an indication that to many Americans, the depiction of war could be used for purposes other than moralistic or pacifistic instruction. Where once democracy had been placed in opposition to militaristic monarchism, it now could be contrasted with a more powerful menace. The aggrandizing totalitarian states of Europe, strengthened by new technology and given direction, momentum, and purpose by ideologies which seemed completely foreign to the American experience, served as convenient counter-examples to the democratic faith.

Although the films of World War I produced in the World War II period took "historical" rather than contemporary events as their subject matter, their primary noneconomic purpose was clearly one of rekindling the democratic fires of a new generation. The films of the immediate prewar years were made with increasing technological sophistication and in the wake of economic depression. They nevertheless shared with their predecessors the conviction that democracy was the only political and social system fit for all the peoples of the world.

Louis de Rochemont's *The Ramparts We Watch* (1940) implicitly compared the two wars as national crises. The picture included newsreel shots for "reality" and was seen by many critics as a preparedness proposal. *Ramparts* was nowhere as lurid as that preparedness epic of earlier days, *The Battle Cry of Peace,* but it was unequivocal in its contrast between "democratic principle" and "might makes right." The bias of Henry Luce and *Time* (the *March of Time* team collaborated on the film) was apparent on an international scale. While German restrictions on shipping during the Great War were emphasized, British restrictions passed without notice. Domestic political favoritism appeared with a shot of young Wendell Willkie's military identification card, accompanied by the voice-over "future leader." While it is an exaggeration to regard *Ramparts* as simply an entry in the 1940 presidential campaign, its militance was meant to contrast with Roosevelt's cautious moves in foreign policy since the German invasion of Poland. The film implied that there was just so much a democratic peace-loving nation could take. Wilson was portrayed in an unfavorable light as a compromiser driven to war by public opinion. The closing sequence featured a patriotic toast and the playing of the national anthem.[23]

Gearing up for a new war. Padre Pat O'Brien exhorts James Cagney to be a man in *The Fighting 69th* (1940).

The Ramparts We Watch was grimly internationalist in approach and stressed the duty of every citizen to defend his democratic rights. De Rochemont's cast of amateurs and little known professionals probably enhanced the film with their sometimes halting paeans to democracy. *Ramparts* tended to regard "small-town America" as the backbone of the nation. Without actually going into the trenches, the picture suggested a minuteman tradition that should be equal to any new tasks.

Also in 1940, Warner Brothers released a commercial film called *The Fighting 69th*. Like *The Lost Battalion,* the Warners' picture supposedly was based on the exploits of a regiment made up from the New York City area. But where *The Lost Battalion* crudely had tried to reconstruct actual events, *The Fighting 69th* was almost completely fictionalized in its treatment of historic personalities. It featured James Cagney as a tough Brooklyn kid who turned coward in battle. Regenerated by the Catholic chaplain (played by Pat O'Brien, who held a copyright on Irish priest and cop roles at that time), the kid showed his guts (literally) by falling on a live grenade to save his comrades. The film closed with an emotional appeal by O'Brien for a restoration of American ideals.

With *The Fighting 69th,* the movies definitely returned to patriotic and democratic themes. "Warner Brothers have chosen a fit time to lay this cinematic wreath at the feet of New York's 'Fighting 69th,'" wrote a *Life* staffer.[24] Although some critics regarded the picture as high Irish hokum which simply moved the Cagney-O'Brien relationship from the East Side to the Western Front, others accepted it as valid drama. Aesthetically, *The Fighting 69th* seems a mere series of clichés today, but its appearance in 1940 was significant. Hollywood by this time was tooling up for the wholehearted attacks on the Axis powers that were to come. In this context *The Fighting 69th* was not only a blunt reminder that the nation was a land of ethnic minorities who were patriotic in the best melting-pot tradition, it was also an augury of the future.

Before devoting itself almost entirely to a new war, the industry paused once more in those gloomy pre-Pearl Harbor days to present *Sergeant York,* a film that, in its way, is probably as much a motion picture classic as *All Quiet on the Western Front.* For years producer Jesse Lasky had had the idea of doing a film biography of Alvin York, the Tennessee backwoodsman who had earned the Congressional Medal of Honor by capturing 132 German soldiers practically singlehandedly in the Argonne in 1918. Other projects intervened, but finally Lasky cornered York and appealed to him to discuss a "historical document of vital importance to the country in these troubled times." According to Lasky, York had to be tricked into signing the film contract, something the Tennessean "really didn't want to do."[25] York was appeased somewhat when he found that the title role had been assigned to Gary Cooper.

Sergeant York, appearing only five months before Pearl Harbor, was an immediate hit and won Cooper an Oscar for the year's best performance by an actor. The film was a true biographical study which made much of York's mountain background; his war heroics were reserved for the final reels. "By showing what he found in the U.S. worth fighting for," wrote one sympathetic reviewer, "the picture becomes Hollywood's first solid contribution to national defense."[26] *Newsweek*'s review gave the most significant reasons for the film's popularity:

> ... In such times, and in less capable hands, the story of the conscientious objector whom General Pershing was to call "the greatest civilian soldier of all time" might have been a jingoistic, flag-waving cross between *Billy the Kid* and *The Fighting Sixty-Ninth*. Instead, it is an engrossing and humorous record of the American way of life in a backwoods community, as well as a timely drama of the inner struggle of a simple, deeply religious man who weighs his horror of killing against what he feels is the greater necessity to stop all killing .... [27]

Here was a production which matched the moment. Cooper's screen personality, an almost unique blend of shy reticence and virile power, was perfectly suited to the role of a Tennessee mountain man. His York was straight from Jacksonian America–a man who chased women, guzzled booze, and enjoyed a good fight until he "got religion." With his pacifist convictions struggling against his patriotic impulse, York used his skill with a rifle to win the Medal of Honor. *Sergeant York* was one part sturdy yeoman and one part Leatherstocking in khaki. This historic connection made the film the most convincing, if not the most profound, of all the motion pictures of the warrior-democrat.

In the film, York rationalized the inner conflict of pacifism with patriotic duty by arguing that he had to kill to save lives. His taking of the German prisoners was depicted as a triumph of frontier daring and courage. "Down in that thar ravine is where we done captured the last batch," said the sergeant. "They all surrendered, all 'cept one. I had to tech him off. I hated to do hit but couldn't take no chances." The Germans were compared to a series of turkeys York had earlier "teched off" one by one during a mountain turkey shoot.[28]

In spite of the contention of some that *Sergeant York* was a film with no preparedness ax to grind and not specifically aimed to motivate a military buildup, Cooper's portrayal tended seriously to compromise pacifism. Further, the picture included a sequence in which Cordell Hull, York's Congressman, looked into a bleak future. "Some day, your people may ask you to serve them again," he said to York. "None of us can tell what we may be called on to do in years to come."[29] *Sergeant York* comfortably straddled the gap between two wars by presenting the democratic faith in its most favorable light–as the most prized possession of those who were peaceful and Godfearing, yet who were capable of righteous power when aroused.

Alvin York points to his cinema self, Gary Cooper, during the premiere of *Sergeant York* at New York's Astor Theater (1941).

v

Sergeant York was far more sophisticated in its delineation of democratic idealism than were previous films like *The Unbeliever* or *The Big Parade*. But it shared certain presuppositions with earlier efforts. Americans on film continued to respond to crisis by reaching deep into both themselves and their traditions for the faith needed to sustain them. The country's most cherished convictions, in cinematic terms, remained idealistic, egalitarian, and humanitarian, whether they appeared in 1917 or 1941.

These convictions were also, to a much less sophisticated degree, parallels to the optimistic progressive histories that dominated American historiography during the interwar years. These histories, while not without their critics, gained a wide audience by stressing continuity, progress, and achievement. But common sense sketched a somewhat different picture. Gene Wise has demonstrated that when Frederick Jackson Turner was unable to reconcile his frontier thesis with the newer forms of American life emerging in the new century, he escalated his rhetoric into the realm of symbolic idealism.[30] Possibly the consistent democratic idealism of the cinema version of America at war stands as proof that such symbolism is the last refuge for unresolved ambiguities in our national character.

The cracks in the mirror of democracy were exasperatingly obvious, even at the time. Many of the screen's dramatic convictions were nothing more than a compound of mythology and irrational romanticism. Historically, the omnipresent gap between idealism and realism in American society has become from time to time too large for a significant number of Americans. The ensuing tensions have been primary in generating, as two examples, the Civil War and the serious domestic crises of the 1960s.

But where flesh-and-blood armies often stalemate, myths can move mountains. Whether it issued forth as exhortation, didacticism, or soothing balm, what is striking is the powerful persistence of the idea, repeated in a thousand films to the point of triteness but yet continually renewed, that America's heritage was truly one of freedom and equality. In short, this heritage included a faith more than important enough for which to fight.

7

The Trumpet Calls: Commitment and Sacrifice

i

The coming of war to America was preceded by the rise of cinematic jingoism and followed by a flood of motion pictures advocating commitment and sacrifice. At the commencement of the war Americans were encouraged by the screen to be neutral. This neutrality appeal was intertwined with ritualistic incantations about pacifism. So long as American interests and lives were not perceived to be involved, the cinema would display all the indignant self-righteousness and virtuous moralism of the Progressive Era.

But the appeal for neutrality rapidly vanished as national prejudices, ethnic ties, and emotionalism asserted themselves. Preparedness, the movement to strengthen national defense, did not envision American soldiers being pulverized like the hapless victims of Verdun and the Somme. Instead, it was a nationwide movement, somewhat weaker in the Middle West than in other areas of the country, which focused on an appropriate stance vis-à-vis the warring powers which might be called "militantly defensive." Film echoed this shift in national sentiment; the trumpets of preparedness, at first muted, came to drown out the pacifistic hymns of neutrality.

When it became evident that the pressures of unrestricted German U-boat warfare would not break the Messianic impulses of an aroused Wilson administration, American filmmakers produced a crescendo of films thundering for the utmost in democratic sacrifice. The cinema shared this zeal with the great majority of the organs of public opinion in the United States; the occasional dissenter, like the *Masses,* was snuffed out by government fiat. The transition from a flimsy neutrality to an aroused, phobic militancy took less than three years and was conditioned to a significant degree by the nation's film industry. By 1917 any modes of film entertainment that had nothing positive to say about the country's war involvement had vanished from the national screen.

The American motion picture industry was not prepared for the war. Old newsreels and picture-postcard views of famous European scenery were made to suffice until the public interest could be assessed and actual footage could be accumulated. Documentary views of war predominated during 1914 and early 1915, simply because producers had no ideas upon which to hinge a fictional war story. Although cooler heads cautioned that there were no "real" pictures of the war available, people flocked to see scenes of maneuvers and parades. "The public knows as well as the exhibitors themselves that actual pictures from the front are impossible," wrote one bemused critic, "but they seem glad of pictures of mimic war if the real article cannot be obtained."[1]

There were two contrasting views on the desirability of showing war to American moviegoers. The first was an extension of the socially polite attitude toward violence–ignore it. Some observers felt that scenes of European combat were so frightful that they literally would nauseate the audience. "Moving picture audiences are fond of a little killing now and then," said one, "but they are not fond of wholesale butchery . . ."[2] The opposite opinion held that war scenes were indeed horrible, but that they conveyed the "truth" and hence must be shown. Orrin G. Cocks, the Advisory Secretary of the National Board of Censors, defended the Board's approval of realistic war films by arguing that Americans must be shown that war "is far from being a game of ping-pong . . ."[3]

Underlying the turmoil of readying films with new plots, locales, and characters for the screen was President Wilson's neutrality request. Motion picture patrons were asked not to demonstrate in favor of either side when war scenes were shown. In line with Wilson's policy, the National Board of Censors urged producers to provide captions preceding war scenes asking for no expression of partisanship. "We further suggest," the censors optimistically added, "that scenes which tend to arouse race hatred because of their realism and horrible detail be treated in a restrained manner."[4]

Although "real" war initially held the stage, commercial producers were quick to regroup. For a brief moment, they took Wilsonian neutralism to heart. *Be Neutral* reportedly was made in forty-eight hours in 1914 to support this ideal. It showed four men discussing foreign war; the argument grew violent and in the commotion a factory burned down, illuminating an obvious moral. *Neutrality* depicted a German and a Frenchman living in continuing amity in the United States. It was an obvious attempt to ameliorate the growing tension among America's national minorities. But these efforts to exalt neutrality, while honest enough in conception, did not offer audiences what they wanted.

Dramatic content at first lent itself to the religious, pacifistic, and humanitarian impulses so common to Progressive America. These impulses attacked all war, but the intent was to display abhorrence toward the current conflict. Films of this nature were in the best tradition of Victorian melodramatic sentiment. *One of Millions* provided an allegorical look at war in the Napoleonic era; it showed the brutality and senseless waste and preached understanding. *Powder* fictionalized its warring countries ("Gravonia" and "Sasofen") but got down to business by presenting a munitions manufacturer as one of its central characters. The hero was a "humanitarian propagandist" who spent his time crusading against munitions interests. When the munitioneer's son was killed by one of his own shells ("Brandite"), the manufacturer renounced war and went into Red Cross work. In the wake of the war, the armaments industry would not get off so lightly.

The seeds of partisanship lay dormant in the approach of films like these, and their maturation made the neutral criticism of war impossible. In their rush for immediacy, producers tried to fasten pacifistic ideals on the current struggle, with the inevitable result that dramatic convention demanded and produced villainy, irrespective of the worthy cause. An intangible target called "war" was an unsatisfactory one for screen devotees who, conditioned to living theater, were used to taking their villains in human form. The prime example of pacifism breeding partisanship was *In the Name of the Prince of Peace,* directed by J. Searle Dawley, who had been responsible for *One of Millions.* In *Prince of Peace* a nun revealed the identity of her father, a member of the invading German army, and he was executed on a church altar. Dawley thus had it both ways by dramatizing religious desecration yet pinpointing the invader-villain.

The culmination of this genteel and remonstrative view of war was Thomas H. Ince's *Civilization.* Ince was attempting with some success to cash in on the early popularity of films that decried war. He certainly was no pacifist himself, as his later war films were among the most bloodthirsty and patriotic of their kind.[5] Ince showed *Civilization* to President Wilson, who consented to appear in a special "foreword" to the film. William Cochrane, the press representative of the National Democratic Convention, later maintained that the picture aided Wilson in his 1916 campaign.

The wicked king gets the bad news in Thomas H. Ince's *Civilization* (1915).

Ince boasted that *Civilization* "was the first picture to show the methods of modern warfare."⁶ This assertion was more than ludicrous; not for a decade would the commercial film even begin to come to grips with modern military technology. War in *Civilization* was combat straight from the Civil War, courtesy of *Birth of a Nation*; Ince's film featured cavalry charges, waving flags, and the entire apparatus of a war of movement. The film's tone was set by the title "Can we call ourselves civilized when we shut our eyes against the command of the Prince of Peace? 'Love they neighbor as thyself?'," and by its dedication to "that noble band of earnest workers, who are bravely striving to bring about everlasting Peace . . ."⁷ A warmaking king was shown the horrors of war by Christ come to earth; he quickly renounced war. The religious theme dominated the entire film, right down to the inordinate capacity of the Judeo-Christian God for revenge (the king was made to suffer for causing war). A plea for human rights accompanied this theme and could be read as a prescription of democracy to cure the ills of monarchical Europe.

Even if *Civilization* had an effective message, it came too late. It was received well enough; Ince was an early master of press agentry and also contrived a full orchestration with solo and choral voices for the film. Religious impulses would remain to serve the cause of democracy, but pacifism as a motive force for movie drama was dying. Concrete evidence of this came with films like *A Nation's Peril*, which depicted a female pacifist becoming so aroused by the national danger that she led men to the recruiting office. Another Ince production, *The Coward*, was concerned with the Civil War, but its story of a young man made brave by war was a tenet for the times. War in this film was really "death and glory . . . hand in hand." The hero's cowardice was cured by the "blood of his father . . . the shadowy hands of past generations of fighting men shatter the fetters of cowardice."⁸

When pacifism became exposed to ridicule, it was dead as a serious movie theme. Such was the case with *Perkin's Peace Party*, a satire on the Ford Peace Ship. The film depicted a professor and his coterie, bunglers all, failing in their efforts to stop the European war, The tension of impending strife split the religious pacifism and humanitarianism of a picture like *Civilization*, discarding useless ideals but retaining those which were malleable. A democracy at war could employ movie conceptualizations of religion and humanitarianism; for pacifism there was no place.

ii

Preparedness pictures waxed full as pacifist films waned, the increasingly favorable acceptance of the former contributing to the decline in popularity of the latter. For some years prior to 1917, the American military had cooperated with motion picture producers in providing men and material to lend "authenticity" to films. Some, such as *The Submarine Pirate*, were even submitted to government officials to pass inspection. *The Hero of Submarine D-2*, in which the hero had himself shot out of his submarine through a torpedo tube to rescue the fleet, was made with military assistance and gloried in the display of new technological devices. This "authenticity," coupled with the dramatic and skillful manipulation of European war themes, provided a readymade platform for the commercial preparedness film.

Beginning in 1915, the public underwent a barrage of preparedness pictures. The gospel was disseminated by organized interest groups as well as professional producers, and it took the form of features and serials. A group of businessmen financed *Defense or Tribute?*, a film that showed the Founding Fathers worrying over the plight of modern America. The audience was given the choice of defending itself or submitting to invasion and subjugation on the scale of the Roman conquest of Gaul and the French Reign of Terror. The serials included *Liberty,* in which the Mexican border troubles augured greater dangers, and *My Country First,* which featured a "wonderful weapon of preparedness."[9]

These warmups merely paved the way for the impresario of preparedness, J. Stuart Blackton. More than any other man, Blackton systematically and purposefully put the preparedness idea before the American movie public. This immigrant Englishman from Sheffield possessed an engaging personality set off by the sartorial sense of a dandy. After his success with Vitagraph, he had himself styled a Commodore of the Atlantic Yacht Club. He counted Theodore Roosevelt, his neighbor at Oyster Bay, among his friends and "blind pacifism" among his enemies.[10]

J. Stuart Blackton, preparedness advocate, in his uniform as Commodore of the Atlantic Yacht Club.

Blackton had begun as a newspaper cartoonist, but readily transferred his talents to the nascent movie industry after a chat with Thomas Edison. One of his first productions was a two-minute film showing the destruction of Admiral Cervera's fleet in the battle of Santiago Bay. It was made in a bathtub and cost $1.98. But is was *Tearing Down the Spanish Flag* that Blackton never forgot. Filmed the day after the declaration of war with Spain, the picture showed only a hand (Blackton's) tearing down the Spanish flag from its pole and substituting the Stars and Stripes. The enthusiastic audience response stayed with the young producer through the years. When the Republicans became the party of preparedness, Blackton saw an opportunity to combine his political inclinations[11] with the well-remembered lessons of the Spanish-American War.

Blackton's masterwork emerged a full half year before *Civilization* and may have done much to weaken the box-office effect of the Ince production. It possessed a wonderfully ambiguous title, *The Battle Cry of Peace*, and it was a pivotal film in every sense. Historians of the neutrality period have mentioned it as the prime example of the preparedness film. The French ambassador Jules Jusserand called it more effective than an army of conferences. *Battle Cry* polarized preparedness and antipreparedness emotions and incidentally grossed millions of dollars.[12]

A book entitled *Defenseless America,* written by Hudson Maxim of the machine-gun Maxims, was the basis for the film. This munitions connection raised the protest that *Battle Cry* was munitions propaganda. Henry Ford waged a publicity campaign against the picture and traded newspaper salvos with Maxim and Blackton. There is no evidence that either Maxim or Blackton intended directly to profit from the sale of munitions, although such an assumption is easy to make. Both were ardent if not fanatic patriots, and both denied unequivocally that pacifism had played or should play any part in the American experience. Blackton called Ford "spineless" and claimed *Battle Cry* had been produced only "to further the interests of practical preparedness."[13] The entire fray resulted in a libel suit from the producers that dragged desultorily and inconclusively through the courts for years.

The film itself was in five parts. "The Warning" featured Maxim himself, among other celebrities, in the role of prophet of doom. "The Invasion" depicted an unnamed enemy landing in New York Harbor. "In the Hands of the Enemy" detailed the enemy bombardment and capture of the Greater New York area. "The Price" Blackton modestly described as an "allegorical masterpiece of inspired symbolism." In this section "Columbia, crushed and bleeding, captive of the God of War, finally (throws) off the yoke by Virtue of the Spirit of America revivified." Part Five, "The Remedy," dealt with the obvious solutions to these indignities. The picture was crammed with actual political and military leaders, a tribute to Blackton's charm and his ability to move in high circles.[14]

Blackton claimed during the film's production that no "racial animosity" would be created by the final result. "We shall depict no nation as the invader."[15] This assertion was reiterated in the film's official program and was superficially the truth. The enemy was never named, but their battle dress was suspiciously Teutonic, right down to the spiked helmets, and their demeanor matched the atrocity stories which had recently emerged from Belgium and Northern France.

Few were fooled by all this. One critic sarcastically remarked that the enemy was "certainly not Portuguese."[16] Nevertheless the picture was a great commercial success and drew celebrity audiences everywhere. It was endorsed by the American Legion, the American Red Cross, the National Security League, and the Army and Navy Leagues. Although Blackton grossly overestimated his potential audience at 75,000,000 people, he was crystal clear on his purpose: "To rout with ridicule the peace-at-any-price folk."[17]

America in danger. Hudson Maxim giving the warning in *The Battle Cry of Peace* (1915).

The Battle Cry of Peace, as Blackton himself later said, deliberately advocated United States entry into the war. The picture's more sensational aspects were toned down by the extensive official support rounded up by the producers. Almost the only leading preparedness advocate missing was Theodore Roosevelt, and he refused to appear because, he said, "When you have the Army, Navy, Church, and State, you don't want anything else." Roosevelt offered the ultimate justification for the film:

> Every good American should be grateful to Mr.Blackton for having produced "The Battle Cry of Peace." Every uninformed but well-meaning American should attend the exhibition and profit by it. The men who oppose it . . .are thoroughly bad Americans and are engaged in an action hostile to the vital interests of the United States.[18]

Not everyone bought this facile generalization of the meaning of Americanism. "There is something in this film which makes decent people recoil from it," wrote the *New Republic's* critic. "The appeal is nauseating without being properly effective."[19] There was a strong popular reaction against the film, apart from such polite liberalism, but controversy merely fed the box office. With *The Battle Cry of Peace*, the trend toward militancy and away from the religious, pacifistic, and humanitarian disavowal of conflict was firmly fixed. Its producers depended on the power of suggestion imbedded in imagination and dramatic narrative. This narrative far outweighed the commercial possibilities of films like *One of Millions* or *Civilization;* and, as Arthur Link has noted, *Battle Cry* was *sui generis*–thoroughy American in conception and production.[20]

Blackton's greatest success was followed by *The Fall of a Nation*, the brainchild of the Reverend Thomas E. Dixon. Dixon, who produced and wrote the screenplay, previously had written *The Clansman*, which as both novel and stage play had provided the basis for Griffith's *Birth of a Nation*. *The Fall of a Nation* owed much to Blackton's spadework, but it carried the attack on pacifism even further. The film pilloried the pacifism and fundamentalism of William Jennings Bryan, recently resigned as Secretary of State, and directly equated pacifism with cowardice and national disloyalty. Again an insidious but readily identifiable force worked to render America defenseless, and again the enemy bristled with Kaiser-like mustaches. A simplified historicism contrasted the European and American political order. The captions included phrases like "the blood-red soil of crowns" and "the poison of kings."[21] The emphasis was clearly on the virtues of democracy, with a prologue describing America as a refuge for Europe's dispossessed. *The Fall of a Nation*, like *The Battle Cry of Peace,* was more than a preparedness tract; it was a militant antipacifist polemic.

Dixon's picture was a sensation. Ten prints were made originally; these had to be supplemented by forty more in September, 1916. The musical accompaniment was equally popular. Victor Herbert's original score went into large editions. As with other patriotic spectacles, audiences included official dignitaries. Although Dixon and Woodrow Wilson had been classmates at Johns Hopkins, the producer was naturally enough unable to enlist the President's approbation. Not only was Wilson striving to hold the line at preparedness, but he had been drawn into a public squabble over the racism stippling *Birth of a Nation* and was twice shy.

The movie tide was running strongly and irreversibly toward international commitment by the end of 1916. Blackton and Dixon were in the van of the shift of producers toward militaristic and chauvinistic themes. The Motion Picture Producers of America, heretofore an industry promotional organization, was quick to enlist. The voices of those who protested the depiction of war as a necessary duty whose rewards were more glorious than lethal were lost in the rising clamor for commitment. Blackton himself never apologized, and he later even boasted that war movies were "the most deadly cargo that crossed the Atlantic during the whole war."[22] Clearly the movies had emerged as a pliable and effective weapon in the eternal battle of ideas. Their suggestion of international involvement had swept away all contending cinematic arguments months before America declared war, just as they were to do during 1939-1941.

iii

A careful student of the activities of intellectuals during the war has remarked that eventually academics became, in effect, "tools of the war machine."[23] They could be charged with culpability because they failed to meet their own high standards of critical aloofness. Filmmakers did not have such a stable system of professional ethics. Unlike the intellectuals, their war involvement was shaped both by the ideal of patriotism *and* the motive of profit. Their participation, while not crucial to the waging of the war, was an integral element of the war mosaic. Arthur Link has argued that the power of war "propagandists" has been overrated, and that "it is doubtful if they played a major role." "In the final analysis," Link concluded, "American policy was determined by the President and public opinion, which had a great, if unconscious, influence upon him."[24] One is then bound to ask, What influenced public opinion? The answer lies in part with the American motion picture industry.

Film executives at first were nervously concerned that essential materials, such as cellulose, might be denied them. But they organized well and eventually were rewarded by seeing motion pictures classed as an essential industry, with some minor restrictions. The 10 percent admissions tax imposed by the government did little if anything to curb attendance, and most of the large producers waxed prosperous. Their products were part and parcel of the wartime economy.

Even critics who downplayed film's wartime influence admitted that the industry played a key role in the Liberty Loan campaigns. Eminent movie personalities toured the country drumming up funds and dramatized appeals were screened in the nation's theaters as well. Wilson lauded the industry for its work in this regard, and film executives never were loath to point to their contributions. The Fourth Liberty Loan may serve as a convenient example. It began on September 28, 1918, and was budgeted for three weeks. Movie people contributed services and materials estimated to be worth around $1 million. The campaign included thirty-five different productions averaging 370 feet apiece. The government was impressed and paid $50,000 for four thousand duplicates.[25] These films were replete with the clichés of the virtues of the American fighting man and the vices of the barbarous German soldier. One memorable clip showed a group of Yanks overrunning a German position and tearing down the German flag. The American leader, his exertions complete, then appealed for the loan, climaxing his pitch by screaming *"Banzai!"* It was the Japanese actor Sessue Hayakawa, then at the height of his American popularity.[26] Not all the Liberty Loan films, however, were of war scenes. Some showed domestic enthusiasm for the Loan program in the form of mass parades and rallies.

The Liberty Loan films were a form of dues-paying. Producers knew that without these tangible proofs of their patriotism any further marketing of films for profit would be severely curtailed. Pictures were rushed into production at an even more rapid clip than usual, but the payoff was sometimes worth the effort. Cecil B. De Mille proudly remembered, apropos of his *The Little American,* that it "was timely, as I knew it would be."[27] To the sincere movie fan it appeared that the film industry more than fulfilled its vow to be an integral part of the war effort. Some filmmakers even carried their screen themes into their private lives.

De Mille had the Paramount Studios designated a Home Guard recruiting station. He himself became a captain, his brother William a sergeant. Others, not so mercurial, simply shifted with the times. Typical of these was Carl Laemmle of Universal, who at first favored Henry Ford's Ark of Peace idea, later supported the decision to enter the war, and ended by contributing to German relief following the Armistice.

The war films of the 1917-18 period formed a mixed collection. Most critics agreed that their aesthetic value was negligible. Terry Ramsaye said the war was "a big show, but monotonous. It had delivered its entire dramatic and emotional punch when the world went to screaming at the top of its voice in 1914. By 1917 we had grown used to the shouting." In short, the war had "slight entertainment value," and its depiction on film "contributed nothing whatever to the art of the motion picture."[28] Since the war films comprised a very small percentage of the country's total film production, producers were not always immersed in our overseas adventure. Jack Warner, one of the Warner brothers, later remembered that

> There was an emptiness somehow, a striving with no patriotic meaning, during the war years . . . . All of us were busy in the dog-eat-dog world of the motion picture, scratching up nickels and dimes here and there, not always aware that the rest of the world was on fire.[29]

William C. De Mille recalled that his and his brother's war pictures were not particularly successful, because "our people were too close to the tragedy in real life to want any part of it as entertainment."[30]

Inevitably filmgoers became more and more satiated with war scenes. In the same month America entered the war, one critic remarked:

> The "war stuff" thrills us no more. It is just like the newspaper headlines of the real conflict. At first they stirred up every emotion within us. Later they merely aroused our curiosity. Now we have become blasé and bored with warfare. It requires a slaughter of hundreds of thousands and the sinking of squadrons of ships to cause a quiver of the eyelash.[31]

Producers responded to this boredom by deemphasizing the impersonal mass movements of war and sensationalizing personalities and events. Instead of moving toward bigger and better spectacles war films descended rapidly to the ridiculous. While some of these efforts generated enthusiasm or controversy, film periodicals such as *Photoplay Magazine* and *Motion Picture Magazine* paid little attention to them. It was as if the industry regarded its war feature films as necessary patriotic exercises, but hardly crucial to its profit margin.

Against these limited indications of growing audience noninvolvement with cinematic war stand the numerous accounts of enthusiastic response to war films. A general scanning of exhibitors' replies in one trade magazine indicates that war films were doing a good business, although this publication was pro-industry and hence may not have included bad reports.[32] Overall, it appears that the total war commitment of the motion picture business led it to produce films the reaction to which cannot be neatly categorized. Some met with great emotional response, while others generated only apathy. But the commitment did not cease during the war. It intensified even as its ingredients grew stale.

iv

There was almost no opposition to the excesses to which this commitment drove producers. If audiences might be apathetic, they were also generally tolerant of this type of fare. Further, there was little danger of something contrary to national goals appearing on the screen. Official censorship at both national and local levels strictly defined the scope of cinematic war. Although it is a great exaggeration to say, with Gertrude Jobes, that "a picture without a war background was taboo,"[33] there were more than enough war films to make a lasting mark. In a review of Griffith's *Hearts of the World* young Kenneth MacGowan pondered their power. "Here we have an art of pure emotion which can go beneath thought, beneath belief, beneath ideals, down to the brute fact of emotional psychology," he wrote, "and make a man or a woman who has hated war, all war, even this war, feel the surge of group emotion, group loyalty and group hate."[34]

A patriotic historicism, a predilection for historical analogy, underlay film's call to arms. Some features extolled the deeds of national myth-figures, implying a clear connection with the present. Typical of these were *Betsy Ross*, which limned the exploits of our earliest flagmaker, and *The Birth of a Race,* which purported to trace the descent of the black man from biblical times, highlighting his wars along the way. Their message was one of simple patriotism, measured by deeds of valor.

However, recent events were more highly valued, probably for their familiarity and their shock effect. Judging by film's attention to these topics, the two most emotionally charged issues of the neutrality period concerned the German invasion of Belgium and the sinking of the *Lusitania*. The first issue gave ample opportunity to attack the German character and will be treated later. The second was more immediate, since it involved Americans and notions of American sovereignty. A dramatic cartoon, *The Sinking of the Lusitania,* was a novel success highly praised for its realism. It was painstakingly drawn by Winsor McCay, the creator of "Gertie the Dinosaur," and depicted German ruthlessness toward helpless civilians. *Lest We Forget* contained a plot centered around the *Lusitania* disaster starring an actual survivor, Rita Jolivet. *Lest We Forget* provided a good example of the road religion and humanitarianism took once they shed pacifism. The film blended recent history with mysticism in a plea for revenge. There was a conscious manipulation of sacred objects: one soldier saluted the American flag in the trenches, while another, mortally wounded, cradled it in his arms. The executed English nurse Edith Cavell wafted down with a halo around her head. The hero enlisted to "avenge the one I love." When he reached the front, he soon found himself covered with the "glorious mud of the trenches:" Humanitarianism easily shaded into patriotic blood lust at the film's end. After the title "We must avenge our dead" came a shot of the Statue of Liberty and the word "PAX."[35]

Americans chided the Germans for showing only films of victory on the grounds that it was "only building up the false hopes of the nation."[36] Films like *Lest We Forget* showed the ultimate hypocrisy of this idea: American films ended universally in victorious achievements. Yet scenes of victory alone soon lost their power.

A Committee of the Associated Motion Picture Advertisers sought to fight public apathy toward the war by making films of the "dangers that confront the nation."[37] This cause was endorsed by leading filmmakers as well as by the War Department. Such pictures were to be patriotic without being gruesome, since the depiction of wholesale carnage was thought to hinder recruiting.

> To be both safe and successful in showing war pictures they must all be of a patriotic nature. Patriotic enthusiasm is now running high; and the high and noble principles which underlie the people's duty, hide from them the dangers which they too well know they have to face, and from which they never shrink at duty's call; but to have the dangers flaunted in their faces, without the inspiration of the high patriotism desired only has a deterrent effect.[38]

To film patriotic acts in a dramatic context without shattering the brittle structure of Victorian gentility was nearly an impossible task. Filmmakers who attempted this middle road were mostly unsuccessful. If their films showed no conflict, they lacked drama; if they showed conflict without bloodshed, they lacked realism; and if they showed gore realistically, they were too gruesome. Adolph Zukor's solution was to entice movie patrons with soporific pictures which would push war into the background.

> Now is the time for the exhibitor to make his house the court of happiness and gladness for his locality, where his patrons will gather to relax the tensions of the times, which fact he should bring out in his advertisements in newspapers, slides, etc. In so doing, he will not only benefit himself, but will be performing a patriotic service for his community . . . .[39]

But it was the rare war film which could perform this service. The pressure was on, applied primarily from public organizations. Ohio, for example, rigorously censored films within its borders. A member of the Ohio censorship board explained that "any picture tending to diminish enthusiasm and cut down recruiting should not be shown."[40] Proof of the lengths to which film censorship would go was the case of *The Spirit of '76*. This film was the creation of Robert H. Goldstein, who produced and wrote the script. The plot was set during the Revolutionary War, and it included scenes of British Redcoats slaughtering women and children in the Wyoming Valley. Fed by official complaints, rumors soon began to circulate that the picture had been financed by German aliens, that Goldstein was an agent provocateur, and even that he served the interests of international Jewry. The power of history on celluloid, combined with the exigencies of wartime, transcended a century and a half and made it a crime to depict an ally doing barbarous deeds. Goldstein was convicted of violating Title XI of the Espionage Act and sentenced to ten years in a federal penitentiary on appeal. He was accused of attempting "knowingly, willfully, and unlawfully to cause insubordination, disloyalty, mutiny, and refusal of duty, in the military and naval forces of the United States." Circuit Judge Hunt tacitly admitted the power of the motion picture in wartime when he added, "The picture might be a truthful representation of historical fact, and yet . . .be calculated to foment disloyalty or insubordination among the naval or military forces."[41]

Producers, faced with this kind of mentality, naturally overreacted in the other direction. Military aid in production was easy to come by, and filmmakers competed for the technological devices which would lend a touch of realism to their work. Realism was further served by casting well-known veterans. Arthur Guy Empey made himself an instant movie star by fictionalizing his war experiences in cinematic form with *Over the Top*. Empey himself appeared at his film's opening, and in a speech at intermission urged his audience to report "impatriotic (*sic*) utterances" to the police.[42] Not quite so blatant was Bert Hall, an ex-flyer who rather unconvincingly portrayed the hero of *A Romance of the Air*. Hall also plugged his film in personal appearances. Empey and Hall were not themselves symbols of war's brutality, but adventure films such as theirs inevitably included battle scenes which were made subordinate to individual heroism. Thus gentility was being undermined even as its chivalric aspects were being paraded. Casual cruelty became fashionable and hence accepted. Typical was this suggestion to exhibitors of the war film *Missing*: "Clip the casualty lists from the local paper of the nearest city issue and mark the 'missing' sections, lettering the announcement of the play above with reference to the lists."[43]

Film followed film with presentations of a catalog of heroic variations. The central theme, of course, was win the war–but the variety of ways to achieve this aim was, on celluloid at least, almost endless. Blackton continued his attack on pacifist "mollycoddles" with *Womanhood, The Glory of the Nation*. He asked his viewers to consider what a nation of 100 million Bryans would be, compared with the same number of Roosevelts. Romantic adventures by the dozen preached solidarity with and revenge for the Allies. Humanitarianism was at times injected into war adventure, *The Spirit of the Red Cross* being the most prominent example. That God was on our side could not be doubted. Until *The Unbeliever*, He made a frequent and often telling appearance on battlefields. Pictures drawn from "real life" had their day, such as the highly successful *My Four Years in Germany*, taken from the autobiographical account of Ambassador James W. Gerard by the Warner brothers.

All of this merely anticipated the nadir of the war film, which was reached by the vitriolic and emotion-baiting attacks centered mainly upon German militarism. Chief among these was *The Kaiser, the Beast of Berlin*, which counted Gerard among the celebrities at its opening. The film featured ads the least inflammatory of which was "WARNING: Any person throwing mud at this poster will *not* be prosecuted."[44] One Jake Myers, in charge of putting up the film's promotional posters in New York City, reported continuous attacks on the menacing head of Wilhelm II. Exhibitors received the following message:

> If you are an American, play this picture. If you are a pro-German it will go a long way toward converting you. Greatest possible opportunities for linking up patriotic societies, Boy Scouts and decent Americans in your community who realize that Uncle Sam is in the war to stay until the Hohenzollern is crushed to earth and the Hun swept into oblivion.[45]

The Beast of Berlin spawned a host of imitations. A critic of one of these, *To Hell With the Kaiser!*, sighed that it was "so easy in times like these to pack houses by appealing to popular passions . . . ."[46] It was a long way from *Civilization* to *The Beast of Berlin*, yet the two films featured much the same emotional appeal, with the exception of the pacifistic aspect. The difference, to put it crudely, was a question of whose ox was being gored. An America in arms was not the America of the 1914-17 years, whose people had been able to regard war as spectators instead of as participants. The movies, perhaps more than any other medium, reflected this change most clearly, as they would again during World War II. Motion pictures were a firm index of the war-spawned hysteria that gripped the nation. The film fare of the war period indicated convincingly that religion, humanitarianism, and democratic thought had an extensive capacity for manipulating vicious emotions.

There is evidence that the motion picture industry was headed for even more strict control from Washington when the Armistice came. Yet there is nothing to indicate that the cinematic frenzy of 1918 could have been sustained for any appreciable period of time. The hate pictures quickly became ludicrous and then embarrassing. All war pictures by November, 1918, were falling off as profit-makers. A trade magazine urged producers to use "after-the-war characters."[47] Caught with titles like *Red, White and Blue Blood* and *Break the News to Mother,* public relations men were quick to emphasize that these were not war stories. Fred J. Balshofer, a pioneer movieman, remembered that on Armistice Day he completed final work on a "six-reel all-out anti-Kaiser picture." The market was dead, and he lost $80,000.[48]

As the dust settled, the industry turned to its more normal pursuits. Only sporadically in the next two decades would the film look at war's aftermath. The intensity of the commitment had for the moment left everyone breathless, and the cinematic final accounting was slow in coming. A great part of the commitment had been the unceasing call for sacrifice. This sacrifice had now been made, and it demanded justification.

v

That index of wartime sacrifice most in tune with the general nature of the earlier war films was the picture whose plot featured returning veterans. These films contrasted the veteran's wartime tribulations with his reception upon his return. They offered no real comment on the nature of the war, but instead sought to justify the sacrifices made by their heroes and to redeem them by various means. The accent was on the individual and on time-worn dramatic themes, while the American war role went unquestioned.

Frank Borzage's critically acclaimed *Humoresque* (1920) told of a young Jewish musician who gave up his career to serve in the army. Wounded in both arms, he despaired of performing again until he was forced to use his arms to aid his girl. As one reviewer put it, he suddenly discovered "that his imagination has held him in check and that his ailments are not as real as he has led himself to believe."[49] This theme of redemption through love actually had little to do with the war. War merely served as a convenient mechanism for generating the ingredients of drama and was not part of the drama itself.

In this convention, recovery from war injury verged on the miraculous. *The Enchanted Cottage* detailed the agonies of a war cripple who was cast out by his friends, family, and sweetheart. Living in a remote cottage, he met a homely girl; their love for each other transformed them into handsome human beings. In *Shootin' For Love* Hoot Gibson played a shell-shocked veteran who feared guns and was branded a coward. With his sweetheart in danger, he rose to the occasion. These plots extolled love as the great healer. They marked the definite reemergence of gentility and also can be seen as an attempt to ameliorate intolerable aspects of wartime sacrifice.

Other films of this type strained even further for credulity. *Sonny* had a soldier masquerading as his dead comrade and living with the comrade's family. *Out of the Ruins* was a tale of love in wartime, in which a soldier faked his own execution and reunited with his girl. *Closed Gates* featured a millionaire who suffered from war-induced amnesia, only to be cured by a Red Cross nurse. And finally, there was *Face Value*. This picture was built around a member of "'The Broken Faces'–France's society of scarred heroes–forced to parade their glorious wounds in a yearly appeal for charity." The hero was mutilated in the face, in a modest way. Here there was no miraculous transformation, as in *The Enchanted Cottage*, but flashbacks allowed the leading man his original physiognomy, and his girl accepted him in the end. This saccharine view of war was caught in two titles. As the hero waited to jilt the girl, believing she could not love him mutilated, the title commented: "The zero hour that soldiers know–waiting to make the supreme sacrifice." When the deed was done: "But in love as in war, we 'carry on'–hiding our heartaches with a smile."[50]

A second type of veteran was he who came home physically intact to find his sacrifices unappreciated. The hero of *The Flag Maker*, a late Blackton production,

Depression bitterness in the war film. Richard Barthelmess bleakly confronts a jobless future as Gordon Westcott looks on in *Heroes for Sales (Breadline)* (1933).

returned to find his job and his girl appropriated by a slacker. All the old Blackton ingredients were present. A new technological device called "natural vision" was much advertised. The U.S. Navy even lent its cooperation, but the picture was a failure. In *The Last Parade,* two buddies returned home, one to his job and one to bitter unemployment. This picture fused the rising themes of the depression and gangsterism by having the unemployed veteran become a criminal.

The Depression finally conquered the mild sentiments of the earlier veterans' pictures with *Heroes For Sale,* also called *Breadline.* This film showed a nation's ungratefulness to unemployed ex-soldiers. It depicted a veteran's cruel descent from unrecognized war hero to hobo. In these pictures the war was more in focus than in the melodramas of redemptive love. The veteran was regarded as a man who had paid his social dues by serving in uniform. The injustice was not that of the war itself, but the fact that his martial service went unrecognized when the veteran returned to civilian life. *Heroes for Sale* nevertheless managed a climactic affirmation of traditional American ideals.

A final variant on the veteran theme was only tangentially connected with the war. These were the aviation pictures, made in part to capitalize on the glamorous aura surrounding the new technology. In this group were *The Lost Squadron* and *The Last Flight,* made in the early thirties and using action footage from such earlier and more spectacular films as *Wings* and *Hell's Angels. The Lost Squadron* followed returning aviators as they came home to the same job market the doughboys had found. The heroes eventually hired out as movie stuntmen, and a heroic sacrifice ended the film. *The Last Flight* was that of a group of war-worn aviators drunkenly carousing through post-Armistice Europe. They were characterized as "spent bullets," trained warriors whose *raison d'être* had vanished with the coming of peace. Nothing emerged from this film beyond a vague sense that some message about war and its waste was being presented.

vi

Early films which had decried war on religious, humanitarian, and pacifistic grounds contained a highly traditional vision of war in that all war was seen as fundamentally useless because it was morally wrong. Once national interests were perceived to be involved, this vision vanished–although many of its elements later appeared as part of vastly different themes. It gave way to a strident call for preparedness, a call which heightened to a militant shriek once American lives became an issue.

With no demand for war films in the wake of the Armistice, producers were chary of stories directly involved with war. The postwar era romanticized the returning veteran, making him a misunderstood hero who finally achieved due recognition. The misunderstanding was dramatic convention; the recognition was an indication that America's role in the war, as well as the wisdom of the war itself, went unquestioned. The Depression, while bringing a more bitter tone, arrived just as films about veterans, never very numerous anyway, were fading into memory. Only one movie, *Heroes For Sale,* effectively blended the futility of faithful wartime service with the desperation of a type made familiar by the Bonus

Army. Broader and more significant themes relating directly to the nature of the war were becoming popular. The call for commitment would come again, but this time in response to a new crisis.

The American film industry clearly assisted in shaping and reflecting ideas, attitudes, and values toward the impending crisis and toward the war itself. There is little doubt that producers such as Blackton and Dixon aided in exacerbating already inflamed emotions or that the hate films of 1918 did the same, until they exceeded even their broad dramatic license. Likewise, the lingering romanticism of the films about veterans of the twenties or the deepening bitterness and despair of the few the following decade produced are an obvious reflection, if not of a national mood, then of what filmmakers though was a responsive mental set toward the war and its aftermath.

8

What Price Adventure?

i

Many Americans, whether combatants or not, saw the American involvement in World War I as grand adventure. In part this attitude was fostered by the literary arts, but it was rapidly taken up by the film. The literature the war produced is usually regarded as one of protest and disillusion, centered on the mindless cruelty of rampant militarism, the empty promise of wartime idealism, and the great mocking face of war itself. While it is true that some postwar novelists and poets left the trenches with their minds full of "horror, dehumanization, numbness, and absurdity,"[1] there was another side to the war experience. Less sophisticated and running counter to the more critically acclaimed works, the literature of this side is not widely ready today. It flourished as the war was being fought; over four hundred of these "war narratives," accounts of the experiences of common soldiers, were published in the years 1917 and 1918. Their keynote was romanticism and idealism, and no picture of what the war meant to Americans can be complete without their inclusion.[2]

The romanticism and idealism of these war narratives were paralleled in the postwar adventure films which used the war as a backdrop. Almost all the films made during the war years were from both necessity and conviction romantic adventures. They shared the simplistic moral dualisms of the Progressive Era. The interwar period, thanks to improved film technology and more sophisticated audiences, saw films which told a story in smoother film language. But some of the most popular films of the interwar period, which were admired at the time for making a "statement" about the war, were really quite ambiguous in their attitude. This ambiguity stemmed from a reliance on adventure themes, which made acts of heroism and deviltry almost mandatory. Richard Whitehall's contention that images of World War I are more those of "mass slaughter" than of "wild whooping heroics" is not borne out by the film evidence.[3] Not until 1930, and then in only a very few films, did moviemakers come to realistic grips with modern war in a mood of disillusionment which approached that of literature.

While our better novelists and poets were moving readily to an appreciation of war as the archenemy of modern society, moviemakers rarely picked up the cue. One student of the World War I novel has isolated five general literary themes: support of wartime idealism; disillusionment with the effects of the war; antimilitarism; isolationism; and the breakdown of Victorian cultural values.[4] Of these five, war adventure films displayed mostly the first, although they sometimes passed from idealism to disillusionment–but *only in terms of individual characters*. Protagonists were still heroes, made more heroic because they did a necessary job in an effective way. Militarism was seen as an exclusive vice of the Central Powers. Isolationism was too sophisticated an idea for film presentation (and at any rate would have unnecessarily encumbered a plot line). Finally, the entire output of the motion picture industry shared in redefining American cultural values.

The general tone of the industry's attitude toward depicting war on film may be characterized as mildly benevolent. A good portion of the public apparently shared this tolerance. The *Nation* was alarmed by the statement of a Los Angeles educator that the movies "should carry the message of pride and patriotism,"[5] yet the educator was voicing the approbation of the millions who enjoyed *The Big Parade, What Price Glory?,* and *Wings*. The *National Board of Review Magazine* gave positive support to pictures with "patriotic themes," such as *Havoc, Yanks,* and *The Spirit of the USA*.[6] The ultimate and perversely logical extension of this line of thought was attained through the argument that films of war created the hope of peace. A survey of 1,149 British schoolchildren showed that after viewing such war films as *The Big Parade* and *What Price Glory?*, 95.7 percent tested out as "antiwar."[7]

The war adventure films did not go unopposed. Both genteel liberalism and unrestrained radicalism attacked the genre, but there is no indication that Hollywood heeded the central premise of its critics: that war films put such a veneer of heroism and glory on battle that war would become popular and "normal." War in this guise, said the critics, was simply putty for movie scenarists. It hence was a moral evil to present deadly combat as adventure. "Films must pay their way," John Galsworthy complained from across the Atlantic, "and ordinary knowledge of human nature assures us that they could not possibly pay their way in any country if they really got on the nerves of their audiences."

> Reproduction of one-millionth part of the horror and misery which every day of the war brought would be enough to ensure the utter failure of any of these films. They are, therefore, in no sense educational, for they cannot tell anything even remotely like the truth. Indeed, to tell the truth about war in a film would be quite impossible . . . .[8]

Galsworthy's voice was that of traditional liberalism. To have social value, an organ of mass communication must transmit information that is both useful and truthful. All the rest is hypocrisy and serves society ill. But the box office was not listening.

Liberals were agitated to the verge of paranoia by the undisguised government involvement in the production of many war adventure films. Some liberal writers verged on radicalism by positing a class structure whose predominant members (the "ruling class") consistently used film to prepare the public for further conflict. Cooler heads, such as Oswald Garrison Villard, could still become inflamed over the one-sided movie view of war. Villard unburdened himself in a reply to a New England librarian who had protested against "the military propaganda going on in the movies":

> I sympathize deeply with the writer. I do not go to the movies very often but not in a year have I seen a newsreel which did not play up the military or the navy. I have never seen a Hearst movie yet that did not contain deliberate propaganda of this kind. The last time I went we were shown a fleet of submarines maneuvering on the Pacific Coast in preparation for the defense of the country, obviously from the wicked Japanese . . . .
> . . .It may be replied that the imperialists and militarists and their friends control the movies and the radio, and our crowd do not. I cannot see that that is a convincing argument. It ought to stimulate us to try to get our material into the movies and on the radio.[9]

Where men such as Villard could reflect with a degree of detachment that the pro-war film could be checked by "our material," radical critics were unsparing in their criticism of war adventures. In this view, the industry at its mildest worked hand-in-glove with the "militaristic, Red-baiting" ogres of the Hearst and MacFadden press. At its worst, Hollywood was either reactionary or a superpatriotic backer of the status quo. It was true, said a *New Masses* reviewer in a display of somewhat confusing logic, that *All Quiet on the Western Front* showed men being "marshalled (*sic*) and mangled and murdered." However, "the carnage is not offensive, it is attractive, it stirs participation."[10]

Certainly after the postwar decade the moviemakers remained adept at manipulating symbols of patriotism and militarism on the screen. The existence of a continued thread of war adventure films, which during the thirties thinned but never broke, suggests a continuing audience which was at least receptive if not responsive to these symbols. Scholars weaned on progressive thought complained that these films ignored the economic factors involved in war and thus, as one sarcastically remarked, they were "similar in effectiveness to the 'pacifism' of the American Legion."[11] One study indicated that feature films and newsreels during the years 1930-31 had a ratio of "war to peace items" of twelve to one. By 1935 this had shrunk to a still significant eight to one. Its author quietly concluded that "feature pictures do not present peace as attractively as they do war."[12]

Bits and pieces of various films presented various aspects of this mood. The director and the editor of *Body and Soul*, a melodrama of lovers in a war setting, decided to change their closing scene because it was dulled by "too much propaganda about the war."[13] The hero of *Mata Hari* told the dancer-spy he adored her as a "sacred thing" after "God-Country-Honor."[14] The French protagonist of the first production of *Seventh Heaven* casually compared his deadly flamethrower to the water hose with which he formerly had sluiced down the Paris streets. Two of the central characters of *Today We Live*, another romantic melodrama, killed themselves on a suicide mission motivated by patriotism and love. All of these–the search for action, the box-office value of heroic patriotism, the casual approach to suffering and death, and the drama of meaningful sacrifice–joined with the occasional film which tended to regard war as glorious good fun (such as *Suzy*) to lend credence to the claim that the war adventure film consistently sublimated any serious examination of the war experience in favor of conventional dramatic themes.

ii

Romance aside, the movie war may be subdivided three ways: the war at sea, on land, and in the air. Of these arbitrary groupings, adventure films using the Navy as a setting were relatively rare. This was due primarily to the fact that the war from the American standpoint was not a naval war, with one exception–that of the convoys. Needless to say, the drearly tedium of convoy duty in the North Atlantic did not appeal to producers conscious that there were better themes available. *Convoy*, despite Navy cooperation in its production, was a box-office disaster. Besides, the Navy was notorious as a males-only service; Army and Air Corps personnel could always count on women nurses conveniently at hand, while a woman at sea was nautical poison.

There were a few tries. *Behind the Door,* an early postwar film, involved an appropriately villainous U-boat commander. *The Seas Beneath* (1931) featured a "mystery ship" as a decoy for a German submarine. A young submarine officer drove his explosive laden boat into the enemy defenses in *Hell Below*. Submarine chasers–the tiny swift craft developed as an anti-submarine weapon–were the heroes of two films released in the late thirties, *Submarine Patrol* and *Thunder Afloat*. Each of these was a standard tale of derring-do. The latter was typical of the kind of picture which gave the left-leaning press constant cause for criticism. It was produced with the approval and assistance of the Navy Department, which lent the producers the remaining sub-chaser fleet for authenticity. *Time's* critic was enraptured, calling the film "as exciting as a periscope rising off starboard, as dramatic as the prayerful waiting of men trapped in a delicate mechanism at the bottom of a turbulent, exploding sea. . ."[15] The release date of *Thunder Afloat* was advanced at the request of a preparedness-minded government.

The naval pictures featured individual heroics, patriotic commitment, and self sacrifice. The fact that very few were made, all centered around the submarine, emphasized technological novelty as well as romantic danger. These films remained unadulterated by any serious commentary on the war.

The war was considered to be poor box office in the wake of the Armistice, and khaki-clad heroes were slow to appear on the screen. *Honor First,* a tale of two French brothers (one a hero, the other a deserter), came to the exhibitors in 1922 with the suggestion to "play down the war angle."[16]

But even before *Honor First* had ventured so cautiously into the trenches, the Metro people had proven that war could be profitable if the casting was right. Out of the Metro back lot came a swarthy bit-player who seemed, to scenarist June Mathis, the ideal man for the role of Julio Desnoyers, the protagonist of a best-selling novel by Vicente Blasco-Ibáñez. And so it was that young Rudolph

Valentino lent his undeniable presence to *The Four Horsemen of the Apocalypse*. The film was a great success (earning over four million dollars) and established the postwar formula of placing the newer romantic leading men in dangerous combat situations. *The Four Horsemen* was thought to be the utmost in realism, thanks to the writing of Miss Mathis and the skilled direction of Rex Ingram, but today Julio's love affair, dutiful enlistment in the French army, and sacrificial death seem high melodrama. The war scenes received praise on aesthetic grounds, but they were backdrops for individual action, not protagonists in themselves.

The individualism and heroism continued undiluted in the industry's next big war film, *The Big Parade*. The plot was adapted by Laurence Stallings from his story "Plumes." Stallings's love-hate affair with war, so evident in his documentary *The First World War* nine years later, was the most conspicuous feature of the film. He burned with the desire to show war as it actually was, and this compulsion carried over into the picture. "The war stuff is magnificent," applauded Gilbert Seldes.[17] All agreed that "realism" in the war film had reached its height. Robert Sherwood was amazed that the war scenes actually resembled war, while the Boston *Transcript* was pleased that there was a "minimum of affected flag-waving."[18] "In every sense of the word," wrote one admirer, *"It is the war!"*[19]

But was it? The same enthusiastic reviewer unwittingly put his finger on one of the reasons *The Big Parade* was more dramatic adventure than war analysis:

> It is the first production that I have ever seen that has caught the *spirit of national pride* that makes the United States army the greatest fighting organization on earth–that subtle yearning to acquit themselves *honorably* in doing *that which the situation demands,* that brings *heroes* out of the slums and the mansions of wealth alike.[20]

Honor, duty, heroism–these are all themes common to the war adventure. All are capable of manipulating emotion. When he saw the film, Alexander Woolcott observed among his neighbors in the theater pity for dying doughboys and satisfaction in scenes of German deaths. *The Big Parade's* honor, duty, and heroism were manifest on an individual plane–that of friendship and democratic solidarity. War brought out the best emotions of which an American could be capable. Transformed into attributes, these became loyalty, devotion, and a dedication to service. The hero's war was an intensely personal one: "I came to fight–not to wait and rot in a lousy hole while they murder my pal."[21] He and a friend bayoneted and killed Germans, but some critics saw the film as "antiwar" because he could not knife a young German face to face. The entire action sequence ended as he cheered his comrades on in their attack on the German positions. The scene was one of patriotic sacrifice overcoming the horrors of war, not vice versa.

The man who, along with Stallings, put his stamp on *The Big Parade* was director King Vidor. To gain a sense of the war, in which he had not been an active participant, Vidor screened reel upon reel of Signal Corps combat footage. The film was his first major project; although he personally realized little from it, its success was considerable. *The Big Parade* cost $245,000 to produce and took in $1.5 million at New York's Astor Theater alone. By 1930 it had grossed over $15 million. Vidor's directorial skills were evident throughout the film. His well-known decision to time the advance of American doughboys through the Argonne Forest by metronomic rhythm and his shots of truck convoys speeding to the front lines have earned their praise. But Vidor had no inclination to overcome Stallings's penchant for emphasizing individual heroism.

Director King Vidor with the three doughboy comrades of *The Big Parade* (1925): Tom O'Brien, Karl Dane, and John Gilbert.

The story was simple: Under the pressure of military service a rich youth, a steelworker, and a bartender became fast friends. The wealthy hero's class ostentation was battered down by the inevitable romance (a classic one with a French girl, played by an actress named Renée Adorée) and by his devotion to his comrades. In this Vidor prefigured, in a war setting, the class leveling aspects of the American Dream which emerged in full flower in 1934 with his socialist parable, *Our Daily Bread*. Vidor's war, as much as it is anything, is a pressure cooker for egalitarianism and the realization of social community. The hero's devotion was displayed by killing the Germans who "murdered" his friend. The sacrifice was made in the form of a leg wound. The reward was the girl. Vidor's touch made the trite story line appealing, while his sense of combat (the dreamlike, insistent rhythm) gained from the Signal Corps material was true to the memory of the many AEF veterans who commented on the picture. Producer Irving Thalberg was convinced that *The Big Parade* marked a significant departure from earlier war films:

> The only difference between it and the other war pictures was the different viewpoint taken in the picture. We took a boy whose idea in entering the war was not patriotic. He was swept along by the war spirit around him and entered it but didn't like it. He met a French girl who was intriguing to him, but he wasn't really

serious about her. The only time he was interested in fighting was when a friend, who was close to him, was killed. It was human appeal rather than patriotic appeal, and when he reached the German trenches and came face to face with the opportunity to kill, he couldn't do it. In other words, a new thought regarding the war was in the minds of most people, and that was the basis of its appeal....[22]

Irving Thalberg, the production wizard behind *The Big Parade (1925)*, snapped on the MGM lot in 1932.

Thalberg was mistaken. The theme of war as a democratic leveller stretched back in movie time at least to Ince's *Civilization*. Rich boys democratized by war had been prominent in earlier films, such as *The Unbeliever* and *The Lost Battalion*. If *The Big Parade*'s hero "wasn't really serious" about his French girl, why did he return to her at war's end? And if the film's appeal was "human" rather than "patriotic," why Woolcott's observations? *The Big Parade* was flawed as a statement about the war by the individualism Thalberg regarded as its primary virtue. Years later Budd Schulberg put it nicely when he called it "second-rate perfection."[23] While in Gilbert Seldes's terms the film gave American audiences the "spectacle of the war,"[24] it gave little else. As long as individuals stood apart from the mass and were made *special* through devices of romance or action, the cinema could never come to grips with twentieth-century warfare. The protagonists faced a rational, if horrible, situation and dealt with it in a necessary and rational way. *The Big Parade* was thus a prisoner of dramatic convention and, judging from its reception, so was its audience. Although English and French audiences naturally tended to resent the film on chauvinistic grounds, its real difficulty lay in its misapprehension of war itself. "No film dare show what (war) resembled," wrote Iris Barry. *The Big Parade* "wreathes machine-guns in roses."[25]

Hard on the heels of *The Big Parade* came another Stallings vehicle, *What Price Glory?*, taken from the successful Broadway play which Stallings co-authored with Maxwell Anderson. Although the screenplay was done by J.T. O'Donohue for the Fox organization, the shift in authors did little to erase the ambivalences of *The Big Parade*. *What Price Glory?* was never sure of itself, seeming to condemn war at one moment and worship it the next.

After a Far East sequence establishing the main characters, the film began with a florid title deprecating war–"Civilization dedicated to destruction–fields of production drenched with blood." One of the brawling Marine protagonists, Captain Flagg, later remarked bitterly after a battle which involved American casualties that "There's something rotten about a world that's got to be wet down every thirty years with the blood of boys like those...." But Flagg tipped his hand in the closing scene, where Stallings's (or O'Donohue's) fascination with war was most evident. The Captain and his nemesis-friend, Sergeant Quirt, were ready to leave the inevitable French girl. "This war and glory racket is sorta like a religion," Flagg said, as he and Quirt answered the bugle call to battle.[26]

Favorable critics lauded the "realism" of *What Price Glory?* just as they had done for *The Big Parade*. But the conscious chauvinism of the film obscured any statement concerning the war. Flagg and Quirt were Marines before they were anything else. One reporter was not being too overly hyperbolic when he said a Marine in the audience almost jumped to salute when the rough-hewn Victor McLaglen appeared as Flagg. The formula worked just as it had for *The Big Parade*. If *Parade*'s depiction of "ordinary" civilian-soldiers seemed to fit an image of the American fighting man, so did the depiction of two brawling, lusting spirits in Marine uniforms. Flagg and Quirt were professionals, but they were also frontiersmen. Audiences everywhere were pleasantly shocked by the evident profanity mouthed by the actors to the silent camera. Because of this essentially romantic attitude toward the war, which reduced mass combat to a virile donnybrook, the film's key scenes of brutality (including the famous title scene) only counterpointed the dangers of battle. They did not illuminate war's futility so much as its fascination.

After *What Price Glory?*, war adventures sought new and more exotic themes. Only *The Lost Patrol* remained to fight on land, and it was a picture of the desert war in the Middle East. In the words of one reviewer, it displayed "ardent enthusiasm for the glories of wartime heroism."[27] The attention of movie audiences in the late twenties was drawn to a more exciting, more daring mode of combat. The war in the air was at last appearing on the nation's screens.

iii

The first aviation epic was also the best. Wartime pictures dealing with aviation never had been able to handle the technological aspects of aerial warfare. But Paramount Studios took the gamble that the success of *The Big Parade* and *What Price Glory?* could be repeated in the clouds. In 1926, filming began on *Wings*.

The airplane, both as mechanical novelty and as military weapon, was the central character. The original story for *Wings* was done by John Monk Saunders, a former pursuit pilot, and the direction was entrusted to William Wellman. Like Vidor and Raoul Walsh, the director of *What Price Glory?*, Wellman was a young man–but one with a past. He had been a combat flyer with both the Lafayette Flying Corps and the Army Air Service. With Saunders and Wellman behind the camera, the outcome naturally enough emphasized the dynamics of aerial combat. An insipid romantic quadrangle could not detract from the breathtaking action sequences. The film could not have been made without the cooperation of the War Department, which in the interwar years had little else to do. San Antonio's Kelly Field was chosen for the outdoor shooting, and Army pilots converged from Langley Field, Virginia; Selfridge Field, Michigan; and Crissy Field, California. Scott Field in Illinois contributed balloon crews and equipment. Since there were sequences of ground warfare in the picture, Fort Sam Houston was called upon to supply explosives, artillery, tanks, trucks, and soldiers. Wellman oversaw the whole mass with patient aplomb, holding up production for days on end to get the right weather for cameraman Harry Perry. The wait was worth it. The aerial action sequences remain classics today, and footage from *Wings* found its way into several lesser efforts, such as *Now We're in the Air, The Legion of the Condemned, Young Eagles,* and *The Eagle and the Hawk.*

A brawlers' war. Victor McLaglen and Edmund Lowe confront each other as Dolores Del Rio referees in *What Price Glory?* (1926).

Director William Wellman, pilot Dick Grace, and writer John Monk Saunders on location for *Wings* (1927).

Paramount expended $2 million on its gamble and won; the film was a success. *Wings* trod heavily on war memories: the two young heroes were matched against the deadly "Flying Circus of Captain Kellerman," and the planes were not models but real planes, although many were of a different vintage that the actual wartime craft. The picture was received with great enthusiasm. *Time*'s reviewer may have been lukewarm ("The audience gulped down the plot as conventional but reliable stuff, watched with waning interest while spinning, swerving, dodging planes grew into confused monotony against a background of unpicturesque ether"),[28] but others were not so reserved. These critics praised the film as a first-rate action thriller packed with "realism."[29]

Just as with the earlier epics, some critics felt the realistic depiction of military violence in *Wings* was actually an aid to peace. But the film's concern with aviation confirmed the traditional adventure theme. The two central characters were only "youth answering the challenge of war."[30] Both were eager to fight after their flight training, and both became decorated heroes, with the attendant Paris leave, easy women, and nightclub brawls. There was a strongly romantic current of knightly chivalry running through the picture, interlaced with the brash bonhomie which passed for outlining young America's exposure to decadent Europe. Individual air duels were dangerous, never futile—more sport than war. *Wings*, like its earth-bound predecessors, never came to grips with the idea of mass death, even in its sequences that reproduced the St. Mihiel offensive. When Americans died in heroic charges against German trenches, their deaths were graceful, stately, and meaningful. It was a continuation of the adventure-film cycle with a different setting.

Wings received a strong boost from the coincidence that the year of its release was the year Lindbergh successfully dared the Atlantic. The public became and remained aviation-conscious. Little wonder, then, that Paramount's triumph became the industry's opportunity. For the next decade, the war adventure film was given over to aerial exploits. The groundlings were henceforth reserved for more sober themes.

The Lone Eagle rushed through production to capitalize on Lindbergh's nickname. It contained little else than its air scenes. *Captain Swagger* was an American pilot in French service whose name indicated his view of the war. The hero of *Hard Boiled Haggarty* spent more time boozing and wenching than he did flying—Captain Flagg in goggles. John Monk Saunders co-authored the script of *The Legion of the Condemned* for Paramount, but the film was only a tricked-up imitation of *Wings*.

This first spate of productions indicated the trend. *The Sky Hawk* told of British aviators eager for combat. The wounded hero downed a Zeppelin in a thrilling finale, a sequence which, like most of the aviation action segments, ignored war to emphasize danger and glory. The arrival of sound helped to motivate the audiences of *Young Eagles,* a film that contained clips from *Wings* to accompany a farfetched plot. Even more unbelievable was *Hell in the Heavens,* which reduced the war to individual combat between two opposing aces. Cut from the same cloth were potboilers such as *Cock of the Air* and *Crimson Romance*. The stories of all these films could have been played out against any war, or even against the background of the western. They merely used war as an action device, nothing more.

The long production difficulties of *Hell's Angels* delayed until 1930 the arrival of the most adventurous aviation film of all. The young and aviation-conscious Howard Hughes sought to make a motion picture to "glorify and perpetuate the exploits of the Allied and German airmen of the World War."[31] Trouble over casting and the arrival of sound hampered the project, and the impatient Hughes eventually directed the air sequences himself. *Hell's Angels* rivaled *Wings* in scope of action, but Hughes did not use the services of the War Department as Wellman had. He simply scoured the country for stunt pilots and barnstormers. The film was completed as a silent with synchronized sound effects for about $3 million. But Hughes scrapped both script and leading lady, gambling on making the film over into sound. By the time *Hell's Angels* underwent a splashy premiere ($11 a ticket) in June, 1930, at Grauman's Chinese Theater in Hollywood, another million had been added to production costs. Again critics were impressed by the spectacle of war in the air and less than enthusiastic about the tale of two brothers, one of whom killed the other to prevent the Germans from getting intelligence information. But Hughes's dedication to the film, to help finance which he sold his chain of movie houses, paid off. *Hell's Angels* eventually earned over $8 million.

The success of *Hell's Angels* was not due to any statement about the war. Although the aerial sequences were convincing, individualism and heroic devotion to duty dominated the film. Not the least of the factors drawing attention from the war itself was the presence of the new leading lady, Jean Harlow. While some aestheticians faulted the story for its "lurid banalities,"[32] others could call it an "outstanding war picture."[33] Clearly, a significant part of the public preferred war portrayed as heroic adventure.

The possibility that the air war contained brutality as well as chivalry was ignored until the thirties. Saunders turned his pen in this new direction in 1933, writing the original story for *The Eagle and the Hawk*. This film traced the breakdown and suicide of a pilot who could not stomach the war. In this it seemed an abrupt departure from the war-as-adventure theme. The ending was made coldly cynical by having the pilot's gunner-observer riddle the body with bullets and then crash the plane to give the illusion of a proper warrior's death. Yet nihilism never penetrated the film. The tension between conscience and devotion to duty was broken not by a concrete realization of war's absurdity but by suicide, which in this case was almost a *deus ex machina* solution.

Equally willing to accept war's brutality but not its absurdity was *The Dawn Patrol* (1930). Saunders, who practically monopolized the plot market for the aviation film, did the initial story for this picture also, foreshadowing the war weariness but not the cynicism of *The Eagle and the Hawk*. The characters again were British pilots, the time the autumn of 1915. The clash was once more between conscience and duty. Duty won as the hero died a sacrificial death in the place of a friend. The film was made believable by a shift in roles: a young squadron commander was promoted to a position where he was forced to send men out on dangerous missions. But the picture could in no way be called pacifistic. To depict war's viciousness and nothing more was simply to enhance the danger, emphasize the courage, and sanctify the sacrifice.

The moviemakers came perilously close in *The Dawn Patrol* to making simply another war adventure. An optional ending, which remained unused, provided for the hero to survive the final plane crash and ensconce himself comfortably in a German hospital. There was also a girl in the script, but she later vanished in the film. What remained was a morally sound but rationally senseless devotion to duty which was given the gloss of high courage. Duty was treated as the highest virtue; there was never any talk about disobeying orders. The grim business of war was made tolerable by this strict perversion of morality and by sportsmanship. Courtney, the embittered squadron commander, advised a young replacement: "If you should lose, be a good loser, just like you would in school."[34] It is possible that director Howard Hawks intended this scene to be bitterly ironic. If he did, the final sequence undercut this intention. Courtney bravely "went West" on a suicidal mission, and in a last courtly gesture saluted the man who shot him down. The face of modern war does not look benignly on bravery such as this–it simply swallows it whole, and the sacrifice becomes an empty mockery. *The Dawn Patrol* was unwilling to take the final step, whether the producers were afraid of audience response or for some other reason. It remains a film without ultimate conviction, although its original viewers probably did not regard this failing as important.

A remake of *The Dawn Patrol* appeared in 1938, but it had little of the grim purposefulness of its predecessor. *Life* called it a "smashing drama of suspense."[35] An historian of war films has given it high praise, calling it "the most satisfying of all the films involving World War I aviation."[36] *Newsweek* admired it as an "argument against war."[37] *Dawn Patrol* followed the earlier version very closely, but there were noticeable differences. The two central characters this time were played by Errol Flynn and David Niven, two actors of charm who unavoidably gave a dashing air to the whole proceedings. Also, the film was made in the shadow of another war, and perhaps in spite of itself continued the theme of noble and loyal sacrifice. Thus the final speech did not quite ring true: "A gallant gentleman died this afternoon. And for what? What have all these deaths accomplished? So many fine chaps who have died and are going to die in this war, and in future wars."[38]

Nevertheless the remake was popular. Various groups applauded the film as displaying the futility and tragedy of war. The DAR, the General Federation of Women's Clubs, the National Board of Review, and the National Council of Jewish Women were only a few of those who were cultivated by the studio (Warner Brothers) and who responded favorably. Presumably they saw the picture's brutality as awful and its depiction of duty as awe-inspiring; no one was willing to criticize the uneasy coexistence of these two themes. Major Brand, Courtney's predecessor as squadron commander, could ejaculate: "It's a slaughterhouse. . .and I'm the butcher!" And the sensitive Courtney could share this exchange:

Courtney: "How did Hollister go?"
Squires: "He was trying to help Thornburgh"
Courtney: "Like a man. . .I'm very glad."[39]

iv

The war adventure film during the interwar years changed in emphasis, if not in outlook. Whereas audiences in the twenties could expect a rousing yarn of battlefield or airborne heroism replete with danger and romance, movie patrons of the thirties were more liable to be exposed to a film which was self-conscious in making a statement about the war.

There is no difficulty in pinpointing films like *The Four Horsemen of the Apocalypse, The Big Parade, What Price Glory?, Wings,* and *Hell's Angels* for the romantic adventures they were. The dozens of lesser efforts fall easily into the same category. But many critics were convinced that in the two *Dawn Patrols* and *The Eagle and the Hawk* they were seeing pictures which were pacifist in both intent and result. The main implication to be drawn from this is that the American public–at least that public which saw these pictures (and they numbered in the millions)–tended to regard duty and honor as essential and nonnegotiable virtues. So essential were these moral values to the *Dawn Patrols, The Eagle and the Hawk,* and in a much less noticeable way to the other adventures, that they were not excluded even when they obviously flawed the picture's intent.

When men fight, the basic pacifist appreciation is not why they fight or how degrading the fighting is. The truly pacifist film, it may be argued, would find neither virtue in duty nor glory in honor. The individual in the pacifist film should be representative, or he becomes special. To become special in a war film was to be heroic. Courtney was a special man; so was the decorated air ace of *The Eagle and the Hawk*. Their deaths were tragic, but they were not meaningless. The motion picture in this particular respect was not equal to the uncompromising power of the postwar pacifist novel.

9

Film against War

i

The debate on whether a film about war could present a message of peace was never decided during the interwar years. The dividing line between the "pacificist film" and other types of war pictures was perilously thin, perhaps nonexistent. For this reason, the films discussed in this chapter have been selected in a largely arbitrary fashion. Yet they do share some themes in common.

In most of these pictures, all produced in the thirties, war was the protagonist. War created the dramatic climate, and the existence of men in this climate was at the sufferance either of blind fate or of forces completely beyond their control. The plots reacted against militarism, authoritarianism, patriotism, loyalty, honor, and duty. These shibboleths were seen as pernicious at best. At their worst they were the instigators of the ultimate degradation of intellectual and moral man. The soldiers in these dramas were battered indiscriminately by the vagaries of war. No one was special, no one was heroic, in the sense that the adventure films had stressed individualism and heroism. But even these pictures had their central characters, some of whom, either by their bewilderment, anger, pride, or negative attitude toward their dilemma, may be called antiheroes.[1]

It is not difficult to explain why these films, whose intent was to be explicitly "anti-war" (even if the result was not), were made when they were. The economic caution of Hollywood undoubtedly played a role: not until the popular reception of Erich Maria Remarque's novels was assured did the industry commit his war trilogy to the screen. Also, a significant portion of the American public was isolationist and aggressively anti-war during most of the decade, and thus was presumably more receptive to this type of film. The educated public favored the new revisionist histories of the war, while popular books and political disclosures (the Nye Committee) did much to spread the anti-war gospel. Finally, the onset of the Depression, which brought with it films of despair and bitterness, may have made the anti-war film more acceptable.[2]

Certainly there had existed an audience for the anti-war film in the twenties, but it had been submerged in an ocean of prosperity and progress. As a result, war as adventure was by far the predominant theme in films of the period. There was a small and almost insignificant countercurrent of protest, but to little avail. Comments such as this one from a Pittsburgh resident fell on deaf ears:

> In the motion picture current-events series at present there seems to me to be a distinct intention to accustom the public to the idea of war-like preparation. Prospective soldiers, drilling with a one-man movement, new sorts of bombs, new kinds of projectiles, a new variety of battle airship—and even the German army goose-stepping past Hindenburg—a representation which met with loud applause. Why?[3]

Why, indeed? Some critics based their arguments against war pictures on the premise that the presentation of war on film was morally repugnant, but others saw in the war film the hope of peace. The results of a symposium conducted in 1931 among French intellectuals showed this schism clearly. The participants were asked to respond to two questions: (1) Should the war film be considered as actual propaganda against war or publicity for war; and (2), Of what value was the war film as pacifist propaganda? Perhaps inevitably, the French were divided. "When a war film is good," ran one contention, "it can only create the desire to make war." But André Maurois countered that war films were "excellent propaganda against war, providing they are true." Others claimed that war films, in keeping the idea of war before the public, conditioned people in the notion that war was an unavoidable aspect of man's existence. "Does a spectacle of evil invite horror or temptation? " queried Marcel Ayme. As long as war was presented as spectacle, the temptation to participate was omnipresent. Ayme concluded that

> In order to make it a pacifist propaganda, one would have to show the picture of life in the trenches and not that of death. The real pacifist propaganda film would show men tired with ennui, killing their lice, scraping the mud from their clothes, and looking at desolate plains in front of the trenches. Success would be complete if the audience fell asleep in their seats, but no one would have the courage to go and see this.

Most of the French agreed with John Galsworthy that it was impossible to give a "true" picture of war on the screen. Besides, questions of nationalism were present even when adventure themes were not. "If one showed war impartially, as it is in all its reality," claimed Henri Barbusse, "such films would never be passed by the censor."[4]

The thrust of the French symposium seemed to be more in the direction of a fatalistic toleration of eternal war than in that of eager acceptance of the ability of a new art form to preach pacifism. Although none of them attacked the studio system directly, many of the French intellectuals implicitly questioned whether it was possible in a competitive economic situation to present successfully films which ran counter to the theme of war-as-adventure. Certainly the French regarded the American film industry as morally culpable in its continuous production of war dramas which paid little or no attention to "true" war. Yet it is probably a mistake to call such films "pro-war." Although this flat assertion allows one a convenient point of departure which makes one's favorite war films "really pacifist," it misses the point that, in making the war adventure film, producers were not really thinking about war, just as the audiences in viewing these films probably tended to ignore war, except when it intruded into the plot. The notions concerning war displayed in such pictures were not so much "pro-war" as they were part of an accepted pattern in a moral universe. The anti-war film rearranged this pattern by taking war from its blurry background setting and presenting it in stark contrast to the dreams and aspirations of civilized man.

In general, those American intellectuals who thought about the film at all tended to regard audiences as victims of "pro-war" propaganda. The only way propaganda could be combated in a democracy, asserted one concerned educator, was to "inoculate students with the vaccine of critical judgment."[5] Hollywood was stereotyped as a place where Machiavellian profiteers manipulated symbols of war in the service of darker things to come.

This view received some scholarly sanction in 1939, when Winifred Johnston published *Memo on the Movies,* her study of war propaganda.[6] Johnston's research was undocumented, but it appeared in the guise of scholarship and was published by a university press. Its appearance was a strong indication that at least some intellectuals accepted the radical critique of the war film. Johnston was convinced that economic interests controlled the content of war propaganda films for their private benefit. She outlined the features of the war adventure film which made it propaganda, identified the symbolic motivations (such as honor, liberty, and duty) of many of the plots, and chided the simplicity of dramatic convention, which demanded a hero-villain syndrome. Yet she herself was as stereotypical as the films she criticized. She maintained that America had entered World War I "after three years and more of high-pressure propaganda paid for or incited by financial and political interests profiting by that hoped-for participation." The motion picture industry was indistinguishable from these "interests." "War is the 'last play'–the reserved move–in the ruthless progession of power politics," she said. "Motion picture history from 1914 to 1939 becomes understandable only when its incidents are considered as a series of moves in this deadly game." Motion pictures were being made to serve "dark and destructive ends."[7]

In such a paranoid atmosphere, the anti-war film of the thirties was welcomed as ultimate realism. But several jarring notes intruded. The same studio system which churned out war adventure films was also responsible for the anti-war films. Further, several of the anti-war films were praised by the industry itself. *All Quiet on the Western Front* won an academy award in 1930 as the best picture of the year. Was this merely a sop to the critics of the war adventure film, a concession made to allow the industry to pursue its true capitalistic and militaristic inclinations? Those who trained heavy proletarian guns of class antagonism against Hollywood forgot that the majority of Americans were middle class in both thought and behavior. This broadening audience was moving steadily in the direction of cultural conformity; because these people made the war adventure film profitable, the industry continued to make war pictures depicting heroism and noble sacrifice. But this was also the audience that welcomed Remarque to the screen. The final implication to be drawn from the anti-war films of the thirties is not that they were a needed antedote to a surfeit of "pro-war" films. It is that by this period Americans were ready to accept an alternative view of war, one that did not supplant adventure but rather coexisted with it in uneasy tension.

ii

Several films tried to combine adventure and romance with an anti-war viewpoint. These aspects were so antithetic that films which contained them were hopelessly confused. Others were so stereotyped in their view of war that they failed both as entertainment and as message. At the grossest level, producers clung to a traditional view of war that went back in screen time to *One of Millions,* even as they emphasized danger and romance. Typical of this approach was the first *Seventh Heaven,* the film with the flamethrower-as-firehose, which interspersed shots of the French mobilization in 1914 with the titles: "War is hunger!"–"War is panic!"–"War is separation!"–"War is lust!"–"War is death!"[8]

But underneath the triteness lay a growing acerbity. *The Enemy*, a silent released in 1928, was a rather commonplace romance set in wartime Central Europe. The script direction for one scene showed rising bitterness: "The flag and the banner and the whole hokum spirit of patriotism has Carl and Pauli in its grip." A professor who functioned as a father-intellectual figure had the final say. "Our enemy is not France or England nor are we theirs," he thundered. "The enemy, the real enemy, is HATE. . . . . Hate is a manufactured product, sold to all nations as patriotism and glorfied by a flag." *The Enemy* was equally bitter in showing profiteering in food.[9] Yet its romantic burden, carried by the winsome Lillian Gish, was in abrupt contrast to the film's view of the war. Like a wagon pulled by an unmatched team of horses going in opposite directions, *The Enemy* made little progress.

Suffering from the same difficulty was *Surrender,* a romance set in a German castle used to house French prisoners of war. It had the advantage of the new sound technology. Along with the Franco-German love story went this dialogue between Germans of different generations:

> Dietrich to Reichendorf (wearily): "Father, it is impossible to compare such things. Everything was different in your days. You fought with music playing and flags flying–gloriously–*magnificently!* (Pause) The war we're fighting is different–entirely different . . . . A war impossible to describe to you!"[10]

This different war–war as an active yet sinister element in reshaping men's lives–cropped up in a variety of films, but none showed the trend more strongly than *Aces of Aces* and *They Gave Him a Gun*. The former dealt with the transformation of a sensitive young sculptor opposed to war into an aviator-killer. Although he originally donned a uniform because his girl mistook his convictions for cowardice, the sculptor was quickly brutalized by the war itself. Surviving numerous aerial engagements, he was left to wonder if his medals were worth the men he killed to win them. *They Gave Him a Gun* was even more explicit. Produced late in the period, this film fused war weariness with the popular gangster theme. Its basic premise was that war as the quintessential form of antisocial action was a training ground for civilian crime. The plot followed a timid bookkeeper through his military-inspired metamorphosis into gangland killer.

By 1937, scriptwriters and directors could afford to speak frankly about militarism and war. After one sobering training-camp experience in *They Gave Him a Gun*, "the men stand listening grimly. All are harder now, subtly brutalized." The bookkeeper at first claimed he was no butcher, but after the war, proud of his new occupation, he bragged to his friend: "While a lot of the other kids were at college or picking up a trade, I was in France getting *my* kind of diploma."[11] These attitudes were clear enough, but they appeared amid the conventional romantic triangle. More seriously the film weakened its argument against war by having two friends undergo the same battlefield experiences, with one emerging good, the other bad. This tended to put the blame for the bookkeeper's criminal misdeeds less on militarism and war than on psychopathic imbalance. The film was nevertheless welcomed as a "stark, super-realistic preachment against the evils of war as they apply to the individual."[12] "For those with an abiding hunger for peace and its ways." enthused the *Literary Digest,* "the picture is superb."[13]

The most popular target of the films which searched for individual villains behind the war itself was the munitions industry. The public had been alerted both by revisionist historiography and by the sensational disclosures of the Nye Committee investigations to suspect the darkest motives from armaments manufacturers. The Depression temper was extremely hostile to this type of industrialism; the day when the munitioneer hero of *Powder* could renounce war and devote himself to humanitarian pursuits had long since passed. *The World Moves On* (1934) was a family epic, obviously influenced by the highly successful *Cavalcade,* that included World War I within its scope. It contained actual newsreel footage for "realism," and its family of cotton merchants was used primarily as mouthpieces for opposing views on war-spawned profiteering. It was, in the words of one reviewer, "pretentious."[14] The villains were given lines such as "War is nature's pruning hook. One of nature's ways of eliminating surplus people."[15] *The Man Who Reclaimed His Head* was a journalist hired to write pacifist articles to ennoble an employer enmeshed in munitions deals. This film crudely burlesqued the rapacity of munitions makers. It reached some kind of apogee of simplicity, insinuating that a munitions ring meeting on a yacht had engineered the war.

Neither the films which sought simplistic solutions for the question of war causation nor those which merely substituted "war" for the individual as the conventional screen villian held the final answer for the anti-war film. The picture which more than any other combined aesthetic brilliance, sympathetic performances, technological expertise, and an intuitive insight into the nature of modern war was not among them.

iii

Critics have been almost unanimous in conceding that *All Quiet on the Western Front* was the finest American picture made about World War I. In part this judgment reflects the liberalism of most movie experts, but it also recognizes the artistic skills of a film which stands today as a true motion picture classic. The story was adapted from the novel by Erich Maria Remarque and imaginatively translated to the screen by director Lewis Milestone. The result is usually ranked with the German G.W. Pabst's *Westfront 1918*, also released in 1930, as the best pacifist film of war.

The Laemmles, Carl Jr. and Sr., in 1927, almost three years before they took a chance with *All Quiet on the Western Front*.

The original gamble that a film about the horrors of war, and nothing else, would be a success was taken by Carl Laemmle of Universal. Laemmle, whose sympathy for the plight of postwar Germany already has been mentioned, along with his son Carl Jr. also gambled on Milestone as director. Milestone was of European stock (*Time* described him as a "chunky Russian who once worked in a raincoat factory")[16] and had served in the Signal Corps during the war. His sympathy for the complete helplessness of Remarque's German lads, who were decimated by the war with the impersonality of sausage going through a meat grinder, was evident throughout the film. For the principal character among the German schoolboys, Milestone picked a twenty-year-old banjo player named Lew Ayres. In this, as in the rest of his casting, the director acted with great shrewdness. By relying on unknown screen names he did much to focus audience attention away from the actors and onto their situation, which was the war itself.

All Quiet contained many memorable scenes, among them that of a chauvinistic pedagogue haranguing his pupils on the glories of the Fatherland, a civil servant turned martinet mindlessly parading the virtues of military obedience, and several showing the blind terror of modern war. Critics agreed that Milestone's strength lay in the "relentless realism" with which he depicted organized chaos. Out of the many strong scenes, the closing sequence was an especially powerful wedding of social commentary with aesthetic impact. The scene, redone at the instigation of Milestone and Carl Laemmle, Jr., used cinematographer Carl Freund's idea of the last German boy left alive being shot as he reached out of the trenches toward a butterfly. It was a somber and highly convincing finale.

Director Lewis Milestone (upper left) working out details with the scriptwriters of *All Quiet on the Western Front* (1930).

The film's premiere was well attended. Laemmle's gamble was ardently praised, but privately the industry was worried that the picture was too gloomy for the general taste. Several filmmakers felt it was artistically inferior to *The Big Parade*. Because of *All Quiet*'s unrelenting attack on war, *Time*'s reviewer was reduced to calling it a "freak, almost a monstrosity."[17] But it was both more and less than that. Milestone's concern for the common recruit underlay the entire work and infused sympathy for everyman in war into the film. Later in his career Milestone directed other war films, most of which shared the same combination of realism and compassion. Karel Reisz has said that this first film made Milestone "a spokesman for an intellectual climate."[18] Certainly *All Quiet* was one motion picture that attracted and held the attention of the country's best critics. The hack reviewers were satisfied with adjectives like "magnificent," and let it go at that.[19] Others viewed the film as the latest entry in the pro-war versus anti-war sweepstakes and hoped the picture would be used for peace by offsetting the "romance and glamours of battle."[20] But sensitive critics were stunned by what seemed to them to be the totally uncompromising view of the quality of the war experience. The predominant impression the film gave, wrote Alexander Bakshy, was of "life in the raw," a life not so much tragic as it was bestial. "One is staggered, and shaken, and almost ready to sob," he concluded, "but one is not really thrilled."[21] It was, to use a trite phrase, a picture of stunning impact.

All Quiet rapidly became a celluloid celebrity. Laemmle Sr. was mentioned in connection with the Nobel Peace Prize. His product was banned in France until 1962 (the German boys were depicted fighting the equally war-weary French), and even then it was booed. Hitler did not allow the film to be shown in Germany, nor did Mussolini in Italy. Major Frank Pease, president of the Hollywood Technical Directors' Institute, was moved to telegraph the President, the Secretary of War, the Secretary of the Navy, all forty-eight governors, Mussolini, and sundry opinion makers calling for censorship of the film. According to Pease, *All Quiet* was

> The most brazen propaganda film ever made in America. It undermines beliefs in the Army and in authority. Moscow could not have produced a more subversive film. Its continued uncensored exhibition especially before juveniles will go far to raise a race of yellow-streak slackers and dis-loyalists. Domestic statecraft, common sense, and plain everyday patriotism demand instant suppression of such vicious propaganda.[22]

In exposing what seemed to many to be the true nature of modern war, *All Quiet* moved the motion picture a step forward as a document of social criticism. Few scenes in cinema history had the power of Milestone's tracking shot down the line of a German trench, the camera looking over the shoulders of the German machine-gunners. In this scene of the French relentlessly being mowed down by a scythe of bullets, the film caught the final impersonality as well as the ruthless efficiency of modern technological warfare. War's continued promotion of senseless carnage dulled every sense but the most fundamental: stay alive. After killing a Frenchman in a shell hole, one young German cried "Oh, God, why do they do this to us?" But later, the healing anesthetic of fatalism overcame him: "After all, war is war." In this setting, duty and patriotic impulse were absurdly futile and irrelevant. The sentiments of the Major Peases were outraged by statements such as "When it comes to dying for your country, it is better not to die at all."[23]

The unequivocal stance of *All Quiet on the Western Front* continued in the next film made from the Remarque trilogy. *The Road Back* (1937) detailed the travails of young German veterans struggling to comprehend their changed postwar world. The Nazi consulate in Los Angeles warned the film's actors that their future pictures might be banned in Germany. Some of director James Whale's friends even believed he had been forced to cut the film under pressure from foreign governments. Others, less suspicious, claimed he merely had shot too much footage. Only the opening sequences of the film were devoted to battlefield action. The rest concerned the painful readjustment to civilian life. *Newsweek* called it a "sincere–if confused–antiwar plea."[24] *The Commentator*'s militantly isolationist critic was unimpressed, however, by what he termed the "biggest, wettest, sickliest fizzle of the year."[25]

The deadly anonymity of modern war. Note the severed hands clinging to the barbed wire in *All Quiet on the Western Front* (1930).

The Road Back was akin to *They Gave Him a Gun,* released at about the same time, in that it viewed war as a fundamental influence in reshaping personality: the grim nadir of environmentalist logic. "You cannot take human beings and train them to be inhuman for four years," said one of the German veterans to his girl, "and expect him to be a fit companion for normal men and women. . . . Don't you realize what they've done to me–to all of us?"[26] What was the true difference, the film asked, between mass murder sanctioned by the state and murder in just revenge? "If a man has been forced to shoot men for three years that have never hurt him," challenged one character, "why shouldn't he shoot a man that has ruined his life?"[27]

The third film in the trilogy, *Three Comrades,* told of German war buddies agonizingly trying to reconstruct their lives after the Armistice. The plot, which included a sentimental love theme, saw the war as a shared experience which cemented friendships. The film constituted an abrupt dilution of the bitterness of the preceding two Remarque stories, a dilution abetted by the casting of suave actors like Robert Taylor, Franchot Tone, and Robert Young in the leads, rather than the relative unknowns who had graced *All Quiet* and *The Road Back.*

Milestone was not the only filmmaker who took a new look at war in 1930. The same year saw the release of two pictures which shared *All Quiet's* purpose if not its technique. *The Case of Sergeant Grischa,* directed by industry veteran Herbert Brenon, was an adaptation of Arnold Zweig's popular novel. It followed the misadventures of a Russian soldier after his escape from a German prison camp. His only goal was to see his mother. He was recaptured and eventually executed– by mistake. The theme that war perverts or annihilates even the simplest and most cherished emotional ties was central to the film, as was the depiction of the cruel and senseless operation of military bureaucracy. But *Sergeant Grischa* was miscast, oversentimentalized, and too highly individualized to be effective.

Robert C. Sheriff,.who later helped to script *The Road Back,* was the author of *Journey's End,* which originally appeared in 1929 as a London play. The play was transformed into a film directed by the same James Whale who later directed *The Road Back.* Both Sheriff and Whale were war veterans. Sheriff had served on the Western Front, whereas Whale actually had spent time as a German prisoner of war. *Journey's End* featured a British officer brutalized into a drunken wreck by incessant war. It failed at the box office where *All Quiet on the Western Front* succeeded–perhaps because its message was relayed by talk instead of action. The film was less cinema than it was photography of a stage play. Whale did not use sound with the imagination of Milestone.

Journey's End was further flawed as a statement against war in that it did not fully retreat from the cult of duty and heroism. The British remained gallant in adversity, an admirable trait which had been made more explicit in films like *The Dawn Patrol*. "As long as society is conceded the right to call upon the individual to perform the supreme sacrifice," one critic remarked bitterly, "so long shall we have this far-from-disinterested cult of heroism, and so long will the 'gentlemanly' Anglo-Saxons glory at the spectacle of gallantry that is unobtrusive and self-effacing."[28] A more radical observer made another point when he described the protagonist of *Journey's End* as more human than bestial, qualities which should have been reversed under war's relentless oppression.[29]

The cycle continued in 1932 with Ernst Lubitsch's *Broken Lullaby,* which had a French veteran seeking out the family of the German he had killed during the war. Lubitsch was an exceptionally skilled manipulator of visual symbols and was much admired by aesthetic critics. The notion that murder was a crime regardless of its saction by the state was explicit in and central to the plot, as was the theme of individual war guilt. Nevertheless, the "Lubitsch touch" gave the film "the synthetic quality which distinguishes propaganda from art."[30] As slick as it was, *Broken Lullaby* was unabashedly pacifist. In spirit if not technique it stood with *The Road Back* in its view of the utter immorality of war.

Morality was also the central issue of *The Road to Glory* which Howard Hawks directed in 1936 from his earlier version of 1926. William Faulkner co-authored the script. Here it was the French who underwent the remorseless destruction of trench warfare. Critics placed the picture with *All Quiet on the Western Front* and *Journey's End* as a "masterly warning sign in the world's unquiet state."[31] But literary critic Mark Van Doren took a rather strange view of *The Road to Glory,* finding that a war without "movement" lacked drama and was "ultimately depressing." Therefore, he concluded, "the story of a war without movement is a story without morality, which is to say without meaning."[32] Van Doren extended this indictment to cover *All Quiet* and *Journey's End*. His argument marked the ultimate dead end for aesthetic criticism of war films – taken logically, Van Doren's rationale meant that any depiction of static trench warfare was meaningless because it lacked drama.

Van Doren's viewpoint is best left buried in the cul-de-sac to which his aesthetic logic led him. *The Road to Glory,* while not the best, was likewise not the least of the thirties films which may justly be called "anti-war" in both intent and execution. These pictures mirrored a desire by a significant part of the American public to see war depicted as brutal, degrading, and senseless–the utmost extension of irrationality. But the films comprised more than this. They may have been acceptable to American audiences for what they omitted as much as for what they said.

iv

All Quiet on the Western Front, the classic of the genre, bears a closer look. Its German boys were all enlisted recruits; officers appeared only as cogs in the war machine. The focus was not so much on militarism as it was on the universality of the common soldier's life. The confused youngsters tossed into a totally incomprehensible situation at first searched for some meaning in their experience. They were puzzled that the military appeared to be able to remodel one's character– their village postman, Himmelstoss, was now an unsympathetic parade-ground martinet. In short, they were civilian-soldiers being acted upon by the alien forces of militarism and authoritarianism.

After they had undergone the first shock of battle, bewilderment was the order of the day. "How do they start a war?" asked an older soldier, then added, "I don't feel offended." The young men could only muster up vague answers. "Somebody must have wanted it." "It must be doing somebody some good." And more bitterly: "Every full-grown emperor needs a war to make him famous."[33] Much of the film's power came from opposing these simple sentiments to the chauvinism and idealism which, in 1930, were well remembered by those not yet middle-aged. Milestone was not above using caricatures to make his point– Himmelstoss was the perfect mindless drillfield loon, while the professor, who even in 1918 ceaselessly urged his students on to war, must be considered a symbol of the "treason of the intellectuals." These figures were played off to great effect against the innocence of the young men.

With all this it may be somewhat surprising to claim that *All Quiet,* as an anti-war film, contained several plot devices that, intentionally or not, made it more palatable to American audiences. First and most obvious, the film was ambiguous in indicating opposition to *all* war. The plot was fixed firmly in time and space: the war was undeniably the historical fact known as World War I. An initial script by George Abbott contained the key scene in which the soldiers philosophize about the war. There was nothing in it nor in the final screen version which indicated universal pacifism as opposed to being against the situation in which the men of World War I had found themselves.[34]

Lest this seem too pedantic, several other factors should be considered. It was long the claim of the American government that the "German people" were not responsible for the war, that they had been led into it by unscrupulous leaders. *All Quiet*, by concentrating its narrative on the "average" civilian-soldier, not only made itself powerful drama but in the process appealed directly to deeply ingrained American sympathies. The democratic faith appeared in the Teutonic mirror. These schoolboys were Americans, except for their spiked helmets and their abysmal leadership. *All Quiet* was made in the wake of the Dawes and Young Plans, which had publicized the postwar needs of the German people to Americans. Milestone's film, apart from its dramatic force, was thus unintentionally weighted to capture American audiences. Would the film have been as popular if its protagonists had been German officers? *All Quiet* made clear that the war was fought by Germans who shared neither the ideals nor the aspirations of their emperor or their ruling classes.

More to the point, *All Quiet on the Western Front* was about Germans. The horror, the suffering, the disillusion, the bitterness—all were undergone by Germans. *The Road Back* and *Three Comrades* likewise featured Germans. *Sergeant Grischa* was a Russian. The British were the key figures in *Journey's End*. The French were central to both *Broken Lullaby* and *The Road to Glory*. American moviemakers were having their cake and eating it too. They were able to condemn war without involving either the war aims or the war conduct of the United States.

Films such as *They Gave Him a Gun*, with its individualism and its ambiguous approach to militarism, could never indict war in the fashion of *All Quiet* or *The Road Back*. Only two very slight pictures, neither of which received much notice, seemed to indicate that American involvement in the war may have been no more ennobling than that of other nations.

Beyond Victory appeared the year after *All Quiet*. It was an unpretentious story of four doughboys fighting a holding action as their comrades retreated. The hiatus provided a chance for flashbacks in which each one told how he enlisted and to what purpose. The film tended to be ambiguous at the wrong moments, as when one of the soldiers exclaimed, "We're fighting over something that don't exist!" and then exulted over killing more Germans. It nevertheless retained a downbeat ending, with the two survivors contemplating their medals won for "killing a lot of guys."[35] *Beyond Victory* was unpopular, perhaps because its Americans were not the Americans of *The Big Parade, What Price Glory?, Wings,* or those countless other films which extolled the innate virtues of the American fighting man.

The only other picture to reflect direct disenchantment with America's role in the war was *Private Jones,* another low-budget film produced in the depths of the Depression. Its title character was an unwilling draftee whose military experiences comprised, in William Troy's words, a "satire of wartime America."[36] Appearing as caricatures were the shavetail lieutenant, the dollar-a-year man, various YMCA operatives, and the inevitable hygiene lecturer. Jones, unlike the German boys on the Western Front, was not bewildered by all this. As a confirmed draft dodger, he simply wanted out. But the plot of this movie, along with its anti-hero, remained mostly in stateside training camps. Since Jones's convictions were never truly put to the test in the trenches, neither were those of the film. As satire it was a unique attempt. It did acidly what Chaplin's much more gentle *Shoulder Arms* had done in 1918. This was probably a reflection of the Depression temper. At any rate, *Private Jones* did not do well at the box office.

Frank McHugh and Lee Tracy ponder the nonheroic aspects of war in *Private Jones* (1933).

Several conclusions can be drawn from the fact that practically all American anti-war films drew on the war experiences of other nations. Although *All Quiet on the Western Front* was a legitimate masterpiece, its success was not the signal for an exclusive onrush of war-protest pictures. It must be remembered that *All Quiet* was conterminous with the blood-and-thunder *Hell's Angels*, *The Road to Glory* with *Suzy*, and *Three Comrades* with *Submarine Patrol*. The thirties can thus in no sense be classified as a decade in which the American cinema was given over to the anti-war film.

Second, even in the most bitter period of economic depression, America's war involvement–its motives and means–went almost unquestioned by the country's motion picture industry. It seems that moviemakers were willing to dispense anti-war sentiment in doses thought palatable for their mass audience, in films which did not directly indict the war conduct of the American government, military, or public.[37] The unspoken conviction here was that the American involvement was exactly what President Wilson had said it was–a war to extend American democratic ideals throughout the world.

Finally, the question of the success of the anti-war film remains a moot point. The answer is probably a function of the audience more than of the moviemaker. The American cinema, while willing to offer its patrons an alternative vision of war, was unwilling to debate issues that might transgress upon the nation's most sincere ideals. In this the industry cannot be said to have failed, no more than the American people have failed, in preaching introspection for others while eschewing the practice themselves. The awful harvest of war, in this view, was reaped legitimately by those nations that had begun the whole thing back in 1914.

Part IV

The Camera Eye: Images in a Mirror

> Remember, Hollweg, we must find that pretext for war that is to make me ruler of the world.
> —Kaiser Wilhelm II in *To Hell With the Kaiser!* (1918)

> For France always, mademoiselle. She helped us in our struggle for freedom—we can do no less than return her aid.
> —American soldier to French girl in *Escaping the Hun* (1917)

> The world believes Russia sold out her Allies knowingly, but my camera will show that it was the German propaganda of lies that undermined this great country.
> —Donald C. Thompson (1918)

10

The Threat: The Image of the Enemy

i

The images of the shadow-world of the screen are illusions which may or may not contain some basis in fact. What is important is that these images, repeated over and over with but little change in setting, eventually harden into stereotypes. Depictions of ethnic minorities, religions, national characteristics, and other easily stereotyped subject matter are expected by audiences to appear in a certain way. The image thus presented is both reassuring, since it reaffirms to the viewer what he knew before, and self-perpetuating, since it leads the viewer to expect more of the same. It took a filmmaker of rare initiative to depart from such a cycle in the days of the studio system. If he was successful, yet another cycle began.

Many stereotypes have been fostered by the motion picture. The visual immediacy of film has proved ideal for the simplistic depiction of national characteristics. The visual image of the German soldier, for example, is common coin today on movie screens and television sets, but it is often forgotten that Americans were first introduced to aspects of this image by the films of World War I. Films depicting an enemy nation, whether made during or after the war, tell us much about ourselves. This appears to be true both in a negative sense, i.e., enemy vices were the reverse image of our virtues, and in a positive sense, wherein the enemy was converted to American ideals. Both of these approaches were common.

Who was the enemy? Prior to 1917, this question never was answered clearly. Such producers as Blackton, the progenitor of *The Battle Cry of Peace,* and such authors as Dixon, who was responsible for *The Fall of a Nation,* certainly had no doubts. But their flirtation with the suggestion that a vague Teutonic monarchism was behind it all was never as explicit as they probably would have liked it to be. The American declaration of war released even moderate filmmakers from this false coyness. During the war years producers operating within the solid boundaries of national hatred chose to identify certain nationalities and individuals as the enemy. In the postwar period, the emphasis switched from the indictment of nationalities to the vilification of certain social classes.

The choice of enemy nationalities was narrowed down rapidly. Austrians were portrayed in only a handful of films. Pola Negri played a courageous Austrian woman in love with a Hungarian officer in the first postwar production of *Hotel Imperial*. Lillian Gish was a more ethereal Austrian in *The Enemy*, having as her main task that of suffering nobly. *The Mysterious Lady* had an Austrian officer falling in love with a lady Russian spy. After much ado about little, the inevitable ending left viewers with the "final presumption. . .that the couple will be at home in Vienna."[1] An Austrian secret agent and yet another feminine member of the Russian spy corps fenced charmingly in *After Tonight*. And *A Woman of Experience* did little more than portray Vienna as a city of gaiety and light, the perfect background for star-crossed lovers. All this romantic folderol revealed that the use of Austrians as enemy material came after the war, and that even then Austrians never were opposed to American ideals. Plots using Austria as a war background settled there for exotic reasons, not because Austrians were in any way deemed culpable for the war in either cause or conduct. Only *The Enemy* hinted at this culpability, and it fell flat at the box office. Most other members of the Central Powers did not even fare so well. Bulgaria and Turkey were of little interest to Americans, and these nationalities were seldom if ever seen. Nationally speaking, only one enemy emerged–Germany.

There were several reasons for the selection of Germany as the enemy. By 1914 American attitudes toward Germany, which had been tolerably friendly since German unification in 1871, had shifted in a more hostile direction. The extensive publicity given German culture, German society, and the German cult of militarism tended to chill many Americans. A series of tensely polite international confrontations–in Samoa, China, the Philippines, and Latin America–seemed to illuminate the swaggering, imperialistic bellicosity of the Germans. Emperor Wilhelm II alienated many Americans by his truculent posturing on the international stage. In short, "at the beginning of the World's War the majority of the American sentiment was opposed to Germany."[2] Anti-German films, then, did not so much create this sentiment as they helped shape it into a more vicious and antagonistic emotion.

The country's considerable German-American population largely was ignored by the celluloid offensive. After 1917, virtually no films appeared that were sympathetic to the problems of this ethnic minority. When German-Americans were depicted, usually they were paragons of American virtue rather than schizoid national figures torn between two conflicting loyalties. The historian of this minority group has mentioned no films dealing with German-Americans.[3] They constitute the forgotten people in film's attack on the foe.

That they were not widely used as figures in film plots is due mostly to the fortuitous existence of evil incarnate in the shape of the fruits of the House of Hohenzollern. In spite of the outrageous attacks on the personal property and persons of many German-Americans by their fellow citizens, film did not advocate directly (with rare exceptions) this sort of thing. It did assist in creating a moral atmosphere in which such excesses were condoned for a period. But why use an ambiguous enemy at home when the perfect enemy existed abroad?

With the enemy thus specifically identified in national terms, moviemakers chose at first to present him individually. Here the choice could only light on one man. With his florid arrogant countenance, his bristling waxed mustachios, and his long record of international bluster and bombast, the Kaiser provided a ready target for celluloid bullets.

ii

Anti-monarchist pictures were nothing new to American audiences. But prior to the war, such films largely were given over to the gentle ridicule of royal and aristocratic ways. Now, with civilization seemingly hanging in the balance, the leader of the Germans appeared as the very incarnation of overweening imperial malevolence. The fact that crowned heads also existed in England and (for a brief period) in Russia was blandly ignored. The way had been prepared for the excoriation of the Kaiser by such films as *Civilization,* whose king wore a spiked helmet and rammed a declaration of war through his rubber-stamp parliament. The comparison of this mythical ruler with the Kaiser was made quite clear when the captain of one of the mythical king's submarines received a message to "Sink liner *Propatria* with full cargo of contraband of war. Passengers used as blind. Disregard sentiment."[4] *Civilization* obviously owed much to the *Lusitania* disaster, which had preceded its release only by a matter of months.

As America went to war, the gloves were taken off–rare was the war film that did not include at least an indirect and derogatory reference to the Kaiser, his family, monarchism, or aristocratic life. To begin with, in cinematic terms, the war was initiated at the instigation of the Kaiser. *Kultur* had Wilhelm decide "the time is ripe" for war. He then induced his "vassal monarch" of Austria to join him.[5] *To Hell with the Kaiser!*, released in 1918, claimed that the German emperor and his "war council" decided to violate Belgian neutrality as early as the spring of 1914. After the United States entered the war, this picture had the Kaiser partitioning the world, with America as the share of the Crown Prince. At the end, the Kaiser was ushered into a Napoleonic island exile, where he went mad and jumped into the sea.[6]

The ridiculous plot of *To Hell With the Kaiser!* may seem today like the merest wish-fulfillment; indeed, many contemporary critics complained about the lurid publicity which attended the film. "The title is sure to offend the tastes of many," sniffed *The New York Times.* "It has a cheap sound, and surrounds the photoplay with an atmosphere of patriotism for the profit of the producers."[7] The next day, the *Times* critic had further thoughts on the matter. "Seriously," he reflected, "(the film) seems a travesty of war and of America's serious purpose in it."[8] But the Kaiser remained indicted. What positive qualities could be given a monarch who on screen divested himself of this line to his Chancellor, Theobald von Bethmann-Hollweg: "Remember, Hollweg, we must find that pretext for war that is to make me ruler of the world."[9]

Portrayed as having maneuvered the world into war to satisfy his own maniacal ambitions, the Kaiser as warlord became more savage animal than man. No duplicity, no deed of cruelty, no act of rapacity was beyond him. In his image were fixed all the woes of a world torn by conflict. The most sensational of the pictures which characterized him in this manner was *The Kaiser, the Beast of Berlin*, a worthy predecessor of the Frankenstein and Count Dracula horror features. The film was treated seriously, reviewed in all the standard publications, and attended

Lawrence Grant as Kaiser Wilhelm in the custody of stouthearted Americans. A publicity still from *To Hell with the Kaiser!* (1918).

by military officers of several Allied nations. It featured impersonations of President Wilson, Generals Pershing, Haig, and Joffre, King Albert of Belgium, and the former United States Ambassador to Germany, James W. Gerard. All were locked in a climactic struggle with the forces of darkness. The picture outdid all its competitors in the shrillness of its advertising: "The Hun reflected in his detestable origin"; "Will you ever buy another German-made article?"; and "How the Hun conceived the war and the Kaiser started it."[10]

The Beast of Berlin was crammed with "atrocities" taken straight from the dubious news releases that accompanied the German violation of Belgian neutrality. "The scenes are said to be historically accurate," the *Moving Picture World* commented smoothly, "and picture a strong, dramatic series of events in a commendable way."[11] Although a print of the picture apparently does not survive, one wonders if this praise was not overly gilding the lily. In one New York theater, for instance, the usherettes were costumed as Belgian peasants, and the programs described the film as "an amazing exposé of the intimate life of the Mad Dog of Europe."[12]

The Kaiser was tagged irrevocably as both war instigator and war criminal. Several films clamored for his immediate punishment. *Wanted for Murder* included a dream sequence in which the hero imagined he flooded Berlin with pictures of the Kaiser which accused Wilhelm of murder. *The Kaiser's Finish* advocated a lynching bee in Times Square, with the emperor as the guest of honor. A subtitle in *Daughter of Destiny* suggested that all the Hohenzollerns be executed. A more sophisticated approach was that of *America Must Conquer* (The King of the Huns), which proposed that all German leaders who avoided execution should be sterilized.

With his abdication, the Kaiser passed ingloriously into the cinema shadows. He seldom appeared on screen again. The script for the first *Dawn Patrol* (1930) had a cartoon of Wilhelm used for British machine-gun practice, but this scene did not appear in the film. The Kaiser's movie legacies to the German people were his bestiality, his ruthlessness, and his rampant sexuality. The most scurrilous films about Germans depicted them as lusty barbarians issuing from the depths of the primeval forest. If looting, killing, and mindless destruction were their business, rape was their sport.

Naturally enough, the Kaiser set the example for this insolent and ham-handed sexuality. A still picture from *The Beast of Berlin* showed the German ruler fondling a young maiden's hand, over the caption: "We all know his Majesty's weakness for soft, white hands, and we shuddered."[13] In *The Great Victory* the Kaiser ordered that all widows and unmarried German women were to submit to German soldiers for the purpose of repopulation. Wilhelm was given an illegitimate son in *The Kaiser's Finish*. This youth, who resembled the Crown Prince, became a U.S. Secret Service operative. The royal bastard was able to penetrate the High Command's headquarters and dispatch all hands.

With their emperor leading the way, the German army spent as much time molesting women as it did in razing Europe. *Motherhood* was the story of a Prussian officer forcing his attentions on a married peasant woman, with a child the result. Many of these attacks took place in Belgium, fusing the notion of the violation of a woman's body with that of an attack on a neutral country. In *The Maid of Belgium,* a young girl lost her memory after witnessing Teutonic rape and murder. But Belgian women were not the only victims. A French girl was rescued in the nick of time from Hunnish predators by an American in *For France*. This film also included scenes of the humiliation of a peasant woman by a Prussian officer. *After the War* featured a French lass who had a baby by a German father. Yet another, this one in Normandy, was tortured by Germans in *On Dangerous Ground,* made about five months before the American declaration of war. Finally, a French girl enjoyed a love-hate affair with a German officer in *A Daughter of France*. Untypical in that it showed a German as a lovemaker rather than a sexual aggressor, this picture included the suggested program phrase: "She hated the Hun, but she loved the man as he was."[14]

The intensity of this wartime hatred is indicated most explicitly by both these films and their advertisements. That the American people were willing to tolerate this crude sexuality in their visual mass medium was a signal warning of the decay of late Victorian gentility and a measure of the depths of national emotion. Further, this type of sexual stereotyping was capable of national transference. Its plasticity is indicated by many films of World War II which added the Japanese to the Germans as sexual aggressors. As a nation (we are by no means alone in this) we seem to demand the display of cruder components of sexuality as part of the holocaust of war. Sexuality thus becomes a perverse militarism and an acceptable outlet for our own unresolved sexual tensions.

Things began to get serious when *American* women became the prey of the Boche. In *Adele,* the heroine was an American nurse who was captured and humiliated by German troops. Theda Bara, the original vamp, shed her usual exoticisms to play an American girl trapped in Germany at the outbreak of the war. Miss Bara managed to avoid a lusty Prussian in *When Men Desire,* although "exposed to his violent embraces," as one trade journal put it.[15] The belle of *For Liberty* was an American girl living in Berlin who narrowly avoided a villainous seduction when her attacker was shot at the last moment.

The Unpardonable Sin managed to combine the rape of Belgium with the spoliation of American women. An American mother and one of her daughters, caught in Belgium at the start of the war, suffered "the fate implied in the title of the photoplay." They were seized in a convent by German soldiers, and both became pregnant. Another daughter went to Belgium to search for them, but she was reserved for a happy ending after escaping "only the limit of the invader's brutality."[16] Since the film was not released until after the Armistice, audiences gave it short shrift, but this was probably due more to weariness of war themes than to a rejection of the sexual caricature.

Even Mary Pickford, then in the middle of her long and successful screen career, was persuaded to make a film that further darkened the German image. The picture was *The Little American,* released in the summer of 1917. Miss Pickford played an American girl aiding Belgian refugees who was captured by the Germans and accused of spying. After several adventures, including the threat of rape, she emerged triumphant. The mere conjunction of this symbol of American innocence and purity with the gross sexuality of a Prussian colonel was an indication of the dimension the American film industry had achieved in its depiction of Germans on the screen.

Once audiences were accustomed to the crude suggestion (but never the actual on-screen consummation) of sexual lawlessness on the part of the Hun, no war-related subject was barred from the nation's theaters. Without ever directly violating social taboos of the period, the movie industry was able to present unlimited German brutality as much by inflection and innuendo as by showing the actual transgressions. The imaginations of the audience could fill in the rest. One of the more sensational scenes in *To Hell With the Kaiser!* had a group of nuns forced to wait on the imperial forces. The heroine of *Escaping the Hun* barely was saved from being raped by "coarse and vulgar-looking" German privates.[17] This film pulled out all the stops. Not only did it indict the Kaiser and the officer caste; it also made provision for a scene showing German soldiers shooting a woman and then impaling her baby on their bayonets. (This may have been too much even for the producers–this scene was described as "optional").[18] From these high points, *Escaping the Hun* proceeded to show German aviators bombing a hospital and German civilians viciously mistreating prisoners of war.

Most of the films of the war period endorsed the axiom that the wearer of a German uniform was invariably a drunk, a looter, or a rapist, following the cue of his emperor. The American government encouraged this imagery in its Liberty Loan campaigns. Germans were caricatured in the grossest manner imaginable. They behaved like subhuman forms of animal life, with every appetite rapacious and compulsive. "In the Fall, a celebration in New York," read a caption in one Liberty Loan film, "and all American women will belong to German soldiers."[19]

There is considerable justification for the attitude that all this crudity was merely an irrational outpouring of vilification that contained little or no thought. On the other hand, the constant production of films that pilloried the Kaiser and his people was a suggestion that a good share of the American public acquiesced in a certain image of Germany. While the United States and Germany remained at war, this image was, ironically enough, closely linked with an image popular in Germany itself. But where many Germans saw in the prehistoric *Volk* only the simple goodness and purity of a hardy forest existence, Americans in their movie theaters received a vision of a primeval and destructive horde. German civilization, in this view, was only a thin veneer that vanished in the searing heat of war. Although many movie patrons did not know it, their Germany was that of Nietzsche, not of Goethe, and the Germany army they saw moved according to the principles of Attila rather than Von Moltke. At its extreme, the indictment of Germany extended from the Kaiser through the simplest uniformed peasant boy to the German civilian population. If this image was too irrational to enjoy favor for long, it was nevertheless a staple of the war era.

iii

"Such war pictures as were made," wrote William C. De Mille in later years, "showed a surprising fairness in depicting our opponents."[20] The brother of Cecil B. De Mille credited this fairness to the restraint the industry applied out of consideration for the feelings of German-Americans. It has been indicated how this doctrine of "surprising fairness" dealt with the Kaiser. At first, the condemnation of the German people lagged behind the excoriation of their leader. As the preparedness fever heightened, however, it became increasingly difficult to avoid the tendency to editorialize.

After the declaration of war, the floodgates opened. Some national leaders tried to stem the tide, recognizing the tragedy of the Great Crusade before praising its glory. The President himself protested against one of the most sensational new releases, William Randolph Hearst's Japanese-baiting serial *Patria*. (Mexican-baiting came later.) This epic followed the adventures of Patria Channing (Mrs. Irene Castle) through a series of international intrigues directed at the United States. Wilson asserted that "the character of the story disturbed me very much."[21] *Patria* became enough of a *cause célèbre* to be discussed by the Council of National Defense. It was almost unique, however, in that it faced west, toward California, and was infused with Hearst's hatred for cheap Japanese and Mexican labor.

Patria's less-than-flattering imagery of alien powers was an ominous portent. Almost within a year Wilson had cause to repeat his strictures. This time the film at issue was taken from the account of a member of the government's own ambassadorial corps, James W. Gerard. *My Four Years in Germany* caused the President more anguish. "I have been very much distressed that Mr. Gerrard should have put his narrative into that form," he wrote to Henry Morgenthau. "Movies I have seen recently have portrayed so many horrors that I think their effect is far from stimulating."[22] *My Four Years in Germany* included several scenes of German prison-camp brutality. Warner Brothers, the studio responsible, blandly claimed the atrocity shots had come from captured German newsreels, but these scenes had been staged by director William Nigh in Grantwood, New Jersey. Nigh further eschewed subtlety when he included a scene likening the Kaiser and his advisers to crooks parceling out the spoils.

Gerard's memoir set the brothers Warner on the road to solvency. *My Four Years* cost a mere $50,000 to produce; it grossed over eight times as much. Gerard himself appeared at the film's crowded New York opening. Called upon for a speech, he claimed the movie had been a vivid illustration of Prussian brutality and asked the multitude to back the President. An approving industry journal left no doubt as to the reasons for the picture's popularity:

> Starting with Mr. Gerard's arrival at the German Imperial Court, July 3, 1913, and his presentation to the Kaiser, the picture follows the important events that came under the personal observation of the American representative down to the time when he was given his passports after the declaration of war between Germany and the United States. This résumé of the influences that brought America side by side with the Allies should be seen by everyone. Its chief merit is its authenticity. It reveals the German emperor and his advisers in their true light—a lot of ruthless savages, whose lust for conquest has made them lower than the beasts.[23]

Gerard never had second thoughts about the film taken from his experiences. Over thirty years later he was still congratulating the Warners on their initial success.[24] Nor did anyone else have second thoughts on the subject of Germany's treachery within the family of nations. *The German Curse in Russia* argued that only the "German propaganda of lies" was responsible for the fall of the Russian ally.[25] To Teutonic brutality thus was added the image of stealth and duplicity. *Pershing's Crusaders* showed the Kaiser's soldiers "creeping upon her *(sic)* prey!" This film included a preface that intoned the international vices of the Hohenzollerns and, by implication, of the people over whom they ruled.[26]

There was little concern over the inconsistency of depicting a nation which could exemplify, on the one hand, brute force and, on the other, wily perfidy. The government's *Official War Review* vacillated wildly between these extremes. Germans were presented as Hunnish destroyers who remorselessly shattered a centuries-old cathedral near Chatillon. Yet almost in the same breath they were described as a "motley crew"—men who "skulked" behind barricades and fled before righteous American arms.[27] This tendency was not due to any uncertainty over the true character and purpose of the German people and their leaders. It merely indicated the encyclopedic nature of the blanket condemnation of things

German, a trend also highly evident in other areas of American life.

The mailed fist of savage war and the velvet glove of devilish intrigue were together the basic ingredients of the wartime German image in America. The fist had been shown even before America's entry by films like *Bullets and Brown Eyes*, a picture that imaginatively showed the fury of the Huns as they despoiled Poland in a fictitious war. *The War Bride's Secret*, made to capitalize on the fame of the pacifist film *War Brides*, contained none of the latter's pacifism but had enough German-inspired carnage to satisfy even the most ardent preparedness advocate. The re-enactment of Belgian atrocities, such as in *Who Goes There?*, *The Belgian*, and *The Heart of Humanity*, usually could be counted on to inflame sentiment in an audience.

The Hun took by force what he could not win by stealth. Or at least he tried, until overcome in the end. Such was the fate of that Prince of Prussians, Erich von Stroheim, in *The Heart of Humanity*. The appearance of von Stroheim's close-shaven bullet head on the screen meant that German arrogance and treachery were on display at the local theater. Inevitably, the bestiality of von Stroheim and the rest of the Teutonic horde spiraled into infinite proportions. Although baby-bayoneting was not especially *de rigueur* (in view of the doubts of the producers of *Escaping the Hun*), children once out of the crib were fair game. A German officer cold-bloodedly murdered an American boy in *For Liberty*. *Till I Come Back To You* showed Belgian children being transported across the Rhine to become slave labor in munitions factories. Such scenes of mistreatment of children were certain to be a goad to a nation like the United States, which tended to pamper its middle-class young and to urge the extenuation rather than the attenuation of adolescence.

Americans became heroes when they performed acts identical to those that, committed by Germans, were the apex of villainy. In *Fields of Honor*, two French girls married for love. The German couple suffered, the American couple prospered. An American Secret Service agent performed deeds of heroic double-dealing in *Berlin Via America*, masquerading as a German aviator. Yet a German spy, attempting to sabotage the British fleet at Gibraltar, came to an ignominious end in *Inside the Lines*. *False Faces* was a melee of spies, culminating in the extermination of the German, played by Lon Chaney, who was just beginning his rise as an impersonator of bizarre characters. It was not the deed that determined the degree of criminality or immorality involved, but the nationality of its perpetrator.

Still, a few films ran against the grain. These did not display an all-encompassing enmity toward Germany. Instead, they anticipated the later argument of Carl Laemmle, who viewed the German people as essentially good. They simply had been "misled by a fool Kaiser, thirsty for power, and compelled to become part of his war machine."[28] The saving virtues of these "common Germans" were twofold: democratic and artistic. The cry of the German democrat in *The Unbeliever* was symptomatic of the first approach. So was *The Zeppelin's Last Raid*, which centered on a "thoughtful little band of Germans," the "Legion of Liberty." Their aim was to bring democracy to the "misguided subjects of the Kaiser." The effort was noble but futile–their leader perished heroically in the crash of his dirigible.[29]

More subtle was the idea of the redemptive character of the artistic conscience. Here beauty and truth were mingled with democracy, the point being that the sensitivity of the cultured aesthete could brook no authoritarian system of government. Von Stroheim, as a typical Prussian, met his end in *The Unbeliever* when he destroyed the violin of a "good" German soldier. In *Lest We Forget,* the heroine was aided in her escape by another German soldier who turned out to be "Fritz Muller, the cymbal-player of the Comic Opera."[30] This note was still being sounded in 1932 in Lubitsch's *Broken Lullaby,* where the Frenchman was bound to the German he had killed through their common love of music.

This light bow in the direction of a universal artistic humanism did not save the German people at the Armistice. In general, they were included with their leaders in films calling for revenge. *Beware!* demanded assurance that Germany would never again become an international menace. It put the Kaiser on trial and proceeded to trace German barbarism back through Frederick the Great to Attila the Hun. Germany was described as a "degenerate nation." *Beware!* closed by recommending that the Germans remain "wards of civilization" until they recovered their sanity. *Why America Will Win* sought reparations, German demilitarization, and Allied occupation. Reparations in the form of cession of territory also were the answer for the makers of *Why Germany Must Pay,* a film whose new title proved more satisfying than its original, *The Great Victory*. This picture cast President Wilson as a vengeful Old Testament prophet, less the international conciliator than the righteous redresser of the grievances of mankind. There is circumstantial evidence that the President may have viewed *The Great Victory* (in its original title) aboard ship on his first journey to Paris.[31]

The films calling for revenge were an indication that the German image in America remained highly unflattering in the first year of peace. These pictures marked the high point of vilification and were worthy companions of *The Beast of Berlin* and *To Hell With the Kaiser!* In terms of setting part of the nation against the Treaty of Versailles, they may have had some effect. But producers were quick to realize that the day had ended where the German people, from Kaiser to commoner, could be used as universal villains. With the unnatural hothouse temperature of the war years declining into a placid normalcy, Germany and her poeple moved temporarily into cinematic limbo.

From time to time there appeared evidence that America was slow to forget. The Germans were called blasphemers in *The Love Light* for using the phrase "Gott mitt Uns! (*sic*)"[32] The taunt in *The Unbeliever* that Germany was a "nation of vulgarians" remained as a haunting refrain,[33] as did the German quote "Might Is Right" from *Lest We Forget*.[34] The first popular postwar film depicting Germans, *The Four Horsemen of the Apocalypse,* proved that little of the bouquet of the vintage war years had been lost. Its Germans were so ruthless and barbarous that they could have stepped right from the set of *The Beast of Berlin*.

As the twenties rolled on, the image of Germany in defeat came in part to supplant the familiar stereotypes of the war years. With the Kaiser and his military minions cast down from high places, a new sympathy arose, dictated by the struggles of the Weimar Republic. The martial image became softened and blurred. It remained to be seen if it could be erased.

iv

Such was the popularity of *The Four Horsemen of the Apocalypse* that it was re-released in 1926 to cash in on Rudolph Valentino's premature death. On this occasion, a respected critic was moved to remark:

> The Prussians in 1914 did very much the same thing as they did in 1870. The officers were overhearing fighters, making the most of every luxury they could find, being careful even to spare a fine château so that if they managed to forge ahead to where the structure was they would be sure of a comfortable billet. In picturing this scene, with all its greed and cruelty, Mr. Ingram has stayed within bounds. . . .[35]

The château was saved, but only to indulge Prussian militarism. Here was the image that persisted, even as nonmilitary aspects of German life were being handled sympathetically. The prime characteristic of the German nation was seen as unquestioning obedience to authority, particularly military authority. This feature purposefully was stressed as the opposite of democracy. Thus audiences reacted with cheers when one of the doughboys in *The Big Parade* spit on a German sniper he had killed, and thus a scene in *What Price Glory?* showing captured Germans goose-stepping in formation seemed wholly believable. The first *Seventh Heaven* spoke in florid tones of "Invading Armies—gray-coated hordes—a tidal wave of death."[36] Always the hordes were dull, regimented martinets serving sinister purposes. The imagery was overpowering. *Lilac Time*'s Germans were a "flood of field gray sweeping on through the night," while the Allied troops were a "surging sea."[37] Postwar Germans were not as prone to maraud and rape as was the average 1918 German horde, yet they could exult in killing, as did the aviators who dropped bombs on London in *The Sky Hawk*.

Slowly aspects of the image began to change. The evil of militarism remained, but by 1929 it began to be overlain with a certain continental suavity rather than glutted with primeval rapacity. This suavity could now be conveyed in the scratchy dialogue of the new sound technology; exotic accents became good box office. Major von Friedrich, arch-villain of *The Sky Hawk*, was described as "shaven to the scalp; a monocle adorns his eye; a cultured voice, a charm of manner, are in direct contradiction to the severity of his militaristic bearing."[38] Such a creature could function adroitly as either a smooth cocktail companion or a deadly battlefield opponent. *Three Faces East,* made twice within five years, was a story of German espionage in London. The second time around the spy was played by von Stroheim, now the mastermind rather than the brute. "The story is highly theatrical," commented *Time*, "but, in view of what is known of the actualities of international espionage during the war, not excessively romanticized."[39]

The convention requiring a villain led to the emergence of the Hun from the forest into the drawing room. At times, as in *The Seas Beneath,* the spy could even be female. But usually it was the male, a cultured purveyor of guile and menace, who titillated movie patrons. The menace, as its historic cause receded in memory, often was coated with the sugar pill of romance and even light comedy.

Rendezvous, a late picture in the genre, was a lighthearted look at a nest of German spies in wartime Washington. The job of infiltrating the highest levels of government called for considerable charm and savoir-faire. So did that of impersonating a German baron, but this was accomplished successfully by a British officer in *Lancer Spy*.

If the polished German made a satisfactory screen villain, he did not entirely replace his militarist brother. Most of the time, militarism was linked with the cold haughtiness of aristocratic caste. In *Surrender*, the son of a German count was described as a "true Prussian of 35–arrogant, with sabre cuts on cheek from too much duelling." Another son was given to bemoaning the fate of the Prussian aristocracy. Six years before Jean Renoir's classic *Grand Illusion*, *Surrender* included this speech, made by an officer-aristocrat upon hearing of the Armistice: "Master and servant–love and lust–truth and falsehood–all these old distinctions–they're all in the discard. . . ."[40] In like manner, *The World Moves On* contained an aristocratic lament: "Whoever wins this war–we are all ruined–WE ARE ALL RUINED!"[41]

Director D. W. Griffith scouting German locales for *Isn't Life Wonderful?* (1924).

Clearly the members of the upper strata of German society were on their way out. What remained on screen was an amorphous something, the "German people," who apparently were all the rest of the population–those who did not sport monocles or sword scars. The recognition of their problems was slow to come, but it finally arrived in 1924, when D.W. Griffith presented *Isn't Life*

Wonderful? His story was a simple one concerning the struggle of the postwar dispossessed in Germany. Its stark simplicity was made more tolerable by typical Griffith romanticism. The location scenes were shot in Berlin and its surrounding environs, and American audiences for the first time were able to see the dreariness of the Weimar existence. Most of the central characters were Polish, but Griffith used them to condemn the Kaiser for the war, implying that common people simply had been misused pawns. Griffith introduced his tale by saying that "The story is laid in Germany only because conditions there were most favorable for showing the triumph of love over hardship." "Where there is LOVE, there is HOPE and TRIUMPH," one title blared, "which is what MAKES LIFE WONDERFUL."[42]

With *Isn't Life Wonderful?* Griffith was more the sentimentalist than the analyst of war causation. Yet his sympathetic treatment of postwar Germany, for whatever purpose, was a definite change from the steady diet of anti-German vitriol which had poisoned American screens for years. Some, like Lillian Gish, believed the film was an apology for Griffith's earlier anti-German epics, such as *Hearts of the World*.[43] *Isn't Life Wonderful?* received a good critical reception. Its appearance coincided with the willingness of many Americans to see the mass of Germans as duped participants in an aggressive war. As dupes, they became understandable as well as pathetic. "Years of war and hell," complained a man forced to steal potatoes to feed his family, "beasts they have made us."[44] Griffith gave his young couple a happy ending, an intimation that all would be well with the shadow of monarchy gone from the land.

Romanticism was one avenue through which average Germans passed into cinema respectability. As one-half of a wartime love interest, the presence of a German man or woman could ensure conflict, yet the necessity for a happy ending tended to ameliorate their role as an enemy. In *Barbed Wire*, the volatile Pola Negri played a French girl who fell in love with a German prisoner of war. "He shows her how his people have been made to suffer as much as the French," commented one industry magazine, "and teaches her brotherly love."[45] Rin-Tin-Tin's mistress, a German nurse, proved to be a suitable romantic entanglement for an American aviator in *Dog of the Regiment*. Love, as the cliché had it, conquered all–even national boundaries.

A second route to American sympathies lay in the humanistic presentation of the enemy. In films of this kind, the enemy was capable of fear, love, anger, disillusion–emotions common to any people in war. *The Enemy*, although its protagonists were Austrian, was one of the first films to give citizens of the Central Powers emotions that were neither vicious nor depraved. Reviewers thought its story dull but convincing. The ultimate in humanism was reached with John Ford's *Four Sons,* the syrupy story of a Bavarian mother who sacrificed three of her boys to Mars. The four sons were pictured as highly devoted to their mother. The only one who survived had emigrated to America and had fought as a doughboy. Ford was careful to set the idyllic village life of his family, living with "people gentle and kind,"[46] apart from Prussian militarism. The war was something foisted on the peaceful village by aristocratic arrogance. The picture's villainous Prussian colonel got his comeuppance, committing suicide at war's end. *Four Sons* was abetted by Ford's soft-focus photography, which made the village as gingerbready after the war as it had been before, and by a bravura performance by Margaret Mann as the mother. The film's emphasis on the universality of mother love and its careful disassociation of the common people from their military leadership smoothed the way for a modest success.

By 1930 films had become more sympathetic to Germany. In *Young Eagles,* for example, a German and an American, former aerial antagonists, became friends after the war. *All Quiet on the Western Front* put the finishing touches on the trend begun by *Isn't Life Wonderful?* six years previously. It is significant that among *All Quiet*'s sympathetic characters there was not one representative of German authoritarianism. The later appreciation which praised these characters because "they appear to us not so much as Germans but as merely human beings about whose fate we feel a deep and tragic concern"[47] missed the point slightly. As mentioned previously, it was probably the "German-ness" of the characters that led American audiences to sympathize with their plight. Certainly Germans paid attention to the nationality of the movie's soldiers. A British observer reported that many Germans objected to the film because "there are so many cowards in it."[48]

The trend continued into the thirties, with screen attitudes toward the average German softening while the censure of militarism and authoritarianism held firm. The theme of universal war guilt preached by *Broken Lullaby* was not matched during the decade, perhaps because some American critics resented its "pro-German" slant. *Ever in My Heart* also was called "pro-German," but its protagonist, a German-American professor spying against the Allies, met a satisfactory end when his wife liberally dosed both of them with poison. *The Road Back* and *Three Comrades* continued the idea of two Germanies, one for the aristocrats and one for the people. In the former, German troops argued that they, the "common soldiers," could stop the war. After the Armistice the commoner Weil and the officer von Hagen shared this exchange:

> Von Hagen: "Now your time begins, Weil."
> Weil: "It can't be quite so futile."
> Von Hagen: "And not quite so fine."
> Weil: "You call it fine to kill a million men so that a few can have the chance of heroism?"
> Von Hagen: "Heroism begins where reason leaves off."
> Weil: "And how far has your heroism brought you?"
> Von Hagen: "At least it's brought me to a great memory!"
> Weil: "To a memory! To a terrible responsibility!"[49]

v

But even as *The Road Back* was being filmed, the image of a new Germany began to darken the improving picture of the old. *The Road Back* offered, in symbolic terms, the choice between humanistic anarchy and authoritarian order. *The Enemy*, back in 1928, already had had the vision that Germany could never shed its cloak of militarism. Its final shot showed "little Kurt goose-stepping at the head of his kids' army, which has grown considerably, down the street."[50] The finale in *The Road Back* was a montage of rearming shots, what *Time* called "the reawakening of German military mania."[51] *Three Comrades* contained a strong motif of Hitlerism rising out of a beaten Germany.

In 1939 the story of Edith Cavell, the English nurse executed in Belgium in 1915 by Germans, again came to American theaters. *Nurse Edith Cavell* was the work of Herbert Wilcox, an Englishman who had done the story previously in 1928 as *Dawn*. *Dawn* had created considerable controversy in both England and Germany, but circumstances denied Wilcox this box-office bonus the second time. *Nurse Edith Cavell* was seen in America after Hitler's invasion of Poland, a fact which certainly colored its reception. Wilcox's Germans, driven inexorably by a sense of duty, duly executed the heroic nurse, but the more favorable side of the German image would have been lost even had Edith Cavell somehow miraculously survived. With the new war the cinematic idea of the two Germanies vanished, and there remained only the military monolith of painful memory.

The Ramparts We Watch implicitly accused Germany of aggression in World War I. One of its characters asserted that Germans only understood war. For the German people, "frightfulness was an accepted principle of warfare."[52] But the Germans were no longer the primeval scourge of civilization. Instead, they were mechanized, merciless robots who catered to a fanatic's ideology and ignored all moral codes. In the script for *Yankee Doodle Dandy* (1942), George M. Cohan was given a speech in which he said, "It always happens when we get too proud for patriotism. Some evil nation tries to destroy us. Then we want to make sure our flag is still waving." By the time these sentences reached the screen, the "evil nation" had become a "thug nation" that "blackjacked" its opposition.[53] These gangland terms indicated the German people were no longer predators in the manner of the original Huns. They had become twentieth-century outlaws.

vi

According to film, Germany was to all intents and purposes the only enemy America faced in World War I. As such, she was vilified from her Kaiser to her lowest peasant soldier during the war years. The German image of militarism, although it moved through various permutations with monarchism, aristocracy, and modern dictatorship, never softened on the American screen. It simply acquired the glossy sophistication of menacing decadence. For a period between the wars, the German people were viewed more as victims than as perpetrators of the war. But the coming of a new and greater conflict again erased any differences between rulers and ruled.

The comparison which comes most readily to mind is that with film's treatment of Russian communism in the decade following 1945. Communism was analyzed by many American films of the period as monolithic, power-hungry, and duplicitous to a fault. The sexual rapacity of the German menace, interestingly enough, tended to be transmuted into an intellectual seduction of idealistic young men (witness *Conspirator* and *My Son John*). At any rate, these later films are an indication that the strong stereotypes of the movie screen do not necessarily require the impetus of a shooting war.

These simple and often repeated images of Germany and of German life have left a residue of stereotypes which persist today in both motion pictures and television. It is difficult to estimate how much these films of World War I altered American views of Germany. It is sufficient to say that, taken as a whole, they did nothing to improve the image and a great deal to distort and defame it. As a vehicle for promoting international understanding, something fondly dreamed of by early supporters of the motion picture, the American film in this regard must be rated a conspicuous failure.

11

The Friend: The Image of the Ally

i

The image of the Allied powers on America's screens naturally was more favorable than the picture of the enemy. But the increase in favor did not mean a corresponding increase in the reliability of the Allied images presented. There was a certain polemical advantage connected with showing Germany warts and all, but much to be lost by displaying the less noble side of the Allies. Siegfried Kracauer's findings, based on later movie material, that screen images of "in-group peoples"[1] were more reliable than those of "out-group peoples" will not hold for films of World War I.

Certainly in time of war the enemy may, in Kracauer's language, be classed as an "out-group," while friends reasonably may be termed "in-groups." Testing the reliability hypothesis against the films in this study indicated no increase in the reliability of pictures that concerned the Allies. The Allied nations received more favorable treatment, to be sure, but the national typing that was the central characteristic of films concerning the enemy still occurred–only this time in an amicable rather than a hostile direction. Stereotyping, while not exclusive with the film, nevertheless had enough staying power on screen to ensure as distorted a picture of the friend as of the enemy.

Whereas the Kaiser was a perfect symbol for the hated Hun, moviemakers conjured up no one to symbolize the exemplary purpose of America's partners. Instead, films showing the Allies at war concentrated on specific national traits, when they were not involved with the intricacies of romance or adventure. Eventually three nations–England, France, and Russia–came to be seen as our primary allies, although the American screen view of each country was decidedly different. Just as in films about the Germans, movies of the Allies helped to implant, strengthen, and nurture stereotypes that persist today.

Other nations also received attention, but not nearly to the degree of the leading three. Belgium came first because she lay in the path of the initial German juggernaut and because her suffering was considered symbolic of the agonies of the civilized world under German barbarism. The hopeless but heroic resistance of the little nation inspired several dramas. The title *Till I Come Back To You,* for instance, was taken from King Albert's pledge to return to his people. The Belgian effort was seen as a glorious sacrifice worthy of a just revenge. So ran the theme of *The Belgian* and others of its ilk. While Belgium remained a symbol of courageous innocence, she did not rise to the role of participant in a crusade.

The Italian image on American screens was slower to develop. Eventually films of Italians fighting against the Austrians began to filter into the United States, and producers were able to assess the qualities of this latecomer to the Alliance. What emerged, for the time, was a grudging but not wholehearted acceptance of Italy. The Italians had at least four factors working against them: they had an international reputation (somewhat deserved) for "jackal diplomacy" and were hence considered less trustworthy than the other Allies; as a relatively new nation, they did not enjoy the historical ties with America that Britain and France did; they had been part of a new wave of immigration from Southern Europe that did not have a good reputation in the United States; and they were engaged against Austria, a nation that, as noted, was not regarded as the primary enemy. *The Official War Review,* pressing for superlatives, could only call the Italians "sturdy men" engaged in a "war of magnificent distances."[2] Virtually no major dramas were produced during the war with Italians as central characters. When they did appear after the war, it was usually in insipid romantic plots. Mary Pickford's *The Love Light* (1921), a box-office disaster, cast her as an Italian girl from a simple fishing village. The war was an agent of romantic turmoil in which Miss Pickford served her country by turning her German husband in to the authorities. *The White Sister* was no less saccharine. Made three times, in 1915, 1923, and 1933, it was the story of a woman who, thinking her Italian hero dead, took the veil. *The Doomed Battalion* treated the war seriously, but its protagonist was Austrian. Italians were featured as the enemy.

The Balkans, cockpit of the war, were given little attention. Not until 1933, with *Storm at Daybreak,* did Hollywood enter the area. This picture showed Serbs and Hungarians in opposition, and re-created the assassination of Franz Ferdinand. But *Storm at Daybreak* was essentially a romance, in which an elderly husband killed himself to ensure his young wife's happiness with her lover. Once again, irreconcilable moral conflict was resolved by that simplest and most final of dramatic conventions—death. "What would have become of Hollywood without the War is appalling to imagine," *Time* sarcastically remarked. "When gangsters, showgirls, Broadway colyumnists (*sic*) and the inmates of reformatories are momentarily exhausted, there is always the Archduke Ferdinand and the affair at Sarajevo . . . ."[3] The movie war went nowhere in the Balkans.

In the Far East, things were little better. Although *Patria*'s anti-Japanese fulminations caused it to be banned in some sections of the United States, Orientals continued to tend more toward villainy than heroism. The region consistently was seen as a sinister place peopled by shifty characters whose principles were as crooked as their countenances were inscrutable. In the popular serial *Pearl of the Army*, for example, Pearl White clashed with vaguely Oriental spies out to destroy the Panama Canal. Rarely, and within limits, could Orientals be heroic. China was the focus of *For the Freedom of the East,* as an American and a German diplomat contested the question of a Chinese alliance. The Chinese heroine renounced her American lover to work to save China from "the crushing hand of the Hun."[4] The Japanese, in the person of the popular Sessue Hayakawa, were featured in *The Secret Game,* a story of an attempt to spirit Americans across Siberia to fight on the Russian front. Hayakawa played "Nara-Nara," a Japanese detective who fell in love with a suspected Caucasian woman spy. In the best Oriental fashion (as construed by Americans), he committed suicide in the end to save the girl for the stalwart (and Caucasian) hero.

Oriental characteristics, like those of other peoples peripheral to the central theater of the war, were etched crudely and shallowly on American screens. The sexual patterns presented by Orientals were ambiguous: on the one hand, American fears of miscegenation would not permit an overt display of true love between "yellow" and white–thus Hayakawa's suicide. Oriental sexuality could be suggested, however, in the same sinister tones as less inflammatory characteristics. Where the Huns assaulted the virgins of the world (the rape image was overpowering), Orientals were seen as seductive. The end result was the same, but the method indicated a racist sexual division in the minds of many Americans.

Producers had little knowledge and less understanding of the customs and institutions of these faraway lands, and this ignorance was reflected in their pictures. Countries like Serbia, China, and Japan remained exotic locales in which to place a romance or an adventure. Their relationship to the war was incidental.

ii

In the case of Britain, the situation was entirely different. Depictions of English lords, butlers, cockneys and colonels were common fare to American theatergoers before the war. This nation, which took so much of its culture in the dramatic arts from England, was thoroughly familiar with the conventional stereotypes. With the coming of war, it proved to be an easy task to place these stereotypes in new settings.

A highly sophisticated psychological study of motion pictures at mid-century concluded that in British-made films the essential plot featured the conflict of forbidden impulses with conscience.[5] Hollywood films of the English at war were not concerned with the delineation of forbidden impulses, but they were saturated with conscience. The Hollywood Englishman was conscience personified in his view of his place in society and his duty to that society. This trait was presented as a virtue, one which was applauded by moviemakers and, by implication, their audiences as well. Although pictures of the English in peacetime situations were, to use Kracauer's phrase, "extremely vulnerable" objectively due to the exigencies of the market and other factors,[6] war films displayed certain English character traits which were highly admirable regardless of the bias involved. In this respect, England was the most admired of all the other nations involved in the war. It thus may be assumed that the most pronounced virtues of the English were not only cherished idealistically by Americans. They were assumed to be part of this country's heritage as well.

The British were seen in a variety of guises. Members of the tweed-and-briar pipe set were depicted on American screens as plucky heroes well before April 1917. They could appear as suavely heroic double-agents, as did H. B. Warner in *Shell 43*. Or they were shown as self-sacrificing members of the aristocracy. Where war accentuated German class pride, it integrated the English upper classes into the total war effort. D.W. Griffith's *The Great Love,* an otherwise bland story of a wartime romantic triangle, included vignettes of high-born Englishwomen, such as the Dowager Queen Alexandra, Lady Elizabeth Asquith, and Lady Diana Manners, serving the Cause. The English, along with members of the Empire, also filled the bill when it came to romance. *Bonnie Annie Laurie* was a tale of another romantic triangle concerning a Scots lass, a Scotsman, and a doughboy. *Waterloo Bridge,* the plot of which must be awarded a prize for endurance if nothing else, was the story of a love affair between a London prostitute and a Canadian soldier. There was nothing unique in these portrayals of spies, *sans-culotte* royalty, and lovers–they simply etched the British in human, if entertaining, terms.

Few warrior Britons went unaccompanied by their girls. An army of plots focused on English aviators and their amours. One of the most popular was *Lilac Time,* which cast Gary Cooper, of all people, as the Englishman and pert Colleen Moore as his French peasant girl. The picture's British pilots were presented as a devil-may-care crew, tossing off toasts like "Here's to us flying in the Heavens at five, and frying in Hell at six."[7] Much the same panache went with the hero of *The Sky Hawk*, who despite an injury singlehandedly outfought a German zeppelin. *Today We Live* centered on a triangle concerning an Englishwoman and English and American aviators, one of the flyers being played by the all-purpose Cooper. This picture was filled with noble self-sacrifice. In order for Cooper to get the girl, two Englishmen successfully completed a suicide mission.

Less action-filled themes placed the English in preposterous plots with farfetched romantic entanglements. *True Heaven* had an English officer falling in love with a female German spy, while *Chances* was a tale of two English brothers in love with the same girl. This latter film starred Douglas Fairbanks, Jr., who also was featured as a British member of another romantic triangle in *Captured!* Here the British sense of duty was again uppermost. The English on screen were almost as versatile as Americans, heroic, romantic, and dependable to a fault. This dimension was enhanced by the new sound technology, the stiff upper lip sounding much better than it looked. But like most of the Americans they were one-dimensional figures, slaves to dramatic convention.

Few plots departed from the norm. *Whom the Gods Destroy,* made in 1916, cast the English as the benevolent protectors of Irish rights. Purposefully or not, it was released in virtual synchronization with the Easter Rebellion. The picture caused an uproar; theater riots attended its showing, and the Friends of Irish Freedom vigorously protested its depiction of "Irish patriots as traitors."[8] Yet the fact that such a film was made indicated the scope of English popularity in the United States. After the war, as indicated above, this popularity did not waver. When English virtues came under assault in more serious films, they held firm.

Pictures indicating that all was not well with the English in war were slow to reach American screens. *The Side Show of Life*, released in 1924, attracted little attention, probably because it was an unbelievable story of a circus clown who became a wartime general. Not until 1930 were the English shown in serious adversity. In that year both *Journey's End* and *The Dawn Patrol* cast aside romantic trivia to concentrate on the war itself. *Journey's End* dissected the lives of British officers as they endured the carnage in a front-line dugout. Despite the continual pounding of shell-fire and the absurdity of their situation, the officers emerged as creatures of high courage–possessing not the daring elan of romantic adventurers, but the will compounded of bulldog tenacity and honorable devotion to duty. They reflected the high moral conscience of "doing the right thing," even though such action led to their deaths. To these Englishmen, a sense of duty was the supreme virtue.

The same theme illuminated *The Dawn Patrol*. Here British pilots were engaged in an endless aerial war of attrition, a situation which matched the absurdity and futility of *Journey's End*. Duty was the rationale for all the butchery, and the English became heroic in their reaction to their grim circumstances. The remake in 1938 vulgarized the theme by adding more dash and charm to the protagonists, but it contained the essentials of the image. Dialogue added for the British version of the later picture indicated American attitudes. In one sequence, Squadron Commander Courtney bolstered a young flyer's mettle:

> Donny: "I like the comparison about this . . . and a game at school."
> Courtney: "And that comparison goes for the whole war, Donny . . . a big noisy game (more dialogue) . . . All through the centuries the instant old Britain's in any kind of trouble every kid . . . every lad . . . is up and at 'em just you . . . ready to give 'em. . . give . . . to give it to them."[9]

The scene was intended as a show of cheery bravado, but the stiff upper lip could be glimpsed through the veil of irony. The English never lost their sense of self.

The pinnacle of praise for the sturdy little island was reached in 1933 when Fox brought out *Cavalcade*. This blockbuster, featuring an almost all-English cast, was taken from Noel Coward's successful play. The entire film was an epic devoted to the English national spirit. It proved extremely popular with American audiences. The picture won an Oscar as best production of the year, and Frank Lloyd's direction earned him one as well. The story was loosely woven around the lives of a "typical" English family from the Boer War to 1932. Included was a long sequence in which England faced up to the demands of world war. Nothing indicated the tone of the picture so well as the final toast of the married couple, given by the wife:

> Now, let's couple the future of England with the past of England. The glories and victories and triumphs that are over, and the sorrows that are over, too. Let's drink to our sons who made part of the pattern and to our hearts that died with them. Let's drink to the spirit of gallantry and courage that made a strange heaven out of unbelievable hell, and let's drink to the hope that one day this country of ours, which we love so much, will find dignity and greatness and peace again.[10]

There was a strong sense of class in *Cavalcade*, far stronger than anything in films praising the British as heroic lovers. The upper middle class, to which the movie's family belonged, was depicted as responding to wars out of a sense of duty and service, while the lower classes simply accepted crisis and conflict as a *fait accompli*. Thus the family butler: "We have to have wars now and then to prove the top dog."[11] But the classes around which English society really moved saw a decided and awful difference between the Boer War and World War I. One surmise which comes from viewing *Cavalcade* today is that its depiction of the upper echelons of English society was highly congenial to American audiences, as were the attendant virtues of these elites. The lower classes in *Cavalcade*, used mostly for comic relief, appeared as something indigenous to England. There was, however, a sequence indicating a war-induced shift in class relationships in favor of the laboring class. It is highly probable that part of the reason for the picture's popularity in this country was its ability implicitly to link English class virtue with American aspirations.

Britannia Forever. The Armistice Day celebration in Trafalgar Square from Frank Lloyd's award-winning *Cavalcade* (1933).

Although not everyone greeted *Cavalcade* with open arms, the picture was a critical as well as a popular success. It was seen by one reviewer not as a "flag-waving melodrama," but as a "hymn to what is best in a national spirit."[12] The British liked the film as well as did the Americans. There is no doubt that *Cavalcade* smoothly submerged patriotism in a sea of social obligation. Yet the upper classes' concern for the defense of social and political order amounted to an especially subtle brand of patriotism that, to Americans, seemed the apex of conscientious national service.

The success of *Cavalcade* put the capstone on the American cinema's attitudes toward England at war. Throughout the years of both war and peace, the English image on the American screen never wavered. While the common comedy stereotypes abounded still, the number of English villains were few, and the English spirit in adversity proved to be a triumph. England stood alone as the most admired country outside America's borders. That she did so was testimony not only to strong historical and cultural bonds, but also to a sense that English society contained ingredients both admirable and worthy of emulation.

iii

If the English image tended to be composed of solid and responsible citizens, the French tended to appear on American screens in a much lighter vein. Wolfenstein and Leites found that French-made films at mid-century stressed the conflict between human wishes and the nature of life itself.[13] The earlier American view of the French at war contained no such existentialist maunderings. Nor could it have, given the primitive state of film art at the time. France, like England and Russia, was a country which was characterized rather than analyzed.

The French movie industry thrived under the onus of war. Appreciative French audiences favored martial themes with a heavy dose of romance. The American depiction of France varied little from the Gallic introspection. The gloss on otherwise banal themes came during the war years from a vigorous historicism that emphasized the traditional friendship between America and France. *Joan the Woman* updated the story of the Maid of Orleans by making it a flashback in the mind of a wounded soldier in the trenches. The film's director, the flamboyant Cecil B. De Mille, described his work as an "age-old call to a modern crusade."[14] The *Official War Review*, in a burst of panegyrics, identified Château-Thierry as the place where "our khaki-clad men proved themselves equal to the greatest fighters in the world and linked again in history the names of America and France."[15] The feature film *Lafayette, We Come!* included the classic statement supposedly uttered by someone on Pershing's staff: "Lafayette, we are here!"[16]

American audiences had been seasoned to actual war footage when *Heroic France* appeared in 1916. Familiar scenes and famous personages were its ingredients, which caused the compilation to be criticized for being twice as long as it need have been. The picture pressed on with its demand for U.S. intervention, sounding the tocsin of history at every opportunity. As the war continued, the image grew of a beleaguered France, one of the original sponsors of American liberty, now in need herself. Not that the French lacked suitable patriotic purpose; a Frenchwoman shot by the Germans breathed her last in *Escaping the Hun* with the words, "It is good to die for France." But France did need help, and the American film industry thought she deserved it. "For France always, mademoiselle," declaimed one American cinema stalwart. "She helped us in our struggle for freedom—we can do no less that return her aid."[17] *Lest We Forget* also made much of the historical relationship between France and America, with a view to justifying American intervention.

Throughout the entire period of this study, the image of France was far more feminine than that of any other country. There was much historicism in this as well, going back to eighteenth-century conceptions of the Goddess Liberty. Just as in the case of Belgium, France was often depicted in sexual terms–as a female violated by the savage German male. But she also held the seeds of a better future. In *Lest We Forget*, the hero and heroine adopted a French war orphan, the "child of victory: France his mother and his father all the poilus who have defended him."[18] As long as the war continued, these images of traditional friendship and the well-known patriotic fervor of the French were uppermost in American theaters.

With peace came a change in the French image. Gallic froth bubbled to the top, replacing the stale effusions of an historicism for which there was no longer any need. The image remained feminine, but instead of the cold dead marble of a patriotic monument, moviegoers were treated to the zestful celebration of French *joie de vivre*. Usually Frenchwomen were depicted as pert, saucy, and temperamental enough to fly into an attractive rage. Major war films of the day were incomplete without such a hellion. *The Big Parade* and *What Price Glory?* each had theirs, but love inevitably tamed and redirected passionate emotions. *Marianne,* described as a "musical war comedy," cast Marion Davies as a "peppery French peasant girl" enduring American soldiers camped near her home.[19] French girls could also figure in more lachrymose stories, such as *The Woman I Love,* a trite tale of two French aviators and the wife of one of them.

The lighter side of America's screen vision of Gallic nature was nowhere better displayed than in *Suzy* (1936). Ostensibly, the war was going on while Cary Grant as a French aviator, Franchot Tone as an Irish inventor, and Jean Harlow as a Broadway showgirl transplanted to Europe whirled sprightly through the pirouettes of light comedy. The film was loaded with snappy repartee, and Grant's portrayal of the French warrior was one with his normal smooth, witty screen image. High patriotism and courage, along with the war itself, were assumed as facts of life and hence relegated to the background.

But the French image was more multifaceted than the English. Alongside the aura cast by the gallant warrior and the tempestuous spitfire was another dimension that praised French republicanism. To many Americans, the French stood almost alone in the interwar period as an egalitarian island in a European ocean of aristocratic privilege. Thus the hero of the second *Seventh Heaven* (1937) stressed his insignificance even as he did his patriotic duty. In the original *Seventh Heaven* there was a strong proletarian theme, extending to forms of address such as "citizen" and "comrade" among French enlisted men. Apart from its love story, this twice-told tale of a French street-cleaner and his girl won praise from critics for its depiction of the common people of France at war.

The American view favored the Gaul as a sort of democratic radical. He could be touched with proletarian wisdom, as was the hero of *Seventh Heaven,* or he could be a more cerebral leftist, as was *The Man Who Reclaimed His Head*. The title role in the latter film was that of a radical French journalist with pacifist leanings. But it was *Surrender,* with its direct contrasting of the French and German images, that outlined France most sharply. It was true, the picture asserted, that the French nation was a melee of disorganization, but its people could and would fight when given cause. "France has no knowledge of efficiency," crustily declared an aristocratic Prussian. "It is her greatest weakness." The French hero, however, more than compensated for this failing. Throughout the film he proudly described himself in turn as an engineer, a republican, and a sergeant. As the script put it, he was "young, handsome, impulsive and gay"– words that might have fit almost any French movie character of the interwar years. But underlying all this bonhomie was a proud attachment to egalitarianism. To his German girl, the Frenchman conveyed his deepest sentiments. "You're an aristocrat and a Prussian–I a Frenchman and an enemy. You think, from your proud eminence, that I and my kind are dirt. . . ."[20]

Here was the more serious but still flattering side of the French image. It reached beyond futility to tragedy in *The Road to Glory*. This picture concerned itself with members of a French unit facing certain death by obeying orders to stand their ground. Some critics thought the film ambiguous, one calling it "neither patriotic poppycock or (sic) pacifistic preachment."[21] Yet *The Road to Glory* marked the inclusion of the French with the British and the Germans as victims of a war grown meaningless and absurd.

Not as one-dimensional as the English image, the French image on American screens was likewise not as strong. While the French could be admired for their irrepressible enjoyment of life, the suspicion existed that they might take things a little too casually. Theirs were the laughter, the tantrums, the passionate love affair–more sober themes generally were the property of the English and the Germans. Fully as patriotic as any nationality, Frenchmen were nevertheless fiery rather than resolute, people who were more comfortable on the boulevards than in the trenches. They lacked the sense of superior class which illuminated Prussian arrogance and English duty, and they reveled in their republicanism. This was a congenial theme to American audiences, and it made the postwar view of the French fully as popular as had the hands-across-the-sea historicism of the war years.

iv

The Russian image was clouded if not obscure. The historical bonds that existed between America, Britain, and France largely were lacking in the case of Russia. In addition, it was wellknown in this country that Russia was the most autocratic of all the Allied nations. It thus seemed that Russian aristocrats led by the knout rather than by example, as did their English brothers. Likewise, the fervent republicanism of the French seemed beyond echo in the Russian experience. Complicating the situation was the Russian Revolution, which tended to confuse moviemakers to whom the damnation of autocracy and the celebration of democracy had become almost instinctive.

Siegfried Kracauer found that in later films about Russia Hollywood indicated little concern for Russian reality. "American screen portrayals of Russians conform to what Americans imagine faraway Russians to be like," he remarked. "Russia is far off."[22] The Russian image in American films of World War I probably was no more distorted than that of the English or the French, but it was more ambiguous. This was due not to any lack of geographical propinquity, but to the historical passage of Russia from autocratic monarchy to constitutional government to revolutionary anarchy to nonhereditary dictatorship in less than twenty years. The confusion attendant on this rapid change was reflected in American films.

As early as 1915, R. R. McCormick of the *Chicago Tribune* sponsored documentaries of the Russian armies in action. The czarist aspect of Russian political and social organization was overlooked in favor of emphasizing Russia's contribution to the alliance. Some films even imaginatively pictured a democratic Russia. *Under False Colors,* made as the Kerensky government teetered on the brink of disaster, featured the "Princess Olga" leading her country's fight for freedom. In a grimly ironic denouement, the main supporter of the successful Russian revolutionists was revealed to be an American millionaire.

The onset of revolution initiated some paeans to democracy like *Under False Colors,* but it also led to movies which depicted a Russia shattered by German propaganda. Donald C. Thompson of *Leslie's Weekly* was an old Russian hand who had made Russian visits in 1907, 1915, and 1916. He returned about November, 1917, from his latest trip with film of his journeys. These scraps were pieced together and given lurid titles such as *Bloodstained Russia, German Intrigue,* and *Treason and Revolt.* Eventually Thompson's footage was made into *The German Curse in Russia.* "The world believes Russia sold out her Allies knowingly," Thompson declared, "but my camera will show that it was the German propaganda of lies that undermined this great country." His imagery was very much like that used later by Winston Churchill when the British leader likened the German-assisted entry of Lenin into Russia as the injection of a plague bacillus into a living organism. "When the Russians forget politics and German propaganda," ran one of Thompson's titles, "they are more than a match for the Germans."[23]

The Thompson film was praised as fact, not fiction. Advertisements boasted it as "the real story of the Russian revolution."[24] An industry publication suggested that exhibitors arrange free morning performances for school children and drape theater lobbies with American and Russian flags.[25] *The German Curse in Russia* received wide distribution, giving credence to the notion that the Romanovs had fallen through no action of their own.

German intrigue was seen as not the only cause of the revolution. Conveniently ideal in dramatic terms was the *éminence grise* of the monk Rasputin. Contemporary with other films that sought to analyze or idealize the revolution came *Rasputin, the Black Monk.* This film portrayed the *starets* as the complete sexual athlete, a voracious lover who spent more time in the boudoirs of the royal palace than in advising the Czar. The holy man's connection with the revolution appeared very vague indeed. Yet the picture intimated that with the shadow of Rasputin gone, Russia was saved. It ended with Kerensky persuading the Duma to remain in session, while the Czar was arrested and exiled. "The day of Russia's long-sought freedom dawns clear and bright," exulted one reviewer.[26]

Rasputin, the Black Monk was greeted with loud enthusiasm at its New York opening by an audience which included many Russians.[27] The first night was so crowded that police reserves had to be summoned to bring order. Several reviewers commented on the veracity of the film. Its reception seemed to indicate that many Americans as well as Russian emigrés thought political and social reforms, if not revolution, were long overdue within the Romanov domains.

At the same time that World's William Brady was presenting *Rasputin, the Black Monk,* director Herbert Brenon of the Fox organization was making *The Fall of the Romanoffs*. This film also centered on Rasputin. "Whatever Rasputin's responsibility for the revolution in history," soberly commented *The New York Times,* "there is no doubt that his dramatic career lends itself excellently to the purposes and requirements of the movie director."[28] Brenon, like D. W. Griffith, quoted "reliable sources" from time to time to help give the touch of authenticity to his picture. Brenon drew on the experiences of a renegade Russian named Sergius Truvanov, who as "Father Iliodor" had played a tangential role in the early days of the revolution. Truvanov played himself in the film, and wound up exposing Rasputin's plot to dominate Russia through the Czar and Czarina. *The Fall of the Romanoffs* was given a posh premiere in the grand ballroom of the Ritz-Carlton Hotel before 600 guests. Brady was in attendance, and he made several disparaging remarks about Brenon's work compared to the World release. The battle of words culminated in a short fist fight between the two in the hotel lobby, more an indication of the nature of the film industry than of the merit of either picture.

Rasputin continued to intrigue American moviemakers. The unhappy postwar American intervention in Russian affairs and the establishment of the Bolshevik state made it all the more important to pinpoint scapegoats. Rasputin was perfect for such a role. He made another bow in 1933 in *Rasputin and the Empress,* a film which was plagued by production difficulties and finished in four months at a cost of a million dollars. In spite of the presence of three Barrymores–Lionel as Rasputin, Ethel as the Czarina, and John as "Prince Chegodieff," the picture received poor reviews and ended slightly in the red. Charles MacArthur, who wrote the script, remarked that on film the Czar and Czarina "became Mr.and Mrs.Hoover." The picture's preface read: "This concerns the destruction of an empire, brought about by the mad ambition of one man. A few of the characters are still alive. The rest met death by violence." One of the "characters still alive" sued MGM for libel. The case eventually was settled out of court. Part of this mishmash was the plot of the film itself–turgid, incredible, and in parts simple nonsense. Richard Watts of the *New York Herald Tribune* wrote that it achieved one feat: it managed to libel even Rasputin.[29]

Apart from the unfriendly depiction of Russia's leaders and their advisers, the Russian people tended to be treated as a vast herd which dimly recognized the benefits of democracy and which should be guided in that direction by more advanced nations. But they were ill-served by their leaders. Even Kerensky, in *British Agent,* was presented as a vain autocrat. Further, Russians shared with Germans a primeval and warlike past. In the first *Hotel Imperial,* for instance, Russian soldiers from the general on down were indicted as womanizers, looters, and drunkards. *Captured!* featured a Russian prisoner who became a rapist-killer, and *Noah's Ark* contained a villainous Russian who welcomed the coming of war. Once in a while a *femme fatale* would pierce this image, as did the beautiful Constance Bennett, who played a Russian spy in *After Tonight*. There was also room for Ruritanian romance, given the right casting. Fans of John Barrymore could see The Profile as a Russian peasant (?!) riding the rollercoaster of revolution in *Tempest* (1928). But most of the time the Russian symbolized a heavy coarseness coupled with a quasi-oriental sense of mystery.

These pictures, all made between 1927 and 1934, did little to endear the new Soviet state to American audiences. Stalin had consolidated his hold on the Soviet party apparatus by this time. While the excesses of enforced collectivization and the first five-year plan were not immediately known in the West, many Americans were appalled at Lincoln Steffens's comment describing the Soviet Union as a model for development. The heavy hand of dictatorship began to be seen as indistinct from Czarist autocracy. Sensationalizing Russian authoritarianism, in either guise, and slandering common Russians concurrently, gave ominous undertones to what was at best the ambiguous treatment of a former ally. The economic and engineering assistance given Russia by the United States, which drew the two countries toward the American recognition of the Soviet state in 1933, was a trend ignored by American film.

The idealized Russian peasant soldier. Chester Morris and Betty Compson in *The Case of Sergeant Grischa* (1930).

There was nevertheless a brief thaw in the Russian image. It marked an interim point between the hopeful criticism of the old Russia and the realization that the

Soviet Union was not exactly a workers' paradise. The picture was *The Case of Sergeant Grischa,* directed by Brenon. Brenon's soft touch made the film fail to have the impact of either *All Quiet on the Western Front* or *Journey's End,* both produced in the same year. But the story of a simple Russian soldier mistakenly executed by a bumbling military bureaucracy was a departure from type. This thaw, however, did not impress America's left-wing press. The *New Masses* critic complained that "sympathy with a single plight or individual case is not sufficient when mass plights, social agonies, human debacles thunder."[30]

The thaw did not last. *British Agent,* which appeared in 1934, indicated that the new Soviet state was as unattractive to moviemakers as had been its autocratic predecessor. The plot, although ostensibly based on the wartime experiences of British diplomat R. H. Bruce Lockhart, was sheer hokum. It has a British diplomat, during the days of Allied intervention in Russia, fall in love with no less than Lenin's secretary. Although not essentially a war picture, *British Agent* looked backward to the czarist era and was firmly anti-Soviet. While one reviewer saw "the suggestion of a great brave shaking of the world underlying the whole,"[31] the film was not appreciative of Russia's new masters. The Brest-Litovsk Treaty was regarded as high treachery on the part of the Soviets, and the revolutionary rabble were depicted as "uncouth murderers of the innocent." Scenes of the brutality of the Cheka were shown, and the hero summarized everything by calling Russia a "traitor nation."[32] In short, the days when Russia as a wartime ally sought a just democratic society had vanished.

v

Postwar American screen views of the three main wartime allies diverged sharply. In part this was due to the maxim that politics, and particularly wartime international politics, produces strange bedfellows. It was also due to the notion that each of three countries reacted differently to the democratic impulse, that most cherished of American ideals. The English responded nobly, lessening class differences and serving willingly in the crisis. The French, while proudly egalitarian, were not so profound, preferring the earthly pleasures to rigorous idealism. The Russians, never highly regarded to begin with, betrayed their revolutionary chance for democratic government. As a result it was the English who carried home the laurels, followed closely by the French. The Russians trailed along, a distant and uncertain third.

American films reflected the strong historical bonds connecting the United States with both England and France. The necessarily simplistic approach of film to complex details of national character inevitably glossed over certain aspects of the Allied nations to concentrate on others. So it was that the English maintained their customary stiff upper lip and strong sense of social obligation; the French appeared as both merrily sexual and fiercely patriotic; and the Russians, in the end, merely sacrificed one set of brutal overlords only to be burdened with another. These images of "in-group" nations were not necessarily more accurate than those of Germany, but they were friendlier. Even the early treatment accorded Russia was cautiously optimistic. Such kindness would not fall to her lot again until the halcyon days of World War II, with films like *Mission to Moscow* and *North Star*.

All of these films point to several attitudes held by a considerable portion of American audiences. The anti-democratic tendencies of Russia, like those of Germany, were despised and ridiculed. Also, the French attitude toward war might evoke a certain envy, but not emulation. Finally, and most admired, was the ability of the English to suffer through nobly. It is significant that no film of the stature of *Cavalcade* appeared to sing the glories of the French or Russian character. A unity in war, the image of the Ally fragmented readily into vastly different components with the coming of peace.

12

We Ourselves: The Image of the Home Front

i

In its efforts to put the war on film, the American motion picture industry did not neglect the people at home. The perfection of the doughboy in performing his duty by defending his flag and capturing or killing Germans was duplicated by the folks he left behind. The call for patriotic sacrifice extended far beyond the Ardennes; it sounded in stateside training camps, public rallies, and in bond drives. The call crossed the doorstep of American homes and filtered into the commonalities of family life. The films that trumpeted forth the summons to participate reflected "reality" to the extent that they were both spurred on by the national war effort and sought to subsume the entire populace in that effort. They provided a firm index to the attitudes and ideals of a home front at war.

Many films issued during 1915-1917 had pressured American audiences to dedicate themselves to strengthening the country's defenses. One example from the many concerned the Triangle Film Corporation, which decreed that advertising for its production *The Flying Torpedo* be built around "preparedness" rather than "war features." The picture dealt with an invention which repelled an unnamed invader of the Pacific Coast in 1921. Triangle attacked the "peace-at-any-price man" and suggested that *The Flying Torpedo* could give exhibitors a chance to declare "Patriotism Week" at their theaters. According to the company, the government cooperated wholeheartedly in the promotion of the film by establishing recruiting stations in movie houses, lending actual torpedoes for exhibition, and arranging patriotic parades.[1] Here, as in so many other instances, films by offering their version of "reality" actually generated it.

By 1917, audiences were used to cinematic appeals to their loyalty, patriotism, and spirit of self-sacrifice. With the coming of the crisis, fully as much attention was paid to the home front as to the boys overseas. Not surprisingly, almost all of the films that created an image of the home front were produced in the years 1917-1919. As the external threat vanished, so too did the image invented to combat that threat. American attitudes turned inward upon the nation itself afford an opportunity to study through film the sacred ideals of a country at war. These ideals, while not necessarily accurate, were nonetheless so widespread on film as to indicate their popular acceptance.

Essential to the image was the notion of the value of hard work for the cause. No one was exempt from demands upon his devotion. The final title of *America's Answer* was addressed to home audiences and congratulated them on the fruits of their labor that they had just seen transmogrified on screen into mighty weapons of war. Both the government and private producers poured out miles of film destined for domestic consumption which showed the nation flexing its industrial muscles. Typical was the short documentary *The Making of Hundred Ton Guns,* filmed at the federal arsenal in Watervliet, New York. "These grimy, unknown men...hold in their hands the defense of the nation," ran the fulsome praise.[2] *Over Here* showed the building of a cantonment at Fort Pike, Arkansas, to house 40,000 men. The project took fifty-two days. The film that recorded its progress impressed one reviewer with the magnitude of the cantonment and the speed with which it was completed.[3] The Committee on Public Information ceaselessly ground out short subjects on almost anything connected with the war, from the making of fuses to Navy torpedo boats zipping through their exercises. Home participation was encouraged by the filming of innumerable parades and titles boasting of the number of pledges gained to support various war-connected causes.

Aiding the war effort could mean more than holding down a simple war-industry job. Films such as *Home Defense,* which chided the ineptitude of the Home Defense organizations, were rare because the war was seen as serious business. More common were pictures like *For the Freedom of the World,* which left no stone unturned in its attempt to inspire dedication and hard work. Audiences were invited to heed the lessons learned at great cost by other nations, with Belgium and France being the favorite examples.

Moviegoers received exhortations to pull in the belt and think of the boys overseas. *The Patriot,* featuring the Broadway favorites Mr. and Mrs. Sidney Drew, was a lighthearted look at the problems of conserving food. "The picture will make an excellent comic number for a patriotic program," said an industry publication, "for, in spite of its comedy, it carries a real lesson."[4] More sober was *The Food Gamblers,* which labeled commodities speculators as traitors. This picture, although not directly concerned with the war, contained a strong strain of muckraking progressivism promoting wartime austerity. The same emphasis appeared in *The Profiteers,* made after the Armistice.

The primary concern still remained the fighting man. Films were devoted to his recruitment and training in addition to depicting his eventual heroism under fire. *Pettigrew's Girl* was standard. It told of the romantic misadventures of a Southern recruit in a Northern training camp. Usually, however, moviemakers waited until the Armistice to make comedies about training-camp life, such as *23½ Hours Leave.* Every effort instead was directed toward giving encouragement to those who would see actual combat. *Joan of Plattsburg* was a one-girl den mother for the raw recruits of the New York camp. Inspired by reading the story of Joan of Arc, the young lady casually rounded up a spy ring between rounds of entertaining the boys. In *Johanna Enlists*, a young girl helped inject enthusiasm into the men of a training camp established near her father's farm. This Mary Pickford release was greeted cordially. The only offense, *The New York Times* ominously remarked, was the appearance of several matinee idols in uniform.[5]

It was up to the female nobly to bear the brunt of home front sacrifice while her man was away. Problems of women left alone were examined in a trivial way by Cecil B. De Mille's *Till I Come Back To You*. D. W. Griffith's *The Girl Who Stayed at Home* applauded feminine courage as it sought to popularize the draft. The women were not allowed to sulk passively, either. Their role was that of active participation in the war effort. The heroine of *Doing Our Bit* scoured urban slums to recruit soldiers and economize on war materials. In *Her Country's Call* a young girl made a career of taking male jobs, freeing men for military activity. Nor were women confined to nonmilitary tasks. Mrs. Irene Castle, one-half of the famed dance team, organized her own army in *Patria*. The daughter of a munitions contractor formed a "Girls' Aviation Corps" in *Her Country First* and managed to catch a gang of spies in the bargain.

Probably the height of selfless dedication to duty came with *The Gown of Destiny*, a picture whose unintentional humor pointed up the extremes to which the motion picture industry would go in urging everyone to do his part. A male dress designer was considered unfit for military service. He thereupon devoted himself to "creating beautiful things." One of the designer's dresses so inspired a man who saw his girl wearing it that he wasted no time getting to the recruiting station.

Literally everyone was encouraged to "do his bit" by the film industry. From babes in arms to octogenarians, from fey dress designers to the most manly exemplars of democratic virtue, all were included in a vast consensus vis-à-vis the purpose of the war. Films of the home front tried to fasten a unity of purpose onto one of the most heterogenous of nations, and to a considerable extent they were successful. Their success, that is, their continuance as economic products, reflected an audience acquiescence in both wartime goals and patriotic ideals. The crisis of war seemed compelling enough for the cinema to insist that no one be allowed to shirk the cause of the moment. Devotion to the central aim of winning the war was rewarded; deviation from this goal was punished. The long months of preparedness advocation reached fruition in these pictures of domestic America at war.

ii

In a democracy, none could shrink from the task at hand. Films such as *18 to 45* went to great lengths to show that the draft was the most equitable method of apportioning military service. It was a tautology that pacifism was tantamount to draft-dodging. The pacifist was the primary non-alien target for the film industry. He was despised and ridiculed without mercy. Even some films made prior to American entry had taken this tack. In *Perkins' Peace Party*, for example, a simpleminded peace advocate and a friend drove a symbolic Model T to New York City with the purpose of sailing to Europe to stop the war. After several bungling adventures, the two decided to return home. "Perkins never again attempted to interfere with the war in Europe," the film condescendingly ended. "He decided that the best thing to do was to remain at his own fireside."[6]

A standard plot line featured the conversion of pacifists into militant defenders of liberty. *Draft 258* concerned a girl and her two brothers. The elder brother spoke out against the draft and inevitably (so strong was the tautology) became entangled with a crew of the Kaiser's spies. Finally he was made to see the light, and he and his brother received the plaudits of their sister as they marched off to war. A conscientious objector likewise underwent a change to willing warrior in *The Man Without a Country*. Douglas Fairbanks, rising fast to the heights of popularity, lent his all-American charm to another anti-pacifist picture, *In-Again, Out-Again*. Fairbanks was able to convince his pacifist girl friend that her ideological mates were secretly peddling war supplies to the enemy. This picture centered on the munitions industry in New Jersey, a topical choice since the region had been experiencing sabotage. Pacifists were caricatured as senile dreamers meeting under a picture of William Jennings Bryan. The brash impetuosity of the Fairbanks screen character was played off against these doddering milquetoasts. Audiences loved such Fairbanks quotes as "Your puny, pussyfooting policies are pulling the punch out of Preparedness!"[7] He was a younger, more blithe Teddy Roosevelt come to the screen. One of Fairbanks's biographers has called him a "popular philosopher" during the years 1917-1920.[8] The phrase aptly described his role in *In-Again, Out-Again*, where he acted out the growing anti-pacifist convictions of his audience.

Some of the films condemning nonmilitancy were by today's standards exceptionally cruel. In *Over There*, for example, a congenital coward who fainted at the sight of blood was shamed into enlisting when his ex-fiancée handed him a white feather. She finally realized he was a "real man" when he returned the feather stained red with the blood he had shed heroically in France.[9] Other offerings reached the incredible to make a point. The tramp-hero of *An Honest Man* was rejected when he offered himself for military duty. After a Horatio Alger deed of returning $50,000 to its rightful owner, the tramp became a soldier.

The stigma of the draft dodger corrupted everything around him. *Shame* was the story of the disgrace shadowing the family of such a creature. A slacker tried to seduce a woman whose husband was in France in *The Other Man's Wife*, but the villain received his just deserts in the finale. There was even a *Mrs. Slacker*. Her cowardly husband had married her merely to claim exemption from the draft. Ashamed, his wife donned a uniform, stumbled upon a German plot to dynamite a reservoir, and inspired her husband to "be a real fellow after all."[10] The same material was used in *The Slacker*. The last scene showed the reformed cad departing in khaki as his patriotic wife bid him good-bye through her tears.

It often took a woman to put backbone into a spineless coward. A Red Cross worker succeeded in getting her brother to enlist in *For Valour*, while a girl shamed her supposed husband into uniform in *The Service Star*. The latter film had a mother hiding her son from the draft. But other mothers heroically accepted the loss of their sons in battle, as did the Gold Star matrons of *We Can't Have Everything*. This was a typically vacuous but successful De Mille production involving a romance between a soldier and a Red Cross worker. De Mille knew a good plot when he had one, and he soon repeated himself with *For Better, For Worse*. The twist in this one had a woman refuse to marry a pediatrician when he chose to care for crippled children rather than go into combat. Instead, she married a man who went to war, but all ended satisfactorily. The doctor's predicament (he really wanted to enlist) was treated sympathetically. The picture was not released until April, 1919, a fact that the canny De Mille probably took into account when he created the character of the doctor. Yet the film was true to the times in giving the women of the home front suitable patriotic fervor.

Beyond loyal and courageous women stood America's children. An indulgent nation watched approvingly as its youth provided examples worth emulating. Today these films seem like the most vicious kind of manipulation of young innocence, but during the war they were taken in stride. There was the chance for kids in uniform to show their stuff, as in *Boy Scouts to the Rescue,* a serial which included a sequence of German spies succumbing to the intrepid youngsters. If the local scout unit was lacking, a boy could always organize his own Home Defense unit, as did *Bobby of the Home Defenders*. The young hero of this film performed his duty well after being rejected by army recruiters, who told him he could best serve his country by keeping an eye on the pacifists. His activities so shamed his parents that they became staunch patriots. Then there was Bud of *Bud's Recruit,* who set a worthy example for his elder brother by trying to enlist.

Nor were little girls less devoted to the cause. The Lee twins, moppet stars of the Fox organization, encouraged a suspected slacker to do the right thing in *Smiles*. For added effect, they assisted the hero in capturing German plans. The twins were at it again in *Doing Their Bit,* in which they provided examples of self-sacrifice for their elders. Here the villain was the "decadent son of a society leader," and the hero was an honest workman in a munitions factory.[11] Child actors often were used to urge men to enlist, as was the little heroine of *The Volunteer*. Madge Evans played herself in this film, taking the platform at a recruiting rally to plead for volunteers. The depth of this trend were attained when children were given vicious emotions to parade on screen. A toddler in *Dolly Does Her Bit* advised her neighborhood pals to shame their fathers and brothers who were still at home, while she herself aided the Red Cross. Even more cruel was *A Little Patriot*. Here a child, after imagining she was Joan of Arc, urged her friends to spit on those whose fathers were slackers. She led her own father to the recruiting station and returned home to organize her schoolmates into a military company. Needless to say, her band of little patriots ended by capturing a spy.

Certainly these pictures of the home front projected an image which was sharp and clear. Most importantly, everyone was expected to support the cause. For those who did not, there remained the choice of reform or of universal execration. The cardinal sin was the refusal to be involved—the reason for refusal was irrelevant. In the lexicon of the film world, pacifism was synonymous with cowardice. Any deviation from the norm was considered criminal in both a moral and legal sense. Any punishment suited such trespasses, the harsher the better. In this regard the motion picture industry proved itself to be perhaps the most intolerant of the mass media, none of which won medals for the dispassionate relaying of information or attitudes.

It was significant that the motion picture image of the home front was all-inclusive. Film synthesized the national will to fight in simple and well-defined terms. Continued audience toleration of such trite themes indicated a strong national consensus in favor of the cinema's version of "reality." Since the synthesis included both sexes, all ages, and virtually every important ethnic group (even, at times, the German-Americans), deviancy tended to stand out. The solidarity of the home front was composed of a wall of celluloid armor reinforced by the sense of external crisis. The crisis was permitted to become internal as well, both because dramatic convention demanded it and because of the notion that the depiction of skulduggery close to home would help to close the ranks even more.

iii

As it turned out, the legion of spies, turncoats, and pacifists that infested movie America from 1917 to 1919 were after material things. They were bent on either appropriation or destruction. To begin with, the screen world was populated with inventors, each one having created a miraculous super-weapon of war. Initially, these weapons were deemed too awful for anyone to have at his command. Thus *War O'Dreams,* made in 1915, was concerned with a powerful explosive called "Trixite." The deadly stuff could be guided to its civilian targets by "ether waves"–not a bad anticipation of today's homing devices. The inventor was grateful when he found that his horrible creation had only been a dream. But inventors rapidly took sides, placing their brain children at the service of nationalism. The Triangle Company bragged about its accurate depiction of the scientific accouterments to war featured in *Shell 43*. Patriotic men and patriotic boys, the company felt, would find alike that the film had "educational value."[12] The explosive in *The Greatest Power*, created by two lovers, was named "Exonite." The woman wanted the United States to have the weapon, but the man, a pacifist, resisted. The upshot was this blurb from an industry publication: "Conrad, disgusted at the methods of the alien spy (Bernard), gives his consent to have Miriam offer the formula to the government. The complete understanding is followed by an early marriage."[13]

Film was suited perfectly to presenting secret formulas, magic industrial processes, and miracle inventions. *The Secret of the Submarine* was a serial which described a marvelous method for drawing oxygen from sea water to allow for indefinite operation beneath the waves. Another serial, *My Country First,* cast Germans as villains even before America declared war. Enemy agents were trying to obtain "the most wonderful explosive in the world," which a young inventor was trying to offer to the United States.[14] Needless to say, the fadeout saw the explosive in the hands of the government and the girl in the arms of the inventor.

With the coming of war, the possession of inventions which could be put to military use became even more critical. In *The Kaiser's Shadow* an American laboratory whiz concocted a "ray rifle" that became a bone of contention between German and American agents, with the inevitable ending. *Wolves of Kultur,* a popular serial, turned the tables by having a man and woman successfully pursue the German inventor of a new torpedo. All this flummery about super-weapons revealed that Americans took an inordinate pride in their inventiveness and originality; it should not be forgotten that Thomas Edison was himself a motion picture pioneer. The syndrome was so prevalent that it even could be parodied, a rarity during the war years. Mack Sennett made a contribution with *An International Sneak,* a slapstick comedy involving a new high explosive. *The War Bride of Plumville* was a satire of munitions profiteering. It dealt with enemy war contractors unsuccessfully attempting to muscle in on the "Plumville Iron Works," which turned out to be a producer of cast-iron hitching posts. The common ingredient in all these films, whether serious thrillers or incongruous farces, was that the powerful weapon, if it existed, ended up in the possession of the government, ostensibly destined for satisfactory use against the enemy.

Few pictures were concerned with the preservation of life itself, as opposed to the protection of material goods. An exception was *Love and the Law,* in which one of New York's finest foiled the attempt of saboteurs to blow up a troop train. Generally articles of war were more precious. The prize in *Her Country's Call* was a cache of ammunition saved at the last moment from Mexican desperadoes. Munitions manufacturers, who later were to become cherished whipping boys for the movie industry, were seen during the war years as patriotic servants. Thomas Ince's melodramatic *Claws of the Hun* showed an American munitioneer and his son grappling with sundry German spies. The son, who had not been allowed by his mother to enlist, was derided as a slacker by fiancée and friends alike. He nevertheless exposed the spy ring and was permitted to go to war, the manufacture of munitions once again proceeding unhindered.

Moviemakers proved adept at bringing topical subjects to the screen. For a while, the nation worried over the threat of shipyard sabotage. *Alias Mike Moran* was the story of a draft dodger who hired a man to substitute for him in the trenches. Eventually the slacker found work in a shipyard, regained his manhood, and redeemed himself in France. J. Stuart Blackton's *Safe For Democracy* turned out to be a sermon on how to avert the destruction of the country's shipyards. Blackton, ever sensitive to the temper of the times, retitled this post-Armistice release *Life's Greatest Problem* and issued ads describing it not as a war story, but as "an echo of the war."[15] In this case the villains were IWW agitators, who throughout the war were pictured as the equivalent of alien saboteurs. *The Road to France* was a typical mélange of patriotic shipyard work endangered by outside forces. Witness this plot outline:

> Tom Whitney, well connected but a social derelict because of his weakness for drink, is released from the draft because of an old football injury, but a policeman persuades him that he can still do his bit in the shipyards. He takes a job in the yard owned by the man to whose daughter he was engaged in happier times. Three German propagandists seek to foment a strike to delay the work, and largely through Tom's efforts the plan goes amiss and the strike is called off. Rehabilitated by work, the launching of the *Liberty* is a forecast of his own rebirth.[16]

Equally topical was the concern over the German nautical menace. A popular serial with unconnected episodes called *Grant, Police Reporter* contained a sequence about a German submarine base in New England. *As in a Looking Glass* had a hero dedicated to supplying the United States with a superior navy and a villian conspiring to secure the plans for the enlarged fleet. Then there was *The Hero of Submarine D-2,* who ruined a plot by German agents to destroy an American naval installation.

The submarine constituted for many citizens an unknown but deadly weapon with assumed capabilities far beyond its actual powers. Thus the intrepid reporter Grant was confronting a towering menace in the middle of New England. The stealthy and secretive operations of the submarine made for popular if farfetched drama. German spies were caught sending messages to a submarine off the coast of Oregon in *Over Secret Wires,* an early production that had no hesitation about identifying the enemy. Another German spy (presumably the country was permeated with them) was found signaling to U-boats off the shores of New England in *Daughter Angele.* This one, however, proved to be an American traitor in the employ of the Fatherland.

The war could not be waged without precious metals, so moviemakers also gave attention to the danger of subversion in the nation's mines. An average handsome New York millionaire was the innocent dupe of Enemy Agents in *Love in a Hurry.* Unknowingly selling them precious titanium, the patriotic plutocrat was forced to pursue them to England in order to give them their just deserts. Cowboy star Tom Mix was pressed into service in *Mr. Logan, USA,* in which spies posed as cowboys in an attempt to destroy valuable tungsten mines. Mix, perhaps because he was able to detect Teutonic accents beneath the bandannas, was able to squelch the threat with his customary flair. A Western mine, the resources of which were not revealed, was the focus of spy activity in *The Spirit of '17.* Mary Pickford's brother Jack, in the central role, had little difficulty in enlisting the aid of residents of a veterans' home in rounding up the Germans.

Lumber also was vital to the war effort. *The Source* cast the popular Wallace Reid as a "well-born man who has become a drunkard." Shanghaied to a Vermont lumber camp, he asserted his manhood by opening a dam closed by "German influences." In this case the reward was beyond even that usually given to home front heroes. Reid won not only the girl, but a place in the lumber business and a check for $20,000. German agents even conspired to wreak havoc on sugar-cane plantations in Hawaii, perhaps trying to bring America to her knees by denying her sweets. The film *The Marriage Ring* was a routine romance which ended with the cane fields safe for Uncle Sam.

Through its movie cameras, the American public saw itself successfully resisting all onslaughts on its domestic riches. German agents, no matter how sly their plans or how nefarious their purposes, invariably came to grief when confronted by staunch heroes and heroines. The plots of films showing the dedicated defense of brilliant inventions, munitions plants, shipyards, naval bases, mines, and lumber camps were more than dramatic clichés. They showed those items Americans regarded as most necessary to the waging of the war. If people were expendable (unless they happened to be the leading man or leading lady), things were not.

This accent on materialism comes as no surprise. But the combinations of materialism and idealism displayed in these pictures of the home front illuminated two contrasting facets of the American character which seem to fuse successfully only in time of war. Ideals could be maintained at a fever pitch only by making the threat immediate, and this could be done only by placing the enemy in the very laps of the folks at home. For a time, it must have seemed that there were more Germans operating in the United States than in France.

iv

With official government agencies joining in hysterical spy hunts during the war, it was little wonder that the film industry cheerfully parlayed the mania into a source of lucre. The British had foreshadowed the symptoms as early as 1915, and the idea that a Prussian fifth column lay waiting for the right moment rapidly became widespread in the United States.[17]

The obvious source for a fifth column was the German-American community. The government itself was nervous about the situation and sponsored a film called *The Immigrant* (1915), which sought to instill patriotism in citizens of German background.[18] This ameliorative approach, with few exceptions, went by the boards in 1917. German-Americans headed filmdom's list of domestic suspects and indeed were often indistinguishable from native German agents. *The Spy,* a prototype, attempted to lay bare the German government's spy network in this country in a highly melodramatic manner. It came complete with false whiskers, sliding wall panels, and other indispensable apparatus of cinematic espionage. The opening night audience was enthralled.

Once an internal danger was recognized, it made little difference, in dramatic terms, whether that danger originated from alien or domestic sources. *The Prussian Cur,* an early effort by director Raoul Walsh, caused a sensation which eventually led to its withdrawal from exhibition. The most offensive scenes were those showing "loyal Americans," hooded and robed in the style of the Ku Klux Klan, attacking "pro-Germans."[19] A few German-Americans emerged as heroes, but only in contrast to other and disloyal German-Americans. *Me und Gott* focused on a former Prussian officer who incongruously had gravitated to the ownership of a delicatessen in Hoboken. The martinet demanded that his son, a hard-working electrician, help him destroy munitions plants. But the boy, a pacifist turned patriotic American, resisted and all ended well. D.W. Griffith, under the pseudonym "Granville Warwick," helped write the story for *The Hun Within,* which pictured the same kind of father-son conflict. Only this time it was the son who became a German agent. The film was well received critically and cleared about $24,000, a fair return for the period.

Clearly, in the moviemakers' scheme of things no one of German descent could be trusted. The idea of the omnipresence of German operatives in the United States inspired many films to "expose" their system. *The Eagle's Eye,* a giant serial of twenty episodes, ran through the entire catalog of German misdeeds. It included defamatory impersonations of Count Von Bernstorff, Captain Franz von Papen, Dr. Heinrich Albert, and Karl Boy-Ed, all recently revealed to the public as plotters against the welfare of the United States. One theater owner in New York City did not show the serial for fear it might offend his German patrons—certainly a rarity for 1918. But this was but a mote in *The Eagle's Eye*. The picture had been produced with government approval and was given a special showing before the Committee on Public Information. A former chief of the Secret Service, William J. Flynn, had written the story and had acted as an adviser on the film. His efforts were lauded at the premiere as "the ideal of patriotic propaganda toward which all active American societies had been striving for the past three years."[20] The threads connecting the serial's episodes were composed of the efforts of a group of patriotic Americans known as the "Criminology Club" to unearth German spies. The club was convinced (and the producers sought to convince viewers) that hundreds of enemy agents were pursuing their heinous purposes throughout the country.

The combination of cloak and dagger (*The Spy*) with pseudo-realism (*The Eagle's Eye*) insured that during the war years American audiences were inundated with a deluge of spy plots. *The Evil Eye* suggested that the Kaiser personally controlled the activity of every agent. *Who Was the Other Man?* invented a "Black Legion" of undercover Germans. Its claim to distinction lay in its presentation of the arch-villain as a turncoat American Secret Service man, something which must not have amused Chief Flynn. Sturdy heroes overcoming shifty multitudes of spies were the familiar staples of pictures like *The Highest Trump, Berlin Via America,* and *I'll Say So*.

Nor did women confine themselves to wrapping bandages and baking cookies when the Boche was at the gate. A French female operative combined with a stern-jawed American agent to get the job done in *The Kaiser's Shadow*. An innocent woman was stigmatized as a spy in *Madam Who?*, but she effortlessly exposed the real spies for the law. *Lafayette, We Come!* went one step further and presented an American girl pretending to be a German agent. And if all this wasn't enough, *Madam Spy* put a government agent in drag to coax the villains into a trap.[21]

Women, by virtue (or handicap) of their sex, could not be counted on to overcome the enemy by themselves. Usually they functioned best with a hefty leading man in tow. Left alone to defend the country, they were sometimes hare-brained enough to be mistaken as enemy agents, as was Billie Burke in *In Pursuit of Polly*. "One is fortunately at liberty to gaze upon Miss Burke instead of thinking about the story," one critic commented acidly.[22] Female innocence was a constant temptation for movie Germans; the heroine of *Shifting Sands* was barely able to resist a German blackmail threat if she did not consent to spy for the Fatherland. Another charmer, herself the daughter of an American agent, almost married an enemy in *Luck and Pluck,* but she was saved at the penultimate moment. The trip to the altar was consummated in *No Man's Land,* where the girl unknowingly married a German spy, one Henry Miller (already revealed to the audience as "Heinrich Mueller"). Mueller was even more shifty than the average home-front antagonist, since he employed "celestial servants" to do his dirty work—alas, to no avail.[23]

A girl clearly had to be careful with whom she fell in love. Ethel Barrymore quickly renounced her lover in *The Greatest Power* upon learning of his duplicity. The young wife of a Senator was suspected falsely of being a double agent in *Secret Code,* thus compromising her husband. The real spy was another woman. *Suspicion* was a morality tale aimed at women whose husbands were involved in war work. Its story was of a lonely wife unwittingly romancing a would-be saboteur.

The inevitable end of those who succumbed to Teutonic blandishments was presented in *Wife or Country*. Here the wife of a high-ranking member of the Justice Department became entangled with German agents. A genteel death by way of poison was her reward.

In the world of film, almost anyone old enough to tell secret plans from knitting instructions could be an enemy hireling. These blackguards, men or women, were found in the highest reaches of government and in the most remote locales of rural America. They could be friends, relatives, or lovers. At times they were husbands or wives. All of this, by the standards of the time, made for cracking good drama, but it also helped to darken the image of the home front with the shadow of paranoia.

v

As the tides of crisis receded, the image of the home front dissolved. The crystal clear likeness of the screen version of wartime domestic life vanished overnight. It would not be seen again for two decades. Then, another international menace would give it new life within a different pattern.

At rare intervals in the interwar period pictures were released which included aspects of domestic America at war. But their plots were varied, their box-office success limited, and their concern for weathering a crisis already past was nil. A Belgian refugee unconvincingly prated about self-sacrifice to the home folks in *The Charmer*, shown in 1925. Three years later appeared *A Ship Comes In*, the sentimental story of an immigrant whose son lost his life in the war. Its tone was more that of its contemporary *Four Sons* than of any wartime film.

The following decade produced *Private Jones*, whose acerbic views of the domestic military establishment owed more to depression bitterness than to a sense of historical actuality. An escape in another direction was provided by *Rendezvous*, a picture that gave the *coup de grâce* to the international menace. *Rendezvous* boasted deft and breezy performances by William Powell and Rosalind Russell, Powell as a newspaperman turned cryptographer-lieutenant and Miss Russell as a suffragist. Even the Germans almost faded from the picture; the "bad guys" out to break Washington's codes were scripted as "Marshovians."[24] There was no atmosphere of crisis as the stars went through their paces, only the witty nonchalance of a film which knew it could well afford an attitude of *savoir faire*.

The urgency underlying the image of the home front had vanished long before *Rendezvous* appeared. The pictures that made up the image suggested that a great majority of the American public were both rapid and efficient in closing ranks behind the war effort. Excluded from the domestic consensus were all enemy aliens, most German-Americans, and anyone who did not register wholehearted support for America's war aims. The only explicit exception to this attitude did not appear until 1933, when *Ever in My Heart* presented sympathetically the plight of a naturalized German professor and his American wife. This film weakened its argument, however, by having the professor become a German spy on the western front.

In addition these films, most of which have long since crumbled into celluloid rubble, provided America with a daguerrotype of an ethical system which rapidly was vanishing. The simplistic solutions to internal problems, the caricatures of the slacker, the coward, and the villainous knave, the rewards of political right-thinking and the punishments of ideological agnosticism—all these harked back to a calmer, more measured pace of life. Even as the nation careened into the problems and responsibilities of the twentieth century, its motion picture industry disseminated, for all its heroics and dramatics, wistful attempts to touch the past. It was a past freighted with materialism as well as idealism, but it was a useful past. It was a point of reference from which to repel the spies, saboteurs, and double-agents whom dramatic convention demanded must populate the country.

Civilian life remained the backbone of the democracy. Defense of country began at home, not in France. For the young gentlemen who fought valiantly on foreign fields, the motion picture had only praise and adulation. But the task was no less arduous or demanding for those who stayed at home. The film played its wartime part in internalizing the national will and purpose. It did its job in simple and universal terms and, since no opposition was allowed to appear, its efforts must be judged an unqualified success.

Part V

The Camera Eye: Variations on a Theme

> It is the mothers, wives and maids betrothed, who, neither following the camp nor fighting in battle, constitute at home an army of woman's constancy and love, whose yearning hearts make men brave and patriotic.
> —Grover Cleveland
> (1905)

> Georgie's war was no different from that of the average doughboy–a lot of hardship, a lot of laughs, and a lot of ladies.
> Title insert in
> *A Soldier's Plaything*
> (1930)

13

War and Women

i

"War is a man's business," bitterly remarked the female principal of *The Story of Vernon and Irene Castle*. "Women only do what they're told."[1] Indeed, the common tendency of most cultures is to blot out female roles in time of crisis. Over and over again, cinematic war was presented as the aggregate of male experience. Women were present, of course, but they were there to be worshipped, fought over, defended, or violated. Women were excluded from the final camaraderie that made the threat of death the supreme male adventure. Thus the battling Quirt and Flagg, arms about each other, left their girl and struggled toward the front at the end of *What Price Glory?* The young protagonists of *Wings* were bound together by their common background and the romance of aerial war. And the two *Dawn Patrols*, with their depiction of lasting friendship in the face of almost certain death, remain the classic examples of the persistence of male bonding in crisis.

The friendship, loyalty, and devotion among men provided the staple for dozens of war plots. The test of manhood was not how one behaved toward the opposite sex, but toward one's brothers. The measure of maleness was taken from the relationship which helped to define the friend or the antagonist–not the mother, wife, or sweetheart. Only the rarest films, such as *All Quiet on the Western Front*, escaped this convention. As Karel Reisz perceptively has pointed out, the realistic depiction of death as a meaningless finality rather than a glorious finale tended to make men "break faith with (their) innate instinct of brotherhood."[2]

The traditional role of women in war was one which, for lack of a better term, may be defined as "inspirational passivity." Anthropologist Lionel Tiger has observed that under emotional stress, a community will allow its males to assume the most significant roles. "Adult males and females seeking defense from without or the maintenance of peace and order within respond positively to appropriate males and negatively to virtually all females."[3] Women might be exemplary, but they were seldom complete models for wartime heroism. Nevertheless, they provided males with reasons both for fighting and for fighting like gentlemen. This impossible ideal remained a rallying point from where the war could be viewed in the best possible terms until it was erased by the cynicism of the twenties. The country went to war with women in its hip pocket. Nothing more illuminates this attitude, which a later day has rather unkindly labeled "male chauvinism," than this statement made by former President Grover Cleveland in 1905:

> In actual war it is the men who go to battle, enduring hardship and privation, and suffering disease and death for the cause they follow. They are deservedly praised for bravery and patriotism. It is the mothers, wives and maids betrothed, who, neither following the camp nor fighting in battle, constitute at home an army of woman's constancy and love, whose yearning hearts make men brave and patriotic. They teach from afar lessons of patient fortitude, and transmit through mysterious agencies, to soldiers in the field, the spirit of endurance and devotion. Soldiers who have fought, and those who praise or eulogize them, never forget to accord to woman the noble service of inspiration she has thus wrought with womanly weapons wielded in her appointed place.[4]

Prior to World War I, women themselves (except for those almost universally regarded as eccentrics) did not contest this traditional definition of their wartime role. Feminist Vita Scudder could remark in 1911 that "Most of us. . .hold (war) to be a real value, and still thrill unabashed to martial strains. . . ."

> Even the most recalcitrant grant the value of an army. . . . Military life affords a unique training in the very virtues most needed by a democratic state: humility and self-effacement; courage, and swift power of decision, . . .the qualities of subordination and of leadership. We all hope to foster these qualities through the opportunities of peace, but so far our success is so imperfect that we can hardly disregard the help presented by the crises of war.[5]

Women never were any real impediment to America's going to war. Those few who did protest did not seriously challenge the family structure, regarded by one authority as central to the question of feminine autonomy.[6] More significantly, the vast majority of American women did not question either motive or method in connection with the war.

Organized women, although lukewarm to the European war, rapidly enlisted in the cause once the United States was involved. While America boasted its fair share of militant suffragists, pacifism was not one of their primary concerns. Only the most militant eschewed war work. Most of the leading feminists, such as Carrie Chapman Catt, hoped the war would be a "good argument for suffrage."[7] "Men. . .are as hysterical as women, only they show it in a different way," wrote Mrs. Catt. "Women weep and men fight."[8] This particular logic held that since the war was avowedly for democracy, and since true democracy implied woman suffrage, the war ultimately would be beneficial to American women.

Thus most women shared the male view of women as "natural pacifists," yet they also shared the militant sense of duty and the fervent idealism that animated their male counterparts. It is debatable whether the postwar world saw a reduction in their aroused militancy. With feminism at its "moral pinnacle" in 1920, all opposition seemed overcome. Yet women, once granted a place in public life, were not spectacularly different from men in their opinions on military issues. Jane Addams, for one, was to regret deeply the fact that many female members of Congress enthusiastically supported increased military appropriations.[9] The advances of women in the interwar period can be measured: as an increase in percentage of the labor force, as a small but growing increment in the professions, and in the increased divorce rate. But true feminine autonomy, as the sixties seem to have demonstrated, remained a will-o'-the-wisp.

The motion picture played an integral part in presenting women first in their traditional wartime role and then, as scenarists stretched for dramatic effect, as active participants in the conflict. It is to the movies, as much as to any other medium, that Americans owed the new vision of the partly emancipated woman. If she was not yet sexually free, she was divested of crinolines and scented handkerchiefs. While she was not yet "Rosie the Riveter" of World War II fame, she nevertheless could play a central role in the war effort. War on film was still a "man's business," but some women were losing their passivity and emerging as compatriots in the cause. The fact that women began to serve as adjuncts to a game formerly and exclusively male is one firm index of America's passage into the twentieth century.

ii

The most unwavering image of women in war films was that of the mother. If at times she grieved over her lost soldier boy, her role also was interlaced with the idealization of motherhood as a biological sanctification of the national spirit. Mothers, in fact, ran children a close second in the American lexicon of much-indulged ideal types. The country that could give the world Mother's Day (in 1907) was fully capable of stereotyping its movie Moms to the point of nausea.

Originally, mothers were linked with the fatherland-nation for which they bore sons to fight. Their fertility was sacred and their gentle saintliness revered. But this concept was more European than American. Feminist leaders in the United States tended to emotionalize the mother-child relationship instead of bowing proudly to Mars in the name of national service. Thus Alice Stone Blackwell reacted against the war in Europe by pleading for the "wishes of the mothers" to be heard.[10] In the scale of pacifism versus patriotism, the maternal instinct became doubly utilitarian.

It was as preachers of pacifism that women first reached America's wartime audiences. The culminating and the most sensational film of this kind was Lewis J. Selznick's *War Brides*, produced in 1916 and starring the famous tragedienne Alla Nazimova. Selznick paid his star $1,000 a day for thirty days and figured it was worth it; the picture grossed $300,000. Nazimova's hysterionics were perfectly suited to her role of a peasant wife rebelling against a mythical government's edict to marry and breed children for the army. She committed suicide upon hearing the King declare that war was perpetual. In retaliation, the nation's women took a page from *Lysistrata* and vowed to produce no more children until war was outlawed. *War Brides* was hysterically emotional and generated much debate, but it was rapidly withdrawn from circulation after America declared war.

Patriotism overtook maternal pacifism with *The Battle Cry of Peace*. J. Stuart

The tragedienne Alla Nazimova resists suspiciously Teutonic aggressors in *War Brides* (1916).

Blackton, an old hand at working both sides of a question, smoothly dedicated the book written from the scenario of the film:

> To the Mothers of America. . . . This story is dedicated with respect, reverence and admiration, and with the earnest prayer that their eyes may be opened to the peril which menaces, and will continue to menace, them, their children, and their loved ones, until the present state of "unpreparedness" has been remedied.[11]

Blackton made his point even more blatantly with *Womanhood, the Glory of the Nation,* released just before America went to war. Although moderate reviewers found the film unbelievable,[12] the industry press applauded it as an "inspiring appeal to chivalry."[13] Then there was Thomas E. Dixon's "Loyal Legion of American Women," who enticed enemy sentries away from their posts in *The Fall of a Nation.* In films such as these, femininity and nationhood were virtually inseparable.

Of all the nations to which the image of the courageous woman and spiritual mother could be appended, France was the most obvious. Cecil B. De Mille was among the first to mine this profitable vein with *Joan the Woman,* a worshipful treatment of the Maid of Orleans which earned back twice its cost. Opera star Geraldine Farrar's Joan was the epitome of fiery patriotism, in every way the exemplar of national spirit. Miss Farrar later admitted she had been pro-German at the beginning of the war but came to believe that she "never played any screen

Woman as a national symbol in a masculine world. Geraldine Farrar reprimands her captains in *Joan the Woman* (1916).

part that inspired my love and enthusiasm as did this beautiful story." She called *Joan the Woman* "the greatest of all pro-Ally propaganda."[14] The film was a ringing appeal for a crusade on behalf of France, as De Mille himself admitted. Praise came from all quarters, including the usually reserved *New York Times* and the unpredictable Vachel Lindsay, who hymned the national spirit inherent in Joan. "The sober mood of America today," sermonized Lindsay, "should be akin to the breed of real men who have knelt to her through the ages."[15]

If Joan of Arc was a little too ethereal for some Americans, they could watch Mrs. Irene Castle portray a less saintly but no less effective national symbol in *Patria*. *Patria*, in fact was her screen name–she was "the last of the fighting Channings."[16] The incredible villainy of exotic Japanese (later Mexican) spies almost did her in, but she organized her own armed force and pressed on in manly fashion. Although she was not a sturdy heroine (she was prone to fainting spells) and did not involve herself directly in fisticuffs or other assorted violence, Patria identified herself with the American flag. In one sequence, she ceremoniously presented the Stars and Stripes to her private army.

Patria Channing solved the problem of how to be both a woman and a militant. The demure passivity that the Clevelands regarded as the essence of American femininity was not in her make-up. With her the war film came down from the clouds of symbolism and offered an alternative to the conception of woman as a national mother-figure. Still intensely patriotic, Patria was presented as particu-

Woman militant. Irene Castle inspects her private army in the tenth episode of the serial *Patria* (1917).

larly American in her initiative and courage. She was only flesh and blood, but her winsomeness made her doubly inspirational as her patriotism made her doubly attractive.

The one screen personality who came closest to embodying American ideals of womanhood during the war years was Mary Pickford. At first glance, Miss Pickford seemed ill-suited to play the role of a Patria, and in fact she shied away from that sort of casting. Her virginal innocence, however, was compatible with object rather than subject parts. In other words, where Mrs. Castle actively portrayed a woman in arms, Miss Pickford, by portraying a girl in danger, could encourage manly heroes to rush to her defense. This was the pattern of *The Little American,* which was effulgently praised by critics who should have known better. Intellectually, the essence of *The Little American* (the canny De Mille again directed) was American womanhood at bay. Miss Pickford, unlike Mrs. Castle, remained less a participant in the shaping of her own destiny than a magnet that attracted all the baser metals of the German spirit. A much lighter film, *Johanna Enlists,* marked the limits of Miss Pickford's screen involvement with the war, with the exception of war-bond shorts and the later failure *The Love Light*. But she remained an ideal symbol of femininity to American fighting men. She sent gold lockets containing her miniature to members of a California unit in France and was assiduous in supplying "her boys" with chocolate and tobacco. Warrior-mother, girl-mother–it all fused into an image of the ideal woman in war.

A glut of films supported the idealization of the mother, yet most of them insisted she compromise maternal instinct with patriotism. Only a Chaplin could get away with parodying motherhood as a national symbol, as he did in *Shoulder Arms*. For the rest, there was only that trite repetition of attitude and belief that was the surest indicator of popular consensus. The mother of *The Coward* was typical, grieving prematurely as he went off to war. This Ince film presented the protagonist as a Momma's boy, tacitly equating womanly pacifism with cowardice. But this picture was only a prototype, concerned as it was with the Civil War. More effective were extravagantly emotional films showing women as hapless victims of the Germans. *Motherhood* had a mother refuse to renounce a baby visited on her by a Prussian rapist. An identical situation prevailed in *After the War,* but here the unwilling matron gave her baby to the wife of her attacker.

War's aftermath tended to tone down the hysterical side of the maternal nature, leaving a residue of grief illumined by an honorable sense of duty. Never did the depiction of the mother, regardless of her nationality, slip from this mold. As the hero of *The Big Parade* went off to war, his mother cried; when he returned minus a leg, she was there to comfort him. The mother of the aviator in *Wings* who did not survive nobly chose to blame "war" rather than any individual for her son's death. And of course *Four Sons* pulled out all the stops, idealizing the mother's role in wartime to the absolute limit. Mother Bernle moved through John Ford's picture sustained by simple faith, able to endure the cruelest shocks for the sake of a happy ending. It was enough for most viewers that the film was a "simple story of mother love," with the aged heroine displaying the "fortitude of a true mother."[17]

With the thirties the portrayal of mothers was darkened by bitterness, but Mom remained a symbol of war's tragedy. Never did she put pacifism before patriotism to become an active opponent of military service. Thus young Paul's mother in *All Quiet on the Western Front* was oblivious to issues of state and concerned only with her son's safety and comfort. *Beyond Victory* showed the mother of a farm lad verbally resisting his enlistment, but doing nothing more. Sexual differentiation was displayed in *Broken Lullaby,* where German mothers softly mourned their sons while a German father was outraged by his boy's needless death. Some films made a maudlin spectacle of a mother's loss, as did *Pilgrimage,* which followed the journey of a Gold Star Mother to France to visit her son's grave. One bored critic called this picture a "résumé of all the mother pictures. . . ."[18] *Cavalcade* marked a small but effective return to the mother as a national symbol, but this speech by the film's matriarch indicated more the bitterness of the depression temper:

> Jane: "Drink to the war, then! I'm not going to. I can't. Rule Britannia! Send us victorious happy and glorious! (*sic*) Drink, Joey, you're only a baby, still, but you're old enough for war. Drink as the Germans are drinking tonight, to victory and defeat, and stupid, tragic sorrow. But don't ask me to do it, please!"[19]

War clearly was the antithesis of motherhood. *Cavalcade* indicated that the use of the mother as a positive national symbol, never very strong in the United States, had vanished from the nation's screens. This may be seen as a mark of national maturity, the sign of a willingness to confront war through the spectacles of realism rather than idealism. "Has it ever occurred to you that there are women in the world who are going to become mothers?" queried the heroine of *The World Moves On.* "And you tell me the world is just getting ready to go to war again."[20] Although mothers continued to be shown as pacifists right up through *The Ramparts We Watch* and *Sergeant York,* they were more the emotional and sentimental counterweights to an unwelcome task that had to be done rather than vigorous proponents of peace at any price.

iii

Young girls had more in common with men in their age group than with older members of their own sex. Maidens and brides faced war courageously, although sometimes with a tear in their eye. They were dutiful; they despised boyfriends and husbands who sought to evade service; and they were patriotic to a fault. "I am not afraid to die . . for Belgium!" proclaimed the stalwart heroine of *The Unbeliever* as she and the hero found themselves surrounded by Germans.[21] Young women were forever bidding brave farewells to their beloveds, assured that the vagaries of the plot would once again return the males safe and sound. *Patriotism, Draft 258,* and *For Valour* were only three examples from the myriad of films showing this familiar procedure.

Inspiration by example was the forte of young womanhood. During the war itself, many producers had not yet arrived at the idea of putting girls in the trenches alongside the men. For them, female characters performed most nobly as bellwethers of democratic sacrifice. For the Prussian villain of *Lest We Forget,* the heroine had only this brushoff: "I have sworn to myself that during the war I will not accept any invitations to dinner."[22] As this young lass certainly knew, dutiful women sometimes dared all, as their devotion to country could expose them as targets of Germanic sexual athletes–yet the ladies persevered. Most felt that service at home was quite as good as service under fire. The heroine of *Seventh Heaven* (1927) envisioned her lover and herself fighting "shoulder to shoulder"– he at the front, she in a munitions factory.[23]

The fascination of war drew many women like moths to a flame. In *The Patent Leather Kid,* the ingenue was tireless in urging her man to enlist. She herself went overseas as a YMCA worker and nurse because, as she said, "lovin' yer country is like lovin' yer mother...you just can't help it." The saucy French lass of *What Price Glory?* was "fascinated by the men...on their way to die."[24] *Lilac Time* featured another French sprite–this one collected German "trophies" such as propellers and fuselage parts.

But the fascination turned to repulsion as the twenties gave way to the thirties. The new movie generation of young girls now condemned war just as their mothers always had done. *Beyond Victory* marked the dividing line. While it contained a young girl who threw herself enthusiastically at an enlistee, it also included a wife, all wisdom in her stupidity as she questioned her husband as to the purpose of the war, and a bride who asked simply: "Why can't they all stop?"[25]

After this, the cycle was complete when the young capitalist-heroine of *The World Moves On* refused to make munitions in her factory.

Moviemakers soon came to be amazingly adept at giving women things to do beyond offering encouragement and setting examples. A two-reel documentary entitled *Woman's Work in War Time* (1917) established the tone by showing suffragists working on farms, in munitions plants, locomotive shops, and on transit lines. It put the war effort before equal rights for women. D. W. Griffith's *The Great Love* contained footage of England's feminine bluebloods working in hospitals and munitions factories. Fiction was even more equal to the challenge. A Canadian woman chucked everything upon hearing of the plight of French and Belgian children in *The Heart of Humanity* and traipsed overseas to care for them. *Shifting Sands* offered the Salvation Army as a possible outlet for the feminine urge to help. And so it went.

The surest occupational champion for women in war was the nursing profession. The introduction of nurses to the screen solved several problems. It put women in the idealized role of ministering to the sick; it got them into dangerous battlefield situations; and it was a device that brought romance to the trenches, it being difficult to conduct a love affair across three thousand miles of Atlantic Ocean. The genre owed much to the real-life martyrdom of the English nurse Edith Cavell, whose sacrifice was interjected whenever a lagging story needed a hypodermic. Impersonations of Miss Cavell appeared in *The Great Victory, Lest We Forget* (where she appeared equipped with halo), and several other features. She was the central character of *The Woman the Germans Shot*, which received favorable reviews for its predictably sentimentalized treatment of its subject. Movie men being what they were, she was provided with a young English lover. Herbert Wilcox's *Dawn*, an English-made film seen in America, told the story again, as did another and later Wilcox production, *Nurse Edith Cavell*. Wilcox always denied that the latter picture was pacifist propoganda, but this continually reiterated story of the execution of a woman of firm moral principle had no other purpose. *Nurse Edith Cavell* was popular with the isolationist press and was urged on high school classes for their edification.

The Cavell episode was essentially a moral drama, but the tales of battalions of Red Cross workers hurrying to the front to find their men had neither the tone nor the empathy of the English nurse's story. Angels of mercy began winging their way overseas almost with the declaration of war. Joining the Red Cross was the one sure way to get in on the action, as attested by the feminine leads of *The Highest Trump, Bonnie Annie Laurie, Adele,* and countless other pictures. Every preposterous plot angle possible was introduced, including marriage at a base hospital in France in *We Can't Have Everything*. The genre even earned a mild parody from Marie Dressler in *The Cross Red Nurse*. In straining for dramatic effect, producers unwittingly were pulling young women from the world of the demitasse and the drawing room. If the emotions paraded by these girls were conventionalized, their situations were not.

The nurse continued as a plot staple after the Armistice. She, along with the French spitfire, comprised most of the romantic possibilities for Yanks in France. One of the two was usually around to cherish the hero, succor the wounded, and comfort the dying. *The Crowded Hour* had both the girlfriend and the wife of one

Lothario pack up and follow him to the front. This picture enraged Gilbert Seldes, who viewed the idea of a girl in a dugout as "appalling hokum."[26] Equally divorced from common sense were films like *The Mad Parade*, which was advertised as having "the first all-woman cast in motion picture history," and *Corporal Kate*. "In bestowing due praise upon the women of the Allied Nations for their services in the Great Conflict," ran the opening title of the latter film, "let us not forget those who, as canteen entertainers, heiped their soldiers endure war's tragedy."[27]

At the apogee, about 1930, women were almost indistinguishable from men as warriors. *She Goes to War* injected a young society maiden right into the trenches, where she was able to kill a German machine-gunner. *War Nurse* was just what its title said it was, a sassy version of What Women Do When War Comes. Nurses fell in love, underwent battle damage, and endured till the happy ending. Things were grimmer in 1930 than in 1918, but the role of healer remained paramount. "You'll learn to look at men without arms, or legs, without faces, and you'll smile," said the matron to a rookie nurse. Why? "Because they need you."[28]

During the Depression decade, war heroines lapsed back from the trenches into the bedroom. This was in part due to the rise of tour-de-force women stars who specialized in boudoir escapades. Sound films let words carry much of the dramatic weight which had been borne by combat sequences in the silents. But the trend may also have been a result of the patterns of realism emerging in films with predominately male casts. American audiences could not digest a steady diet of somber war themes, but a feminine lead in a film where the war served as *deus ex machina* generally was box office. *Born to Love,* starring Constance Bennett as an American nurse who had an illegitimate child by an aviator, was a good index of the change. The front-line nurse made a small comeback in *Army Surgeon* (1942), but by that time she was on duty for a new cause.

The visualization of women in nurses' uniforms at least had the echo of actuality to commend it. But fantasy overcame all obstacles with the spy pictures, which began in deadly seriousness during the war and ended in the thirties as breezy, nonchalant window dressings for screen personalities. Women were ideal for cloak-and-dagger work—not danger, but only the threat of danger, could make them alluring as well as give them a chance to do their bit. *Sylvia of the Secret Service,* an early and popular serial, set the pace by sending its heroine on the trail of diamond thieves, who were operating to who knew what purpose. A flood of films followed, all putting women into situations which demanded their ingenuity as well as their charms. *Daughter of Destiny, The Belgian, Till I Come Back to You, Somewhere in France* (November, 1916), *Vive La France, Lafayette, We Come!, The Firefly of France*—these were some of the productions presenting women using both wit and beauty to overcome enormous odds.

The plots may have been tortured out of all relation to reality, but one thing was certain—women were becoming *involved.* They were busy doing such things as rescuing their lovers from German execution squads (*Arms and the Girl*), being trained as counter-espionage agents (*Follow the Girl*), betraying their stepfathers as spies (*War and the Woman*), personally exterminating German agents (*An Alien Enemy*), and falling in love with mysterious foreign men (*Souls in Pawn*). For these women, war was not merely an emotional cul-de-sac; it was life itself.

The spy game proved well suited to postwar female stars, and many films simply used the war as a setting for romantic or seductive doings. There was Marion Davies in *The Dark Star,* hustling about with plans for Turkish forts; her audience laughed in all the wrong places. Betty Compson played a dancing girl who outwitted German spies in *New Lives For Old;* she returned as a British double agent in *Inside the Lines* (1930). Helen Twelvetrees used her bedroom talents for her country in *A Woman of Experience* and was rewarded for her service.

War is Hell. Greta Garbo dallies with Ramon Novarro in *Mata Hari* (1931).

Constance Bennett, in addition to her lachrymose appearance in *Born to Love,* was seen in *After Tonight* as a Russian spy and in *Three Faces East* (1930) as a British operative. Spy roles attracted the biggest names in the business. The bigger the name, the more the war and woman's role in it faded into the background. Marlene Dietrich played a Mata Hari type to critical applause in *Dishonored,* but the kudos were for her, not her role. Greta Garbo assayed the part of the actual Mata Hari in the movie of that name, which turned out to contain one of the most ridiculous plots in a genre not known for a sense of actuality.

As the thirties progressed, the tragic and fateful overtones of female spy stories like *Till We Meet Again* lost favor. "War is pushed aside," as *Newsweek*'s critic sketched this picture, "and (the film) becomes a game of love between opposing secret service operatives."[29] This was overly familiar material. More popular were the lighthearted portrayals of women in the spy game, such as that by Myrna Loy in *Stamboul Quest* (a picture in which Miss Loy rather unconvincingly endured a bout of madness and life in a nunnery before the happy ending) and by wisecracking Rosalind Russell in *Rendezvous*.

Having begun as the constant and patriotic companions-in-spirit of the male warrior, young American women moved rapidly into war-related occupations such as nursing and spying. The role of women in modern war was given a certain visual immediacy by these unrealistic films. In reality most American women did not capture spies, conduct bedroom acrobatics in the name of patriotism, or gun down Huns in the trenches. The dull routine of wartime factory work earned only a few documentary treatments during the war itself. Most of middle- and lower-class American womanhood remained immersed in home and family for the duration, an immersion that drowned the fires of wartime dramatics. Because of this, the screen's portrayal of women in war has an unreality perhaps greater than any other series of images discussed here. This unreality mirrors the national uncertainty over the increasing complexity of feminist issues in a society which was engaged in redefining a significant part of its moral code.

Hence the marked difference in the cinematic view of distinct feminine roles. It is important to note the sharp schism between the view of mothers in war and the view of younger (and thus romantically eligible) ladies. Where the mother worried, the girl encouraged; the loss belonged to the mother, the happy ending to the girl. While motherhood remained corseted in the bonds of Victorian conventionality, America's young women were striking out on new paths.

iv

The final instances of the role of women in war were quite peripheral to the war itself. These were the pictures which were sheer romance, the war usually being used as an excuse to separate lovers before their final reunion. "Boy meets girl, boy loses girl, boy wins girl," that trite formula with endless variations, found a world war to its liking. Women as romantic objects, unburdened by the necessity of acting as nurses, spies, or other sorts of war auxiliaries, were tossed about like flotsam on the tides of war. Romantic films marked a continuation of woman's traditional role as a sexual ballast to the militant madness of men. Although most of the films mentioned previously contained the element of romance, their women were more active ("liberated" is not quite the word) and were not content merely to sit and suffer.

A prime example of the solely romantic type of film was *The White Sister*, the tale of a maiden who became a nun upon thinking her lover dead. It was produced three times in less than twenty years, with Viola Allen, Lillian Gish, and Helen Hayes in the title roles. The plot was a guaranteed tearjerker that successfully opposed moral obligation to love. Actresses in parts such as this were expected to suffer magnificently; as one script described the process, "Louise registers utter despair, but makes an attractive picture."[30]

Ideal roles for the display of traditional femininity included those in *Missing*, where two women agonized over the fate of a missing soldier; *The Maid of Belgium*, which had a young girl undergo amnesia as a result of Hunnish depredations; *Fields of Honor*, whose emigrant heroine endured attempted rape and the death of her sister to win her artist-soldier-hero; *The Unpardonable Sin,* which was what one can imagine; and *Sweetheart of the Doomed,* about a social butterfly who fell in love with a French spy. These pictures and many more did not pierce the crust of Victorian convention as some of the more war-related films were beginning to do.

The leader of this approach to war via the tender avenue of romanticism was D.W.Griffith. So overriding was the sentimental streak in Griffith's nature that even his "serious" war pictures, such as *Hearts of the World,* were infused with it. The great director was fond of younger women, the type suitable for romantic leads. He had no use for older women, having inserted a sarcastic title in *Intolerance* to the effect that reform was the only outlet for women who had ceased to be attractive. The screen personalities of the girls Griffith chose for the leads in his war pictures tended to overshadow the stories themselves. As a result, few of his war films are remembered today as incisive examinations of the war experience.

Griffith had high hopes for a "motion picture history" of the war when he first sailed for Europe in March, 1917. He later summoned his leading players to join him and commenced shooting reel after reel of film. Although he was one of the very few moviemakers allowed at the front, the final edited results of Griffith's war footage were almost subsumed in his sticky plots. On the surface the stories of the pictures made at least in part from this footage–*Hearts of the World, The Great Love, The Greatest Thing in Life,* and *The Girl Who Stayed at Home*–were trivial if full-blown endorsements of the Allied cause. Lillian Gish, for one, later recanted her part in these films, although admitting that they were "good stories and deeply moving ones."[31]

Hearts of the World was a tale of a French peasant girl (Miss Gish) enduring endless hardships when her village was over-run by the Boche. Lillian and her sister Dorothy, who played an elfin sprite, dominated the film. Although the picture was liberally interlaced with brutality (Erich von Stroheim was on hand), Griffith allowed his girls to walk away with the honors. The director himself remained a captive of his own sentimentality. At the New York premiere of *Hearts of the World* he became so emotional in his plea to support the Allies that he broke down and was unable to continue. His film proceeded to have a checkered career. It was censored in some cities, including Chicago, and many critics labeled its sentimental approach to war as mawkish rather than inspiring. Lillian Gish later claimed that Griffith never forgave himself for making the picture.[32]

The Great Love concentrated on the noble women of wartime England. This movie was so wooden that Lewis Jacobs called it a "glorified newsreel."[33] The plot, when it could be glimpsed through the fog of "real life," concerned a trite romantic triangle of which Lillian Gish again was an apex. *The Greatest Thing in Life* was the third of the films to cast Miss Gish and Robert Harron as young lovers caught up in war. The title of the film meant "love." *The Girl Who Stayed at Home* extended the romantic wartime triangle to a quadrangle, but did little else. The best comment on all these pictures came from a reviewer of *The Greatest Thing in Life:* "Little Lillian Gish is shown to beautiful advantage in three or four close-ups of a new type which idealize her expression."[34] Griffith's concern for the Allied cause was consistently undercut by his idealization of young women; for him the war existed to give tragedy and triumph to their lives.

Postwar films of this type retained Griffith's sentimentality but several added a more cavalier view of women as sexual objects. *Women of All Nations,* a spin-off from the popular Quirt-Flagg rivalry in *What Price Glory?,* and *Whirlwind of Youth* were typical examples of male lust inviting feminine acquiescence. But the standard female model was always available: there was Mary Pickford in *The Love Light,* Lillian Gish in *The Enemy,* and Corinne Griffith in *Six Days,* all striving to be the best of women in the worst of worlds. Less well-known actresses did their turn of suffering also. Gertrude Olmstead bravely carried on in *Puppets* while her man was overseas; Marguerite de la Motte mistakenly believed her fiancé to be *The Unknown Soldier;* Dorothy Mackaill met and overcame obstacle after obstacle as she tracked down a German spy in *Convoy;* and Virginia Valli worried over the cowardice of her sweetheart in *Judgment of the Hills.*

The genre by 1930 had worked its way so far from the war that any appearance of shellfire or wounded soldiers seemed the merest accident.[35] It was deemed more important to provide a showcase for the impish Colleen Moore or the sensual Pola Negri than to give much attention to the war. Miss Negri, in fact, was capable of reducing war causation to a question of sexual rapacity, as she did in *Hotel Imperial* (1927). Films with titles like *Seventh Heaven, The Dark Angel,* and *Shopworn Angel* (all made twice to capitalize on the new sound technology) cast the war as some dark cloud hovering over lissome creatures of sweetness and light. One review described them all when it touted the second *Seventh Heaven* as a classic in the "lachrymal school of drama."[36]

During the thirties, women in love proved to be better box office than women in war. Sentiment and convention tended to freeze the new American vision of woman at a point somewhere between traditionalism and emancipation. American moviegoers liked their girls courageous but not afraid to cry; passionate but romantically loyal; intrepid but occasionally helpless. Thus audiences were treated to *Waterloo Bridge* and its American girl stranded in London; *Born to Love* and its American girl pregnant in London; *Body and Soul,* and its French girl stranded (and maybe pregnant) in bed; and *A Farewell to Arms,* the first among Ernest Hemingway's stories to reach the screen, and its English girl pregnant in Italy. Several other films used the war as a backdrop for the inevitable triangular affairs, and one (*The Story of Vernon and Irene Castle*) put Fred Astaire and Ginger Rogers through some "real life" paces of love and heroics. Romance and danger being the staples of good drama, women in war represented generous portions of both–with the palm going to the stories of romance.

v

If cinematic war was man's business, it was woman's opportunity. While her role as a mother bound her to home, family, and the genteel emotions associated with those relationships, she was able to find a more satisfactory ideal self as a wife and sweetheart. Movie portrayals of damsels battling German rapists dressing picturesquely modest war wounds, and trailing spies were a distinct departure from the vision of Grover Cleveland and his generation. The visual presentation of women in war spread the notion of increased feminine potential throughout the country.

Yet women never could shed the essence of their femininity. They might fire guns, wrestle saboteurs, and play with bombs, but they never achieved independence. As the turmoil of war subsided, receding first into revered memory and then into a dim past, females continued to move through the cinema conflict in dime-novel stories of tragedy. They were consistent symbols of the goodness that had vanished from a world at war. Not for them was the action-filled environment in which their elder sisters had reveled. They needed only a man to fulfill themselves. Even Lenin's girl secretary in *British Agent* finally avowed she was "too much of a woman" to be a Soviet patriot and an idealist. "You can't let political opinions come between us," pleaded her British lover[37]–and she didn't. Her story made a fitting epitaph.

14

War and Humor

i

Comedies using World War I as backdrop may seem at first glance to be misplaced in time and space. Yet their humor seldom was derived from the war itself. These films retained most of the comic mechanisms found in standard slapstick comedies or polite drawing room farces. Comic art is far more rewarding in terms of social analysis than is tragic art.[1] War comedies in fact contained social and intellectual themes that may be examined in the context of comic art. By asking the question "What was so funny about the war?" we may not arrive at answers to why the war was so funny, but we may achieve some idea why Americans laughed.

In essence, the comedies of World War I used military "comic heroes" to explore questions of authority within the democratic system. In this guise, clowns in uniform commented endlessly on all of American society. That society, in spite of the boast and brag of its egalitarian tradition, has been like any other society a hierarchy of superiors, inferiors, and equals. Comedy has been called that "sanctioned doubt" which allows the claims of superiors to be deflated and the preposterous behavior of inferiors and equals to be reassuring.[2] In a sense, the society that denies itself comic art operates on artificial social planes. Comedy, while doubting, can close the gap between social theory and social practice by bestowing implicit approval on hierarchical social structures.

Most of the producers of these comedies probably never considered authority to be a central issue in the success of their films. Their comic heroes were clowns who specialized in exposing social vices to movie audiences who were both well aware that the vices existed and in agreement as to the need for exposure. Although they also were used to reject as well as support authority, the screen comedians who dueled against the authoritarianism of military life usually were harmless "safety valves" for moviegoers unable or unwilling to confront the growing bureaucratic impersonality of the twentieth century. In most of the war comedies authority received many blows to its pride and dignity, but it was never overturned. The comedies discussed in this chapter betrayed an uneasiness about military authority, a fear that the stern social gradations of uniformed life might be fastening themselves upon the rest of society. In upholding the shadow if not the substance of the egalitarian dream, these films were evidence that many Americans felt the dream threatened by forces over which they had no control.

In supporting authority, then, war comedies like other comedies made whatever threatened the social order appear ridiculous. In this way moviegoers could purge themselves of social tension while the actual hierarchy remained unscathed. Many of the pictures in this chapter thus may be described as "conservative," in the sense they advocated no social change. Institutions remained imperturbable under comic assault. If an individual soldier was a gross incompetent, the army remained the ideal of patriotic militancy.

All this seems quite removed from the war itself. In fact, producers never attempted what today would be called a "black comedy"—the examination of war's horror, futility, and absurdity through the devices of comic art. It would take a Hiroshima to produce a *Dr. Strangelove*. For this reason, comedies of World War I seldom ventured into the trenches, and if they got there the war was reshaped to fit comic routines, not vice versa. Instead, the comedies usually took place behind the lines or in training camps. This was an indication that the halo of serious purpose cast its aura around the battlefield itself, and that the fighting still was seen as part of a sacred cause well after the war had ended.

True to national ideals, the American comic hero was raffishly proletarian. Almost inevitably, in the military social structure, he was an enlisted man, one who blithely ignored the etiquette of military convention to comment endlessly on the foibles of his superiors, from corporals to generals. He at times was an example of the "comedy of reason," an ironic bird of discord piping notes that cast doubt on the social order. Thus a select few of the war comedies rose above their conservative function to offer the merest suggestion of the need for social change. The proletarian comic hero could more often play the fool, reassuring audiences by his blunders. Neither comic mode contained a hint of social revolution, which was the hallmark of a type of comic art not yet adapted to the screen.

Comedy plays an innately social function as a salve to soothe society's wounds. Democracies rightly value it among the most precious of their treasures, since it is so necessary to explain the incongruities which inevitably appear in professedly egalitarian social systems. Hugh Dalziel Duncan has explained it thus:

> We learn in comedy that the virtues of superiors are not so great after all, the humility and loyalty of inferiors are not without limits, and that friends and peers sometimes deceive us. But guilt lightens in laughter as I admit that if they are rascals, so too am I. We begin by laughing at others only to end by laughing at ourselves. The strain of rigid conventions, of majestic ideals, of deep loyalties, is lessened, for now they are open to examination. They can be questioned, their absurdities can be made plain. Now that we can openly express our vices, there is hope for correction. At least we now have company in misery; we are no longer alone and can take heart for another try. For when all is said and done, what do we have but each other? So long as we can act together we have all the good there is in life.[3]

There have been many attempts to explain film humor, but since nothing renders comedy less humorous than the explanation of it, this chapter does not attempt to analyze why some war comedies were funny and some were not. The central issue instead is the question of how authority is regarded by a democratic society. Even the crudest slapstick humor was not as far removed from this issue as one might think. When Mack Sennett exulted that "*Of course* comedy is a satire on the human race," he was talking about authority. "Our specialty was exasperated dignity and the discombombulation of authority," he remembered. "We whaled the daylights out of everything in sight with our bed slats, and we had fun doing it."[4]

Superficially, movie clowns provided an escape from everyday concerns. As early as 1914, a traveler in Europe reported a great demand for film comedies as an antedote to the horrors of war.[5] "Comedy is the thing," another observer noted two years later. "The soldier wants his thoughts to be taken away from the serious work ahead of him."[6] But the sloppy incompetence of most movie clowns went further than this, registering deeply with the American spirit. In their guise as pseudo-warriors, these funny-men took upon themselves the fear of not measuring up to the demands of a military organization caught up in a world war. They thus served as comic scapegoats for the society at large.

The comedies of World War I reflected a nervousness over the inadequacies of American social organization and the fear that these inadequacies were increasing rather than decreasing. The military was seen as a microcosm of society as a whole. Its well-ordered ranks, its unquestioning obedience to higher authority, and its meticulous attention to trivial details were aspects made for parody, just as they were uncomfortable reminders that the snake of social class continued to slither about in an egalitarian Eden.

ii

Germany was of course the most obvious target for democratic ridicule. Things German were lampooned mercilessly both during and after the war. Everything from cartoons to full-length features vented democratic spleen on a nation seen as the perfect symbol of rigid authoritariansim and imperial arrogance. Cartoon hero Happy Hooligan was one of the first to enlist, bombing "Kaiser Bill" in *Doin' His Bit*. Mutt and Jeff went to war in *The 75 Mile Gun* and *The Kaiser's New Dentist*. In the first of these, Ham Fisher's intrepid duo captured a German "Big Bertha." In the second, they tried to yank the Emperor's tooth with a minimum of professionalism and a maximum of pain. The hallmark of these cartoons, as well as that of many comedy features, was a series of escapades depicting insouciant democratic ingenuity grappling successfully with blundering Prussian authority.

The grosser melodramas defaming Germany earned their own parodies. Universal, the studio which had been responsible for *The Kaiser, the Beast of Berlin*, followed up with *The Geezer of Berlin*, a farce whose *dramatis personae* included the Kaiser, the "Clown Quince," "Von Turpentine," and "Von Bethman Bowlegs." Its producers probably were pleased when one correspondent described their work as "utterly witless."[7] Another reviewer soberly warned that "there is always the danger of treating too lightly the serious side of this tremendous conflict." However, he continued, "as to caricaturing the Kaiser and his bloodthirsty crew there can certainly be no objection to that, except that it lets them off too easily."[8] Cross-eyed Ben Turpin was in agreement when he hammed it up as the Kaiser in *Yankee Doodle in Berlin.* Nor did the counteroffensive stop at the Imperial Court. An early Harold Lloyd comedy, *Kicking the Germ Out of Germany,* kidded the excesses of spy pictures.

The foolish German enemy needed to be offset by handsome heroes. These Adonises were often on hand in light comedies to win the girl after the fun had subsided. *The Submarine Pirate,* an early Keystone comedy made with Navy assistance, was such a picture, so popular that it was used by the Navy Department to encourage recruiting. *Madam Spy* (1918) got some good laughs from a man impersonating a German baroness, and *Luck and Pluck* did the same with acrobatic George Walsh doing in a German agent. These were all "safe" humorous films showing the conservatism of war comedy. More marginal were the nonsensical caperings of *An International Sneak,* a Sennett spy parody. Equally light in touch was *The War Bridegroom,* which had its heroes treat the draft with casual aplomb, and *The War Bride of Plumville,* with its gentle satire of munitions-making. Nevertheless, all these films ended satisfactorily—institutions remained unscathed, heroes and heroines emerged unruffled, and all was peaceful—except in the Sennett films, which often climaxed in a burst of happy chaos.

Just as the Germans served as foreign butts of crude jokes, pacifists were the domestic lightning rods which attracted seasoned farceurs. *In-Again, Out-Again* and *Perkins' Peace Party* were examples of movies which owed much of their humor to their caricatures of pacifism. In *I'll Say So,* the hero comically overcame the machinations of his girl's pacifist-guardian, who was trying to force her to marry a Prussian. A less vicious brand of comedy was used to get laughs from those institutions which, though deemed necessary, seemed to infringe on individual liberties. Typical of this approach was *Home Defense,* a one-reeler that kidded overage and undertrained civilian warriors.

But even comedy had its serious purpose. Many of the comedies made in the 1917-1919 period performed the dual function of providing amusement as they sought to teach moral and patriotic lessons. *Too Fat to Fight* followed the antics of a fat man as he tried to reduce to meet the Army's specifications. Here as in so many other features, comic art fit itself nicely into the institutional mold, upholding rather than challenging authority. This tendency was especially true of the training-camp comedies, such as *Pettigrew's Girl* and *Come On In.* The former, filmed near Camp Kearney in California, was a standard tale of a rookie's misadventures. *Come On In* combined a short man's attempts to enlist with a spy chase. The tone of its humor may be gauged by the names of its characters: "Count Von Bumstuff," "Professor G. Wottan Orphul-Schmell," "A. Schlobb," and "Otto B. Schott." Yet one reviewer thought the burlesque "never becomes offensive" and was "not overdone."[9]

Against this glut of comic art which lampooned aspects of authoritarian behavior while leaving its institutional principles intact, one film stood out. Almost all of the war comedies ignored the war itself, concentrating on trivial comic incidents. In this atmosphere Charles Chaplin turned his talents to a true war comedy. The result, while not a telling blow to war-bred institutionalization, hit both broader and deeper than its peers. *Shoulder Arms,* the individual production of a comic genius at the height of his powers, was certainly the best comedy to come out of the war. Chaplin shed part of his Little Tramp character for this film but retained enough to make clear the irrational qualities of army life. This picture, only three reels long, followed Chaplin's peregrinations from a bumbling, awkward recruit through his exposure to trench life and battle to his ultimate capture of the Kaiser and the Crown Prince. Chaplin's mimic skills made hilarious the visualization of the discomforts of the trenches and the real dangers of warfare, but the picture had its intentionally disrespectful moments. The censors banned the original ending, in which Chaplin was to receive the thanks of the Allies at an enormous Lucullean banquet, with the King of England snipping a button off Charlie's uniform as a souvenir. Yet what survives, if it does not quite rate the extravagant praise bestowed upon it by some cinema historians, is an excellent example of the purgative powers of comic art.

The little film was completed in midsummer of 1918, but Chaplin's friends urged him not to release it while the war lasted. He nevertheless chose to open in New York on October 20. The comedian was under some pressure from the public, because in spite of his well-publicized Liberty Loan campaign tours, he had not volunteered for military service. *Shoulder Arms* thus may have been a form of dues-paying, although Chaplin's talents ensured that the apologia came encased in thorns.

Audiences weary of melodramatic war themes and inconsequential fluff about training camps and spies gave *Shoulder Arms* an excellent reception. Chaplin was not above burlesquing Germans for comic effect, but he also hit out at the absurdities of war which continually confronted men powerless to alter their destiny. Only in the final part, with the madcap capture of the Hohenzollerns, did the picture disintegrate into pure farce. The consistent symbol of Chaplin's humor was authority, whether it was vested in an American drill sergeant or in a pipsqueak German martinet. The comic response to authority was interspliced with Chaplin's characteristic nonchalance, which at times was almost cruel–as in his keeping a chalk tally of Germans he had shot. But mostly he laid about him on all sides with the sharp knife of satire. He laughed at the image of women as national symbols; he laughed at trench life (viewed as perpetual residence in three feet of water); he laughed at the standard leave-taking scene which had become the indispensable ingredient of war plots; and in all this, audiences laughed with him. As a true comic genius, Chaplin made impossible situations bearable even as he attacked the processes which had led to the situations in the first place.

Chaplin himself revealed in later life the deep emotions which had driven him to make the film. He postulated the existence of forces beyond anyone's control: "We were caught in an avalanche of mad destruction and brutal slaughter–we had started a haemorrhage of world proportion, and we could not stop it." He despised war-bred authoritarianism: "America was cast into a matrix of obedience and every thought was secondary to the religion of war."[10] And he approached the war with a bitterness which made for high comic art:

The war was now grim. Ruthless slaughter and destruction were rife over Europe. In training camps men were taught how to attack with a bayonet–how to yell, rush and stick it in the enemy's guts, and, if the blade got stuck in his groin, to shoot into his guts to loosen it. Hysteria was excessive. Draft dodgers were being sentenced to five years and every man was made to carry his registration card. Civilian apparel was a dress of shame, for nearly every young man was in uniform and, if he was not, he was liable to be asked for his registration card, or a woman might present him with a white feather.[11]

Charles Chaplin burlesques the well-turned-out doughboy for *Shoulder Arms* (1918).

Chaplin regarded authoritarianism as the ultimate sin of rampant nationalism. With the Nazi experience fresh in his mind, he evolved in his autobiography an organic theory of authoritarian growth, likening incipient authoritarianism to cells which lay dormant but which "can be activated quickly in every country."[12] He was the first serious modern comedian to grapple with this problem. World War I gave him the opportunity to confront it face to face, and this he did in *Shoulder Arms* with mixed results. More than any other comic artist, Chaplin bit deeply into the idealistic façade of the Great Crusade. His humor, like most great comedy, was edged with a pathos to which the country was beginning to respond. In early 1917, *Shoulder Arms* could have been a box-office disaster; by late 1918 it was able to capture the mood of a considerable segment of the population. But even Chaplin was unable, or did not choose, to confront the institutionalization which gave authority its cutting edge. While he remained a proletarian comedian in his soldier's disguise, Chaplin did not find his humor so much in burlesques of class antagonism as he did in set sequences which cast him as a poet of reason confronting a completely unreasonable world. This confrontation might include authority as an antagonist, but authority was seldom diminished thereby. Comic necessity gave it stamina–it always survived to face another round of pratfalls.

No other war comedy made either during or after the war approached *Shoulder Arms* as comic art. It immediately was recognized as a remarkable achievement, the "perfect handling of a delicate subject."[13] Chaplin's picture holds up well today as a prime example of the rationality of humor. It was an egalitarian sermonette delivered in the most difficult circumstances.

iii

To provide a comic footnote to Chaplin was not an easy task, but a number of undaunted filmmakers continued to issue war comedies throughout the twenties. By the time of the Depression, the genre had largely died off, killed by its own repetitions and the emergence of lighter farces set in more modern surroundings. In general, the postwar fun reverted back to training camps or behind the lines, although now and then a battle scene was done up in slapstick fashion. The same comic modes which ridiculed other aspects of society made familiar war fare as well.

Ethnic humor held high favor. The film world was in its heyday of degrading ethnic minorities, although it is only fair to point out that in this movie magnates differed little from society at large. Where Chaplin and lesser lights took delight in leveling their social superiors, the ethnic films assured audiences that minorities were harmless fools and that their shenanigans constituted no threat to the social order. Several war comedies featured whites in blackface–by today's standards the epitome of condescending racism but widely accepted then. *Ham and Eggs at the Front,* originally conceived by the young Darryl Zanuck, put an all-white cast in blackface. Its portrayal of Negro soldiers hewed to the popular Sambo stereotype. *Variety* coolly commented that the "mere idea of a colored regiment at the front should be sufficient to draw business with proper exploitation."[14] Moran and Mack, white men billed as vaudeville's "Two Black Crows," appeared in *Anybody's War* as blacks lured into enlisting by promises of food, music, and plenty of sleep. Occasionally an actual Negro would be presented, but only in character. Stepin Fetchit, for example, reprised his familiar role in *The World Moves On.*[15]

Jewish comic figures likewise were common coin. They moved effortlessly from urban ghettoes to trench life. *What Price Glory?* had one, the small, big-nosed "Lipinsky." So did *Wings,* which featured "Schwimpf" as its butt of all jokes. The Irish ran a close race with the Jews. *Corporal Kate* set some kind of record by including Irish, Jewish, and Negro stereotypes in mindless profusion. Supposedly, films such as this promoted the melting-pot ideal, but in reality they used ethnic minorities as comic scapegoats in the service of a stable society. Typical were two "Izzy Murphy" films featuring George Jessel: *Private Izzy Murphy* and *Sailor Izzy*

Murphy. The first strained for laughs by inserting a Jewish boy into New York's Irish Sixty-ninth Regiment, while the second was even more trivial.

Postwar comedies of military life were most at home in the training camps. There the lines of authority were clear and the differences between sloppily democratic civilians and drill-field soldiers could be treated most broadly. All these pictures used traditional comic idioms. *Hayfoot-Strawfoot* cast boyish Charles Ray as rookie "Ulysses S. Grant Briggs," the fumbling inheritor of a family's proud military tradition. This picture was archly conservative, in that its humor was derived from the blunders of a lad trying frantically to institutionalize himself. Much the same theme was present in *23 ½ Hours Leave,* where the post's commanding general appeared as the authority figure. The comic hero finally won the general's daughter, thus signifying that all was well both in the camp and in the rest of society. When this film was remade in 1937, however, its traditional humor had been outdated by more current topics.

As the twenties wore on, it became evident that little more than slapstick could be expected from military comedies. *Rookies* proved to be profitable for MGM, with lumbering Karl Dane and pint-sized George K. Arthur as a Mutt and Jeff pair of boot-camp antagonists. "There is something inherently funny in sassing military discipline," mused *Time*'s critic.[16] Indeed there was–so long as the discipline ultimately was not destroyed in the process. *Top Sergeant Mulligan* was a pale imitation which involved two recruits in a plot centering on mistaken identities, and like most of the war comedies, its story could have been placed anywhere at any time.

Individual comedy stars usually assayed at least one film with a war setting during their careers, since the institutional background was too rich in comic possibilities to pass up. Hoot Gibson combined action and humor in three light war tales: *Shootin' for Love, Blinky,* and *The Gentleman from America.* Larry Semon, whose stock in trade was a sad-sack approach to humor, was not as successful with *Spuds.* Marion Davies tried her hand at a war musical comedy, *Marianne*, a mishmash which piled slight songs atop the usual comic stereotypes. Whey-faced Harry Langdon, in the period of his declining popularity, played a fumbling doughboy in the initial sequences of *The Strong Man.* Even less satisfactory was Langdon's talkie *A Soldier's Plaything,* made in 1930. There was nothing original in this picture–most of its comic sequences were lifted from *The Better 'Ole* (discussed below) and the stock authority figure appeared, disguised as a captain. One title insert subconsciously gave away a universal comic formula. In describing the military adventures of Langdon's handsome pal, it read: "Georgie's war was no different from that of the average doughboy–a lot of hardship, a lot of laughs, and a lot of ladies."[17]

Another comedian on the downgrade was Buster Keaton. In *Doughboys,* Keaton displayed little of the comic inspiration of his earlier films. This story of a rich and reluctant draftee accidentally attaining heroic stature was stale and unworthy material. Keaton himself had gotten to France with the AEF, but he had not seen action. He claimed that his war memories, particularly those of his training-camp days, served as the basis for *Doughboys*. What comedy there was in the film came from Keaton's dead-pan expression and the pro-egalitarian theme of a rich boy being democratized by the Army. Here authority was in the service of class effacement and thus maintained itself with ease.

Even further removed from actual war were the antics of comedy teams like Wheeler and Woolsey or Laurel and Hardy. The first pair appeared in *Half-Shot at Sunrise,* which was largely a rehash of old vaudeville routines. Military police and a blundering, pompous colonel served as the feckless authority figures. Laurel and Hardy, however, were at their humorous best in *Pack Up Your Troubles,* being seen in sequence as unsuccessful draft dodgers, unwilling front-line heroes, and humanitarian caretakers of a homeless little girl. Nevertheless, the war seemed tailored for their comedy instead of vice versa.

Compared with such comic talents, the remaining war comedies were even more forced and artificial. Screen comedy was crude, since the silent camera depended on elaborate mannerisms and detailed sight gags to register humor and the sound camera was in its infancy. More gentle fun, like that in *The Goodby Kiss* (a late Sennett film) was relatively rare. Many complained about the cruder comedy films, calling them a "perversion of humor."[18] Such critics objected to the exploitation of human weakness and frailty, but they merely were shoveling sand against the tide. Most audiences responded favorably to the rough-and-tumble brawling of films like *The Big Parade* and its two sequels, *The Cock-Eyed World* and *Women of All Nations.* Take two or more doughboy comrade-rivals, mix with an artificial sense of danger, add a love interest, and leaven with generous doses of thwarted authority. These were the ingredients of plodders such as *Her Man O'War, Hard Boiled Haggarty,* and *Two Arabian Knights,* the last a Lewis Milestone picture showing none of the sensitivity that blossomed forth three years later with *All Quiet on the Western Front.* Audiences nevertheless laughed at Milestone's fantasy of two escaped POW's gravitating to Constantinople. He won an Oscar for comedy direction and continued to regard the picture as a favorite.

By 1930 it was evident that the genre had reached a dead end. Moviegoers were more bored than amused by trite comic routines. Pictures sporting titles like *Flying Luck, Tin Hats, Buck Privates, Riley of the Rainbow Division, Lost at the Front,* and *Finders Keepers* were harbingers of the end of the cycle. Although authority continued to be worried by handsome devils and their comic sidemen, patrons were tiring of the quasi-war setting. It was too familiar, which tended to make it contemptible rather than funny. Producers even resorted to actual events for themes, but this approach also was unsuccessful. *Legionnaires in Paris,* a film distantly based on the tenth convention of the American Legion in Paris in 1927, proved to be just another comic disaster.

Slapstick was becoming more palatable to movie audiences in plots with contemporary backgrounds. Although Paramount enjoyed some success with its highly slapstick Wallace Beery–Raymond Hatton series—*Behind the Front, We're in the Navy Now,* and *Now We're in the Air*—coarser forms of comedy were taking leave of the war and moving to greener, more lucrative pastures. *The Better 'Ole,* appropriately enough starring Sidney Chaplin, Charlie's talented brother, provided one last glimmer of originality. The film was based on the popular play by Bruce Bairnsfather and Arthur Eliot, which in turn had been taken from Bairnsfather's cartoons of the hapless Bill and Alf. The two British Tommies were the spiritual godfathers of Bill Mauldin's Willie and Joe and displayed much the same attitudes. One reviewer thought the "unfailing humor" of the comic pair was "typical of the rank and file in all the armies."[19] Most of the film's comedy came from its cockney sass and bounce and the perseverance of its heroes in the face of innumerable obstacles. Here there were no fools as authority figures, simply Chaplin as Old Bill getting into and out of hilariously incongruous situations.

The Depression produced plenty of comedy, but practically none of it drew upon the war experience. In part this was due to the rise of new comic talents to favor. The unpredictable anarchist caperings of the Marx Brothers and the misanthropic waspishness of W. C. Fields usually called for plots alien to military life, although the Marxes' *Duck Soup* (1933) is still cherished today as an antimilitarist parody. But it was also because the tendency to ridicule military authority through the circumstances of the war had temporarily reached an impasse. Authority now was either grimly responsible (the *Dawn Patrols*), bitterly condemned (*All Quiet on the Western Front*), or admired (in numerous adventure films). The democracy still took its pokes at pompous generals and foghorn-voiced drill sergeants, only now they were corporation executives and society matrons. A rare film like *Sky Devils* could try to bring back the pratfall and the roughhouse, but its chipper wisecracks belonged to the new sound era of film comedy.

iv

So the war survived attempts to make it funny. Even though the contrived screen humor presented to American audiences was comic distortion, the purpose of the nation's comic art went beyond a few moments of illusionary amusement. Democratic comedy, in fact, proved to be a bulwark of the egalitarian dream. Invariably, America's comic war heroes were "little men"–average guys with no distinguishing characteristics, save perhaps their ethnic personalities and their ability to become entangled in absurd situations. Keaton's aristocratic "Elmer Stuyvesant" in *Doughboys* was an exception which proved the rule. Although the nation's movie clowns were not proletarians in the sense political theorists might use the term, it is fair to describe them as such because of their role as mouthpieces for depicting concern over and exasperation with authority and the claims of social class.

War comedies did not view the war as a laughing matter. The Great Crusade had not been conducted to be defamed by a few pies in the face or a well-placed kick in the rear. For this reason, no satires of the war itself–of its brutality, insanity, and meaninglessness–were forthcoming. *Shoulder Arms* was a noble attempt, made more so by the fact that it was issued while the war still raged, but it did not directly address itself to the aims and methods of the conflict. Either America's screen comic art was incapable of such a satire, or American audiences were not yet ready to see sacred ideals and institutions seriously challenged through the use of humor. The first possibility was unlikely, given men with the universal comic wisdom of Chaplin and Keaton. More probably, the nonexistence of true war comedies was absent proof of the nation's tendency to regard its conduct of the war as irreproachable.

What audiences preferred, then, were comedies with the ingredients of war in them. Uniforms, guns, drill sergeants, and now and then a little shellfire–these were sufficient to provide the illusion that somewhere, just off screen, a real war was taking place. In fact, what was taking place was the age-old ridicule of authority, placed in an ideal military setting. War humor attacked the pernicious arrogance of the authoritarian mind with every ego-deflating weapon at the hands of its proletarian clowns. In their average comic heroes, Americans found surrogates who satisfactorily pricked balloons of hot air which theoretically had no place among the cool breezes of a democracy.

But screen comedy held no final rebuttal for the inchoate forces which were slowly coalescing into The Lonely Crowd. Humor could irritate its main target; it might even delay the growth of institutionalized authoritarianism, but it could never completely quash it. Nor was this its primary purpose. Because the country's war comedies could never shake the sacred shackles of national institutions, they never seriously challenged authority. The recruits with two left feet, the white-toothed singing doughboys, and the stentorian topkicks were all permanent enlistees in a hopeless war, one that had little to do with World War I.

Conclusion

This study has examined America's experience in World War I as it was presented in motion pictures. While the focus has been on World War I throughout the period 1914-1941, the larger intent was to explore the usefulness of film as valid historical evidence. If this usefulness becomes evident, then the fresh insights that war films of the period provide us may help to reshape some of our ideas concerning American attitudes toward the conflict.

The motion picture provides one key to the better understanding of American society in the twentieth century. By 1920 the movie house was a local fixture in practically every geographic area and social enclave in the country. The entertainment and information transmitted by the film was "popular" in the sense that movies literally saturated the nation with visual images that conveyed ideas, attitudes, and values. Most historians of high thought have tended to ignore these popular currents of thought as mundane and trivial, yet these currents reach far greater numbers of people than are contained within the rather severely circumscribed area of traditional studies in intellectual history. Thus the ideas conveyed by film carry two possibilities: they may be intellectually causative in themselves, serving as progenitors and guides for action; or, they may be fairly accurate reflectors of the tone of American culture as a whole.

The movies in this study suggest that certain popular consensuses about the war were at least partly shared by the movie audience, which in its turn formed a substantial portion of the national population. This statement becomes plausible in the context of American culture when the following facts are examined. First, the American film audience throughout our period was huge, numbering in the tens of millions. Second, the country's film industry, geared as it was to maximize profit, aimed repeatedly to present those themes thought most appealing to its mass audience. Finally, the films of World War I, analyzed extensively, are seen continuously to repeat such themes as related to the war experience. Quite obviously, exceptional instances in every case may be cited in the attempt to prove that film did not totally blanket the land with its simplistic approach to the war. Nevertheless the examination of the celluloid evidence provides us with a broad base from which to reassess the social, moral, and intellectual earthquake that marked America's passage into the twentieth century.

The intellectual history of the World War I period and its aftermath, as written thus far, tends to be an examination of the reaction of intellectual elites to the conflict. The study of film moves the scholar into the study of society as a whole, not just of those elites that have been assumed to have spoken for the entire society or to have set its tone. World War I films yield certain insights into the burgeoning mass culture of the war and postwar years. More traditional forms of evidence, such as manuscripts, diaries, biographies, autobiographies, and monographs, have all been utilized to construct studies of the period, but all these sources, while perfectly feasible as historical evidence, are far more narrow in the scope of their audience than is the film. This is not to argue for historical causation on the grounds of numbers alone, but merely to indicate a serious methodological gap between the study of intellectual "prime movers" and the assumption that vast populations supposedly followed their lead.

The study of film requires a break with the practice of relying on literary, or written, evidence alone. Film is one with literature in its ability to promote, advocate, and reconfirm ideas, attitudes, and values. It differs from literature, however, in myriad and important ways. The visual media lack the finesse and the delicate shadings that allow literary art to more fully delineate our perspectives. Films are relatively crude forms of communication, particularly in their commercial context. They provide a congeries of images that flash transiently across our minds, leaving only a partial perception of what has been. Yet they tend to repeat acceptable themes, until what was once only a submerged memory may become part and parcel of the thought patterns of everyday life. Because it is such fertile ground for ideas–for their initiation, repetition, distortion, and communication– film is also fertile ground for research in intellectual history.

These ideas may not be grand. They may not contain the sweeping insight of universal genius, but they are no less significant for this. If the movies that contain these ideas are in themselves inaccurate historically, this is no reason to ignore them. The untruth as well as the fact may help shape historical analysis. Everyone remembers the great liars of our nation–history would be composed of duller stuff were Parson Weems, Davy Crockett, and their ilk to be forgotten. So it is with the motion picture. Objectively and aesthetically, much of its history has been odious in the extreme, particularly to those intellectuals who see themselves as creators of climates of opinion and custodians of what is best in the national heritage. On intellectual grounds, the record of the film shows much to dislike and precious little to respect. Historians have responded to this situation by either ignoring the film altogether or relegating it to a relatively unused corner of the area of intellectual and social history.

Yet the motion picture, despite its record, shows us far more than just outright lies and shallow distortions. Like most other forms of communication, it is able to evoke mental images that may be pondered, dissected, and analyzed. These images are made more vivid by their visualization, but they are no less usable as evidence for this. The depiction of the villainous Hun on the nation's screens, for example, helped foster an entirely new set of visual images of German militarism. In short, film is part of the structure of American culture. Motion picture analysis as a method of isolating and defining ideas should take its place with the now familiar literary analysis centering on the essay, the novel, the poem, and the short story. Only a generation ago the use of this type of literary evidence was an innovation, yet it proved to be highly productive in terms of studying the national character.

Each angle of perception on the mammoth and confused historical event we call World War I has revealed new dimensions. The novelist may see the experience differently from the general writing his memoirs; the aviator differs from the sailor, the nurse from the amputee, and the German from the American. The historian, trying to cull some sense from the whole, must of necessity be rigorously selective. So the film differs with other media. The power of its evidence rests primarily on the fact that in the first half of the twentieth century the motion picture was interwoven into the very fabric of our society to a greater extent than almost any other form of mass communication in that pre-television era.

The incredible and fascinating plasticity of the film was shown by the documentaries and semi-documentaries of the war. Truth on film sometimes had many sides. The same slices of film that were used to proudly unveil American military might in *Guarding Old Glory* were used a generation later to make the point that the practice of war was expensive, amorally lethal, and corrupt. The motion picture was truly an intellectual gadfly, endlessly providing whatever fantasies audiences wished or filmmakers thought they wished. On occasion movies may have generated fantasies or half truths of their own accord, such as the repetitive hymns to American valor sung by the Committee on Public Information. The many truths of films purportedly factual gave shape to the varied audience consensuses concerning the war itself.

National ideals, which were both stripped to the bare essentials and buffed to a bright gloss by the film, paraded in an undiminished splendor on the nation's screens. Such disparate commercial films as *The Hun Within* and *The Patent Leather Kid,* made in 1918 and 1927 respectively, shared the same ideals. Yet this nine-year period, according to many sources relying on standard evidence, was one of dramatic change in our society's attitude toward the war. However, these films and many others indicate that ideals regarding the nation's war involvement continued practically undiminished among a significant part of the population.

The commercial feature film, at first so ardent in its support of the war, eventually reached a position of studied ambiguity toward the conflict, an ambiguity sometimes realized in a single film, such as *Beyond Victory*. Yet no medium in our history, not even the Hearst press trumpeting the call to arms in 1898, had matched the vivid and almost unidimensional summons of the cinematic fanfare of the war years. Heroes were never more heroic, heroines never more appealing, villains never more evil. These conventions so perfectly matched the tenor of the times that it is difficult to tell where film left off and reality began. The war adventure film exploited every favorable approach to those dramatic clichés most admired by Americans. The movie theater was the theater of democracy, not only because it catered to a fair cross-section of the public, but also because it was everyman's arsenal of democratic idealism. Patterns of democratic thought, illuminated with the high courage that our idealism seemed to indicate was the birthright of every American as well as his responsibility, were models of martial behavior. These patterns were the more readily understood for being trite and simplistic. Their endless repetition indicated that their screen presence touched a common chord in their audiences.

Likewise, film gives us fresh insight, on the scale mass culture society demands, into the postwar attitudes toward the conflict. Where for the involved nations of Europe the war was nothing less than a political, economic, social, intellectual, and moral holocaust, the tale of the film conveys the feeling that many Americans continued to view it as the supreme adventure of the democratic conscience. The appearance of a whole generation of democratic samurai in European trenches was enough to render tangled international problems understandable as well as soluble. From Wallace Reid to Richard Barthelmess to Gary Cooper may mark a change in the image of popular leading men, yet all bore the burden of democracy's war with little or no change in idealism. Where other less popular forms of evidence showed a mounting repulsion with the war and its results, and even with the American role in the war, motion pictures continued to outline the war experience in honorable and heroic terms.

This is not to say that film was without its pacifistic or isolationist impulses. The earliest presentations of the war, as far back as 1914, had been based on the ideals of ethical Christianity. But these rapidly gave way to more robust appeals to nationalism and the democratic spirit. War as tragedy did not really reappear on American screens until the Depression decade. Yet even then this tragic vision was tempered by the unwillingness or inability of the film to criticize American participation. Those films usually regarded as firm indices of a shift away from militarism in the United States, such as *All Quiet on the Western Front* and *The Dawn Patrol*, did not directly criticize America. Germany began to be treated more sympathetically, and European Allies lost some of their noble character that had helped to cement wartime bonds, but the American role went almost unchallenged. The image of the United States as a redresser of European wrongs survived to fuel yet another drive for international involvement.

The thirties generally have been seen as a decade when Americans recoiled from the responsibilities of world power and tended to view World War I as at worst a debacle and at best a mistake. The most acerbic critics of national policy viewed the war as a Machiavellian machination engineered in the name of power politics and economic gain. More moderate analysts saw only a series of blunders and mistakes that took lives without recompense. Yet film continued to indicate a certain popular ambiguity toward the American role. Traditional ideals survived alongside the newer viewpoints. These ideals seemed almost indestructible, and they gained new life with the rising antipathy toward totalitarian regimes.

The evidence of the motion picture was no less articulate in limning national characteristics. American attitudes toward other countries appeared in sharp focus througout the period. England, France, Russia and Germany each received thorough, if not careful, cinematic treatment. In each case, the leaders and the people of these countries were presented in terms understandable to Americans at the simplest visual level. The English were sketched in terms most congenial to

American ideals of national service and self-sacrifice. Films such as *Cavalcade* showed that Americans felt more than the passing fancy of a military alliance toward their North Atlantic neighbor. The French, although romantically democratic, were much less dependable, while the Russians, as indicated by the vacillating nature of their treatment on American screens, were almost incomprehensible. Above all, the war experience fastened a militarist image on Germany that even films of the caliber of *All Quiet on the Western Front* were unable to erase. All these cinematic perceptions of national characteristics had one thing in common: American ideals provided the firm yardstick of measurement, a form of national subjectivism that responds well to historical analysis.

No less rewarding is the harvest of images reaped from the presentation of sexual or social groups, such as women or the military. Movies offer various ways of analyzing popular attitudes toward these groups and toward various roles played within the groups. American society contained certain patterned appreciations of mothers, sweethearts, and wives that emerged into bold relief in war films. In the case of the military, the ancient practices of comic art afford useful evidence regarding American attitudes toward authority. In short, through film we may examine the imagery that was being offered to the American public, imagery that Americans relied upon to help explain not only the friend or the foe, but themselves as well.

It is not too much to claim for the motion picture a primary role in the popular dissemination of intellectual material. Film constantly strives to find the dead center of the views, intellectual and otherwise, of its audience. In this lies its greatest popularity and profit. It is not argued that through motion picture evidence we arrive at the appreciation of something called a "mass mind," but it is suggested that intellectual life, in its causational as well as its reflective aspects, may exist outside the university classroom, the elitist salon, and the halls of government. The films of World War I strongly suggest this is indeed the case. Film speaks both for and to a world that is largely inarticulate, and it is waiting to be heard.

Notes

Preface

1. Harold Cruse, *The Crisis of the Negro Intellectual* (New York: William Morrow and Company, Inc., 1967), p.221.
2. Quoted in Robert E. Spiller et al., *Literary History of the United States*, 3d ed. rev. (New York: The Macmillan Company, 1963), p.931.
3. One scholar claims World War I has been underrepresented in films made in the post-World War II era; see Garth S. Jowett, "The Concept of History in American Produced Films: An Analysis of the Films Made in the Period 1950-1961," *Journal of Popular Culture* 3 (Spring 1970): 800,809.

Introduction

1. Jacques Barzun and Henry F. Graff, *The Modern Researcher* (New York: Harcourt, Brace and World, Inc., 1957).
2. Ibid., p. 133.
3. Arthur M. Schlesinger and Dixon Ryan Fox, eds., *A History of American Life*, vol. 12, Preston William Slosson, *The Great Crusade and After, 1914-1928* (New York: The Macmillan Company, 1931), p.393. Other general histories with the same approach to film include George E. Mowry, *The Urban Nation, 1920-1960* (New York: Hill and Wang, 1965); John D. Hicks, *Republican Ascendancy, 1921-1933* (New York: Harper and Row, 1963); William E. Leuchtenburg, *The Perils of Prosperity, 1914-1932* (Chicago: University of Chicago Press, 1958); George Soule, *Prosperity Decade: From War to Depression, 1917-1929* (New York: Harper and Row, 1968); Arthur S. Link, *Woodrow Wilson and the Progressive Era, 1910-1917* (New York: Harper and Row, 1963;* and Robert M. Crunden, *From Self to Society, 1919-1941* (Englewood Cliffs, N.J.: Prentice-Hall, Inc., 1972).
4. Joseph Wood Krutch, *The Modern Temper: A Study and a Confession* (New York: Harcourt, Brace and World, Inc., 1956), p.126. This work was originally published in 1929. See Paul F. Lazarsfeld and Robert K. Merton, "Mass Communication, Popular Taste and Organized Social Action," in *The Communication of Ideas*, ed. by Lyman Bryson (New York: Harper and Brothers, 1948), p.98, for the view that the social role played by mass media has been overestimated. The historian may agree with Lazarsfeld and Merton and still assess as considerable the social and intellectual role of film.

5. Mass media literature, both theoretical and substantive, is far too vast to be examined here. Bryson's (n4) is a solid collection. An introduction that is flawed by its textbookish and banal style is Erik Barnouw, *Mass Communication: Television, Radio, Film, Press: The Media and Their Practice in the United States of America* (New York: Rinehart and Company, 1956). Malcolm W. Willey, "Communication Agencies and the Volume of Propaganda," *Annals of the American Academy of Political and Social Science* 179(May 1935): 194-200, outlines some characteristics of modern mass communication.

6. Arthur Weigall, "The Influence of the Kinematograph upon National Life," *Nineteenth Century* (April 1921): 661.

7. "Our Motion-Picture Films Encircling the Earth," *Literary Digest*, September 28, 1918, p.78. England, judging from calendar year 1917, was by far the leading recipient, with 30,000,000 feet. Other leading customers included Italy (16,000,000), Russia (15,000,000), Canada (14,000,000), France (11,000,000), Australia (10,000,000), Argentina (6,000,000), Japan (2,375,000), and China (1,320,000).

8. Davidson Boughey, *The Film Industry* (London: Sir Isaac Pitman and Sons Ltd., 1921), p.xvii. Boughey estimated the weekly film requirements of world cinemas at about 1,500,000,000 feet.

9. In no case did American films outnumber foreign competitors in foreign countries by less than two to one. In the important markets, namely those of Europe, Argentina, Australia, and Japan, the ratio was more often four to one. The United States could also claim four times as many theaters as the next country. There were only five nations in the twenties which had even 10 percent of the total number of American theaters. Charles Merz, "When the Movies Go Abroad," *Harper's Magazine*, January 1926,pp.159-65. For a thorough breakdown of international film markets during the decade, see C. J. North, "Our Foreign Trade in Motion Pictures," *Annals of the American Academy of Political and Social Science* 128 (November 1926): 100-108.

10. Hicks, *Republican Ascendancy*, p.172, argues in passing that foreign audiences rarely realized that Americans took as entertainment what foreigners believed to be stark reality depicted on the screen. Daniel Boorstin, as late as 1960, remarked upon the contrast of a near-empty USIA library in Bangalore with the full movie theaters nearby playing American products. *The Image: A Guide to Pseudo-Events in America* (New York: Harper and Row, 1964), p.242.

11. These estimates are taken from Mowry, *The Urban Nation*, p.4; Leuchtenburg, *The Perils of Prosperity*, p.196; and Gertrude Jobes, *Motion Picture Empire* (Hamden, Conn.: Archon Books, 1966), p.123. See also Carl Laemmle, "From the Inside," *Saturday Evening Post*, August 27, 1927, p.130. Laemmle was head of Universal Studios. Statistical data by year may be found in the *Film Daily Yearbook of Motion Pictures*, passim.

12. Terry Ramsaye, "The Motion Picture," *Annals of the American Academy of Political and Social Science* 128 (November 1926): 1-19. Ramsaye was not a professional historian, but he wrote prolifically about film history. He was editor of the weekly trade magazine *Motion Picture Herald* from 1931 until his death in 1954.

13. Robert S. Lynd and Helen Merrell Lynd, *Middletown: A Study in Modern American Culture* (New York: Harcourt, Brace and World, Inc.,1929),pp.358, n20; 359, n22. The Lynds remark that this total included people from the surrounding countryside; even so, the figures seem impressive.

14. J.F. Steiner, "Recreation and Leisure Time Activities," *Recent Social Trends in the United States*, Report of the President's Research Committee on Social Trends (New York: McGraw-Hill Book Company, Inc.,1933), pp.912-57.

15. Frederick P. Keppel, "The Arts in Social Life," in ibid., p.993.

16. I. C. Jarvie, *Movies and Society* (New York: Basic Books, Inc., 1970), pp.4-5, n9, recapitulates this argument. Jarvie, a sociologist, knows of "nothing comparable from the point of view of getting inside the skin of another society as viewing films made for the home market."

17. Lottie Briscoe, "The Great War," *Motion Picture Magazine* (February 1915), pp.81-84.

18. Vachel Lindsay, *The Art of the Moving Picture*, rev. ed. (New York: Macmillan Company, 1922), pp.67, 289. This argument also was current in the editorial pages of the industry's trade magazines before and during the war years. In particular, see the *Moving Picture World*, passim.

19. Lindsay, *The Art of the Moving Picture*, pp.65-66.

20. "The War-Time Sanctuary," editorial, *Photoplay Magazine*, October 1917, p.15.

21. Harrison Rhodes, "The Majestic Movies," *Harper's Magazine*, January 1919, pp.183-94.

22. Mowry, *The Urban Nation*, p.4. The ensuing paragraph follows Mowry's argument, which in turn is a reflection of a widely accepted consensus concerning the cultivation of mass taste.

23. Edward F. Stevenson, *Motion Pictures in Advertising and Selling* (New York: Visugraphic Pictures, Inc., 1929), pp.4, 16-19. True to form, this statement, which appeared in a brochure, was attested by eighteen business firms.

24. Mortimer J. Adler, *Art and Prudence: A Study in Practical Philosophy* (New York: Longmans, Green and Co., 1937), p.118.

Chapter 1

1. John C. Greene, "Objectives and Methods in Intellectual History," *Mississippi Valley Historical Review* 44 (June 1957): 71.

2. Daniel Boorstin, *The Image: A Guide to Pseudo-Events in America* (New York: Harper and Row, 1964), pp.264, 287. In line with the homogeneity of his philosophy, Boorstin inveighs against what he sees as an ossified, artificial, and conventional structuring of fields of historical study.

3. Charles Callan Tansill, *America Goes to War* (Boston: Little, Brown and Company, 1938), pp.16-31.

4. Charles Seymour, *American Neutrality, 1914-1917: Essays on the Causes of American Intervention in the World War* (New Haven, Conn.: Yale University Press, 1935), p.149.

5. H. Schuyler Foster, Jr., "Charting America's News of the World War," *Foreign Affairs* 15 (January 1937): 311-19.

6. Frances Winwar, "The World War and the Arts," in *War in the Twentieth Century*, ed. by Willard Waller (New York: Dryden Press, 1940), pp.192-232.

7. Harold D. Lasswell, *Propaganda Technique in the World War* (New York: Alfred A. Knopf, 1927), pp.19, 144-45.

8. James Duane Squires, *British Propaganda at Home and in the United States From 1914 to 1917* (Cambridge, Mass.: Harvard University Press, 1935), pp. 86-104.

9. See, for example, Arthur Ponsonby, *Falsehood in Wartime* (London: George Allen and Unwin, Ltd., 1928), pp.135-39, 181-82; James Morgan Read, *Atrocity Propaganda, 1914-1919* (New Haven, Conn.: Yale University Press, 1941), pp.14-15, 225, 256 n62; Walter Millis, *Road to War: America, 1914-1917* (New York: Howard Fertig, 1970, hardbound reprint of 1935 edition), pp.217-218, 237, 303; and Horace C. Peterson, *Propaganda For War: The Campaign Against American Neutrality* (Norman, Okla.: University of Oklahoma Press, 1939).

10. William E. Leuchtenburg, *The Perils of Prosperity, 1914-1932* (Chicago: University of Chicago Press, 1958), p.197.

11. Thomas J. Pressly, *Americans Interpret Their Civil War* (New York: Free Press, 1965), p.305. It is indicative that Pressly's otherwise excellent historiographical study found no room for the numerous film treatments of the Civil War, in particular David W. Griffith's classic, *Birth of a Nation* (1915).

12. George E. Mowry, *The Urban Nation, 1920-1960* (New York: Hill and Wang, 1965), pp.130-31. The "almost unanimous" idea appears to be drawn largely from a superficial knowledge of the handful of famous "anti-war" films of the period. See Chapter 9 for a critical assessment of this hypothesis.

13. Arthur Weigall, "The Influence of the Kinematograph Upon National Life," *Nineteenth Century*, April 1921, p.671.

14. The *American Film Catalog,* compiled by the American Film Institute and scheduled for publication by the R. R. Bowker Company. The catalog is projected at nineteen sections and is divided by decade into "feature films," "short films," and newsreels for the years 1893-1970. The prospectus indicates remarkable thoroughness of approach. There is a system of cross-indexing. The first volumes have begun to appear. The prices are individually prohibitive, but the entire catalog appears to be a necessity for aiding the film student of the future.

15. Examples of this practice abound; one of the classic cases is the superpatriotic *Victory at Sea* series produced shortly after World War II and still being shown at U.S. naval installations and on some local television stations.

16. See Penelope Houston, "The Nature of the Evidence," *Sight and Sound*, Spring 1967, p.90, for comment on this point.

17. Richard Dyer MacCann, ed., *Film and Society* (New York: Charles Scribner's Sons, 1964), pp.179-82.

18. James Card, "Problems of Film History," *Hollywood Quarterly*, Spring 1950, 288.

19. The best general (though badly outdated) history of the American film is still Lewis Jacobs, *The Rise of the American Film: A Critical History* (New York: Teachers College Press, 1968), which contains both footnotes and an excellent bibliography. Paul Rotha and Richard Griffith, *The Film Till Now: A Survey of World Cinema* (Feltham, England: Hamlyn Publishing Group, Ltd., 1967), has footnotes and useful appendices, but no bibliography. Benjamin B. Hampton, *History of the American Film Industry from Its Beginnings to 1931* (New York: Dover Publications, Inc., 1970), has no footnotes and no bibliography; Maurice Bardèche and Robert Brasillach, *The History of Motion Pictures,* trans. and ed. by Iris Barry (New York: Arno Press and *The New York Times,* 1970), has footnote commentary but no bibliography; Richard Schickel, *Movies: The History of an Art and an Institution* (New York: Basic Books, Inc., 1964), has no footnotes and no bibliography; and Arthur Knight, *The Liveliest Art* (New York: New American Library, Inc., 1957), has no footnotes and a bibliography entitled "100 Best Books on Films." Kenneth MacGowan's entertaining and informative *Behind the Screen: The History and Techniques of the Motion Picture* (New York: Dell Publishing Company, Inc., 1965), and Terry Ramsaye, *A Million and One Nights* (London: Frank Cass and Company, Ltd., 1964) (originally published in 1926) have neither footnotes nor bibliography. Gerald Mast, *A Short History of the Movies* (New York: Bobbs-Merrill Company, Inc., 1971), has no footnotes but a good general bibliography of books and films. All these works are indexed with varying degrees of efficiency. Recent scholarly approaches are Robert Sklar, *Movie-made America: A Cultural History of the Movies* (New York: Random House, 1975) and Garth Jowett, *Film, the Democratic Art: A Social History of American Film* (Boston: Little, Brown and Company, 1976).

20. See n19. Schickel and Knight are film critics. Ramsaye was editor of the weekly trade magazine *Motion Picture Herald* from 1931 to his death in 1954. Hampton began as a newspaper editor, moved to a vice-presidency with the American Tobacco Company, and became first the engineer of the merger that produced Paramount and later a small independent producer. He died in 1932. MacGowan was a movie producer who gravitated to academia, being Chairman Emeritus of the Department of Theater Arts at UCLA at the time of his death in 1963. Jacobs and Rotha are award-winning filmmakers and critics. Mast has been both a child actor and an extra in films.

21. For differing analyses of the relationship between literature and film, see George Bluestone, *Novels into Film* (Berkeley, Calif.: University of California Press, 1971), and Robert Richardson, *Literature and Film* (Bloomington, Ind.: Indiana University Press, 1969). While Bluestone claims film and novels comprise completely separate genres, a position with which I agree, Richardson stresses the similarity in approach between literary and film construction.

22. Bertha Westbrook Reid, *Wallace Reid: His Life Story* (New York: Sorg, 1923); Ezra Goodman, *The Fifty-Year Decline and Fall of Hollywood* (New York: Simon and Schuster, 1961).

23. An engaging work on the star phenomenon is Edgar Morin, *The Stars,* trans. by Richard Howard (New York: Grove Press, 1960). For a discussion of the star as myth, see p.183.

24. See, for instance, Theodore Huff, *Charlie Chaplin* (New York: Henry Schuman, 1951).

25. A running debate concerning the auteur theory has engaged the aestheticians of the film periodicals for years. For an overview, see Charles Glynn, "Auteur Criticism and Popular Films," *Journal of Popular Culture* 4 (Winter 1971): 754-68; McCreary, "Film and History,"p.55.

26. Stanley Cooperman, *World War I and the American Novel* (Baltimore, Md.: Johns Hopkins Press, 1967), p.208.

27. Arthur Edwin Krous, "Literature and the Motion Picture," *Annals of the American Academy of Political and Social Science* 128 (November 1926): 70. Krous, a free-lance scenario writer and film editor, believed that the works of authors such as Maeterlinck, Conrad, Kipling, and Barrie (a list revealing in itself) had little possibility of finding realization on the screen. "The conjunction of motion pictures and literature is rather futile – like trying to discuss music in terms of architecture, for instance, or tennis in terms of football." Those who wrote novels, plays, or short stories with the specific purpose of having them made into movies were in for a rude shock. Many were examined, few were chosen. See Ruth Sapin, "Confessions of a Movie Reader," *Nation,* (September 8, 1926), pp.214-15; and, "A Scenarist Confesses," *Literary Digest,* January 22, 1927, p.27.

28. For commentary on the difficulties of selling script ideas to Hollywood, see Sapin, "Confessions of a Movie Reader"; Bruce Bliven, "Mr. X of the Movies," *New Republic,* January 25, 1922, pp.246-48; and W.H. Tolischus, letter to the editor, "Clio on the Screen," *New Republic,* February 22, 1922, p.373. For problems of the scriptwriting process itself, see I. A. R. Wylie, "Gone Hollywood," *Harper's Magazine* , June 1932, pp.11-20; Philip Wylie, "Writing For the Movies," *New Republic,* December 1937, pp.96-102; and "Perpetual Motion as Discovered by a Movie-Play Writer," *Literary Digest,* November 13, 1920, pp.61-62.

29. Sidney R. Kent, "The Motion Picture of Tomorrow," *Annals of the American Academy of Political and Social Science* 128 (November 1926): 33.

30. D. W. Griffith, *The Rise and Fall of Free Speech in America,* pamphlet (Los Angeles, Calif.: n.p., 1916), pp. 1, 8.

31. Thomas H. Ince, "History and Development of the Motion Picture Industry," undated typewritten MS., Museum of Modern Art, New York City (hereafter cited as MOMA). The MS. has no date, but internal evidence suggests that it was written in late 1921. There is no pagination.

32. Tolischus, "Clio on the Screen," p.373. For a warning on authenticity in historical films, see William H. Hartley, *Selected Films for American History and Problems* (New York: Columbia University Press, 1940), pp.11-15.

33. W. Stephen Bush, "History on the Screen," *Moving Picture World*, February 22, 1913, p.757.

34. "Yale's Movie Version of American History," *Literary Digest*, March 4, 1922, p.43.

35. "The Historian in the Movies," ibid., January 12, 1918, p.27

36. Harrison Rhodes, "The Majestic Movies," *Harper's Magazine,* January, 1919, p.184.

37. I. C. Jarvie, *Movies and Society* (New York: Basic Books, Inc., 1970), p.125.

38. Arthur Gleason, "Gibbon and the Movies," *New Republic,* September 26, 1923, pp.128-30.

39. Irving Thalberg, "The Modern Photoplay," in *Introduction to the Photoplay,* mimeographed typewritten MS. of lecture delivered at the University of Southern California, March 20, 1929, Academy of Motion Pictures Arts and Sciences Library, Los Angeles (hereafter cited as AMPAS), p.68.

40. William Dieterle, "Views on Historical Movies," *New York World-Telegram*, October 13, 1937, p.44.

Chapter 2

1. Barry Ulanov, *The Two Worlds of American Art: The Private and the Popular* (New York: The Macmillan Company, 1965), pp.11-12.

2. See in particular Gilbert Seldes, *The Seven Lively Arts* (New York: A. S. Barnes and Company, Inc., 1962) (originally published in 1924). An excellent survey of early film criticism is

Myron Osborn Lounsbury, "The Origins of American Film Criticism, 1909-1939" (Ph.D. diss., University of Pennsylvania, 1966). I am here using the term "intellectual" to mean one who sees himself and is seen by others as having some presumed ability to comment critically on all manifestations of culture, in whatever form these manifestations may appear.

3. Lounsbury, "The Origins of American Film Criticism,"pp.489-92.

4. Lyman Bryson, "Popular Art," in Lyman Bryson, ed., *The Communication of Ideas* (New York: Harper and Brothers, 1948), p.286.

5. Russel B. Nye, *The Unembarrassed Muse: The Popular Arts in America* (New York: Dial Press, 1970). See in particular the discussion of "elite art" and "popular art," pp.3-4. Further sympathetic discussions of popular culture are Stuart Levine, "Art, Values, Institutions and Culture: An Essay in American Studies Methodology and Relevance," *American Quarterly* 24 (May 1972): 131-65; and Edward Shils, "Mass Society and Its Culture," in Bernard Rosenberg and David Manning White, ed., *Mass Culture Revisited* (New York: Van Nostrand Reinhold Company, 1971), pp.61-84.

6. This argument owes much to John A. Kouwenhoven, *The Arts in Modern American Civilization* (New York: W.W. Norton and Company, Inc., 1967).

7. Ulanov, *The Two Worlds of American Art,* pp.14-15; see also Nye, *The Unembarrassed Muse,* p.4.

8. For an argument for using the auteur theory to judge aspects of popular culture, see John G. Cawelti, "Notes Toward an Aesthetic of Popular Culture," *Journal of Popular Culture* 5 (Fall 1971): 255-68. Bluestone, *Novels into Film*, p.13, claims aesthetic analysis is virtually inseparable from social and psychological analysis, a position with which I disagree.

9. Felix Gilbert, "Intellectual History: Its Aims and Methods," *Daedalus* 100 (Winter 1971): 88. Franklin L. Baumer, "Intellectual History and Its Problems," *Journal of Modern History* 21 (September 1949): 191-203, includes "popular literature of all sorts" in his discussion (p.191) but does not mention film.

10. R. Richard Wohl, "Intellectual History: An Historian's View," *Historian* 16 (Autumn 1953): 66.

11. John Higham, "The Rise of American Intellectual History," *American Historical Review* 56 (April 1951): 471.

12. Gilbert, "Intellectual History: Its Aims and Methods," p.84. Gilbert also argues that even if avenues of communication in all levels of society are studied, the historian of ideas is still confronted with the problem of causation. This problem is a crucial and difficult one for the student of film; see chapter 3.

13. Rush Welter, "The History of Ideas in America: An Essay in Redefinition," *Journal of American History* 51 (March 1965): 602.

14. Ibid., p.610.

15. For speculation on this point, see John Higham, "American Intellectual History: A Critical Appraisal," in *The American Experience: Approaches to the Study of the United States,* ed. by Hennig Cohen (Boston: Houghton Mifflin Company, 1968), p.355.

16. Vachel Lindsay, *The Art of the Moving Picture*, rev. ed. (New York: The Macmillan Company, 1922); Hugo Münsterberg, *The Photoplay* (New York: D. Appleton and Co., 1916).

17. Lounsbury, "The Origins of American Film Criticism," pp. 48-49.

18. See, for example, a debate between S.L.M. Barlow and Robert Emmett MacAlarney (anti-movie) and Burton Rascoe and Sir Gilbert Parker (pro-movie) in "An Arraignment and Defense of the Movies," *Current Opinion,* March 1922, pp.353-54.

19. Lounsbury, "The Origins of American Film Criticism," p.482. Lounsbury also identifies six basic types of critical opinion, 482-89. The arrival of sound, far from being regarded as an extension of the art of film, seems to have discouraged many of the intellectual critics. See "Hollywood Speaks," *Nation*, September 26, 1928,pp.285-86.

20. Harold E. Stearns, ed., *Civilization in the United States: An Inquiry by Thirty Americans* (New York: Harcourt, Brace and Company, 1922).

21. Ibid., p. 212.

22. Harold E. Stearns, *America: A Reappraisal* (New York: Hillman-Curl, Inc., 1937), pp.240-58.

23. Harold E. Stearns, ed., *America Now: An Inquiry into Civilization in the United States* (New York: Literary Guild of America, Inc., 1938).

24. H. L. Mencken, *Prejudices: Sixth Series* (New York: Alfred A. Knopf, 1927), pp.290, 302.

25. Bernard Shaw and Archibald Henderson, "The Drama, the Theater, and the Films," *Harper's Magazine,* September 1924, pp. 425-26.

26. I. A. R. Wylie, "Gone Hollywood," pp.11-20.

27. The writer was Aaron Hardy Ulm, "How Our Films Misrepresent America Abroad," *Literary Digest,* November 26, 1921, pp.28-29.

28. Hortense Powdermaker, "An Anthropologist Looks at the Movies," *Annals of the American Academy of Political and Social Science,* 254 (November 1947): 83.

29. Sapin, "Confessions of a Movie Reader," p.215.

30. See Leo Rosten, "Movies and Propaganda," *Annals of the American Academy of Political and Social Science,* 254 (November 1947): 116-24.

31. Quoted in Nye, *The Unembarrassed Muse,* p.389. See also Hampton, *History of the American Film Industry from Its Beginnings to 1931,* p.359. This book was published originally as *A History of the Movies* (New York: Covici, Friede, 1931). For the routine nature of the industry by 1927, see Carl Laemmle, "From the Inside," *Saturday Evening Post,* August 27, 1927, p.11.

32. Terry Ramsaye, "The Motion Picture," *Annals of the American Academy of Political and Social Science* 128 (November 1926): 19.

33. Katherine Fullerton Gould, "Hollywood: An American State of Mind," *Harper's Magazine,* May 1923, pp.689-96.

34. Parker Tyler, "Hollywood as a Universal Church," in *The American Experience,* pp.287-88. Tyler calls the world of professional entertainment an "economic democracy where the artistic product is without true ethical responsibility, and the human objective is profit and nothing more." Ibid., p.284.

35. But see Jarvie, *Movies and Society,* p.185, where it is argued that advertisements, word of mouth, and critical approbation do not make a film successful. "On the whole I think people are critical and on the lookout." Impressionistically, this statement probably did not hold true for the earlier years of the industry, since the visual product was not being marketed to a sophisticated, media-conscious generation.

36. Powdermaker, "An Anthropologist Looks at the Movies," p.83.

37. Hortense Powdermaker, "Hollywood and the U.S.A.," in Bernard Rosenberg and David Manning White, eds., *Mass Culture: The Popular Arts in America* (Glencoe, Ill.: Free Press, 1957), p.282.

38. "Juvenile Audience," *Nation*, December 7, 1916, p.530.

39. John S. Cohen, Jr., "Books and the Movies," *New Republic,* November 10, 1926, p.343.

40. Kenneth M. Goode and Harford Powel, Jr., "What About Advertising?" in Robert Sklar, ed., *The Plastic Age, 1917-1930* (New York: George Braziller, 1970), p.91.

41. "Morals and Movies," *Nation,* September 18, 1929, 292.

42. J. Stuart Blackton, "Early History," in *Introduction to the Photoplay,* February 20, 1929, AMPAS. See also Weigall, "The Influence of the Kinematograph Upon National Life," p.668.

43. "The Movie and the Masses," *New Republic,* June 8, 1927, pp.61-62. See Mortimer J. Adler, *Art and Prudence: A Study in Practical Philosophy* (New York: Longmans, Green and Company, 1937), p.145, for the argument that mass taste is not determined totally by the masses themselves, but by the "better organized groups" who "approve or disapprove of the movies on other grounds than their entertainment and recreation values."

44. Daniel J. Boorstin, *The Image: A Guide to Pseudo-Events in America* (New York: Harper and Row, 1964), pp.128-29. Such an argument ignores nineteenth-century writers of the caliber of Melville, Ibsen, and Hardy. See also Cohen, "Books and the Movies," p.343.

45. Ramsaye, "The Motion Picture," p.19.

46. Robert S. Lynd and Helen Merrell Lynd, *Middletown: A Study in Modern American Culture* (New York: Harcourt, Brace and World, Inc., 1929), p.381, n6.

47. Richard Sheridan Ames, "The Screen Enters Politics: Will Hollywood Produce More Propaganda?," *Harper's Magazine,* March 1935, p.482.

48. J. Stuart Blackton, "Our Debt to Hollywood," *Motion Picture Director,* October 1926, p.59.

49. Cohen, "Books and the Movies," pp.343-44. The closest a book ever came to being translated literally onto the screen was probably Erich Von Stroheim's *Greed* (1923), which attempted through almost countless reels faithfully to relate Frank Norris's *McTeague.* The full version was never shown commercially.

50. Herbert Butterfield, *The Whig Interpretation of History* (New York: W.W. Norton, Inc., 1965).

51. Jarvie, *Movies and Society,* p.86.

52. Bush, "History on the Screen," p.757. Vachel Lindsay once enthused that "in a photoplay by a master, when the American flag is shown, the thirteen stripes are columns of history and the stars are headlines" (*The Art of the Moving Picture,* p.54).

53. Nathaniel W. Stephenson, "The Goal of the Motion Picture in Education," *Annals of the American Academy of Political and Social Science* 128 (November 1926): 118.

54. Harry Arthur Wise, *Motion Pictures as an Aid in Teaching American History* (New Haven, Conn.: Yale University Press, 1939), pp.112-13, 142-43.

55. Harry C. Carr, "Griffith, Maker of Battle Scenes, Sees Real War," *Photoplay Magazine,* March 1918, p.119.

56. For comment on the inclination of symbol study to lead to aesthetic judgment, see Welter, "The History of Ideas in America,"p.604. Most film historians are aestheticians before they are historians. Pertinent examples include Bardèche and Brasillach, *The History of Motion Pictures;* Schickel, *Movies: The History of an Art and an Institution;* Knight, *The Liveliest Art;* Rotha and Griffith, *The Film Till Now;* Mast, *A Short History of the Movies;* and A.R. Fulton, *Motion Pictures: The Development of an Art from Silent Films to the Age of Television* (Norman: University of Oklahoma Press, 1960). Jacobs, *The Rise of the American Film,* and Sklar, *Movie-made America,* are almost alone in effectively interrelating historical and aesthetic comment. Most of these works now are dated: Bardèche and Brasillach originally published in 1938; Rotha by himself in 1930, although his work has been updated; and Jacobs in 1939. Two works in a class by themselves are Edward Wagenknecht, *The Movies in the Age of Innocence* (Norman, Okla.: University of Oklahoma Press, 1960), a highly readable piece of nostalgia, and Kevin Brownlow, *The Parade's Gone By...* (New York: Alfred A. Knopf, 1968), a hymn to the best work of the silent-film era.

Chapter 3

1. Henry James Forman, *Our Movie Made Children* (New York: The Macmillan Company, 1934), p.279. These conclusions would seem as valid today, especially with the advent of the film media into the home via television. For general comment on the Payne Fund Studies, see Sklar, *Movie-made America,* pp.134-40, and Jowett, *Film, the Democratic Art,* pp.220-29.

2. Herbert Blumer, *Movies and Conduct* (New York: The Macmillan Company, 1933), pp.193-94, 196; Herbert Blumer and Philip M. Hauser, *Movies, Delinquency, and Crime* (New York: Macmillan Company, 1933), pp.197-202; Perry W. Holaday and George D. Stoddard, *Getting Ideas From the Movies* (New York: Macmillan Company, 1933), pp.77-80.

3. Lloyd L. Ramseyer, "A Study of the Influence of Documentary Films on Social Attitudes" (Ph.D. diss., Ohio State University, 1938), pp.156-58. The films used were produced primarily by the Works Progress Administration.

4. Solomon P. Rosenthal, "Change of Socio-Economic Attitudes Under Radical Motion Picture Propaganda," *Archives of Psychology* 25 (April 1934): 46.

5. Nelson L. Greene, "Motion Pictures in the Classroom," *Annals of the American Academy of Political and Social Science* 128 (November 1926): 122-30. Greene was editor of *The Educational Screen.*

6. Adler, *Art and Prudence;* Raymond Moley, *Are We Movie-Mad?* (New York: Macy-Masius, 1938).

7. Ruth C. Peterson and L.L. Thurstone, *Motion Pictures and the Social Attitudes of Children* (New York: Macmillan Company, 1933).

8. Adler, *Art and Prudence*, pp.194-212. Sociologist Hugh Dalziel Duncan's observation is pertinent here. Although art may be discussed using quantitative techniques, we currently know little about the production, distribution, and consumption of art's "symbolic material." See *Symbols in Society* (New York: Oxford University Press, 1968), p.10.

9. *Time*, June 11, 1923, p.15. An attempt to categorize by sex in this instance leads only to complexity, since both pictures featured Rudolph Valentino.

10. Lynd and Lynd, *Middletown*, pp.263-69,200. For the *Chronicles of America* series, see "Yale's Movie Version of American History," *Literary Digest*, March 4, 1922,pp.38, 40, 43.

11. *New York Times*, December 30, 1918, p.7.

12. Sklar, *The Plastic Age*, pp.55, 48.

13. Joseph L. Holmes, "Do War Films Inculcate War, or the Will to Peace?" *Motion Picture Monthly,* November 1930, p.11.

14. Peterson and Thurstone, *Motion Pictures and the Social Attitudes of Children,* pp.24-28, 39-44, 58-60, 65-66.

15. Richard D. MacCann, "Documentary Film and Democratic Government: An Administrative History From Pare Lorentz to John Huston" (Ph.D. diss., Harvard University, 1951), p.74.

16. Kenneth E. Boulding, *The Image: Knowledge in Life and Society* (Ann Arbor, Mich.: University of Michigan Press, 1961), p.45.

17. My argument here follows that of Hugh Dalziel Duncan's theoretical study, *Communication and the Social Order* (New York: Oxford University Press, 1968).

18. Boulding, *The Image: Knowledge in Life and Society,* p.6.

19. Marshall McLuhan, *Understanding Media: The Extensions of Man* (New York: McGraw-Hill, 1964), pp.284-96.

20. Duncan, *Communication and Social Order,* pp.16, 74. Emphasis in original. For the opposite view, that the "medium is the message" in the case of movie audiences, see Jarvie, *Movies and Society,* p.216.

21. Boulding, *The Image: Knowledge in Life and Society,* pp.7, 16.

22. Duncan, *Communication and Social Order,* pp. 13, 10, 85. In the same work Duncan argues (p.191) that the social meaning of an art work lies in how the different and conflicting claims of the actors are resolved. This resolution is Boulding's "change in imagery"; see n21.

23. Jarvie, *Movies and Society,* p.96.

24. Joseph Wood Krutch, *The Modern Temper: A Study and a Confession* (New York: Harcourt, Brace and World, Inc., 1956), p.xiii.

25. Powdermaker, "Hollywood and the U.S.A.," p.289.

26. Budd Schulberg, "Movies in America: After Fifty Years," *Atlantic*, November 1947,p.120.

27. George H. Mead, "The Nature of Aesthetic Experience," *International Journal of Ethics* 36 (July 1926): 382-93.

28. Parker Tyler, *Magic and Myth of the Movies* (New York: Henry Holt and Company, 1947), p.xi. Emphasis in original.

29. But see Paul G. Cressey, "The Motion Picture Experience as Modified by Social Background and Personality," *American Sociological Review* 3 (August 1938): 516-25, for the argument that movies take their specific character from the social and psychological "framework" in which they are experienced. Cressey concedes that it is still possible to discover "certain characteristic circumstances in which the cinema's contribution to ideation and conduct is great" (p.525).

30. Martha Wolfenstein and Nathan Leites, *Movies: A Psychological Study* (Glencoe, Ill.: Free Press, 1950), pp.11-16, 294.

31. James Richard Connor, "Pen and Sword: World War I Novels in America, 1916-1941" (Ph.D. diss., University of Wisconsin, 1961), p.387. Even the historical novel may prove to be a rich source of information about the historical tone of the period in which it was written. See Alastair MacDonald Taylor, "The Historical Novel as a Source in History," *Sewanee Review* 46 (October-December 1938): 459-79.

32. William O. Aydelotte, "The Detective Story as a Historical Source," *Yale Review* (September 1949): 91.
33. Tyler, *Magic and Myth of the Movies*, p.xiii.
34. Kracauer, *From Caligari to Hitler,* particularly pp. 3-11.
35. Welter, "The History of Ideas in America," p.608.
36. Franklin Fearing, "Influence of the Movies on Attitudes and Behavior," *Annals of the American Academy of Political and Social Science* 154 (November 1947): 75.
37. John D. Hicks, *Republican Ascendancy, 1921-1933* (New York: Harper and Row, 1963), p.171.
38. Lynd and Lynd, *Middletown*, p.269.
39. See Dorothy B. Jones, "The Hollywood War Film: 1942-44," *Hollywood Quarterly* 1, no. 1 (1945-1946) (October 1945): 1-19.
40. Connor, "Pen and Sword," p.376. For a good discussion of the problem of devising an adequate measuring scale, which in the current jargon of the historian comes close to "quantification," see Fearing, "Influence of the Movies on Attitudes and Behavior," pp. 78-79.
41. Gilbert, "Intellectual History: Its Aims and Methods," p. 92.
42. Pola Negri, *Memoirs of a Star* (Garden City, N.Y.: Doubleday and Company, Inc., 1970), pp.314-15, 291-92.
43. Ince, "History and Development of the Motion Picture Industry."
44. Irving Thalberg and Hugh Weir, "Why Motion Pictures Cost So Much," *Saturday Evening Post,* November 4, 1933, p. 10.

Chapter 4

1. See in particular Eugene C. McCreary, "Film and History: Some Thoughts on Their Interrelationship," *Societas* 1 (Winter 1971): 51-66; Stuart Samuels, "Film as Social and Intellectual History" (paper presented at the First Meeting of the Popular Culture Association, Michigan State University, April 8-10, 1971); and British Universities Film Council, *Film and the Historian,* pamphlet (London: n.p., 1969), passim.
2. Quoted in McCreary, "Film and History," pp.52-53 n8.
3. I am using the word *documentary* to describe that type of film which was shot spontaneously (which is to say events dictated the shooting, rather than vice versa) and without any special technical preparation. The pictures thus captured are "real" in the sense they were unposed and unplanned. This definition differs somewhat from the traditional idea of "documentary" formulated primarily by the British. This idea also eschews the use of professional actors but pays great attention to composition of shots and to scenic effects. These documentaries are to a certain extent carefully plotted for dramatic content, which their makers hoped would heighten their message. See Paul Rotha, *Documentary Film* (New York: W.W. Norton and Company, Inc., 1939). World War I documentary films of the commercial variety, shot mostly by Signal Corps photographers, clearly are distinct from the school of documentary realism which arose in England during the thirties and quickly spread to America.
4. Iris Barry, "History in the Movies," *National Board of Review Magazine,* April 1941, pp. 4-7.
5. McCreary, "Film and History," pp. 65-66.
6. J. A. S. Grenville and N. Pronay, "The Historian and Historical Films," in *Film and the Historian,* pp. 3-4.
7. Paul Smith, foreword in ibid., p.1.

8. Judith Stafford, "Films on the Second World War," in Grenville and Pronay, "The Historian and Historical Films," p.20.

9. Fritz Terveen, "Film as a Historical Document: Its Limitations and Possibilities," trans. by C. L. Burgauner, in ibid., p. 24. I assume here that when Terveen used the phrase "historical film" he meant films which comprise evidence for the historian. Terveen was the director of the *Landesbildstelle Berlin*.

10. Penelope Houston, "The Nature of the Evidence," *Sight and Sound*, Spring 1967, p. 91.

11. The film referred to here is Leni Riefenstahl's *Triumph of the Will* (1936), a motion picture about the Nuremberg Nazi Party Convention in 1934. For the interesting background on the making of this film, see Siegfried Kracauer, *From Caligari to Hitler: A Psychological History of the German Film* (Princeton, N.J.: Princeton University Press, 1947), pp. 300-303, and David Stewart Hull, *Film in the Third Reich* (New York: Simon and Schuster, 1973), pp. 73-76.

12. Virginia Woolf, "The Movies and Reality," *New Republic*, August 4, 1926, p. 310.

13. Davidson Boughey, *The Film Industry* (London: Sir Isaac Pitman and Sons Ltd., 1921), p. 51. For an example of this type of film, made in connection with the presidential campaign of 1932, see *Herbert Hoover: Master of Emergencies* (1932) in the Prints and Photographs Division, Library of Congress (hereafter cited as LC).

14. This definition follows MacCann, "Documentary Film and Democratic Government," pp. 13-14. A complete discussion of public communication and propaganda is on pp. 10-19. There are, of course, degrees of "goodness" and "badness."

15. W., Stephen Bush, "The Social Uses of the Moving Picture," *Moving Picture World*, April 27, 1912, p. 306.

16. Leo Rosten, "Movies and Propaganda," *Annals of the American Academy of Political and Social Science* 254 (November 1947): 119. Rosten says that propaganda films are those made for the *purpose* of changing attitudes; those that merely dramatize existing situations concerning national heroes, institutions, or prevailing civic emotions, are patriotic (118). This is semanticism at its worst. Specific cases are not at all this clear-cut. Where for example does one put Riefenstahl's *Triumph of the Will?*

17. For the Nazi films, see Kracauer, *From Caligari to Hitler*, pp. 273-307; for the Sinclair campaign, see Selden C. Menefee, "The Movies Join Hearst," *New Republic*, October 9, 1935, pp. 241-42. An excerpt of Sinclair's defense is in MacCann, *Film and Society*, pp. 82-84.

18. For details on the Eisenstein affair, see Ivor Montagu, *With Eisenstein in Hollywood* (Berlin: Seven Seas Publishers, 1968).

19. Abraham Kaplan, "Realism in the Film: A Philosopher's Viewpoint," *Quarterly of Film, Radio and Television*, Summer 1953, pp. 383-84.

20. Horace C. Peterson and Gilbert C.Fite, *Opponents of War, 1917-1918* (Madison, Wis.: University of Wisconsin Press, 1957), p. 93. See in particular their discussion "Purging the Movies and the Press," pp. 92-101.

21. Boorstin, *The Image: A Guide to Pseudo-Events in America*, p. 145. Boorstin presents the curious case of one who fully grasps the illusionary nature of the film ("the movie can (never) give us the nut of the matter"–p. 148), yet he seems to feel that something (the novel?) may eventually and totally delineate "reality."

22. Aldous Huxley, "Where are the Movies Moving?", *Essays New and Old* (New York: George H. Doran Company, 1927), pp. 220-27. Films of course may be *realistic* without being *reality*.

23. Woolf, "The Movies and Reality," pp. 308-10.

24. Seldes believed the movie "can be made great by ceasing to be realistic." "The Abstract Movie," *New Republic*, September 15, 1926, pp.95-96.

25. See in particular Tyler, *Magic and Myth of the Movies*, and McLuhan, *Understanding Media*, pp. 284-96. Lounsbury, "The Origins of American Film Criticism," p. 491, states the problem thus: "Sould the primary attribute of the motion picture be described as 'the *illusion* of reality' or 'the illusion of *reality?*'" Emphasis in original.

26. Boulding, *The Image: Knowledge in Life and Society*, p. 166.

27. Ernest L. Crandall, "Possibilities of the Cinema in Education," *Annals of the American Academy of Political and Social Science*, CXXVIII (November, 1926), 110-11. In spite of the existence of the Prizma and other color processes at the time of World War I, color combat photography, and hence the "rocket's red glare," awaited later conflicts.

28. Bush, "The Social Uses of the Moving Picture," p.305.

29. Orestes H. Caldwell, "Realism in the Movies," *Scribner's Commentator,* April 1941, pp. 95-98.

30. W. Stephen Bush, "War Films," *Moving Picture World,* September 19, 1914, p.1617.

31. Robert C. McElravy, "War Realism," ibid., July 27, 1918, p.540. P.D. Hugon, the director of the English *Pathé Gazette* at the start of the war, said that Americans demanded the real thing in war films. "Americans are not squeamish–they would not even mind seeing actual bayonet fighting in all its horror." "War Films America Wants to See," ibid., October 7, 1916, p. 50. This situation probably had changed by 1918.

32. Gilbert Seldes, "Progress in the Movies," *New Republic,* July 27, 1927, pp. 255-56. See also MacCann, "Documentary Film and Democratic Government," p. 90, for the equation of complete objectivity (a myth in itself) with dullness.

33. "Fake War Movies," *Literary Digest,* November 30, 1915, 1079. I have been unable to establish any meaningful percentage of fakes as opposed to actual war footage. For an assessment of fakery in British films, see Houston, "The Nature of the Evidence," pp. 89-90. For a first-person account of how commercial war movies were filmed, see Austin C. Lescarboura, "Generals of Shadowland Warfare," *Scientific American,* May 5, 1917, pp. 446-47, 456-57, 459-60.

34. Ernest A. Dench, "Following the Movies to the Firing-Line and Back," *Motion Picture Magazine,* October 1916, p. 60.

35. Carr, "Griffith, Maker of Battle Scenes, Sees Real War," p. 23.

36. Newton E. Meltzer, "Are Newsreels News? " *Hollywood Quarterly,* April 1947, p. 270.

37. An excellent general history is Raymond Fielding, *The American Newsreel, 1911-1967* (Norman, Okla.: University of Oklahoma Press, 1972). For an entertaining look at an early newsreel cameraman's experiences with *Pathé News Weekly,* see Fred J. Balshofer and Arthur C. Miller, *One Reel a Week* (Berkeley, Calif.: University of California Press, 1967), pp. 68-73.

38. This opinion is based on viewing the Pathé News Collection, MOMA, and those portions of the *Official War Review* that survive in the National Archives (hereafter cited as NA) and LC. As the war churned on, outright fakes proved unacceptable to seasoned audiences.

39. MacCann, "Documentary Film and Democratic Government," p. 79. MacCann then cites the Sinclair example, p. 87 n21. Here I will offend purists by regarding the "newsreel" and the "news feature" as branches of the same reportorial tree; I use the term "newsreel" to cover both.

40. Boughey, *The Film Industry,* p. 50. See, for example, D.W. Griffith's comment that "the moving picture is simply the pictorial press." *The Rise and Fall of Free Speech in America,* p. 19.

41. William Troy, "Journey to the End," *Nation,* May 30, 1934, p.630.

42. Emanuel Cohen, "The Business of International News by Motion Pictures," *Annals of the American Academy of Political and Social Science* 128 (November 1926): 74-78. Cohen was editor-in-chief of *Pathé News.*

43. Louis R. Reid, "Amusement: Radio and Movies," in *America Now,* p. 34.

44. Alexander Bakshy "The News Reel," *Nation,* January 8, 1930, p. 54. See also "Motion-Picture Newsreels," *New Republic,* April l, 1931, pp. 164-65.

45. Gilbert Seldes, "Newsreels and Pictures," *New Republic,* March 11, 1931, p. 96.

46. Forsyth Hardy, ed., *Grierson on Documentary,* rev. ed. (Berkeley, Calif.: University of California Press, 1966), p. 145. Grierson was no kinder to the commercial film. Excerpts of his criticism may be found in George Pratt, ed., *Spellbound in Darkness: Readings in the History and Criticism of the Silent Film,* vol. 2 (Rochester, N.Y.: University of Rochester Press, 1966), pp. 358-81.

47. Meltzer, "Are Newsreels News? " p. 272. The complete indifference displayed by some newsreel men toward the intelligence of their audience is indicated in John B.Kennedy, "News on the Reel," *Commentator,* February 1939, pp. 42-47. Kennedy's decidedly pro-newsreel argument includes the statement that "when you complain that clichés recur too much in newsreels–remember that nine-tenths of the newsreel audience doesn't know and doesn't care what a cliché is as long as they understand it " (p.43). Further, "everything must be spotted for intensive storytelling" (p.46). See also the lively and anecdotal account of a newsreel cameraman, Charles Peden, *Newsreel Man* (New York: Doubleday, Doran and Company, 1932), which unabashedly admits catering to the entertainment demands of the public.

48. The *March of Time* in the strictest sense was not a newsreel at all, but a news feature. Yet it was periodical, topical, current, and openly (as opposed to covertly) analytic. For information on and

praise of the *March of Time,* see Edgar Anstey, "The Film as Document and News," *National Board of Review Magazine,* April 1938, 8-10; "Making the *March of Time,*" ibid. (November 1938), 8-11; Raymond Fielding, "Time Flickers Out: Notes on the Passing of the *March of Time,*" *Quarterly of Film, Radio and Television,* (Summer, 1957), 354-61. A leftist critique of newsreels in general and of the *March of Time* in particular as "mouthpieces for monopoly capital" is Robert Stebbins and Peter Ellis, "Are Newsreels News?" *New Theater and Film* (April 1937), 12-15, 44-45. A balanced assessment that weighs news interpretation against strict presentation of news is William Troy, "Pictorial Journalism," *Nation* (February 20, 1935), 232.

49. See Hardy, *Grierson on Documentary,* p.201, for Grierson's comments; also Rotha, *Documentary Film,* pp.248-49. Selected issues of the *March of Time* are in MOMA; a file is in the custody of Time-Life Films, Inc., New York City.

50. Menefee, "The Movies Join Hearst," pp.241-42. Even allowing for errors in categorization and observation these percentages seem to comprise a clear indictment of newsreel coverage. The government moved into the newsreel business in 1936, tacitly recognizing the propaganda value of this mode of communication. "'Educational' Newsreels for WPA," *Literary Digest,* August 8, 1936, p.32.

51. Paul Rotha, "The Documentary Method in British Films," *National Board of Review Magazine,* November 1937, p.7. This section is based primarily on Hardy's edition of Grierson's writings and on Rotha, *Documentary Film.* For biographical material on Grierson, see Hardy, *Grierson on Documentary,* pp.13-39. British documentarists such as Rotha and Grierson and Americans such as Robert Flaherty and Pare Lorentz learned much from one another's craftsmanship.

52. MacCann, "Documentary Film and Democratic Government," pp.87-88. Where MacCann stresses subject matter, I see editing as the more crucial aspect of documentary production.

53. Ramseyer, "A Study of the Influence of Documentary Films on Social Attitudes," p.13.

54. Ben Belitt, "The Camera Reconnoiters," *Nation,* November 20, 1937, pp.557-58.

Chapter 5

1. Ernest A. Dench, "Filming Wars–The Hardships and Perils Camera Men Have to Face," *Motion Picture Magazine,* December, 1914, p.82, presents anecdotal evidence that cameras had covered the Balkan Wars of 1912-13.

2. Ernest A. Dench, "Following the Movies to the Firing Line and Back"; Parke Farley, "The War Photographer's Job," *Photoplay Magazine,* February 1915, pp.163-66; Homer Croy, "Maybe *You* Would Like to Take War Movies," ibid., February 1918, pp.97-98.

3. The Central Powers were a little slower getting their films to America than were the Allies, for obvious reasons. The first release of Central Powers material occurred in New York City in September, 1915. Walter Millis, *Road to War: America, 1914-1917* (New York: Howard Fertig, Inc. 1970) (originally published in 1935), p.217. A most useful set of articles that lists many documentary and feature films concerning World War I is Jack Spears, "World War I on the Screen," *Films in Review,* May 1966, pp.274-92, and ibid., June-July 1966, pp.347-65. For the documentaries of the 1914-1917 period, see May, p.281. Less discriminating general treatments are provided by Creighton Peet, "Hollywood at War, 1915-1918," *Esquire,* September 1936, pp.60, 109, and by Peter A. Soderbergh, "*Aux Armes!:* The Rise of the Hollywood War Film, 1916-1930," *South Atlantic Quarterly* 65 (Autumn 1966): 509-22.

4. Harry C. Carr, "Capturing the Kaiser," *Photoplay Magazine,* March 1916, pp.111-12; John Allen Everets, "How I Got to Przemysl and Filmed the Bombardment," *Motion Picture Magazine,*

February 1916, pp.56-65; *The New York Times*, June 30, 1919, p.16; *Moving Picture World*, October 4, 1919, p.163.

    5. Neither documentaries nor feature films were taking notice of the contemporary revisionist histories of World War I causation. See Warren I.Cohen, *The American Revisionists: The Lessons of Intervention in World War I* (Chicago: University of Chicago Press, 1967), passim.

    6. *Motion Picture News*, June 12, 1915, p.75

    7. *Moving Picture World*, June 12, 1915, p.1785.

    8. *The New York Times*, July 11, 1916, p.9.

    9. Ibid., July 6, 1916, p.11; ibid., September 24, 1916, sec.1, p.20; *The Triangle*, 2 (July 20, 1916): 2; ibid., 1 (July 29, 1916): 7; ibid., August 26, 1916, p.1. *The Triangle* was the official newspaper of the Triangle Film Corporation. Surviving files are in AMPAS.

    10. "Training Recruits With Motion Pictures," *Photoplay Magazine*, February 1915, p.42; *The New York Times*, April 10, 1916, p.13; Frank P.Liberman, "A History of Army Photography," *Business Screen*, December 30, 1945, pp.15-17, 94-95; "How the Movies Helped Win," *Literary Digest*, February 22, 1919, pp.25-26.

    11. MacCann, "Documentary Film and Democratic Government," p.283; Earl Theisen, "The Photographer in the World War," *The International Photographer*, November 1933, pp.4-6, 24.

    12. The standard history of the Committee on Public Information is James R.Mock and Cedric Larson, *Words That Won the War: The Story of the Committee on Public Information, 1917-1919* (Princeton, N.J.: Princeton University Press, 1939). This should be supplemented by George Creel, *How We Advertised America* (New York: Harper and Brothers, 1920), and by Creel's official résumé, *Complete Report of the Chairman of the Committee on Public Information, 1917-1919* (Washington, D.C.: Government Printing Office, 1920). Creel's memoirs, *Rebel at Large: Recollections of Fifty Crowded Years* (New York: G.P. Putnam's Sons, 1947), contain nothing new on the subject.

    13. Ramsaye, *A Million and One Nights*, p.785. For a complete listing of the movie organizations behind the war, see *Moving Picture World*, August 11, 1917, p.918; *The New York Times*, July 12, 1917, p.2; and ibid., July 29, 1917, sec 1, p.8.

    14. These films included the following (asterisks indicate the film is deposited in NA): *The 1917 Recruit* (two editions); *The Second Liberty Loan; Ready for the Fight; Soldiers of the Sea; Torpedo-boat Destroyers(*); Submarines(*); Army and Navy Sports; The Spirit of 1917; In a Southern Camp; The Lumber Jack; The Medical Officer's Reserve Corps in Action; Fire and Gas(*); American Ambulances; Labor's Part in Democracy's War; Annapolis; Ship-building; Making of Big Guns(*); Making of Small Arms; Making of Uniforms for the Soldiers; Activities of the Engineers; Woman's Part in the War;* and *The Conquest of the Air*. Some detail may be found in Creel, *How We Advertised America*, pp.119-20.

    15. Pertinent details on the financial, administrative, and organizational aspects of the film activities of the Committee on Public Information may be found in the *Complete Report of the Chairman*. These are summarized in Creel, *How We Advertised America*, pp.117-32.

    16. "Seeing Our Boys 'Over There'," *Literary Digest*, June 8, 1918, pp.28-29. The archival print of this film was severely edited by the Signal Corps in 1936 from its original seven-reel running time to about 56 minutes. Destroyed in the editing were the opening scenes of the volcano and much of the German sabotage. The edited version shows almost no fighting but describes an abundance of parades and maneuvers.

    17. *The New York Times*, July 30, 1918, p.9; ibid., November 2, 1918, sec. 2, p.3.

    18. Ibid., November 18, 1918, p.13.

    19. The name "Allied" was interposed with "Official," the latter giving the impression that the United States was the most involved in the production. Extant issues of the *Review* include nos.9, 18, 19, 27, 28, and 31 (NA) and 11 and 17 (LC). This paragraph is based on those issues. Many portions of these newsreels were included in the seven-reelers, particularly in *America's Answer*. Four newsreel companies–Mutual, Universal, Gaumont, and Hearst-Pathé–paid for the films at a rate of $5,000 per 2,000 feet.

    20. *The New York Times*, July 22, 1918, p.9; the quotations are from nos.18 and 19.

    21. Creel, *How We Advertised America*, pp.222-25.

    22. All prefaced by "Says Uncle Sam:" these titles were *Keep 'Em Singing and Nothing Can Lick 'Em; I Run the Biggest Life Insurance Company on Earth; A Girl's a Man for A' That;* and *I'll Help Every Willing Worker Find a Job*.

23. *Schooling Our Fighting Mechanics; There Shall be No Cripples; Colored Americans; It's an Engineer's War; Finding and Fixing the Enemy; Waging War in Washington; All the Comforts of Home; Masters for the Merchant Marine; The College for Camp Cooks;* and *Rail-less Railroads.*

24. This film may have been issued under the title *Our Bridge of Ships.* See *The New York Times,* August 20, 1918, p.7.

25. MacCann, "Documentary Film and Democratic Government," p.280, n10; Creel, *How We Advertised America,* p.129. Mention also must be made of the CPI's sponsorship of programs of film slides. The Committee also took an active role in promoting American films overseas. For the slides, ibid., pp.129-32; for the work of the Foreign Section, ibid., pp.273-82.

26. Creel, *How We Advertised America,* p.282.

27. Creel defined "educational matter" as "film that showed our schools, our industrial life, our war preparations, our natural resources, and our social progress." Ibid., p.282.

28. Ibid., pp.273-74, 281. Emphasis in original.

29. Mock and Larson, *Words That Won the War,* pp.148-50, claim a print of this film is in NA. I was unable to discover it. For details on the controversy, in which personal animosity played a part, see "Aeroplane Crash Between Creel and Universal," *Moving Picture World,* July 6, 1918, pp.41-42; *The New York Times,* June 24, 1918, pp.1, 20; ibid., June 25, 1918, pp. 1, 24; Jobes, *Motion Picture Empire,* p.182; Spears, "World War I on the Screen," May 1966, 283. This film should not be confused with the one-reel film of the same title released by Warner Brothers in 1934, composed primarily of Signal Corps footage from 1917-1919 and recommended as an educational film by Hartley, *Selected Films For American History and Problems,* pp.172-73.

30. Ernest A Dench, "Preserving the Great War for Posterity by the Movies," *Motion Picture Magazine,* July 1915, p.89.

31. This film, or a film by Lust under the same name, was finally copyrighted in 1934 under the lurid title *Over There: or, Through Hell and Back Again With the Allies.* It should not be confused with the feature presentation *Over There* (Selig-Charles Richman Pictures Corporation, 1917). See also the *National Board of Review Magazine,* July 1928, p.11.

32. *Time,* July 24, 1933, p.43.

33. Ibid., January 30, 1933, p.26. Rule served as a private in the AEF.

34. Ibid., November 19, 1934, pp.28-29.

35. *Newsweek,* November 17, 1934, p.27; see also "On the Current Screen," *Literary Digest,* November 24, 1934, p.28; *New Republic,* December 26, 1934, pp.180-81. Possibly the most perceptive review was by William Troy, *Nation,* November 21, 1934, p.602. This is one of the rare films that may be called a one-man creation, as Stallings co-produced (with Truman Talley), wrote the script, and edited. Stallings's war background is well known and needs no elaboration here.

36. *Time,* December 17, 1934, p.32. A similar film, a quickie venture called *War is a Racket,* was released at the same time but has vanished completely.

37. *New Republic,* December 26, 1934, pp.180-81; ibid., February 6, 1935, p.346.

38. *National Board of Review Magazine,* February, 1937, p.2. See also *Time,* September 27, 1937, p.36. *Digest,* September 25, 1937, p.34. Interestingly, the symbolic national figures did not include a representative of the war ally that sustained the greatest absolute loss of life–Russia.

39. *Time,* July 29, 1940, p.44. I viewed this film at Time-Life Films, Inc., New York City. I am grateful to Mr. Lothar Wolff and Mr. Morrie Roizman of the Time-Life staff for sharing their memories of the film's production; both men worked as editors on the project.

40. *Life,* August 12, 1940, p.69.

41. *Scribner's Commentator,* November 1940, pp.75-78.

Chapter 6

1. The standard work that puts this "democratic faith" in perspective remains Ralph Henry Gabriel, *The Course of American Democratic Thought*, 2nd ed. (New York: Ronald Press Company, 1956).
2. William Troy, "Panorama," *Nation*, August 2, 1933, pp.138-39.
3. Frank Thomas Phipps, "The Image of War in America, 1891-1917: A Study of a Literary Theme and Its Cultural Origins and Analogues" (Ph.D. diss., Ohio State University, 1953), p.2. The professions unabashedly placed themselves at the service of the government for the duration. See in particular Thomas Marley Camfield, "Psychologists at War" (Ph.D. diss., University of Texas, 1969), George T. Blakey, *Historians on the Homefront: American Propagandists for the Great War* (Lexington, Ky.: University Press of Kentucky, 1970), and Carol S. Gruber, *Mars and Minerva: World War I and the Uses of the Higher Learning in America* (Baton Rouge: Louisiana State University Press, 1975).
4. *The New York Times*, October 7, 1917, sec.7, p.2.
5. Creel, *How We Advertised America*, xiii-xiv, frontispiece. I have removed the capital letters in the quotation from the frontispiece.
6. John William Ward, *Andrew Jackson: Symbol for an Age* (New York: Oxford University Press, 1962).
7. *Moving Picture World*, September 28, 1918, p.1928. The ethic of success that accompanied the rise of both real and fictional film heroes is best described in Irvin G. Wyllie, *The Self-Made Man in America: The Myth of Rags to Riches* (New York: Free Press, 1966). Although Wyllie's work is primarily concerned with the 1865-1914 period, films continued to depict this ethic into the middle of the twentieth century. It often was interwoven with democratic idealism.
8. *Moving Picture World*, September 29, 1917, p.2003.
9. Ibid., February 16, 1918, p.1010. My emphasis.
10. Ibid., December 28, 1918, pp.1560-61. For some background information on the making of *The Common Cause*, see Marie Wardall, "Driving the Huns Home," *Motion Picture Magazine*, December, 1918, pp.91-92, 124.
11. *Moving Picture World*, December 22, 1917, pp.1847-48. The actor playing the leading role in *The Pride of New York* was George Walsh; the *World* followed the popular practice of referring to the actor's name intead of to the name of his character. Need I add that the character was an Irishman named Kelly?
12. *Dramatic Mirror* clipping, September 22, 1917, folder, AMPAS.
13. *Moving Picture World*, August 10, 1918, p.892; ibid., March 22, 1919, p.1701.
14. Ibid., December 21, 1918, p.1386.
15. *The Lost Battalion* (McManus Corporation, 1919), LC; quotations are from the film.
16. *The Unbeliever* (Edison, 1918), LC; quotations are from the film.
17. *Corporal Kate* (Producers Distributing Corporation, 1926), LC; quotation is from the film.
18. Dale Van Every, "Marianne," Script ("Dialog Cutting Continuity"), October 10, 1929, in Theater Collection, New York Public Library, Library and Museum of the Performing Arts, Lincoln Center (hereafter cited as NYPL (LC)).
19. *The Big Parade* (MGM, 1925), MOMA; quotation is from the film. Tangential to the war leveling theme and lighter in touch were *Civilian Clothes* (Famous Players–Lasky, 1920), in which a

veteran became a butler to embarrass his society wife, and *This Hero Stuff (Business)* (Russell-Pathé, 1919), which had a modest war hero try to avoid public notice.

20. Cooper's films in this study include *Wings* (1927), *Legion of the Condemned* (1928), *Lilac Time* (1928), *Shopworn Angel* (1929), *A Man From Wyoming* (1930), *A Farewell to Arms* (1932), *Today We Live* (1933), and *Sergeant York* (1941). Among top-billed actors, Cooper was unexcelled at playing the silent yet noble warrior. His film credits in this regard were rivaled only by Richard Barthelmess.

21. *National Board of Review Magazine,* September, 1927, p.8.

22. Pare Lorentz, "Judging the Movies," *Judge,* September 10, 1927, clipping in Richard Barthelmess Collection, vol.XXIII (hereafter cited as Barthelmess Collection), AMPAS. See also ibid., vol.XXIV. It was ironic that *The Patent Leather Kid,* like so many democratic preachments on celluloid, contained a black stereotype character.

23. *The Ramparts We Watch* (Time, Inc.-RKO-Radio, 1940), MOMA; quotations are from the film. Lothar Wolff, who worked as an editor on the picture, has stated that *Ramparts* was conceived as a "parallel" to the 1914 period, and that it was de Rochemont who decided on the device of presenting the message from "small-town America." Interview, July 27, 1971, New York City.

24. *Life,* January 29, 1940, p.32-33.

25. Jesse L. Lasky and Don Weldon, *I Blow My Own Horn* (Garden City, N.Y.: Doubleday and Company, Inc., 1957), pp.253-56.

26. *Time,* August 4, 1941, pp.70-71.

27. *Newsweek,* July 14, 1941, pp.61-62.

28. Aben Finkel, Harry Chandlee, Howard Koch, and John Huston, "Sergeant York," Script ("Revised Final"), January 31, 1941, AMPAS, pp.142-43.

29. Ibid., pp.154-56.

30. Gene Wise, *American Historical Explanations: A Strategy for Grounded Inquiry* (Homewood, Ill.: The Dorsey Press, 1973), pp.179-222.

Chapter 7

1. Bush, "War Films," p.1617; see also *The New York Times,* September 6, 1914, sec.6; pp.1-3; ibid., September 16, 1914, sec. 10, p.2.

2. Robert J. Shores, "The European War–In Grantwood, N.J.," *Motion Picture Magazine,* January 1915, p.71.

3. *The New York Times,* October 23, 1915, p.10.

4. Ibid., August 28, 1914, p.9. See also Arthur S. Link, *Woodrow Wilson and the Progressive Era, 1910-1917* (New York: Harper and Row, 1963), p.148 n.9; William E. Leuchtenburg, *The Perils of Prosperity, 1914-32* (Chicago: University of Chicago Press, 1958), p.14.

5. *Civilization* cost $100,000 and grossed $800,000, a considerable margin for the era. Ince's later films included such saber-rattlers as *Claws of the Hun, The Kaiser's Shadow,* and *Vive La France,* all superpatriotic productions. For background on Ince, who remains an obscure figure, see George J. Mitchell, "Thomas H. Ince," *Films in Review,* October, 1960, pp.464-84.

6. Ince, "History and Development of the Motion Picture Industry," p.29. This remark was penciled in, presumably by Ince himself, in the final correction of the typewritten MS.

7. *Civilization* (Ince-Triangle, 1916), MOMA; quotations are from the film.

8. *The Coward* (Ince-Triangle, 1915), MOMA; quotations are from the film. See also Thomas H.

Ince Collection, Scrapbooks 21 and 22, AMPAS (hereafter cited as Ince Collection). Also combining romanticism with a rising militancy was *A Soldier's Oath* (Fox, 1915).

9. *Moving Picture World,* June 3, 1916, p.1762.

10. There is no biography of Blackton (1875-1941). Snatches of his early career may be glimpsed in Wyndham Martyn, "An Early Believer in Moving Pictures," *Pearson's Magazine,* August, 1915, pp.186-90, and Albert E. Smith and Phil A. Koury, *Two Reels and a Crank* (Garden City, N.Y.: Doubleday and Company, Inc., 1952). Smith was one of Blackton's partners in Vitagraph. Blackton's later career was checkered. From Vitagraph he went to Paramount as an independent producer, and from there he faded into obscurity. After the war he made two patriotic pictures, neither of which was released. He was killed in an automobile accident in 1941. There is some material in the form of clippings in the J. Stuart Blackton Collection (hereafter cited as Blackton Collection), AMPAS.

11. When asked who would receive his vote in the presidential election of 1916, Blackton replied, "Hughes, because I believe he is not too good to give Americans abroad that feeling of security and pride in their flag which is their birthright and of which they are at present deprived." *New York World* clipping dated November 5, 1916, Blackton Collection, AMPAS.

12. *The Battle Cry of Peace* is a crucial film for this history; unfortunately, I have been unable to locate a surviving print. See H.C. Peterson, *Propaganda for War: The Campaign Against American Neutrality* (Norman, Okla.: University of Oklahoma Press, 1939), pp. 202, 239; Millis, *Road to War,* pp. 217-18; Hampton, *History of the American Film Industry,* p.127; and Edwin M. LaRoche, "The Battle Cry of Peace," *Motion Picture Magazine,* October, 1915, pp.81-88.

13. For details on Ford's attacks on the film and the counterattacks of Blackton and Maxim, see *The New York Times,* May 11, 1916, p.10; ibid., August 22, 1916, p.9; Millis, *Road to War,* pp.217-18, 303.

14. J. Stuart Blackton, "The Battle Cry of Peace," *Motion Picture Magazine,* September, 1915, pp.122-23. Among the famous appearing in the film were former President Taft, Secretary of State Lansing, Secretary of War Garrison, Admiral Dewey, Reverend Lyman Abbott and Judge Alton B. Parker. The not-so-famous included members of the GAR, the National Guard, and the regular Army and Navy.

15. Martyn, "An Early Believer," p.190.

16. *The New York Times,* August 7, 1915, p.8.

17. Ibid., August 11, 1915, sec.11, p.4; ibid., September 10, 1915, sec.11, p.1. The general climate in which *The Battle Cry of Peace* was promoted may best be examined in the rare brochure, program, and book in the Blackton Collection, AMPAS. This collection also includes some stills from the picture.

18. Jacobs, *Rise of the American Film,* pp.251-52; Blackton, "Early History," p.20; Letter, Roosevelt to Richard L. Gorman, November 24, 1915, in vol.8 of *The Letters of Theodore Roosevelt,* ed. by Elting E. Morison, 8 vols. (Cambridge, Mass.: Harvard University Press, 1954), pp.989-91. Gorman was the manager of the Majestic Theater in Boston. Roosevelt apparently wrote another letter congratulating Blackton along the same lines. This letter is not included in Morison's collection but is quoted in Norma Talmadge, "Close-ups," *Saturday Evening Post,* May 7, 1927, p.76. Miss Talmadge appeared in *The Battle Cry of Peace* and was elevated to "stardom" thereby. Her article, part of a series, includes background information on the trappings that surrounded the film's presentation.

19. "The Battle Cry of Peace," *New Republic,* October 9, 1915, p.247. The critic may have been Vachel Lindsay, although the style is not quite that of Lindsay's usual film comments. Another possibility is Kenneth MacGowan. See also *The New York Times,* December 25, 1915, sec.5, p.6.

20. Link, *Woodrow Wilson and the Progressive Era,* p.178 n13.

21. *The New York Times,* June 7, 1916, p.11.

22. Blackton, "Early History," p.20.

23. Carol Signer Gruber, "Mars and Minerva: World War I and the American Academic Man" (Ph.D. diss., Columbia University, 1968), pp.1-35, 315-25. Since published as *Mars and Minerva: World War I and the Uses of the Higher Learning in America* (Baton Rouge: Louisiana State University Press, 1975). See also Blakey, *Historians on the Homefront,* and Camfield, "Psychologists at War."

24. Link, *Woodrow Wilson and the Progressive Era,* pp.279-80.

25. A convenient summary of the films made to support the Liberty Loan drives is "Synopsis of

Liberty Loan Specials," *Moving Picture World,* October 5, 1918, pp.122-24. A list of stars contributing to the Fourth Liberty Loan Campaign may be found in *The New York Times,* September 28, 1918, p.2.

26. *Liberty Loan—National Association of the Motion Picture Industry* (believed to be 1918 or early 1919), LC; quotation is from the film.

27. Donald Hayne, ed., *The Autobiography of Cecil B. De Mille* (Englewood Cliffs, N.J.: Prentice-Hall, Inc., 1959), pp.183-85.

28. Ramsaye, *A Million and One Nights,* pp.777-88.

29. Jack L. Warner, *My First Hundred Years in Hollywood* (New York: Random House, 1964), p.86.

30. William C. De Mille, *Hollywood Saga* (New York: E.P. Dutton and Company, Inc., 1939), p.191.

31. Paul H. Dowling, "Battle Business: Nine Kinds of Sudden Death in Filmland Warfare," *Motion Picture Magazine,* April, 1917, p.97.

32. This response may best be traced in the movie review section of *The New York Times,* 1917-1919, passim. See also Rhodes, "The Majestic Movies," p.186; *Motion Picture Magazine,* 1917-1919, passim.

33. Jobes, *Motion Picture Empire,* p.161.

34. Kenneth MacGowan, "Hearts of the World," *New Republic,* July 20, 1918, p.344.

35. Quotes are taken from the script, Leonce Perret, "For This We Fight" ("Lest We Forget"), no date, in custody of the New York Public Library (hereafter cited as NYPL). On the back of the script in pencil is the date "Aug 1917"; *Lest We Forget* was copy-righted on February 26, 1918. Perret also directed. The quotes may be found on p.23, scene 129; p.34, scene 211; p.13, scene 74; p.31-B, scene 197; p.141, scenes 268 and 270.

36. Dench, "Filming Wars," p.91.

37. Ralph D. Casey, "Propaganda and Public Opinion," in Willard Waller, ed., *War in the Twentieth Century* (New York: Dryden Press, 1940), p.440; *The New York Times,* March 16, 1917, p.7.

38. Reverend W. H. Jackson, "War Time Pictures," *Moving Picture World,* August 4, 1917, p.770.

39. Adolph Zukor, "The Motion Picture and the War," ibid., February 2, 1918, p.678.

40. "Ohio Censors All War Films Closely," ibid., May 19, 1917, p.1164.

41. Details of Goldstein's court cases may be found in Mock and Larson, *Words That Won the War,* pp.147-48; James R. Mock, *Censorship 1917* (Princeton, N.J.: Princeton University Press, 1941), pp.179-81; and *The New York Times,* February 3, 1918, sec.1, p.6. See also *United States v. Motion Picture Film* "The Spirit of '76," 252 Fed. 946 (S.D. Cal., 1917); *Goldstein v. United States,* 258 Fed. 908 (9th Cir., 1919). Goldstein's sentence, served in the federal penitentiary at Steilacoom, Washington, was commuted to three years. Zechariah Chafee, Jr., *Freedom of Speech* (New York: Harcourt, Brace and Howe, 1920), p.10,n17; pp.60-61.

42. *The New York Times,* April 1, 1918, p.9.

43. *Moving Picture World,* June 8, 1918, p.1478.

44. *Time,* December 4, 1939, pp.82-83. Emphasis in original.

45. *Moving Picture World,* April 20, 1918, pp.411, 438.

46. *The New York Times,* June 30, 1918, p.6.

47. Spears, "World War I on the Screen," June-July, 1966, pp.347-48.

48. Balshofer and Miller, *One Reel a Week,* p.139.

49. *Moving Picture World,* May 15, 1920, pp.982-83; *The New York Times,* May 31, 1920, sec.14, p.2. Other films in this line included *The Hero* (Lichtman-Preferred, 1922) and *Blaze O'Glory* (Sono-Art, 1930), both trivial efforts.

50. *Face Value* (Sterling, 1927), LC; quotations are from the film.

Chapter 8

1. Cooperman, *World War I and the American Novel*, pp.viii, 85, 97.
2. Charles V. Genthe, *American War Narratives, 1917-1918: A Study and a Bibliography* (New York: David Lewis, 1969), pp.3-4.
3. Richard Whitehall, "One...Two...Three?: A Study of the War Film," *Films and Filming*, August 1964, p.10.
4. Connor, "Pen and Sword," pp.377-86. This analysis dovetails with that of Wolfenstein and Leites for later American films. Americans tend to successfully confront hazards of external situations (standard adventure) rather than life itself (the nature of war). See *Movies: A Psychological Study*, p.298.
5. "Motion Pictures Placed in the Service of a Narrow Patriotism," *Nation*, July 25, 1928, p. 74.
6. "Motion Pictures With Patriotic Themes," *National Board of Review Magazine*, May-June 1926, pp.16-17.
7. "War-Films Create Hope of Peace," *The Motion Picture*, October 1, 1929, p.6.
8. "Untruthful War Films," *Literary Digest*, March 17, 1928, p.27.
9. Oswald Garrison Villard, "Propaganda in the Movies," *Nation*, December 12, 1934, p.665.
10. Harry Alan Potamkin, "Hollywood Looks at War," *New Masses*, August, 1931, p.19; Potamkin, "The Film and the War," ibid., June, 1930, pp.14-15.
11. O. W. Riegel, "Nationalism in Press, Radio, and Cinema," *American Sociological Review*, 3 (August 1938): 514.
12. Edgar Dale, "Movies and Propaganda," in *Education Against Propaganda: Developing Skill in the Use of the Sources of Information about Public Affairs*, Seventh Yearbook of the National Council for Social Studies, ed. by Elmer Ellis (Philadelphia: McKinley Publishing Company, 1937), p.75.
13. "*Body and Soul* Is (Here) Put Together," *Fortune*, August 1931, p.117.
14. Benjamin Glazer and Leo Birinski, "Mata Hari," script, no date (but 1931), American Film Institute Library, Beverly Hills, California, reel 3, no.8.
15. *Time*, September 25, 1939, p.33.
16. *Moving Picture World*, August 19, 1922, p.611.
17. Gilbert Seldes, "The Theater," *Dial*, February, 1926, p.169.
18. "Watching the War From an Orchestra Chair," *Literary Digest*, March 6, 1926, p.40.
19. Robert M. Finch, "The Big Parade," *Motion Picture Director*, November, 1925, p.25. Emphasis in original.
20. Ibid., p.59. My emphasis.
21. *The Big Parade* (MGM, 1925), MOMA; quotation is from the film.
22. Bob Thomas, *Thalberg: Life and Legend* (Garden City, N.Y.: Doubleday and Company, Inc., 1969), pp.82-86, 332-35, 128-29. Thalberg, the production genius of MGM's front office, may have played a role in expanding *The Big Parade* into an epic feature film. See Spears, "World War I on the Screen," June-July, 350-51; MacGowan, *Behind the Screen*, 254; Philip French, *The Movie Moguls: An Informal History of the Hollywood Tycoons* (London: Weidenfeld and Nicolson, 1969), p.57.
23. Schulberg, "Movies in America," p.117.
24. Gilbert Seldes, "The Two Parades," *New Republic*, December 16, 1925, pp.111-12.
25. Iris Barry, "The Cinema: *The Big Parade*," *The Spectator* (London), June 5, 1926, pp.946-47.

26. *What Price Glory?* (Fox, 1926), MOMA; quotations are from the film. For comment on the war experiences of the makers of *What Price Glory?*, see Frank Murray, "What Price Glory?," *Motion Picture Director*, August, 1926, pp.17-18.

27. "On the Current Screen," *Literary Digest*, April 14, 1934, p.36. *Dark Sands* (Record Pictures, 1938) may be mentioned here as an oddity. Filmed largely in North Africa, it had a man (Negro expatriate Paul Robeson) escape from an AEF murder charge to the Sahara. For remarks on Robeson's movie career, see Peter Noble, *The Negro in Films* (London: Skelton Robinson, 1948),pp. 139-47; Daniel J. Leab, *From Sambo to Superspade: The Black Experience in Motion Pictures* (Boston: Houghton Mifflin Company 1975), pp.78-79, 109-15; and Dorothy Butler Gilliam, *Paul Robeson: All-American* (Washington, D.C.: New Republic Book Company, Inc., 1978).

28. *Time*, August 22, 1927, pp.16-17. The theme of the deadly German ace as a standard for American aviators was to be long-lived; witness George Roy Hill's *The Great Waldo Pepper* (1975). Anecdotal material on the filming of *Wings* may be found in William A. Wellman, *A Short Time For Insanity* (New York: Hawthorn Books, Inc., 1974), pp.162-78.

29. *National Board of Review Magazine*, September, 1927; "When War-Planes Flame and Audiences Gasp," *Literary Digest*, November 12, 1927, pp.36, 38, 40, 42.

30. *Wings* (Paramount, 1927), LC; quotation is from the film.

31. Rudy Behlmer, "World War I Aviation Films," *Films in Review*, August-September 1967, p.420. The best background material on the filming of *Hell's Angels* may be found in ibid., pp.420-24.

32. Alexander Bakshy, "Hell's Angels," *Nation*, September 3, 1930, p.254.

33. *National Board of Review Magazine*, September, 1930, p.16.

34. Seton I. Miller, Dan Totheroth, and Howard Hawks, "The Dawn Patrol," script ("Revised"), March 14, 1930, AMPAS. See also Barthelmess Collection, Vol.XXXV, AMPAS.

35. *Life*, December 26, 1938, p.33.

36. Behlmer, "World War I Aviation Films," pp.429-30.

37. *Newsweek* (December 12, 1938), p.25.

38. Seton I. Miller and Edmund Goulding, "Dawn Patrol," script ("Revised Final"), August 4, 1938, 159, AMPAS, Wisconsin Center For Theater Research, Madison (hereafter cited as WCTR).

39. "Dawn Patrol," script, 4, 73.

Chapter 9

1. For a literary comparison based on works about World War I, see Cooperman, *World War I and the American Novel*, pp.155-56, 174.

2. A good introduction to films of the Depression era is Andrew Bergman, *We're in the Money: Depression America and Its Films* (New York: New York University Press, 1971). A rather disappointing analysis on the same topic is Jeffrey Morton Paine, "The Simplification of American Life: Hollywood Films of the 1930's" (Ph.D. diss., Princeton University, 1971).

3. "E.M.A.," "The Menace of the Movies," *Nation*, June 9, 1926, p.634.

4. "War Films: For and Against," *Literary Digest*, August 29, 1931, pp.14-15. I have been unable to find similar symposia among American intellectuals.

5. Dale, "Movies and Propaganda," p.85. For the stereotypical view, see Potamkin, "Hollywood Looks at War," and Tom Brandon, "A Pre-War Film," *New Masses*, May 29, 1934, pp.29-30. For a more balanced assessment, see George Seldes, "The New Propaganda For War," *Harper's Magazine*, October, 1934, pp.540-54.

6. Winifred Johnston, *Memo on the Movies: War Propaganda, 1914-1939,* Cooperative Books, Series 1, no.5 (Norman, Okla.: University of Oklahoma Press, 1939).

7. Ibid., pp.30, 45, 63.

8. Benjamin Glazer, "Seventh Heaven," script ("Shooting Script"), September 7, 1926, Scenes 155-56, Titles 102-6, AMPAS.

9. Willis Goldbeck and Agnes Christine Johnston, "The Enemy," script ("Fourth Temporary Complete"), May 23, 1927, Scenes 158, 221, 223, 231, MOMA.

10. S.N. Behrman and Sonia Levien, "Surrender," script ("Second Draft Screen Play"), August 28, 1931, 68, AMPAS. Emphasis in original.

11. Cyril Hume, Richard Maibaum, and Maurice Rapf, "They Gave Him a Gun," script ("Okayed by Harry Rapf–Producer"), February 9, 1937, pp.7, 10-11, 68, AMPAS. Emphasis in original.

12. *Time,* May 24, 1937, p.55.

13. "How War Made a Man Into a Killer," *Literary Digest,* May 22, 1937, p.28. For an opposite yet isolationist view of this picture, see Don Herold, "Back Talk at the Movies," *The Commentator,* July 1937, pp.123-24.

14. William Troy, "The Unregenerate Art," *Nation,* September 19, 1934, p.336; see also "Argus," "On the Current Screen," *Literary Digest,* July 14, 1934, p.29.

15. Reginald Berkeley, "The World Moves On," script ("Final Shooting Script"), February 21, 1934, p.75, AMPAS.

16. *Time,* May 5, 1930, pp.30, 32.

17. Ibid., p.32.

18. Karel Reisz, "Milestone and War," *Sequence 14,* New Year 1952, pp.12-16.

19. *National Board of Review Magazine,* May-June 1930, pp.5-7.

20. "All's Quiet on the Western Front," *Motion Picture,* March 1, 1930, pp.6-7.

21. Alexander Bakshy, "Stark War," *Nation,* June 11, 1930, p.688.

22. Quoted in George Seldes, "The New Propaganda for War," p.552. Pease made quite a career baiting various "un-Americanisms." For his anti-communist and anti-semitic abuse of the visiting Russian filmmaker Sergei Eisenstein, see Ivor Montagu, *With Eisenstein in Hollywood* (Berlin: Seven Seas Publishers, 1968), p.121.

23. *All Quiet on the Western Front* (Universal, 1930), MOMA; quotations are from the film.

24. *Newsweek,* June 26, 1937, p.23.

25. Don Herold, "Back Talk at the Movies," *The Commentator,* August, 1937, pp.123-24.

26. R. C. Sheriff and Charles Kenyon, "The Road Back," script ("Revised Continuity and Dialog"), n.d. (but 1937), Reel 8, p.4, NYPL (LC).

27. Ibid., Reel 11, p.10.

28. Alexander Bakshy, "Journey's End," *Nation,* April 30, 1930, pp. 524-25.

29. Potamkin, "The Film and the War," pp. 14-15.

30. This film was also known as *The Man I Killed.* For an aesthetic appreciation, see Margaret Marshall, "Propaganda," *Nation,* February 17, 1932, p.212.

31. "New Portrayal of War That Avoids Propaganda," *Literary Digest,* July 11, 1936, p.22.

32. Mark Van Doren, "Stationary War," *Nation,* September 26, 1936, pp. 374-75.

33. *All Quiet on the Western Front,* MOMA; quotations are from the film.

34. George Abbott, "All Quiet on the Western Front," script ("Abbott Version"), November 11, 12, 13, 19, 20, and 21, 1929, Scene 8-E, MOMA. Internal evidence indicates this was not the final script for the film. Abbott was given credit for co-authoring the final script with Dell Andrews and Maxwell Anderson.

35. *Beyond Victory* (RKO-Pathé, 1931), WCTR; quotations are from the film. See also *Time,* April 20, 1931, p.28; *National Board of Review Magazine,* April 1931, p.24. This film was directed by John S. Robertson, but the person most responsible seems to have been character actor James Gleason, who co-authored the original story and screenplay with Horace Jackson and also played one of the American soldiers.

36. William Troy, "A Hollywood Trio," *Nation,* April 12, 1933, pp. 421-22.

37. *Westfront 1918,* a German film (1930), and *Grand Illusion,* a French film (1937), are examples of anti-war pictures that in part indicted the nationality of their makers.

Chapter 10

1. Unidentified clipping, folder, AMPAS.
2. These arguments are distilled from Clara Eva Schieber, "The Transformation of American Sentiment Towards Germany, 1870-1914," *Journal of International Relations* (July 1921): 50-74.
3. Carl Wittke, *German-Americans and the World War,* Ohio Historical Collections, vol. 5 (Columbus: Ohio State Archeological and Historical Society, 1936).
4. *Civilization,* MOMA; quotation is from the film. The kingdom was identified, perhaps by a professional Welsh-baiter, as that of "Wredpryd."
5. *Moving Picture World,* September 28, 1918, p. 1922; see also *Motion Picture News,* August 17, 1918, p. 993.
6. *Moving Picture World,* June 22, 1918, p. 1762.
7. *The New York Times,* June 30, 1918, sec. 3, p. 6.
8. Ibid., July 1, 1918, p.9.
9. Ibid.
10. Ibid., March 10, 1918, sec. 1, p. 18.
11. *Moving Picture World,* March 30, 1918, p. 1867.
12. *Time,* December 4, 1939, pp. 82-83.
13. Still, *Beast of Berlin* folder, AMPAS.
14. *Moving Picture World,* March 30, 1918, p. 1869.
15. Ibid., March 22, 1919, p. 1697.
16. *The New York Times,* May 3, 1919, p. 11.
17. Script, "Escaping the Hun," no date, but believed to be 1917, Scene 7, NYPL (LC).
18. Ibid., Scene 77A.
19. *Liberty Loan - National Association of the Motion Picture Industry,* LC; quotation is from the film.
20. De Mille, *Hollywood Saga,* p. 191.
21. Letter, Wilson to J. A. Berst of Pathé, June 4, 1917, in Ray Stannard Baker, *Woodrow Wilson: Life and Letters,* 8 vols. (New York: Doubleday, Doran Company, Inc., 1939), 7:100.
22. Letter, Wilson to Henry Morgenthau, June 14, 1918, in Baker, *Woodrow Wilson,* 8:213. The President apparently distrusted film as a good conduit for information, although he enjoyed watching certain types of pictures. He refused an offer to use his *History of the American People* as material for movies. Letter, Wilson to William H. Briggs of Harper and Brothers, October 1, 1918, in ibid., p.441. See Also Spears, "World War I on the Screen," May, 1966, p. 288.
23. *Moving Picture World,* March 30, 1918, p. 1863.
24. James W. Gerard, *My First Eighty-Three Years in America* (Garden City, N.Y.: Doubleday and Company, Inc., 1951), 284-85.
25. Jacobs, *The Rise of the American Film,* p. 258.
26. *Pershing's Crusaders* (CPI, 1918), NA; quotation is from the film.
27. *Official War Review,* nos. 11 and 17, LC.
28. Quoted in John Drinkwater, *The Life and Adventures of Carl Laemmle* (New York: G.P. Putnam's Sons, 1931), 215-16.
29. *Dramatic Mirror* clipping, November 17, 1917, folder, AMPAS.
30. Script, "Lest We Forget," p.18, Scene 102.

31. "The President as a Movie Fan," *Literary Digest,* February 22, 1919, pp. 67, 70. There exists no reason to suppose Wilson was affected one way or another if he did view *The Great Victory.* There is no mention of the film in Baker's collection of Wilson's correspondence, and the President's taste ran to romances–Nazimova was one of his favorites. However, such patriotic sermons as *The Slacker* (Rolfe-Metro, 1917) and *Draft 258* (Metro, 1917) were shown on board during Wilson's trip. See also Charles Reed Mitchell, "New Message to America: James W. Gerard's *Beware* and World War I Propaganda," *Journal of Popular Film* no. 4 (1975): 275-95.

32. *The Love Light* (United Artists, 1921), LC.

33. *The Unbeliever,* LC.

34. Script, "Lest We Forget," p.24, Scene 138.

35. *The New York Times,* October 3, 1926, sec. 8, p. 5.

36. *Seventh Heaven* (Fox, 1927), MOMA; quotation is from the film, which included a map featuring Berlin under a hunk of liverwurst and Paris as cubes of sugar.

37. *Lilac Time* (First National, 1928), WCTR; quotations are from the film.

38. Llewellyn Hughes and Campbell Gullian, "The Sky Hawk," script ("Pictorial action and dialog"), no date (but 1929), p. 91, MOMA.

39. *Time,* September 15, 1930, p. 38.

40. Script, "Surrender," pp. 1, 82, 93.

41. Script, "The World Moves On," p. 62.

42. *Isn't Life Wonderful?* (United Artists, 1924), MOMA; quotations are from the film. See also *The New York Times,* December 1, 1924, p. 17. Griffith was deeply involved in financial difficulties as this picture was being made. These troubles hastened his "lockstep to oblivion." See Robert M. Henderson, *D. W. Griffith: His Life and Work* (New York: Oxford University Press, 1972), pp. 252-56.

43. Lillian Gish, *The Movies, Mr. Griffith, and Me* (Englewood Cliffs, N.J.: Prentice-Hall, Inc., 1969), 201-02.

44. *Isn't Life Wonderful?* MOMA; quotation is from the film.

45. *National Board of Review Magazine,* July, 1927, p.10; see also Welford Beaton, "'Barbed Wire' a Great Picture," *Film Spectator,* March 5, 1927, pp. 6-7.

46. *Four Sons* (Fox, 1928), MOMA; quotation is from the film.

47. Dorothy B. Jones, "War Without Glory," *Quarterly of Film, Radio, and Television,* Spring 1954, p.288.

48. "Germany Repudiates a Film," *Literary Digest*, August 30, 1930, p. 17.

49. Script, "The Road Back," Reel 1, p.5; Reel 5, p.6.

50. Ibid., final scene.

51. *Time,* June 28, 1937, p. 51.

52. *The Ramparts We Watch,* MOMA; quotation is from the film.

53. Robert Buckner and Edmund Joseph, "Yankee Doodle Dandy," script, no date (but 1942), MOMA, WCTR, 122; *Yankee Doodle Dandy* (Warner Brothers, 1942), LC, WCTR.

Chapter 11

1. Kracauer, "National Types as Hollywood Presents Them," in Rosenberg and White, *Mass Culture,* p. 274. In fairness to Kracauer, he is speaking of films of the thirties and forties, yet he seems

to imply that his observations fit any situation. He bases his "in-groups" and "out-groups" according to the favor each enjoyed with Americans.

2. *Official War Review,* nos. 11 and 17, LC.
3. *Time,* July 17, 1933, p.34.
4. *Moving Picture World,* October 19, 1918, p. 448.
5. Wolfenstein and Leites, *Movies: A Psychological Study,* p. 295.
6. Kracauer, "National Types as Hollywood Presents Them," pp. 270-71.
7. *Lilac Time,* WCTR; quotation is from the film. See also Behlmer, "World War I Aviation Films," pp. 418-19.
8. *The New York Times,* January 25, 1917, p. 7.
9. Script, "Dawn Patrol," pp. 115-15A.
10. Reginald Berkeley and Sonya Levien, "Cavalcade," script ("Final Shooting Script"), September 19, 1932, AMPAS, 127. *Cavalcade* was no rarity in its emphasis on tradition and family. It was precisely these, according to a character in *Born to Love* (RKO-Pathé, 1931), WCTR, that "made England England."
11. *Cavalcade* (Fox, 1933), MOMA; quotation is from the film.
12. For laudatory reviews, see "'Cavalcade' as a Film Out-shines the Play," *Literary Digest,* (January 28, 1933), 15.
13. Wolfenstein and Leites, *Movies: A Psychological Study,* p. 296.
14. Spears, "World War I on the Screen," May 1966, pp. 281-82.
15. *Official War Review,* no. 11, LC.
16. Spears, "World War I on the Screen," May 1966, p. 282.
17. Script, "Escaping the Hun," Scene 340.
18. Script, "Lest We Forget," p. 39, Scene 254A.
19. *National Board of Review Magazine,* November 1929, p. 18.
20. Script, "Surrender," pp. 38-A, 12, 35.
21. *Time,* August 17, 1936, p. 46.
22. Kracauer, "National Types as Hollywood Presents Them," pp. 258, 272-73.
23. "The German Curse in Chaotic Russia," *Photoplay Magazine,* April, 1918, pp. 32-33.
24. Ibid., p.32.
25. *Moving Picture World,* January 26, 1918, p. 571. Actual film footage of the Russian revolution rarely was shown in American theaters after 1918. The *Official War Review,* no. 27, NA, contains shots of American forces occupying Vladivostok in the wake of the Armistice.
26. *Moving Picture World,* October 20, 1917, pp. 441, 444.
27. Ibid., September 29, 1917, p. 2008.
28. *The New York Times,* September 24, 1917, p. 11.
29. Bosley Crowther, *The Lion's Share: The Story of an Entertainment Empire* (New York: E.P.Dutton and Company, Inc., 1957), pp. 225-29.
30. Potamkin, "The Film and the War," p. 14.
31. *Time*, September 17, 1934, p. 40. See also William Troy, "The Brownings in Hollywood," *Nation,* October 10, 1934, pp. 419-20; Otis Ferguson, "Screen Versions," *New Republic,* September 12, 1934, pp. 131-32; "Argus," "On the Current Screen," *Literary Digest,* September 29, 1934, p. 29; Ames, "The Screen Enters Politics," p. 477.
32. *British Agent* (First National, 1934), WCTR; "traitor nation" quotation is from the film.

Chapter 12

1. *The Triangle,* March 4, 1916, pp. 1 ff.
2. *The Making of Hundred Ton Guns* (Edison, 1917), LC; quotation is from the film.
3. *Moving Picture World,* December 1, 1917, pp. 1336-37.
4. Ibid., September 22, 1917, p. 1845.
5. *The New York Times,* September 16, 1918, p.9.
6. *Moving Picture World,* February 26, 1916, p. 1358.
7. *In-Again, Out-Again* (Paramount-Artcraft, 1917), MOMA; quotation is from the film. See also *The New York Times,* April 23, 1917, p. 7.
8. Alistair Cooke, *Douglas Fairbanks: The Making of a Screen Character* (New York: Museum of Modern Art, 1940), p. 17.
9. *Dramatic Mirror* clipping, October 20, 1917, folder, AMPAS. This film should not be confused with Sidney B. Lust's 1934 documentary of the same name.
10. *Moving Picture World,* April, 13, 1918, p. 282.
11. Ibid., March 8, 1919, p. 1389; ibid., August 10, 1918, p. 892.
12. *The Triangle,* July 29, 1916, p. 5.
13. *Moving Picture World,* June 16, 1917, p. 1838.
14. Ibid., June 3, 1916, p. 1762; *Motion Picture News,* May 27, 1916, pp. 3269-70.
15. *Moving Picture World,* January 18, 1919, p. 389.
16. Ibid., October 5, 1918, p 128.
17. Alaric Flardon, "Producing War Dramas in Britain During Wartime," *Photoplay Magazine,* April, 1915, pp. 138-39. The term "fifth column" is from World War II; its usage nevertheless seems pertinent here.
18. This film should not be confused with the Chaplin picture of the same title, produced the next year.
19. *Moving Picture World,* September 7, 1918, p. 1455.
20. *The New York Times,* January 26, 1918, p. 11.
21. *Madam Spy* should not be confused with the film of the same name released by Universal in 1934.
22. *The New York Times,* September 2, 1918, p. 7.
23. *Moving Picture World,* July 13, 1918, p. 255.
24. Bella Spewack, Samuel Spewack, P.J.Wolfson, and George Oppenheimer, "Rendezvous," script ("Revised Dialog Cutting Continuity"), December 31, 1935, NYPL (LC).

Chapter 13

1. Richard Sherman, Oscar Hammerstein II, and Dorothy Yost, "The Story of Vernon and Irene Castle," script ("Final"), December 16, 1938, with changes dated January 4, 10, 1939, p. 105 AMPAS.
2. Reisz, "Milestone and War," p. 13.
3. Lionel Tiger, *Men in Groups* (New York: Vintage Books, 1970), pp. 104-11.
4. Grover Cleveland, "Would Woman Suffrage Be Unwise?" *Ladies' Home Journal,* October, 1905, pp. 7-8.
5. Scudder, quoted in William L. O'Neill, ed., *The Woman Movement: Feminism in the United States and England* (Quadrangle Books, 1971), pp. 175-76.
6. Aileen S. Kraditor, ed., *Up From the Pedestal: Selected Writings in the History of American Feminism* (New York: Quadrangle Books, 1968), p. 24.
7. Quoted in ibid., p. 287.
8. Quoted in O'Neill, *The Woman Movement,* p. 195.
9. A good statement of duty overriding pacifism is an unsigned editorial in *The General Federation of Women's Clubs Magazine,* June 1917, quoted in ibid., pp. 188-89. See also pp. 89, 92. Representative Jeannette Rankin of Montana, who voted against American involvement in both World Wars, was a much-publicized exception to the less well-known general voting pattern of women legislators.
10. Quoted in Kraditor, *Up from the Pedestal,* p. 287.
11. Book, "The Battle Cry of Peace," Blackton Collection, p. 13, AMPAS.
12. Sutherland Denlinger, "We Go to War," *New York World Telegram,* Metropolitan Weekend Magazine Section, April 3, 1937, p. 6; *The New York Times,* April 2, 1917, p. 11.
13. *Moving Picture World,* April 21, 1917, pp. 449-50.
14. Quoted in Mock and Larson, *Words That Won the War,* p. 132.
15. *The New York Times,* December 25, 1916, p. 7; Vachel Lindsay, "Venus in Armor," *New Republic,* April 28, 1917, pp. 380-81.
16. *Patria* (Cosmopolitan Pictures, 1917), MOMA; quotation is from the film. For undocumented background on the making and reception of this picture, see Mock and Larson, *Words That Won the War,* pp. 143-47. See also *The New York Times,* December 9, 1918, p. 11.
17. "*Four Sons* Wins Photoplay Medal For Last Year," *The Motion Picture,* December 1, 1929, p. 7; *National Board of Review Magazine,* March, 1928, p. 11.
18. William Troy, "Panorama," *Nation,* August 2, 1933, p. 139.
19. Script, "Cavalcade," p. 94.
20. Script, "The World Moves On," pp. 75-76.
21. *The Unbeliever,* LC; quotation is from the film.
22. Script, "Lest We Forget," p. 21, scene 117.
23. *Seventh Heaven* (1927), MOMA; quotation is from the film.
24. *The Patent Leather Kid* (First National, 1927), WCTR; quotation is from the film. *What Price Glory?* (Fox, 1926), MOMA; quotation is from the film.
25. *Beyond Victory,* WCTR; quotation is from the film.
26. Gilbert Seldes, "The Plot and the Picture," *New Republic,* September 16, 1925, pp. 97-98.
27. *Corporal Kate,* LC; quotation is from the film.

28. Becky Gardiner, "War Nurse," script ("Dialog Cutting Continuity"), October 17, 1930, NYPL (LC); see also *Time,* November 3, 1930, pp. 44-45.
29. *Newsweek,* May 16, 1936, p. 42.
30. Script, "Escaping the Hun," scene 414.
31. Lillian Gish, "I Made War Propaganda," *Scribner's Commentator,* November, 1941, pp. 7-11.
32. Gish, *The Movies, Mr. Griffith, and Me,* pp. 201-02. For a later appreciation, see Roger Manvell, "Hearts of the World, 1918," *Sight and Sound,* May 1950, pp. 130-32.
33. Jacobs, *The Rise of the American Film,* p. 386.
34. Hazel Simpson Naylor, "Across the Silversheet," *Motion Picture Magazine,* March 1919, p. 73. Lillian Gish was of the opinion that *The Greatest Thing in Life,* which apparently has vanished, was Griffith's best film. See "Conversation with Lillian Gish," *Sight and Sound,* Winter 1957-58, pp. 128-30.
35. There were so many films on this periphery that some must be reduced to a footnote. Included were *Havoc* (Fox, 1925); *Out of the Ruins* (First National, 1928); *The Battle of Paris* (Paramount, 1929); *Hotel Imperial* (Paramount, 1927); and, as a marginal case, *Lilac Time* (First National, 1928).
36. "Remade 'Seventh Heaven' is a Hit," *Literary Digest* (April 3, 1937), 20.
37. *British Agent,* WCTR; quotations are from the film.

Chapter 14

1. Duncan, *Communication and Social Order,* p. 438. The framework of this chapter is built around Duncan's insights into the nature of comic art.
2. Duncan, *Symbols in Society,* p. 60.
3. Duncan, *Communication and Social Order,* pp. 402-3.
4. Mack Sennett, *King of Comedy* (Garden City, N.Y.: Doubleday and Company, Inc., 1954), p. 90. Emphasis in original.
5. *The New York Times,* December 15, 1914, p. 13.
6. Dench, "Following the Movies to the Firing-Line and Back," 60.
7. *The New York Times,* September 23, 1918, p. 7.
8. *Moving Picture World,* July 20, 1918, p. 453.
9. *The New York Times,* September 23, 1918, p. 7; *Moving Picture World,* September 28, 1918, p. 1926.
10. Charles Chaplin, *My Autobiography* (London: The Bodley Head, 1964), pp. 228, 233. Chaplin's remembrances of the World War I period after a hiatus of over forty years must be treated with some care. They were written after another world war the totalitarian ingredients of which Chaplin had treated with comic art in *The Great Dictator* (1940). Although Chaplin had been active in Liberty Loan drives in the earlier period, the emotion of his autobiography rings true with some of his comic statements in *Shoulder Arms.*
11. Ibid., p. 241.
12. Ibid., pp. 383-84.
13. Julian Johnson, "The Shadow Stage," *Photoplay Magazine,* January 1919, pp. 67-68; for another laudatory review, see *The New York Times,* October 21, 1918, p. 15.
14. *Variety* clipping, March 14, 1928, *Ham and Eggs at the Front* folder, AMPAS.
15. The most spectacular instance of departure from the black stereotype during this period undoubtedly was the famous kissing scene between a white soldier and a delirious black soldier in D.

W. Griffith's *The Greatest Thing in Life*. See "Conversation with Lillian Gish," p. 129; Noble, *The Negro in Films*, p. 39.

    16. *Time*, May 9, 1927, p. 36; see also *National Board of Review Magazine*, May 1927, pp. 16-17.

    17. *A Soldier's Plaything* (Warner Brothers, 1930), WCTR; quotation is from the film.

    18. Fanny Lee McKinney, "The Movies and the People," *Outlook*, May 16, 1923, pp. 882-83.

    19. *National Board of Review Magazine*, September-October 1926, p. 13; see also Charles Reisner and Darryl Zanuck, "The Better 'Ole," script, no date (but 1926), AMPAS.

Bibliography of Primary Sources

For further detail, the interested reader may refer to my doctoral dissertation, "War on Film: The American Cinema and World War I, 1914-1941," on file with University Microfilms, Ann Arbor, Michigan.

Indispensable reference catalogs for this study include the *American Film Catalog* (New York: R.R.Bowker Company, 1970-) and the *Catalog of Copyright Entries, Cumulative Series: Motion Pictures, 1912-1939* (Washington, D.C.: Library of Congress, 1951.)

Abbreviations

AFI	American Film Institute Library, Beverly Hills
AMPAS	Academy of Motion Picture Arts and Sciences Library, Los Angeles
LC	Library of Congress
MOMA	Museum of Modern Art, New York City
NA	National Archives
NYPL	New York Public Library
NYPL(LC)	Theater Collection, New York Public Library, Library and Museum of the Performing Arts, Lincoln Center
WCTR	Wisconsin Center for Theater Research, Madison
WYO	University of Wyoming Library, Laramie

Films

Films form the core of this study. They are here cited as to name, producing company, and year of production. In instances where only dates for films are given, the production company is unknown. Wherever possible, the year of the copyright date is given. Most of the films seem to have been released from two weeks to two months prior to their copyright date, but this was no set rule. When a production company appears in hyphenated form (i.e., "Universal-Jewel"), the second name usually is that of the distributing affiliate, with the exception of producers' names like RKO-Radio and Famous Players-Lasky.

Locations of positive prints of the films are cited by abbreviation. These are not necessarily the only places these prints may be found. Where no location is cited, I have been unable to locate a positive print. In addition, those films I have viewed are marked with an asterisk (*), although I did not necessarily view them in the location cited. Metro-Goldwyn-Mayer is cited as MGM, Twentieth Century-Fox as Fox, and the Division of Films, Committee on Public Information, as CPI. CPI short subjects are not included; the reader may refer to the notes in chapter five.

Ace of Aces (RKO-Radio, 1933) WCTR(*).
Adele (United Picture Theaters, 1919).
After the War (Universal, 1919).
After Tonight (RKO-Radio, 1933) WCTR (*).
Alias Mike Moran (Paramount, 1919).
An Alien Enemy (Hodkinson-Paralta, 1918).
All Quiet on the Western Front (Universal, 1930) MOMA (*).
The American Ambulance Boys at the Front (Documentary) (Triangle, 1916).
America Preparing (Documentary) (1916).
America's Answer (Documentary) (CPI, 1918), NA (*).
America Unprepared (Documentary) (American Defense Society, 1916).
Anybody's War (Paramount, 1930).
Arms and the Girl (Famous Players-Lasky, 1917).
Army Surgeon (RKO-Radio, 1942), WCTR (*).
As in a Looking Glass (World, 1916).
Barbed Wire (Paramount, 1927).
The Bath of Bullets (Documentary) (CPI, 1918).
The Battle Cry of Peace (Vitagraph, 1915).
The Battle of Paris (Paramount, 1929).
Behind the Door (Paramount-Artcraft, 1919.)
Behind the Front (Paramount, 1926).
The Belgian (State Rights, 1917).
Be Neutral (Universal-Powers, 1914).
Berlin Via America (Fordart Films, Inc., 1918).
Betsy Ross (World-Peerless, 1917).
The Better 'Ole (Warner Brothers, 1926), WCTR (*).
Beware! (Warner Brothers, 1919), WCTR (*).

Beyond Victory (RKO-Pathé, 1931), WCTR (*).
The Big Drive (Documentary) (First Division, 1933), LC (*).
The Big Parade (MGM, 1925), MOMA (*).
The Birth of a Race (1918).
Blaze O'Glory (Sono-Art, 1930).
Blinky (Universal, 1923).
Bobby of the Home Defenders (Greater Vitagraph, 1917).
Body and Soul (Fox, 1931).
Bonnie Annie Laurie (Fox, 1918).
Born to Love (RKO-Pathé, 1931), WCTR (*).
Boy Scouts to the Rescue (Serial) (Universal, 1918).
The Brand of Cowardice (Metro, 1916).
British Agent (First National, 1934), WCTR (*).
Broken Lullaby (Paramount, 1932), MOMA (*).
Buck Privates (Universal-Jewel, 1927).
Bud's Recruit (General Film Company, 1918).
Bullets and Brown Eyes (Kaybee-Triangle, 1916).
Captain Eddie (Fox, 1945) (*).
Captain Swagger (Pathé, 1928).
Captured! (Warner Brothers, 1933), WCTR (*).
The Case of Sergeant Grischa (RKO-Radio, 1930).
Cavalcade (Fox, 1933), MOMA (*).
Chances (First National, 1931), WCTR (*).
The Charmer (Famous Players-Lasky, 1925).
Civilian Clothes (Famous Players-Lasky, 1920).
Civilization (Ince-Triangle, 1916), MOMA (*).
Claws of the Hun (Paramount-Artcraft, 1918).
Closed Gates (Sterling, 1927).
The Cock-Eyed World (Fox, 1929).
Cock of the Air (United Artists, 1932).
Come On In (Paramount, 1918).
The Common Cause (Vitagraph, 1918).
Comrades (First Division, 1928).
Convoy (First National, 1927).
Corporal Kate (Producers Distributing Corporation, 1926), LC (*).
The Coward (Triangle, 1915), MOMA (*).
Crashing Through to Berlin (Documentary) (Universal-Jewel, 1918).
Crimson Romance (Mascot, 1934).
The Cross Red Nurse (World, 1918).
The Crowded Hour (Famous Players-Lasky, 1925).

Dangerous Business (First National, 1921).
The Dark Angel (First National, 1925).
The Dark Angel (United Artists, 1935).
Dark Sands (Record Pictures, 1938).
The Dark Star (Paramount-Artcraft, 1919).
Daughter Angele (Triangle, 1918).
Daughter of Destiny (First National, 1918).
A Daughter of France (Fox, 1918).
Dawn (Columbia, 1928).
The Dawn Patrol (First National, 1930), MOMA, WCTR (*).
Dawn Patrol (Warner Brothers, 1938), WCTR (*).
The Dead March (Documentary) (Imperial Pictures, 1937).
Dealers in Death (Semi-documentary) (Topical Films, 1934).
Defense or Tribute? (Radio Film Company, Inc., 1916).
Dishonored (Paramount, 1931).
Dog of the Regiment (Warner Brothers, 1927).
Doing Our Bit (Fox, 1918).
Doing Their Bit (Fox, 1918).
Doin' His Bit (Cartoon) (Universal-Powers, 1917).
Dolly Does Her Bit (Pathé, 1918).
Doomed Battalion (Universal, 1932).
Doughboys (MGM, 1930).
Draft 258 (Metro, 1917).
Dugan of the Dugouts (Anchor, 1928).
The Eagle and the Hawk (Paramount, 1933).
The Eagle's Eye (Serial) (Wharton, Inc., 1918).
18 to 45 (Fox, 1918).
The Enchanted Cottage (First National, 1924).
The Enemy (MGM, 1928).
Escaping the Hun (No company or date, but probably 1917).
Ever in My Heart (Warner Brothers, 1933), WCTR (*).
The Evil Eye (Paramount-Artcraft, 1916).
Face Value (Sterling, 1927), LC (*).
The Fall of a Nation (National Drama, 1916).
The Fall of the Romanoffs (Fox, 1917).
False Faces (Paramount-Artcraft, 1918).
A Farewell to Arms (Paramount, 1932).
Fields of Honor (Goldwyn, 1918).
The Fighting 69th (Warner Brothers, 1940), WCTR (*).
Finders Keepers (Universal-Jewel, 1928).

Find Your Man (Warner Brothers, 1924).
The Firefly of France (Paramount, 1918).
The First World War (Documentary) (Fox, 1934).
Fit to Fight (Goldwyn, 1918).
The Flag Maker (Spoor-Blackton, 1927).
Flying Luck (Pathé, 1927).
The Flying Torpedo (Triangle-Fine Arts, 1916).
Flying with the Marines (Documentary) (CPI, 1918).
Follow the Girl (Universal-Butterfly, 1917).
The Food Gamblers (Eastern Triangle, 1917).
For Better, For Worse (Paramount-Artcraft, 1919).
For France (Vitagraph, 1917).
For Liberty (Fox, 1917).
For the Freedom of the East (Goldwyn, 1918).
For the Freedom of the World (Goldwyn, 1918).
For Valour (Triangle, 1917).
The Fountain (RKO-Radio, 1934).
The Four Horsemen of the Apocalypse (Metro, 1921).
Four Sons (Fox, 1928), MOMA (*).
The Geezer of Berlin (Universal-Jewel, 1918).
The Gentleman From America (Universal, 1923).
The German Curse in Russia (Documentary) (Pathé, 1918).
The German Side of the War (Documentary) (Indian Film Company, Inc., 1915).
Germany's Side of the War (Fifty-fifth Street Playhouse Group, 1928).
The Girl Who Stayed at Home (Paramount-Artcraft, 1919).
The Goodbye Kiss (First National, 1928).
The Gown of Destiny (Triangle, 1917).
Grant, Police Reporter (Serial) (1916).
The Greatest Power (Metro-Rolfe, 1917).
The Greatest Thing in Life (Paramount-Artcraft, 1918).
The Great Love (Paramount-Artcraft, 1918).
The Great Victory (Retitled *Why Germany Must Pay*) (Metro, 1918).
Guarding Old Glory (Documentary) (F.O.Nielson, 1915).
Half-Shot at Sunrise (RKO-Radio, 1930), WCTR (*).
Ham and Eggs at the Front (Warner Brothers, 1927).
Hard Boiled Haggarty (First National, 1927).
Havoc (Fox, 1925).
Hayfoot-Strawfoot (Ince, 1919).
The Heart of Humanity (Universal-Jewel, 1919).
Hearts of the World (World-Comstock, 1918).

Hell Below (MGM, 1933).
Hell in the Heavens (Fox, 1934).
Hell's Angels (United Artists, 1930).
Her Country First (Paramount, 1918).
Her Country's Call (Mutual, 1917).
Her Man O'War (Producers Distributing Corporation, 1926).
The Hero (Lichtman-Preferred, 1922).
Heroes For Sale (Breadline) (First National, 1933), WCTR (*).
Heroic France (Documentary) (Mutual, 1916).
The Hero of Submarine D-2 (Vitagraph, 1916).
Hiding in Holland (Documentary) (Universal, 1919).
The Highest Trump (Vitagraph, 1919).
Home Defense (Paramount-Klever Pictures, Inc., 1917).
An Honest Man (Triangle, 1918).
Honor First (Fox, 1922).
Horses of War (Documentary) (CPI, 1918).
Hotel Imperial (Paramount, 1927), MOMA, LC (*).
Hotel Imperial (Paramount, 1939).
Humoresque (Paramount-Artcraft, 1920).
The Hun Within (Paramount-Artcraft, 1918).
I'll Say So (Fox, 1918).
The Immigrant (Lasky-Paramount, 1915).
In-Again, Out-Again (Paramount-Artcraft, 1917), MOMA (*).
In Pursuit of Polly (Paramount, 1918).
Inside the Lines (World-Pyramid, 1918).
Inside the Lines (RKO-Radio, 1930).
An International Sneak (Paramount, 1917).
In the Name of the Prince of Peace (World, 1915).
Intolerance (Triangle, 1916), MOMA (*).
Into No Man's Land (Excellent Pictures Corporation, 1928).
Isn't Life Wonderful? (United Artists, 1924), MOMA (*).
Joan of Plattsburg (Goldwyn, 1918).
Joan the Woman (Famous Players-Lasky, 1916).
Johanna Enlists (Paramount-Artcraft, 1918), LC (*).
Journey's End (Tiffany-Stahl Productions, 1930).
Judgment of the Hills (FBO, 1927).
The Kaiser's Finish (Warner Brothers, 1918).
The Kaiser's New Dentist (Cartoon) (Fox, 1918).
The Kaiser's Shadow (Paramount-Artcraft, 1918).
The Kaiser, the Beast of Berlin (Universal, 1918).

A Kaiser There Was (Universal, 1918).
Kicking the Germ Out of Germany (Rolin-Pathé, 1918).
Kultur (Fox, 1918).
Lafayette, We Come! (Affiliated-Independent, 1918).
Lancer Spy (Fox, 1937).
The Land of the Free (Lasky, 1918).
The Last Flight (First National, 1931), LC, WCTR (*).
The Last Parade (Columbia, 1931).
Legionnaires in Paris (FBO, 1927).
Legion of the Condemned (Paramount, 1928).
Lest We Forget (Metro, 1918).
Liberty (Serial) (Universal, 1916).
Lilac Time (First National, 1928), WCTR (*).
The Little American (Pickford-Artcraft, 1917).
A Little Patriot (Pathé, 1917).
The Lone Eagle (Universal Jewel, 1917).
Lost at the Front (First National, 1927).
The Lost Battalion (Semi-documentary) (McManus Corporation, 1919), LC (*).
The Lost Patrol (RKO-Radio, 1934), WCTR (*).
The Lost Squadron (RKO-Radio, 1932), MOMA, WCTR (*).
Love and the Law (Film Clearing House, 1919).
Love in a Hurry (World, 1919).
The Love Light (United Artists, 1921), LC (*).
Luck and Pluck (Fox, 1919).
Madam Who? (Paralta, 1918).
Madam Spy (Universal-Butterfly, 1918).
Madam Spy (Universal, 1934).
Made in America (Hodkinson-Pathé, 1919).
The Mad Parade (Paramount, 1931).
The Maid of Belgium (World, 1917).
Making the Nation Fit (Documentary) (CPI, 1918).
A Man From Wyoming (Paramount, 1930).
The Man Who Reclaimed His Head (Universal, 1934).
The Man Who Was Afraid (Essanay, 1917).
The Man Without a Country (Universal-Jewel, 1917).
Mare Nostrum (MGM, 1926).
Marianne (MGM, 1929).
The Marriage Ring (Paramount, 1918).
Mata Hari (MGM, 1931) (*).
Me und Gott (Romayne Super-Film Company, 1918).

The Miracle of the Ships (Documentary) (C.L.Chester, 1918).
Missing (Paramount, 1918).
Motherhood (Mutual, 1917).
Mr. Logan, USA (Victory-Fox, 1918).
Mrs. Slacker (Astra-Pathé, 1918).
My Country First (Serial) (Unity-Pathé, 1916).
My Four Years in Germany (Warner Brothers, 1918), WCTR (*).
My Own United States (Metro-State Rights, 1918).
The Mysterious Lady (MGM, 1928).
A Nation's Peril (Lubin, 1915).
Neutrality (No company or date, but 1914).
New Lives For Old (Famous Players-Lasky, 1925).
Noah's Ark (Warner Brothers, 1929), WCTR (*).
No Man's Land (Metro, 1918).
Now We're in the Air (Paramount, 1927).
Nurse Edith Cavell (Imperadio-RKO, 1939).
The Official War Review (Documentary short subjects) (CPI, 1918).
On Dangerous Ground (Brady-World, 1916).
One of Millions (Dyreda Art Film Corporation, 1914).
The Other Man's Wife (British-American Pictures Finance Corporation, 1919).
Our Bridge of Ships (Documentary) (CPI, 1918).
Our Invincible Navy (Prizma, 1918).
Our Wings of Victory (Documentary) (CPI, 1918).
Out of the Ruins (First National, 1928).
Over Here (Documentary) (World, 1917).
Over Secret Wires (Kaybee, 1915).
Over There (Selig-Charles Richman Pictures Corporation, 1917).
Over There (Documentary) (1934).
Over the Rhine (Universal-Independent, 1918).
Over the Top (Vitagraph, 1918).
Pack Up Your Troubles (MGM, 1932).
The Patent Leather Kid (First National, 1927), WCTR (*).
Patria (Serial) (Cosmopolitan Pictures, 1917), MOMA (*).
The Patriot (Metro, 1917).
Patriotism (Brunton-Paralta, 1918).
Pearl of the Army (Serial) (Astra-Pathé, 1916).
Perkins' Peace Party (Mutual, 1916).
Pershing's Crusaders (Documentary) (CPI, 1918), NA (*).
Pettigrew's Girl (Paramount, 1919).
Pilgrimage (Fox, 1933).

Powder (Mutual, 1916).
The Price of Peace (Documentary) (U.S. Treasury Department, 1919).
The Pride of New York (Fox, 1917).
Private Izzy Murphy (Warner Brothers, 1926).
Private Jones (Universal, 1933).
The Profiteers (Astra-Pathé, 1919).
The Prussian Cur (Fox, 1918).
Puppets (First National, 1926).
The Ramparts We Watch (Semi-documentary) (Time, Inc. - RKO-Radio, 1940), MOMA (*).
Rasputin and the Empress (MGM, 1933).
Rasputin, the Black Monk (World, 1917).
Rendezvous (MGM, 1935).
Riley of the Rainbow Division (1928).
The Road Back (Universal, 1937).
The Road to France (World, 1918).
The Road to Glory (Fox, 1926).
The Road to Glory (Fox, 1936).
A Romance of the Air (Crest-State Rights, 1918).
Rookies (MGM, 1927).
Safe For Democracy (Retitled *Life's Greatest Problem*) (Vitagraph, 1918).
Sailor Izzy Murphy (Warner Brothers, 1927).
The Seas Beneath (Fox, 1931).
Secret Code (Triangle, 1918).
The Secret Game (Lasky-Paramount, 1917).
The Secret of the Submarine (Serial) (American-Mutual, 1916).
Sergeant York (Warner Brothers, 1941), WCTR (*).
The Service Star (Goldwyn, 1918).
Seventh Heaven (Fox, 1927), MOMA (*).
Seventh Heaven (Fox, 1937).
The 75-Mile Gun (Cartoon) (Fox, 1918).
Shame (Noble-Duplex-State Rights, 1917).
She Goes to War (United Artists-Inspiration, 1929).
Shell 43 (Triangle, 1916).
Shifting Sands (Triangle, 1918).
A Ship Comes In (Pathé, 1928).
Shootin' For Love (Universal, 1923).
Shopworn Angel (Paramount, 1929).
Shopworn Angel (MGM, 1938) (*).
Shoulder Arms (First National, 1918), LC (*).

The Side Show of Life (Famous Players-Lasky, 1924).
The Sinking of the Lusitania (Cartoon) (Universal-Jewel, 1918).
Six Days (Goldwyn, 1923).
Sky Devils (United Artists, 1932).
The Sky Hawk (Fox, 1929).
The Slacker (Rolfe-Metro, 1917).
Smiles (Fox, 1919).
The Soldier Man (Pathé, 1926).
A Soldier's Oath (Fox, 1915).
A Soldier's Plaything (Warner Brothers, 1930), WCTR (*).
Somewhere in France (Kane-State Rights, 1916).
Somewhere in France (Triangle, 1916).
Somewhere in Somewhere (Pathé, 1925)
Sonny (First National, 1922).
Souls in Pawn (American-Mutual, 1917).
The Source (Paramount, 1918).
The Spirit of '17 (Morosco-Paramount, 1917).
The Spirit of '76 (Continental Producing Company, 1917).
The Spirit of the Red Cross (James Montgomery Flagg, 1918).
The Spirit of the USA (R-C Pictures Corporation, 1924).
Spuds (Pathé, 1927).
The Spy (Fox, 1917).
Stamboul Quest (MGM, 1934).
Storm at Daybreak (MGM, 1933).
The Storm of Steel (Documentary) (CPI, 1918).
The Story of Vernon and Irene Castle (RKO-Radio, 1939), WCTR (*).
The Strong Man (First National, 1926).
Submarine Patrol (Fox, 1938).
The Submarine Pirate (Keystone-Triangle, 1915).
Surrender (Fox, 1931).
Suspicion (Hoffman, 1918).
Suzy (MGM, 1936).
Sweetheart of the Doomed (Triangle, 1917).
Sylvia of the Secret Service (Astra-Pathé, 1917).
Tempest (MGM, 1928) (*).
They Gave Him a Gun (MGM, 1937).
The Thing We Love (Lasky-Paramount, 1918).
This Hero Stuff (Business) (Russell-Pathé, 1919).
This Is America (Documentary) (United Artists, 1933).
Three Comrades (MGM, 1938).

Three Faces East (Producers Distributing Corporation, 1925).
Three Faces East (Warner Brothers, 1930), WCTR (*).
Thunder Afloat (MGM, 1939).
Till I Come Back to You (Artcraft, 1918).
Till We Meet Again (Paramount, 1936).
Tin Hats (MGM, 1926).
Today We Live (MGM, 1933).
To Hell With the Kaiser! (Metro, 1918).
Too Fat to Fight (Goldwyn, 1918).
Top Sergeant Mulligan (Anchor, 1928).
True Heaven (Fox, 1929).
23½ Hours Leave (Famous Players-Lasky, 1919).
23½ Hours Leave (Grand National, 1937).
Two Arabian Knights (United Artists, 1927).
The Unbeliever (Edison, 1918), LC (*).
Uncle Sam's Defenders (Documentary series) (Mutual, 1916).
Under False Colors (Pathé, 1917).
Under Four Flags (Documentary) (CPI, 1918).
Under the Stars and Stripes in France (Documentary) (Pathé, 1917).
The Unknown Soldier (Producers Distributing Corporation, 1926).
The Unpardonable Sin (Garson, 1919).
The Vanishing American (Paramount, 1925).
Vive La France (Paramount-Artcraft, 1918).
The Volunteer (World, 1917).
Wanted For Murder (Chatham Pictures Corporation, 1918).
War and the Woman (Pathé, 1917).
War Bibles (Documentary) (Pathé, 1918).
The War Bridegroom (Universal, 1917).
The War Bride of Plumville (Essanay, 1916).
War Brides (Selznick-World, 1916).
The War Bride's Secret (Fox, 1916).
The War Horse (Fox, 1927).
War Nurse (MGM, 1930).
War O' Dreams (Selig, 1915).
Waterloo Bridge (Universal, 1931).
We Can't Have Everything (Artcraft, 1918).
We're in the Navy Now (Famous Players-Lasky, 1926).
What Price Glory? (Fox, 1926), MOMA (*).
When Men Desire (Fox, 1919).
When Your Soldier Is Hit (Documentary) (CPI, 1918).

Whirlwind of Youth (Paramount, 1927).
Whispering Wires of War (Documentary) (Pathé, 1918).
The White Sister (Essanay, 1915).
The White Sister (Metro, 1923).
The White Sister (MGM, 1933).
Who Goes There? (Vitagraph, 1917).
Whom the Gods Destroy (Greater Vitagraph, 1916).
Who Was the Other Man? (Universal-Butterfly, 1917).
Why America Will Win (Fox, 1918).
Wife or Country (Triangle, 1918).
Wilson (Fox, 1944).
Wings (Paramount, 1927), LC (*).
Wolves of Kultur (Serial) (Pathé, 1918).
Womanhood, the Glory of the Nation (Vitagraph, 1917).
The Woman I Love (RKO-Radio, 1937).
A Woman of Experience (RKO-Pathé, 1931), WCTR (*).
The Woman the Germans Shot (Plunkett and Carroll, 1918).
Women of All Nations (Fox, 1931).
The World Moves On (Fox, 1934).
Yankee Doodle Dandy (Warner Brothers, 1942), LC, WCTR (*).
Yankee Doodle in Berlin (Sennett-Sol Lesser, 1919).
The Yanks Are Coming (Documentary) (Universal, 1918).
Young Eagles (Paramount, 1930).
The Zeppelin's Last Raid (Paramount-Artcraft, 1917).

Scripts

No bibliography of motion picture scripts exists. Several film libraries maintain script collections, but the collections are by no means thorough. Shooting scripts must be used with care, since they often are revised as the film is shot. For the purpose of research, scripts labeled "Dialog Cutting Continuity" are the most desirable, since they are taken from the final print itself. Dialog cutting continuities thus are not scripts at all, in the strictest sense of the term. They are included here for the sake of simplicity.

Abbot, George. "All Quiet on the Western Front." Abbott Version. November 11, 12, 13, 19, 20, and 21, 1929, MOMA.

Baker, Melville. "Seventh Heaven." Revised final. December 1, 1936, Henry King Collection, WYO.

Bart, Jean (Marie Antoinette Sarlabous), and Ornitz, Samuel. "The Man Who Reclaimed His Head." Continuity and dialog. No date, but 1934, NYPL (LC).

Bibliography of Primary Sources

Behrman, S.N., and Levien, Sonya. "Surrender." Second draft screen play. August 28, 1931, AMPAS.

Bekroff, Percy. "A Soldier's Plaything." Final. November 1, 1930, WCTR.

Berkeley, Reginald. "The World Moves On." Final shooting. February 21, 1934, AMPAS.

——, and Levien, Sonya. "Cavalcade." Final shooting. September 19, 1932, AMPAS.

Buckner, Robert; Epstein, Julius; and Epstein, Philip. "Yankee Doodle Dandy." Final. June 1, 1942, MOMA, WCTR.

Chodorov, Edward. "Captured!" Final. August 19, 1933, WCTR.

Doyle, Laird. "British Agent." Final. September 15, 1934, WCTR.

"Escaping the Hun." No date, but believed to be 1917, NYPL (LC).

Finkel, Aben; Chandlee, Harry; Koch, Howard; and Huston, John. "Sergeant York." Revised final. January 31, 1941, AMPAS, WCTR.

Fitzgerald, Edith, and Taylor, Dwight. "Today We Live." Dialog cutting continuity. April 8, 1933, NYPL (LC).

Fitzgerald, F.Scott, and Paramore, Edward E. "Three Comrades." Okayed by Joseph Mankiewicz (Producer). February 1, 1938, with changes to March 31, 1938, AMPAS.

Gardiner, Becky. "War Nurse." Dialog cutting continuity. October 17, 1930, NYPL (LC).

Garrett, Oliver H.P. "Three Faces East." Temporary. July 26, 1930, WCTR.

Glazer, Benjamin. "Seventh Heaven." Shooting. September 7, 1926, AMPAS.

——, and Birinski, Leo. "Mata Hari." File copy. No date, but 1931, AFI.

Goldbeck, Willis, and Johnston, Agnes Christine. "The Enemy." Fourth temporary complete. May 23, 1927, MOMA.

Hellman, Lillian, and Sharp, Mordaunt. "The Dark Angel." May 31, 1935, AMPAS.

Hughes, Llewellyn, and Gullian, Campbell. "The Sky Hawk." Pictorial action and dialog. No date, but 1929, MOMA.

Hume, Cyril; Maibaum, Richard; and Rapf, Maurice. "They Gave Him a Gun." Okayed by Harry Rapf (Producer). February 9, 1937, AMPAS.

Lord, Robert, and Mizner, Wilson. "Heroes For Sale." Final. June 17, 1933, WCTR.

Milhauser, Bertram. "Ever in My Heart." Final. October 28, 1933, WCTR.

——. "Storm at Daybreak." Dialog cutting continuity. June 30, 1933, NYPL (LC).

Miller, Seton I., and Goulding, Edmund. "Dawn Patrol." Revised final. August 4, 1938, AMPAS, WCTR.

Miller, Seton I.; Totheroth, Dan; and Hawks, Howard. "The Dawn Patrol." Revised. March 14, 1930, AMPAS, WCTR.

Morgan, Byron. "The Last Flight." Final. August 29, 1931, WCTR.

"Pack Up Your Troubles." Dialog cutting continuity. No date, but 1932, NYPL (LC).

Parker, Dorothy; Campbell, Alan; Jackson, Horace; and Coffee, Lenore. "Suzy." Dialog cutting continuity. July 17, 1936, NYPL (LC).

Perret, Leonce. "For This We Fight." (Retitled "Lest We Forget"). August, 1917, NYPL.

Raine, Norman Reilly; Niblo, Fred, Jr.; and Franklin, Dean. "The Fighting 69th." Revised final. January 27, 1940, WCTR.

Reisner, Charles, and Zanuck, Darryl. "The Better 'Ole." No date, but 1926, AMPAS.

Schayer, Richard. "Doughboys." Dialog cutting continuity. August 7, 1930, NYPL (LC).

Sheriff, R.C., and Kenyon, Charles. "The Road Back." Revised Continuity and Dialog. No date, but 1937, NYPL (LC).

Sherman, Richard; Hammerstein, Oscar II; and Yost, Dorothy. "The Story of Vernon and Irene Castle." Final. December 16, 1938, with changes dated January 4, 10, 1939, AMPAS.

Spewack, Bella; Spewack, Samuel; Wolfson, P.J.; and Oppenheimer, George. "Rendezvous." Revised dialog cutting continuity. December 31, 1935, NYPL (LC).

Stewart, Donald Ogden, and Hackett, Walter. "The White Sister." Dialog cutting continuity. March 7, 1933, NYPL (LC).

Trotti, Lamar. "Wilson." Fourth revised shooting final. November 13, 1943, Henry King Collection, WYO.

Van Every, Dale. "Marianne." Dialog cutting continuity. October 10, 1929, NYPL (LC).

Young, Waldemar. "Chances." Final. July 18, 1931, WCTR.

Manuscripts and Special Collections

Major film libraries contain folders of clippings and stills for many of the pictures. The three leading repositories in this regard are AMPAS, MOMA, and WCTR. Manuscripts, memoirs, diaries, and memoranda are extremely scarce for this study. The following are of special interest:

AMPAS. Richard Barthelmess Collection.

——. J. Stuart Blackton Collection.

——. "Havoc." Fox Film Corporation Folder, 1925.

——. Thomas H. Ince Collection.

——. *Introduction to the Photoplay.* Mimeographed typewritten MS. Los Angeles: University of Southern California, 1929.

MOMA. Ince, Thomas H. "History and Development of the Motion Picture Industry." Typewritten MS. No date, but believed to be 1921.

WYO. Henry King Collection.

Dissertations

Most dissertations in history reflect the peripheral relationship of film to historical scholarship. The following were of some help:

Camfield, Thomas Marley. "Psychologists at War: The History of American Psychology and the First World War." Ph.D. dissertation, University of Texas, 1969.

Connor, James Richard. "Pen and Sword: World War I Novels in America, 1916-1941." Ph.D. dissertation, University of Wisconsin, 1961.

Gruber, Carol Signer. "Mars and Minerva: World War I and the American Academic Man." Ph.D. dissertation, Columbia University, 1968.

Heubner, Lee William. "The Discovery of Propaganda: Changing Attitudes Toward Public Communication in America, 1900-1930." Ph.D. dissertation, Harvard University, 1968.

Lounsbury, Myron Osborn. "The Origins of American Film Criticism, 1909-1939." Ph.D. dissertation, University of Pennsylvania, 1966.

MacCann, Richard D. "Documentary Film and Democratic Government: An Administrative History From Pare Lorentz to John Huston." Ph.D. dissertation, Harvard University, 1951.

Paine, Jeffrey Morton. "The Simplification of American Life: Hollywood Films of the 1930's." Ph.D. dissertation, Princeton University, 1971.

Phipps, Frank Thomas. "The Image of War in America, 1891-1917: A study of a Literary Theme and Its Cultural Origins and Analogues." Ph.D. dissertation, Ohio State University, 1953.

Ramseyer, Lloyd L. "A Study of the Influence of Documentary Films on Social Attitudes." Ph.D. dissertation, Ohio State University, 1938.

Scholarly Papers

The Jarvie, Samuels, and Jowett papers were made available to me by Mr. Jowett. The others were supplied by their authors. The Adler, Murphy, and Small papers, while not cited in the text, have been valuable in the formulation of my ideas.

Adler, Les K. "The Counter-Subversive Screen: Hollywood and the Red Image." Paper presented at the Annual Meeting of the Southern Historical Association, Louisville, Ky. November 12, 1970.

Jarvie, Ian C. "Movies and Socialization." Paper presented at the First Meeting of the Popular Culture Association, East Lansing, Mich., April 8-10, 1971.

Jowett, Garth S. "The Motion Picture and the American Mind." Paper presented at the First Meeting of the Popular Culture Association, East Lansing, Mich., April 8-10, 1971.

Murphy, William Thomas. "World War I and the Film of Propaganda." Paper presented at the Annual Meeting of the American Studies Association, Washington D.C., October 22, 1971.

Samuels, Stuart. "Film as Social and Intellectual History." Paper presented at the First Meeting of the Popular Culture Association, East Lansing, Mich., April

8-10, 1971.

Small, Melvin. Comments on Adler paper cited above, Annual Meeting of the Southern Historical Association, Louisville, Ky., November 12, 1970.

Index

Abbot, George, 138
Ace of Aces, 131
Adams, Henry, 9, 35
Addams, Jane, 191
Adele, 150, 197
Adler, Mortimer, 19, 45
Adorée, Renée, 119
After the War, 149, 195
After Tonight, 146, 171, 199
Albert, Dr. Heinrich, 183
Albert, King of the Belgians, 148, 162
Alexandra, Dowager Queen of England, 164
Alias Mike Moran, 88, 181
Alien Enemy, An, 198
Allen, Viola, 200
Allied (Official) War Review, 73-74, 77-78, 152, 162, 167
All Quiet on the Western Front, 30, 46, 51, 94, 116, 130, 132-40, 158, 173, 189, 195, 212-13, 218-19
America Goes to War, 26
America Must Conquer (The King of the Huns), 149
American Ambulance Boys at the Front, The, 70
American Legion, 78, 103, 116, 212
America Now (Book), 37
American Red Cross, 103
American Tragedy, An, 60
America Preparing, 69
America's Answer, 72-74, 77, 176
America Unprepared, 69-70, 80
Anderson, Maxwell, 121
Anybody's War, 210
Arms and the Girl, 198
Army Air Service, 122
Army League, 103
Army Surgeon, 198
As in a Looking Glass, 181-82
Asquith, Lady Elizabeth, 164
Associated Motion Picture Advertisers, 107
Astaire, Fred, 202

Astor, Mrs. Vincent, 70-71
At the Front With the Allies, 69
Austria at War, 69
"Auteur theory," 29-30
Aydelotte, William O., 50-51
Ayme, Marcel, 129
Ayres, Lew, 133

Bairnsfather, Bruce, 212
Bakshy, Alexander, 65, 135
Balkans, in war films, 162
Balshofer, Fred J., 110
Bara, Theda, 150
Barbed Wire, 46, 53, 157
Barbusse, Henri, 129
Barry, Iris, 58, 121
Barrymore, Ethel, 171, 184
Barrymore, John, 171-72
Barrymore, Lionel, 88, 171
Barthelmess, Richard, 218
Bath of Bullets, The, 75
Battle Cry of Peace, The, 92, 102-4, 145, 193
Beery, Wallace, 212
Behind the Battle Line in Russia, 69
Behind the Door, 117
Behind the Front, 212
Belgian, The, 153, 162, 198
Belgium, in war films, 107, 161-62
Be Neutral, 98
Bennett, Constance, 171, 198-99
Berlin Via America, 153, 184
Bernstorff, Count Johann von, 183
Bethmann-Hollweg, Theobald von, 147
Betsy Ross, 107
Better 'Ole, The, 211-13
Beware!, 154
Beyond Victory, 139, 195-96, 217
Big Drive, The, 78-79
Big Parade, The, 30, 46, 51, 53, 80, 91, 96, 115, 118-22, 126, 134, 139, 155, 168, 195, 212

265

Bill and Alf, 212-13
Birth of a Nation, 32, 51, 100, 104
Birth of a Race, The, 107
Bismarck, Otto von, 79
Blackton, J. Stuart, 41-42, 64, 87-88, 101-4, 109, 111-12, 145, 181, 193
Blackwell, Alice Stone, 192
Blasco-Ibáñez, Vicente, 117
Blinky, 91, 211
Bloodstained Russia, 170
Bobby of the Home Defenders, 179
Body and Soul, 116, 202
Bonnie Annie Laurie, 164, 197
Bonus Army, 112
Boorstin, Daniel, 26, 41, 61
Born to Love, 198-99, 202
Borzage, Frank, 110
Boston *Transcript,* 118
Boulding, Kenneth, 47-48, 62
Bourne, Randolph, 37
Boy-Ed, Karl, 183
Boy Scouts to the Rescue, 179
Boys From Your State, The, 76
Brady, William, 171
Brand of Cowardice, The, 88
Breadline. See *Heroes for Sale*
Break the News to Mother, 110
Brenon, Herbert, 137, 171, 173
Brest-Litovsk Treaty, 173
Britain, in war films, 163-67
British Agent, 171, 173, 203
Broken Lullaby, 137, 139, 154, 158, 195
Bryan, William Jennings, 104, 109, 178
Bryson, Lyman, 34
Buck Privates, 212
Bud's Recruit, 87-88, 179
Bullets and Brown Eyes, 153
Buntline, Ned, 9
Bureau of Reclamation, 70
Burke, Billie, 184
Bush, W. Stephen, 32, 59, 62
Butterfield, Herbert, 42

Cagney, James, 94
Capra, Frank, 46-47
Captain Swagger, 124
Captured!, 164, 171
Card, James, 28
Carr, Harry C., 43
Carter, Boake, 79
Case of Sergeant Grischa, The, 137, 139, 173
Castle, Mrs. Irene, 151, 177, 194
Catt, Carrie Chapman, 190
Cavalcade, 132, 165-67, 174, 195, 219
Cavell, Edith, 107, 159, 197
Cervera, Admiral Pasqual, 102
Chances, 164
Chaney, Lon, 153
Chaplin, Charles, 30, 37, 139, 195, 207-10, 212-13
Chaplin, Sidney, 212-13
Charmer, The, 185

Cheka, 173
Chicago Tribune, 68, 170
Chronicles of America. See Yale Historical Series
Churchill, Winston, 170
Cinema. *See* Motion Pictures
Citizen Kane, 51
Civilization, 99-100, 104, 109, 120, 147
Civil Service Commission, 70
Clansman, The, (Book), 104
Claws of the Hun, 181
C.L. Chester Company, 74
Cleveland, Grover, 190, 202
Closed Gates, 111
Cochrane, William, 99
Cock-Eyed World, The, 212
Cock of the Air, 124
Cocks, Orrin G., 98
Cohan, George M., 159
Come On In, 207
Commentator, The, 136
Committee on Public Information (CPI), 71-78, 86, 176, 184, 217
Common Cause, The, 88
Compson, Betty, 199
Comrades, 91
Congressional Record, 28
Conspirator, 159
Convoy, 117, 202
Cooper, Gary, 91, 94-95, 164, 218
Corporal Kate, 90, 198, 210
Cosmopolitan Productions, 37
Council of National Defense, 151
Coward, The, 100, 195
Coward, Noel, 165
Crashing Through to Berlin, 76
Creel, George, 71-72, 74-75, 86
Crimson Romance, 124
Crockett, Davy, 216
Cross Red Nurse, The, 197
Crowded Hour, The, 197-98
Cruse, Harold, 9
Cummings, E.E., 60

Dane, Karl, 211
Dangerous Business, 91
Dark Angel, The (1925), 202
Dark Angel, The (1935), 202
Dark Star, The, 199
Daughter Angele, 182
Daughter of Destiny, 149, 198
Daughter of France, A, 149
Daughters of the American Revolution (DAR), 126
Davies, Marion, 91, 168, 199, 211
Dawes Plan, 139
Dawley, J. Searle, 99
Dawn, 159, 197
Dawn Patrol, The (1930), 125-6, 137, 149, 165, 189, 213, 218
Dawn Patrol (1938), 126, 189, 213
Day, George Parmly, 32
Dayton-Wright Company, 76

Dead March, The, 79
Dealers in Death, 79
Dearborn *Independent,* 38
Defenseless America (Book), 102
Defense or Tribute?, 101
De la Motte, Marguerite, 202
De Mille, Cecil B., 105, 151, 167, 177-79, 194
De Mille, William, 105-6, 151
De Rochemont, Louis, 80, 92-93
"Dialog Cutting Continuity," 31
Dieterle, William, 32-33
Dietrich, Marlene, 199
Dishonored, 199
Dixon, Professor W. MacNeile, 26
Dixon, Reverend Thomas E., 104, 112, 145, 193
"Documentary prejudice," 57-59
Dog of the Regiment, 91, 157
Doin' His Bit, 206
Doing Our Bit, 177
Doing Their Bit, 88, 179
Dolly Does Her Bit, 179
The Doomed Battalion, 162
Dos Passos, John, 60
Doughboys, 211-13
Draft 258, 178, 196
Dressler, Marie, 197
Drew, Mr. and Mrs. Sidney, 176
Dr. Strangelove, 205
Duck Soup, 213
Dugan of the Dugouts, 91
Dunborough, W.H., 69
Duncan, Hugh Dalziel, 47-48, 205

Eagle and the Hawk, The, 123, 125-27
Eagle's Eye, The, 183-84
Easter Rebellion, 164
Eastman House, Rochester, New York, 27
Edison, Thomas, 16, 102, 181
Edison Company, 89
18 to 45, 177
Eisenstein, Sergei, 60
Eliot, Arthur, 212
Empey, Arthur Guy, 77, 108-9
Enchanted Cottage, The, 110-11
Enemy, The, 131, 146, 157-58, 202
Escaping the Hun, 150, 153, 167
Esnault, Phillipe, 57
Evans, Madge, 179
Everets, John Allen, 69
Ever in My Heart, 158, 185
Evil Eye, The, 184

Face Value, 111
Fairbanks, Douglas, 49, 178
Fairbanks, Douglas, Jr., 164
Fall of a Nation, The, 104, 145, 193
Fall of the Romanoffs, The, 171
False Faces, 153
Famous Players-Lasky Corporation, 31
Far East, in war films, 162-63
Farewell to Arms, A, 202

Farrar, Geraldine, 194
Faulkner, William, 38, 137
Fearing, Franklin, 52
Fetchit, Stepin, 210
Fielding, Romaine, 88
Fields of Honor, 153, 200-201
Fields, W.C., 213
Fighting 69th, The, 94
Film. See Motion Pictures
Films in Review, 29
Finders Keepers, 212
Find Your Man, 91
Firefly of France, The, 198
First World War, The, 79, 118
Fisher, Ham, 206
Fitzgerald, F. Scott, 38
Flag Maker, The, 111
Flashes of Action, 78
Flying Luck, 212
Flying Torpedo, The, 175
Flying With the Marines, 76
Flynn, Errol, 126
Flynn, William J., 184
Foch, Marshal Ferdinand, 73
Follow the Girl, 198
Food Gamblers, The, 176
For Better, For Worse, 179
Ford, Henry, 38, 102, 105
Ford, John, 49, 157
Ford Peace Ship, 100
For France, 149
For Liberty, 150, 153
For the Freedom of the East, 163
For the Freedom of the World, 88, 176
For Valour, 178, 196
Four Horsemen of the Apocalypse, The, 45, 80, 118, 126, 154-55
Four Sons, 157-58, 185, 195
Fox Film Corporation, 121, 171, 179
France, in war films, 167-69
Freund, Carl, 134
Friends of Irish Freedom, 164
From Caligari to Hitler (Book), 51

Galsworthy, John, 115, 129
Garbo, Greta, 199
Geezer of Berlin, The, 206
General Federation of Women's Clubs, 126
Gentleman from America, The, 211
Gerard, James W., 109, 148, 152
German-Americans, in war films, 183-85
German Curse in Russia, The, 152, 170
German Intrigue, 170
German Side of the War, The, 69
Germany and Its Armies of Today, 68-69
Germany, in war films, 145-60
Germany's Side of the War, 69
"Gertie the Dinosaur," 107
Gibson, Hoot, 91, 110, 211
Gilbert, Felix, 36, 53
Girl Climbing a Tree, 64
Girl Who Stayed at Home, The, 177, 201

Gish, Dorothy, 201
Gish, Lillian, 131, 146, 157, 200-202
Gleason, Arthur, 32
Goldstein, Robert H., 108
Goodbye Kiss, The, 212
Goodman, Ezra, 29
Gown of Destiny, The, 177
Grand Illusion, 156
Grant, Cary, 168
Grant, Police Reporter, 181-82
Greatest Power, The, 180, 184
Greatest Thing in Life, The, 201
Great Love, The, 164, 197, 201
Great Victory, The, 149, 154, 197
Great War in Europe, The, 69
Greene, John, 25
Grierson, John, 65
Griffith, Corinne, 202
Griffith, David W., 31-32, 49, 63, 104, 107, 156-57, 164, 171, 177, 183, 197, 201-202
Guarding Old Glory, 69, 80, 217

Hackett, Francis, 37
Haig, Field Marshal Sir Douglas, 148
Hale, Edward Everett, 87
Half-Shot at Sunrise, 212
Hall, Bert, 77, 109
Ham and Eggs at the Front, 210
Hamilton, Alexander, 87
Hard Boiled Haggarty, 124, 212
Harlow, Jean, 125, 168
Harper's Magazine, 18
Harron, Robert, 201
Hatton, Raymond, 212
Havoc, 115
Hawks, Howard, 125, 137
Hayakawa, Sessue, 105, 163
Hayes, Helen, 200
Hayfoot-Strawfoot, 211
Hearst, William Randolph, 26, 37, 76, 151, 217
Hearst Metrotone News, 66
Hearst-Selig Company, 68
Heart of Humanity, The, 153, 197
Hearts of the World, 107, 157, 201
Hell Below, 117
Hell in the Heavens, 124
Hellman, Lillian, 38
Hell's Angels, 112, 124-26, 140
Hemingway, Ernest, 60, 202
Herbert, Victor, 104
Her Country First, 177
Her Country's Call, 177, 181
Her Man O'War, 212
Heroes for Sale, 112
Heroic France, 167
Hero of Submarine D-2, The, 100-101, 182
Hicks, John, 52
Hiding in Holland, 69
Higham, John, 36
Highest Trump, The, 184, 197
Hitchcock, Alfred, 49
Hitler, Adolph, 135, 159

Hollywood Technical Directors' Institute, 135
Home Defense, 176, 207
Honest Man, An, 89, 178
Honor First, 117
Hooligan, Happy, 206
Horses of War, 74
Hotel Imperial (1927), 53, 146, 171, 202
Houston, Penelope, 58
Hughes, Howard, 124-25
Hull, Cordell, 95
Humoresque, 110
Hun Within, The, 183, 217
Huxley, Aldous, 61

I'll Say So, 184, 207
Immigrant, The, 183
In-Again, Out-Again, 178, 207
Ince, Thomas H., 31, 99-100, 120, 181
Industrial Workers of the World (IWW), 73, 181
Ingram, Rex, 118, 155
In Pursuit of Polly, 184
Inside the Lines (1918), 153
Inside the Lines (1930), 199
International Sneak, An, 181, 207
In the Name of the Prince of Peace, 99
Intolerance, 32
Into No Man's Land, 91
Isn't Life Wonderful?, 156-58
Italian Battle Front, The, 69
Italy, in war films, 162

Jackson, Andrew, 86-87
Jacobs, Lewis, 201
Jarvie, Ian, 32, 48
Jessel, George, 210-11
Joan of Plattsburg, 176-77
Joan the Woman, 167, 194
Jobes, Gertrude, 107
Joffre, Marshal Joseph, 148
Johanna Enlists, 177, 194
Johnston, Winifred, 130
Jolivet, Rita, 107
Jones, Buck, 91
Journey's End, 30, 46, 137-39, 165, 173
Joyce, James, 53
Judgment of the Hills, 202
Jusserand, Jules, 102

Kaiser, the Beast of Berlin, The, 109, 148-49, 154, 206
Kaiser's Finish, The, 149
Kaiser's New Dentist, The, 206
Kaiser's Shadow, The, 180, 184
Kaplan, Abraham, 60
Keaton, Buster, 211-13
Kent, Sidney R., 31
Kerensky, Alexander, 170-71
Keystone Pictures, 207
Kicking the Germ Out of Germany, 207
Kracauer, Siegfried, 51-52, 161, 163, 169

Krutch, Joseph Wood, 16, 48
Kubrick, Stanley, 10
Kultur, 147
Kuttner, Alfred, 37

Laemmle, Carl, 105, 133-35, 153
Laemmle, Carl Jr., 133-34
Lafayette We Come!, 167, 184, 198
Lafayette Flying Corps, 30, 122
Lancer Spy, 156
Land of the Free, The, 87
Langdon, Harry, 211
Lasky, Jesse, 94
Lasswell, Harold D., 26
Last Flight, The, 112
Last Parade, The, 111
Laurel and Hardy, 211
Lawrence of Arabia, 10
Lean, David, 10
Lee twins, 179
Legionnaires in Paris, 212
Legion of the Condemned, The, 46, 123-24
Leites, Nathan, 167
Lenin, Vladimir, 170, 173, 203
Leslie's Weekly, 170
Lest We Forget, 107, 154, 167-68, 196-97
Liberty, 101
Liberty Loan campaigns, 105, 151, 208
Library of Congress, 27
Life Magazine, 80, 94, 126
Life's Greatest Problem. See *Safe for Democracy*
Lilac Time, 46, 155, 164, 196
Lincoln, Abraham, 86-87
Lindbergh, Charles A., 124
Lindsay, Vachel, 18, 37, 194
Link, Arthur, 104-5
Literary Digest, 132
Little American, The, 105, 150, 194
Little Patriot, A, 179
Lloyd, Frank, 165
Lloyd, Harold, 207
Lockhart, R.H. Bruce, 173
Log of the U-35, The, 69
Lone Eagle, The, 124
Lorentz, Pare, 58, 92
Lost at the Front, 212
Lost Battalion, The, 77, 89, 94, 120
Lost Patrol, The, 121
Lost Squadron, The, 112
Love and the Law, 181
Love in a Hurry, 182
Love Light, The, 154, 162, 194, 202
Loy, Myrna, 199-200
Lubitsch, Ernst, 137, 154
Luce, Henry, 93
Luck and Pluck, 184, 207
Lusitania, sinking depicted in war films, 107, 147
Lust, Sidney B., 78
Lynd, Robert S. and Helen Merrell, 42, 45, 52

MacArthur, Charles, 171

MacCann, Richard D., 28, 66
McCay, Winsor, 107
McCormick, R.R., 170
MacGowan, Kenneth, 107
Mackaill, Dorothy, 202
McLaglen, Victor, 121
McLuhan, Marshall, 47, 61
MacManus, Edward, 77-78, 89
Madam Spy (1918), 184, 207
Madam Who?, 184
Made in America, 74, 87
Mad Parade, The, 198
Maid of Belgium, The, 149, 200
Making of Hundred Ton Guns, The, 176
Making the Nation Fit, 75
Man From Wyoming, A, 91
Mann, Margaret, 158
Manners, Lady Diana, 164
Man Who Reclaimed His Head, The, 132, 168
Man Who Was Afraid, The, 87
Man Without a Country, The, 87, 178
March of Time, 65, 80, 93
Marianne, 91, 168, 211
Marine Corps, 89
Marriage Ring, The, 182
Marx Brothers, 213
Mason, J.C. Bee, 68-69
Masses Magazine, 97
Mata Hari, 116, 199
Mathis, June, 117-18
Mauldin, Bill, 212
Maurois, André, 129
Maxim, Hudson, 102
Mead, George H., 49
Memo on the Movies (Book), 130
Mencken, H.L., 37-38
Metro-Goldwyn-Mayer, 39, 211
Metro Pictures Corporation, 117
Me und Gott, 183
Milestone, Lewis, 30, 133-39, 212
Miracle of the Ships, The, 74
Missing, 109, 200
Mission to Moscow, 174
Mix, Tom, 182
Modern Researcher, The, (Book), 14
Moley, Raymond, 45
Moore, Colleen, 164, 202
Moran and Mack ("Two Black Crows"), 210
Morgenthau, Henry, 152
Motherhood, 149, 195
Motion Picture Association of America, 53
Motion Picture Producers of America, 104
Motion Picture Magazine, 29, 106
Motion Picture News, 29
Motion Pictures: and aesthetics, 34-43; and analysis of World War I, 26-27; as behavioral mechanism, 44-47; as a business, 39-41; as mass communication, 47-50; and democracy, 17-19; as documentaries, 66-67; as historical evidence, 9-11, 27-31, 215-19; and historical methodology, 44-54; as history, 31-33; and intellectuals, 36-43; as newsreels, 64-66; objectivity of, 57-67; popularity of, 16-17; and

propaganda, 59-61; and psychological analysis, 50-52; and quantification, 52-54; and reality, 61-64; subjectivity of, 57-67; and the written word, 41-43
Movies. *See* Motion Pictures
Moving Picture World, 28-29, 148
Mowry, George, 19, 27
Mr. Logan, USA, 182
Mrs. Slacker, 178
Münsterberg, Hugo, 37
Museum of Modern Art, New York City, 27
Mussolini, Benito, 135
Mutt and Jeff, 206
My Country First, 101, 180
Myers, Jake, 109
My Four Years in Germany, 109, 152
My Own United States, 87
My Son John, 159
Mysterious Lady, The, 146

National Archives, 27
National Association for Better Films, 45
National Association of Moving Picture Producers, 86
National Board of Censors, 98
National Board of Review Magazine, 115, 126
National Council of Jewish Women, 126
National Security League, 103
Nation Magazine, 40, 115
Nation's Peril, A, 100
Navy Department, 117, 207
Navy League, 103
Nazimova, Alla, 192-93
Negri, Pola, 53-54, 146, 157, 202
Neutrality, 98
New Lives For Old, 199
New Masses Magazine, 116, 173
New Republic Magazine, 18, 103
News of the Day, 37
Newsweek Magazine, 126, 135-36, 199
New York Herald Tribune, 171
New York Times, The, 26, 69, 147, 171, 177, 194
Nicholas II, Czar of Russia, 170-72
Nigh, William, 152
Niven, David, 126
Noah's Ark, 171
No Man's Land, 184
North Star, 174
Now We're in the Air, 123, 212
Nurse Edith Cavell, 159, 197
Nye, Russel B., 34
Nye Committee, 79, 81, 128, 132

O'Brien, Pat, 94
O'Donohue, J.T., 121
Official War Review. See Allied War Review
Olmstead, Gertrude, 202
On Dangerous Ground, 149
One of Millions, 98-99, 104, 131
On the Firing Line With the Germans, 69
Other Man's Wife, The, 178

Our Daily Bread, 119
Our Invincible Navy, 76
Our Wings of Victory, 74
Out of the Ruins, 111
Over Here, 176
Over Secret Wires, 182
Over There, 78, 178
Over the Top, 108-9

Pabst, G.W., 133
Pack Up Your Troubles, 212
Papne, Captain Franz von, 183
Paramount-Bray Pictograph, 74
Paramount Pictures Corporation, 60, 105, 122-24, 212
Parker, Sir Gilbert, 26
Patent Leather Kid, The, 91-92, 196, 217
Pathé Freres, 76
Pathé News, 66
Paths of Glory, 10
Patria, 26, 151-52, 162, 177, 194
Patriot, The, 176
Patriotism, 196
Payne Fund Studies, 44-46
Pearl of the Army, 162
Pease, Major Frank, 135
Perkin's Peace Party, 100, 177-78, 207
Perry, Clarence Aitken, 45
Perry, Harry, 122
Pershing, General John J., 72, 77, 86-87, 148, 167
Pershing's Crusaders, 72, 74, 78, 152
Peterson, Ruth C., 45
Pettigrew's Girl, 176, 207
Photoplay Magazine, 28-29, 106
Pickford, Jack, 182
Pickford, Mary, 49, 150, 162, 177, 182, 194-95, 202
Pilgrimage, 195
Portnoy's Complaint, (Book), 53
Powder, 98, 132
Powdermaker, Hortense, 38, 40, 48
Powell, William, 185
President's Research Committee on Social Trends (1933), 17
Pressly, Thomas, 27
Pride of New York, The, 88
Private Izzy Murphy, 210-11
Private Jones, 139-40, 185
Prizma color process, 76
Profiteers, The, 176
Prussian Cur, The, 183
Puppets, 90, 202

Ramparts We Watch, The, 80, 92-93, 159, 196
Ramsaye, Terry, 39, 106
Ramseyer, Lloyd, 67
Rasputin, 170-71
Rasputin, the Black Monk, 170-71
Rasputin and the Empress, 171
Ray, Charles, 211

Red, White and Blue Blood, 110
Reid, Louis R., 37
Reid, Mrs. Bertha Westbrook, 29
Reid, Wallace, 17, 29, 182, 218
Reisz, Karel, 134, 189
Remarque, Erich Maria, 128, 133, 135-36
Rendezvous, 156, 185, 200
Renoir, Jean, 156
Republican Ascendancy (Book), 52
Riefenstahl, Leni, 58
Riley of the Rainbow Division, 212
Rin-Tin-Tin, 91, 157
Road Back, The, 30, 135-37, 139, 158-59
Road to France, The, 181
Road to Glory, The, (1936), 137-40, 169
Rogers, Ginger, 202
Romance of the Air, A, 109
Rookies, 211
Roosevelt, Franklin, 93
Roosevelt, Theodore, 70, 101, 103, 109, 178
Ross, Betsy, 86
Rosten, Leo, 60
Roth, Philip, 53
Rotha, Paul, 65
Rule, Albert L., 78
Russell, Rosalind, 185, 200
Russia, in war films, 169-73

Safe For Democracy, 87, 181
Sailor Izzy Murphy, 210-11
Saunders, John Monk, 122, 124-25
Schulberg, Budd, 49, 120
Scudder, Vita, 190
Seas Beneath, The, 117, 155
Secret Code, 184
Secret Game, The, 163
Secret of the Submarine, The, 180
Secret Service, 184
Seldes, Gilbert, 61, 63, 65, 78, 118, 120, 198
Selznick, Lewis J., 192
Semon, Larry, 211
Sennett, Mack, 180, 206-7, 212
Sergeant York, 94-96, 196
Service Star, The, 178
Seventh Heaven (1927), 116, 131, 155, 168, 196, 202
Seventh Heaven (1937), 168, 202
75-mile Gun, The, 206
Seventy-seventh Division, 77-78, 89
Seymour, Charles, 26
Shame, 178
Shaw, George Bernard, 38
She Goes to War, 198
Sheik, The, 45
Shell 43, 164, 180
Sheriff, Robert C., 137
Sherwood, Robert, 118
Shifting Sands, 184, 197
Ship Comes In, A, 185
Shootin' for Love, 110, 211
Shopworn Angel (1929), 202
Shopworn Angel (1938), 202

Shoulder Arms, 30, 139-40, 195, 208-10, 213
Side Show of Life, The, 164-65
Sight and Sound, 29
Signal Corps, 30, 64, 71, 76, 78-79, 118-19, 133
Sinclair, Upton, 60
Sinking of the Lusitania, The, 107
Sky Devils, 213
Sky Hawk, The, 124, 155, 164
Slacker, The, 178
Smiles, 179
Soldier's Plaything, A, 211
Solow, Herbert, 39
Somewhere in France (November, 1916), 69, 198
Sonny, 110
Souls in Pawn, 198
Source, The, 182
Spirit of '17, The, 182
Spirit of '76, The, 108
Spirit of the Red Cross, The, 109
Spirit of the USA, The, 115
Spuds, 211
Spy, The, 183-84
Squires, James Duane, 26
Stalin, Joseph, 172
Stallings, Laurence, 79, 118-19, 121
Stamboul Quest, 199-200
Stearns, Harold, 37
Steffens, Lincoln, 172
Storm at Daybreak, 162
Storm of Steel, The, 75
Story of Vernon and Irene Castle, The, 189, 202
Strong Man, The, 211
Submarine Patrol, 117, 140
Submarine Pirate, The, 100-101, 207
Surrender, 131, 156, 168-69
Suspicion, 184
Sutter's Gold, 60
Suzy, 117, 140, 168
Sweetheart of the Doomed, 201
Sylvia of the Secret Service, 198

Talmadge, Constance, 91
Tansill, Charles Callan, 26
Taylor, Deems, 37
Taylor, Robert, 136
Tearing Down the Spanish Flag, 102
Tempest, 172
Terveen, Fritz, 58
Thalberg, Irving, 32-33, 54, 119-20
Thing We Love, The, 87
They Gave Him a Gun, 131-32, 136, 139
This is America, 78-79
Thompson, Donald C., 170
Three Comrades, 136, 139-40, 158-59
Three Faces East (1930), 155, 199
Thunder Afloat, 117
Thurstone, L.L., 45
Tiger, Lionel, 189
Tin Hats, 212
Till I Come Back to You, 153, 162, 177, 198
Till We Meet Again, 199
Time Magazine, 78, 80, 117, 123, 133, 155, 162, 211

Today We Live, 116, 164
To Hell With the Kaiser!, 109, 147, 150, 154
Tone, Franchot, 136, 168
Too Fat to Fight, 89, 207
Top Sergeant Mulligan, 211
Treason and Revolt, 170
Treaty of Versailles, 154
Triangle Film Corporation, 70, 175, 180
Troy, William, 139
True Heaven, 164
Truvanov, Sergius, 171
Turner, Frederick Jackson, 96
Turpin, Ben, 207
Twain, Mark, 10
Twelvetrees, Helen, 199
23½ Hours Leave (1919), 176, 211
23½ Hours Leave (1937), 211
Two Arabian Knights, 212
"Two Black Crows." *See* Moran and Mack
Tyler, Parker, 39, 50-52, 61

Ulanov, Barry, 34
Ulysses (Book), 53
Unbeliever, The, 89, 96, 109, 120, 153-54, 196
Uncle Sam's Defenders, 69
Uncle Sam series, 74
Under False Colors, 170
Under Four Flags, 72-74
Universal Film Manufacturing Company, 76, 105, 133, 206
Unknown Soldier, The, 202
Unpardonable Sin, The, 150, 201
U.S. Army in Action During World War I, The, 76

Valentino, Rudolph, 53, 117-18, 155
Valli, Virginia, 202
Van Doren, Mark, 137-38
Vanishing American, The, 90
Variety, 210
Vidor, King, 30, 87, 118-19, 122
Villard, Oswald Garrison, 116
Vitagraph, 41, 101
Vive La France, 198
Volunteer, The, 179
Von Stroheim, Erich, 89, 153-55, 201

Walsh, George, 207
Walsh, Raoul, 122, 183
Wanted for Murder, 149
War and the Woman, 198
War Bibles, 76
War Bridegroom, The, 207
War Bride of Plumville, The, 181, 207
War Brides, 153, 192-93
War Bride's Secret, The, 153
War Department, 107, 122, 124
War Horse, The, 91
Ward, John William, 86
Warner Brothers, 94, 109, 126, 152
Warner, H.B., 164

Warner, Jack, 106
War Nurse, 198
War O'Dreams, 180
Washington Sky Patrol, 46
Waterloo Bridge, 164, 202
Watts, Richard, 171
Wayne, John, 49
We Can't Have Everything, 178, 197
Weems, Parson, 216
Weigle, Edwin F., 68-69
Weimar Republic, 154, 157
Wellman, William, 30, 122, 124
Welter, Rush, 36, 52
We're in the Navy Now, 212
Westfront 1918, 133
Whale, James, 30, 135, 137
What Price Glory?, 115, 121-22, 126, 139, 155, 168, 189, 196, 202, 210
Wheeler and Woolsey, 212
When Men Desire, 150
When Your Soldier Is Hit, 74
Whirlwind of Youth, 202
Whispering Wires of War, 76
White, Pearl, 162
Whitehall, Richard, 114
White Sister, The (1915), 162, 200
White Sister, The (1923), 162, 200
White Sister, The (1933), 162, 200
Who Goes There?, 153
Whom the Gods Destroy, 164
Who Was the Other Man?, 184
Why America Will Win, 87, 154
Why Germany Must Pay. *See The Great Victory*
Why We Fight, 47
Wife or Country, 184
Wilcox, Herbert, 159, 197
Wilhelm II, Emperor of Germany, 109, 146-49, 151-54, 157, 159, 161, 206-7
Willie and Joe, 212
Willkie, Wendell, 93
Wilson, Woodrow, 31, 60, 64, 86, 93, 97-99, 104-5, 140, 148, 151-52, 154
Wings, 30, 46, 51, 80, 112, 115, 122-24, 126, 139, 189, 195, 210
Wisconsin Center for Theater Research, Madison, 27
Wise, Gene, 96
Wolfenstein, Martha, 167
Wolves of Kultur, 180
Womanhood, the Glory of the Nation, 109, 193
Woman I Love, The, 168
Woman of Experience, A, 146, 199
Woman's Work in Wartime, 197
Woman the Germans Shot, The, 197
Women of All Nations, 202, 212
Women Who Win, 76
Won Through Merit, 70
Woolcott, Alexander, 118, 120
Woolf, Virginia, 59, 61
World Film Corporation, 171
World Moves On, The, 132, 156, 196-97, 210
World War, The, 78

World War I Motion Pictures: as adventure, 114-27; as air power themes, 122-26; as Allied images, 161-74; as Army themes, 118-21; and biography, 86-87; as comedies, 202-14; and the democratic faith, 85-96; as documentaries, 68-81; as enemy images, 145-60; and the film industry, 104-6; and the Home Front, 175-86; and national commitment, 97-113; and naval themes, 117-18; and neutrality, 97-100; and newsreels, 71-74; and pacifism, 128-41; and patriotism, 106-10; and preparedness, 100-104; and semi-documentaries, 77-78; and women's roles, 189-203
W.W. Hodkinson Corporation, 74, 87
Wylie, I.A.R., 38

Yale Historical Series, 32, 42-43, 46
Yankee Doodle Dandy, 159
Yankee Doodle in Berlin, 207
Yanks, 115
Yanks Are Coming, The, 76
York, Alvin, 94-95
Young, Robert, 136
Young Eagles, 123-24, 158
Young Plan, 139

Zanuck, Darryl, 210
Zeppelin's Last Raid, The, 153
Zukor, Adolph, 108
Zweig, Arnold, 137